AF559641

TRIBAL AGRICULTURE AND ANIMAL HUSBANDRY

(TRIBAL LIFE IN INDIA—3)

Edited by

DEVENDRA THAKUR
D. Litt.
Former Professor, L.N. Mishra College of Business Management
B.B.A. Bihar University, Muzaffarpur

and

D.N. THAKUR
Ph.D.

SECOND REPRINT EDITION

DEEP & DEEP PUBLICATIONS PVT. LTD.
F-159, Rajouri Garden, New Delhi - 110027

TRIBAL AGRICULTURE AND ANIMAL HUSBANDRY
(Tribal Life in India—3)

First Published: 1994
Second Reprint Edition: 2009

ISBN 978-81-8450-106-3 (Vol. 3)
ISBN 978-81-8450-114-8 (Set)

Typeset by THE LASER PRINTERS, 8/15, 3rd Floor, Subhash Nagar, New Delhi-110027.

Printed in India at NEW ELEGANT PRINTERS, A-49/1, Phase I, Mayapuri, New Delhi-110064.

Published by DEEP & DEEP PUBLICATIONS PVT. LTD.,
F-159, Rajouri Garden, New Delhi-110027. Phones: 25435369, 25440916.
E-mail: ddpbooks@yahoo.co.in • ddpubs@gmail.com
Sales Showroom: 2/13, Ansari Road, Daryaganj, New Delhi-110002
Phone/Fax: 23245122

Contents

Preface

India is primarily the land of agriculture and the tribal people being the original inhabitants of this land are not only closely related to agriculture, but they depend almost totally on cultivation. There are a number of social and religious rituals connected with agriculture which explicitly disclose their emotional relation with land and crops in addition to plants and trees.

In ancient time, food gathering and hunting were the chief sources of the livelihood of the tribal community. But, in course of time, as a result of pressure of population, they acquired the skill of agriculture. They cleared the forest and brought land under cultivation. So they consider themselves to be the original owners of the land they cultivate. But the advanced people from outside forced them in many ways to leave the land which created serious problems and Government had to make certain rules relating to the tribal ownership of land. All these facts reveal that the tribal life is chiefly based on agriculture.

Tribal agriculture is closely associated with animal husbandry because it is primarily primitive in nature.

In preparing this volume, we have tried to associate tribal agriculture with animal husbandry. The study starts with land and the tribes and further deals with tribal agriculture and allied sectors. Shifting cultivation is the significant part of the tribal agriculture. It has, therefore, been included in this work. Endeavours have been made to introduce new agricultural technology in the tribal areas. So this aspect has also been a part of this study.

The relation of tribal agriculture with animal husbandry has been described in the end. We would like to extend our regards to all those scholars and friends whose support and sympathy resulted in the competition of this work. Finally, if this work serves any purpose in the welfare of the tribal people, it would bring immense pleasure to us.

Muzaffarpur

DEVENDRA THAKUR
D.N. THAKUR

Introduction: Land and the Tribe

More than 90 per cent of the tribals are dependent on agriculture and allied activities. Land is also the only tangible asset of a tribal family, other possessions being extremely meagre in the present stage of their economy. There are a number of social and religious rituals connected with land which establish emotional ties between the tribal and his land. Thus, land is much more than merely a source of livelihood to the tribal people. One of the important characteristics of a tribal community is its traditional association with a territory. Initially, the community subsisted on food-gathering and hunting in the area under its command. As the pressure of population grew and the community acquired the new skill of agriculture they cleared the forest and brought land under cultivation. The individual tribal considers himself owner of the land he occupies by virtue of his traditional association and his personal effort in making it cultivable. However, pressure from advanced communities in a variety of forms sometimes forces him to leave his land. This did not create a serious problem for him in the early stages or in many areas even as late as the first half of our century when the forests were still plentiful and not fully administered and the pressure of population was not very high with only a moderate rate of population growth. He moved to yet another part of the forest retaining his links with the earlier settlement for some time for ritual purposes and finally settled on the new lands establishing new bonds. The need for additional land for the growing population of the tribal communities themselves was met from the available forests which still provided adequate space for agriculture. This process has continued for centuries.

The tribal areas remained for a long time outside the land management systems of the advanced areas because of their inaccessibility. The tribal communities, therefore, developed their own tradition for management of land. The land ownership amongst the tribals broadly falls under three categories, viz., community land belonging to the village as a whole, lands belonging to a clan and individual holdings. As the British administration consolidated its position in India, they established three main systems of land revenue and land rights, viz., zamindari, malguzari and ryotwari. Some of the tribal areas also came under one of these new systems depending on the system adopted in the concerned British province. A policy of treating some of the tribal areas excluded or partially excluded, however, helped in the continuance of the traditional tribal system for some time and delayed the extension of the new system. Moreover, many of the tribal areas were parts of the Indian princely states. The situation in these States was mixed—some continued with the traditional management systems, some developed their own system while some others adopted one of the newer systems of British India.

The position of land records also varies considerably. In a province like Bihar the tribal areas were also covered by regular settlement operations. In some provinces and many princely States rough and ready records were prepared based on visual estimates without detailed survey. In many areas a system of revenue-based on the number of ploughs or family units (number of hearths) was introduced on the presumption that in the context of extensive availability of land in the tribal areas this would be a dependable criterion for determining the quantum of land utilised. Settlement operations or preparation of land records was expected to be undertaken only at long intervals even in advanced areas. In the tribal areas, even where settlements were taken up, they have been less frequent for a variety of reasons. Nevertheless the tribals continued to clear lands for agriculture as noted earlier and there was considerable divergence between the records and the actual position in the field. In the absence of a settlement or up-to-date record of rights the tribals were at the mercy of petty officials of revenue and forest departments and of the landlords where zamindari had been introduced. Even though intermediaries have been abolished, the state of land records in many tribal areas remained unsatisfactory.

One significant consequence of unsatisfactory state of land records was that the tribal was not legally recognised as owner of the land he cultivated and he could simply occupy it till such time as a superior claim got enforced. Since the new legal system was superseding the traditional custom gradually, the tribal as an individual was unable to stand against the continuing pressure of outsiders. Wherever formal land settlement was introduced for the first time or a new settlement was ordered after a long period it was difficult for the tribal to get his rights recorded. The extent of ownership actually recorded in favour of tribal cultivators in a settlement operation depended largely on the sensitivity of the officer responsible for the operation, the strength of outside interests and consciousness amongst the community about the nature of their operations. In many areas, therefore, dissonance between official records and the field station arose as a result of settlement operations without the tribal even becoming aware about it. Steady dispossession followed these operations in many areas. The tribal moved on to a more inaccessible region and got busy with preparation of fresh lands.

The alienation of tribal lands for a variety of reasons over a long period in the past has resulted in discontentment and even sporadic revolts and rebellion. The pointed attention of the British administration was drawn to this sensitive issue by about the middle of the last century. Consequently two important lines of action were adopted. Firstly, in some cases the community ownership of land was recognised in contrast to the general system of individual ownership which had got currency in the country as a whole. In this way the effective management of land by the community was restored. Secondly, suitable laws and regulations, particularly for the Agency or excluded and partially excluded areas were enacted which prohibited transfer of land from tribals to non-tribals. In some cases, as in Santhal Parganas, transfer could be made only in favour of a person who already held land in the village, thus excluding the possibility of migrants acquiring land but allowing mutual transfers within the village community. In some princely States like Bastar and some Agency areas, the migrants, particularly the officials, were prohibited from acquiring lands in the tribal areas. In view of the fact that in some areas considerable lands had already passed from tribal hands, right of pre-emption was also introduced so that the process could also be reversed even though partially.

A number of important developments after Independence have had far-reaching implications for tribal land and their economy. A substantial area predominently inhabited by tribals hitherto under the Princely States were merged with the new States. One of the important consequences of this merger was that the laws and the rules, many of which were enforced through administrative fiat of the ruler or by simple administrative orders and conventions became ineffective. The new centres of administrative authority were far away from these areas and it took considerable time before their problems could be appreciated at those levels. The vested interests took advantage of this period of uncertainty and indecision at the cost of the tribal interest in the land. The Constitution envisaged scheduling of tribal areas and making special regulations for protection of tribal lands. The earlier regulations prevalent in the excluded and partially excluded areas continued to operate after those areas were scheduled. However, many predominently tribal areas, particularly those forming part of erstwhile Princely States, remained outside the schedule and therefore did not get benefit of protective land laws for quite some time. The reorganisation of States also resulted in many changes in the administrative boundaries. Consequently sometimes different regulations were applicable in different regions in the same State without much coordination. Since regulations were enacted at different times for different areas, certain crucial gaps also appeared which adversely affected the tribal interests. The situation settled down gradually after 1956.

As a determined effort for planned economic development in the country was initiated soon after independence, the tribal areas also received special attention. Some of them began to be opened up gradually. In the meantime the pressure of population in the advanced areas was also growing. It resulted in substantial in-migrations particularly because the tribal areas provided better opportunities in view of their rich natural resources. In a number of areas new industrial and mining complexes were also established which also resulted in acquisition of land for non-agricultural purposes. The reservoirs of many major irrigation projects were located in tribal areas resulting in submergence of extensive lands belonging to tribals. The in-migration of population led to substantial transfer of lands through individual transactions, legal or illegal. The land situation, therefore, continued to deteriorate in the tribal areas.

Before we proceed further to examine the continuing process of land alienation and measures taken by the States for protecting tribal lands in the recent years, it will be useful to review the present state of land holdings in the tribal areas. As we have seen an average tribal family initially had a sufficiently large land holding for supporting itself reasonably even with their primitive method of cultivation. This stage of large holdings is now generally over and the situation has changed considerably with the increasing pressure of population and growing incidence of land alienation. Nevertheless the per capita land holdings for the tribal communities on an average for the country as a whole is comparatively larger than for the general population because of lower pressure of population in the tribal areas as also greater availability of land. The size of holdings, however, varies considerably from one region to another depending on a number of factors like accessibility, quantum of immigration, enforcement of protective laws, etc. The latest comparative figures for holding of tribals and other relate to 1961. According to these figures 29 per cent of the scheduled tribe households had holdings less than 24 acres compared to 34.5 per cent in the general population. The percentage of households having land holdings between 2.5 to 4.9 acres was 25.6 per cent amongst scheduled tribes compared to 22.8 per cent amongst the general population. The percentage of households having 10 acres or more was 20.8 per cent amongst scheduled tribes compared to 21.2 per cent in the general population. This shows that not only the land holdings amongst the scheduled tribes were larger but the difference in the size of holdings amongst the members of the scheduled tribes was comparatively smaller than for the general population.

In the absence of land holding data for the later years, the occupational classifications in the Census can be used to get an idea of the status of land holdings and alienation of lands in the tribal areas. According to 1971 Census there were 84.18 lakh cultivators and 48.32 lakh agricultural labourers amongst the scheduled tribe workers who constitute about nine-tenths of the total working population. The classification of male workers many give a better idea of the real situation since the response of women workers in the Census enumeration is influenced by their household duties which does not get uniformly recorded. Even these cultivators may be having small holdings. Most of them have become agricultural labourers. The position was slightly better in Maharashtra, Andhra Pradesh and Tamil Nadu where 40 per cent to 50 per cent of the scheduled tribe workers were cultivators but the number of agricultural labourers had also grown and about 30 to 40 per cent of scheduled tribe workers were agricultural labourers. In Orissa, Madhya Pradesh and Bihar about two-thirds of the tribals were cultivators but the number of agricultural labourers has risen substantially, more than one-fourth of the tribals having lost their lands and becoming agricultural labourers. The state of landlessness in these States is specially noteworthy because they have large compact tribal area comparable in size and population to the tribal majority states and U.T.s in North-East and they amongst themselves account for more than 50 per cent of the tribal population in the country. Therefore, even though in terms of percentage it appears that only 25 to 30 per cent of the scheduled tribes were agricultural labourers, in terms of absolute numbers and quantum of alienated land the problem had assumed a large dimension. In the middle Indian Tribal Scene Rajasthan appears as an exception with more than 80 per cent cultivators and less than 10 per cent agricultural labourers among tribal workers. In the North-Eastern States where more than 80 to 90 per cent of scheduled tribes were returned as cultivators, the tribals continue to hold on to the land. The number of landless persons amongst the scheduled tribes in these States is insignificant. The same situation also holds in the hill areas of U.P. and Himachal Pradesh.

The above analysis gives a broad state-wise picture of the tribal land holdings in the country. Within each state itself the situation may vary considerably. In the state having large tribal areas the all India pattern of continuing command over land on the one end and high incidence of landlessness on the other, gets reflected as between different regions. The command over land in the more inaccessible regions continues to be undisturbed though many adverse forces are making their presence felt even in these areas. In many regions with the development of communications and intermixing of population the situation has deteriorated. In some of the advanced areas the members of the tribal communities have been rendered completely landless and they may not own even 5 to 10 per cent of the total land area.

The attention to the deteriorating land situation in the tribal areas was pointedly drawn by the Dhebar Commission in 1961. They called for a thorough review of the laws relating to land alienation and for adoption of a uniform approach within and outside the scheduled areas. The Shilu A.O. Committee in 1969 reiterated the observations of the Dhebar Commission, and urged upon the Government to take up vigorous protective measures. A Committee under the Chairmanship of Shri P.S. Appu again went into the question of land alienation in 1972 when Tribal Development Agencies were established in the wake of agrarian unrest in Andhra Pradesh, Bihar and Madhya Pradesh. Elimination of exploitation and effective protective measures were accepted as an integral part of the strategy for tribal development under the sub-plans and highest priority was accorded to this problem.

In the Fifth Five Year Plan, action was initiated on two important lines; viz., updating and preparation of lands records in the tribal areas and review of laws relating to land. The preparation of land records was taken up as a part of the sub-plan programme in many states although it is generally treated as a non-plan activity. It was at different stages at the end of the Fifth Plan and is a continuing scheme in the Sixth. It, however, appears that adequate preparatory work first to ascertain the local tradition and custom and then to orient the land records staff before undertaking these operations has not been done with the result that dissonance may continue or even may arise between the real situation in the field and the land records which we have discussed earlier. Since much work still remains to be done, the States should undertake the necessary studies and sensitivise the personnel. The Tribal Welfare Departments and particularly the Tribal Research Institute should be associated with these operators intimately without any further loss of time.

The process of the review of land laws was initiated in the Fifth Plan following the reference of State Ministers incharge of Welfare of Backward Classes in 1973 who resolved that the existing laws relating to transfer of land should be reviewed and a time bound programme should be prepared for identification of lands transfered legally and irregularly within a period of two years. The Ministry of Home Affairs circulated a model draft for land legislation drawing attention to the possible loopholes. The State Governments have reviewed the land laws and some changes have been made. The review shows that the legal position is not satisfactory even after the various amendments have been made. Moreover in some cases as in Kerala even the law has not been made effective. It is therefore necessary that a time-bound programme which had been undertaken in the beginning of the Fifth Plan, now more than seven years back, with the resolution to be completed within two years or so, should now be completed forthwith. In view of the fact that this is a crucial issue for tribal development we will recapitulate some of the important points of action by the States.

Most of the legislations enacted by the State Governments are intended to ensure that tribal land does not pass on to non-tribal through illegal and fraudulent transactions. However, there are many loopholes which have resulted in whittling down significantly the effect of these legislations particularly in view of some rulings of the High Courts. For instance, the Bihar High Court has held that the period of limitation extended to 30 years under the Bihar Scheduled Areas Regulation, 1969 would be operative prospectively and not retrospectively. This means that all cases of adverse possession having matured into title on the expiry of the limitation period of 12 years before these regulations came into being in 1969 must remain unaffected by the protective measures provided in these regulations. This negates the specific constitutional provision in the Fifth Schedule for giving retrospective effect to any change in an existing law.

The provision of Chhotanagpur Tenancy Act and Scheduled Areas Regulation do not apply to municipal areas. This has had the effect of not only legitimising the massive alienation of tribal land. Another serious issue arises from some Court decisions which held that tresspass did not amount to transfer. If a non-tribal tresspassed into the lands of tribal holders and continued to hold it, the existing provisions which sought to regulate transfer of land by a non-tribal could not be invoked and the aggrieved party would have to seek redressal in a civil court. Many tribals could not avail of this opportunity thereby contributing, albeit involuntarily to legitimisation of tresspass.

The laws relating to land transfers generally regulate transfer of lands from tribals to non-tribals. In some areas inscrupulous elements take advantage of this fact and acquire control over tribal lands through tribal girls in whose names they may get the lands transferred and whom they may just keep or may even formally marry but with a clear intention of grabbing land. Benami transactions in favour of servants is also quite common.

Attention may also be drawn to the practice prevalent in many areas where the transfer of tribal lands may be affected on the basis of wrong declaration or suppression of the information about the caste of the individual who transfers the land. Once the tribal falls in this trap, it becomes difficult for him to get any relief. In some cases the protection of the law has been denied even by some Courts who have held that this protection cannot be invoked by a party which has failed to invoke it at an earlier stage of the proceedings. For example, the Patna High Court have held (AIR 1962, Pat. 72) that the benefit of the provisions of the Bihar Tenancy Act was not available to a party if, having had an opportunity to invoke this benefit at an earlier and appropriate stage of the proceedings, he did not do so. The Orissa High Court has followed this decision (AIR 1977 Ori. 16) in a case where the judgment debtor belonged to the Scheduled Tribes and was entitled to the protection under the Orissa Land Reforms Act, 1960, which makes any transfer by raiyat belonging to a scheduled tribe void except where it is in favour of person belonging to a Scheduled Tribe. The Court held that the judgment debtor could have brought the fact of his membership of a scheduled tribe to the notice of the Court at an earlier stage of the proceedings. According to the Court, there is no obligation cast on the executing Court to make an enquiry as to whether a judgment debtor before it belongs to any of the Scheduled Tribes or Scheduled Castes for purposes of determining whether such judgment debtor is entitled to protection of the Act. In the absence of any provision, fault cannot be found with the executing court for not having made any such enquiry. After the sale has taken place certain consequences, have ensued and the judgment debtor must pay the price of his earlier silence.

The prolonged litigation in which the tribal becomes a party is generally dragged by the more cunning adversary, thereby, neutralising the effect of the laws. In view of the numerous provisions for appeal and revision, a tribal seeking restoration of his land is sometimes forced to go through three levels of legal battle, involving immense expenditure harassment and uncertainty. The limited provisions of legal aid from the Government is not of much assistance to him. In the process of mobilising his own resources to fight the case he may be forced to dispose of his assets or borrow from a money-lender. Even so, he may be no match to the resourceful opponent and many find the battle of litigation a losing one particularly in view of the manoeuvrability of the other party to fabricate documents in its favour sometimes in collusion with lower level functionaries. Further, if the tribal wins the final legal battle and the land is restored to him, the delivery of possession is often delayed for a long time in collusion with the other party. Even where the possession has been formally delivered, it is not uncommon that the tribal may have been prevented from cultivating his land under threat from the same opponent. At times false criminal cases are instituted to demoralise him. In such circumstances, most tribals accept defeat and keep quiet rather than fight.

While action was expected to be taken for plugging the loopholes in the laws and making them effective an equally important task was to identify the illegal and irregular alienation of tribal lands and to take measures for restoration of alienated lands so identified. It is not possible to assess the precise magnitude of land alienation but our analysis in the preceding paragraphs gives the broad dimensions of the problem faced in these areas. Since the present situation is the result of a long process over centuries, the cases in which effective relief can be given will relate to a limited period and they can be identified only by a systematic survey. No such survey has been undertaken in most of the States so far even though the need for such a survey has been accepted and even programmes have been drawn up. The figures given by some of the States of the work done by them for identification and restoration of alienated lands are given on next page.

Sl. No.	*States*	*No. of cases registered*	*Total disposed of*	*In favour of Tribals*	*Against Tribals*	*Cases in which land has been registered*
1.	Andhra Pradesh (April 1980)	49630	46090	—	—	22373
2.	Bihar (upto April 1979)	43335	40416	24430	15973	—
3.	Gujarat (upto April 1980)	17171	8898	8648	250	795
4.	Maharashtra (upto April 1980)	47332	43643	17731	25912	13713

It is clear that the administrative effort so far has been quite inadequate and in some cases negligible compared to the importance and size of this problem. It is only in Andhra Pradesh that a substantial number of cases have been reported where lands have been actually restored. The relief given in Gujarat is negligible. In a number of cases the verdict is given against the tribals. It may not be possible for us to draw valid conclusions from the limited data available but as we shall see in our further discussion we feel that the present state is largely due to indifference shown to the implementation of the law after they have been passed. As we have discussed earlier even the legal situation itself is not entirely satisfactory and the inherent resistance is clear from the fact that even in some cases the law has not been enforced. Whatever may be the law of the land it is the executive action which gives in the required thrust. It is this thrust which is missing in most of the cases and a situation of non-action in relation to land problems continues to exist while the process of alienation of tribal lands continues unabated. The happy situation where this would have meant only his receding back into the forests and clearing some more lands for himself no longer exists; and where it is still happening it is not in the long-term interest of the tribal economy and the economy of the region and the nation as we have discussed while dealing with forests and tribal economy. Consequently, the growing pressure is resulting in development and may lead to further agrarian unrest even in areas not affected so far.

The above review shows that on the formal side various State Governments have taken a number of measures from time to time for protecting tribal lands, particularly in the scheduled areas, some States even altogether prohibiting all transfers of tribal lands. But the total impact of all these measures has not been very significant. Sometimes even progressive measures, like those of land reforms, have adversely affected the tribal communities because those laws did not take into account the special situation in the tribal areas. For example, the lessee of agricultural land in some cases may be a money-lender while the original land owner may be working as agricultural labourer on the land which may be still recorded in his name. The money-lender may acquire the title under the Land Reform Law. Thus, the benefit of the new law accrues to an undeserving person. Many a legal provision have had adverse effect because of their faulty application or incongruous interpretation. It is thus clear that the law relating to the transfer of land including reform laws themselves have some critical omissions or defects which make them rather ineffective or even detrimental to tribal interests. All transfers from tribals to non-tribals should be prohibited and prohibited effectively. Where no such law exists, suitable law should be enacted immediately. Consequently, it will be necessary to critically examine the law and suitably chisel it with reference to the clear objectives set-up in this regard and keeping in view the inherent limitations arising from the socio-economic situation.

We may draw attention to one important aspect at this stage. The tribal generally has a high regard for the word and believes that all others also have the same value. Therefore, he is prepared to put his thumb impression or sign any paper without any reservation. This psychological make up is taken advantage of by the unscrupulous elements who may create documentary support for even fictitious claims. The articulate people are generally very careful in their dealings and they ensure that the property acquired by them is in accordance with the letter of the law which however may be circumvented in suitable ways. It is, therefore, necessary that oral evidence is placed on a higher pedestal and the law of evidence is amended so far as it is applicable to the evidence of members of the Scheduled tribes so as to follow oral evidence to be adduced against all forms of documentary evidence including the registered documents. Such a provision existed earlier in the regulations made for agency areas which enabled the administration to take a realistic view rather than only a technical view of the situation and dispense justice to the tribal. In the scheduled areas in case of a dispute about the ownership of land, it should be presumed that the land belongs to the tribal unless proved otherwise. Therefore, the onus of proof that the land has been acquired by the individual in accordance with the provisions of law, should be on the non-tribal holder of the law.

An important reason for the weakness of the tribals in the new context is that he has to deal with the modern institutions on his own in isolation outside his group without association of those when he may be able to trust. All documentation in support of money and property transactions is required to be authenticated by witness. But the legal provisions in this regard are so permissive that the witness can be picked up by the other parties at will from anywhere. Therefore, these provisions are missed and evidence may be created against the tribal without his knowledge. This has been a major cause of the silent discontent in the tribal areas for a long period. The procedure for advancing of loans, execution of agreements, etc. should be prescribed as to require the payment and formalities being completed in the 'open' where members of the village community should be present and attestation by one or more members of the Community depending on the nature of agreement, should be made obligatory. Any violation of this rule should have the effect of making the transaction or agreement abinitio null and void. In fact, the procedure adopted at the time of settlement follows this principle. Similarly, when Khanapuri is done in the land records, advance notice is given and all possible interested parties and other assemble at the time of the proceedings. The special procedure so adopted for the tribal areas should be widely publicised. Once the broad outlines of a procedure are known to the people and its parameters clear, it will be difficult for any one to take undue advantage of the ignorance of the tribals. These measures will also help in establishing the much needed confidence relationship between the people and the institutions responsible for implementation of the developmental programmes in the tribal areas.

Much of the trouble in relation to land titles also arises from the fact that the owner of the land has no document with him and the records prepared by the revenue official is final. In the institution of tribal areas this put the tribal to great advantage and he is at the mercy of the patwari. This situation needs to be corrected. A Pass Book should be prescribed for keeping record of all lands including standing trees owned by a tribal, which should be kept by the tribal himself. It should be made obligatory for the substance of any agreement or other legal formalities creating a charge on his land, directly or indirectly, to be recorded and duly authenticated in this Pass Book. No liability of any description whatsoever on tribal land should accrue if it is not recorded in the Pass Book. The registration of land transfers should be subject to prior verification by the registration authorities that the conditions of transfer contained in the law have been strictly complied with.

While necessary provisions should be made in the law to cover all these aspects it will be equally important to sensitivise the appropriate branches of regular administration. Many a time the spirit of the law is not fully appreciated by those responsible for their implementation. The rules made under these laws tend to emphasise the formal and procedural aspects only which results in their mechanical operation, Therefore, the rules in these important matters should be elaborate which should give a clear idea of the basic objectives of the law and also indicate possible alternatives along with their implications for guidance of the executive officers. Detailed guidelines should also be given besides bare legal provisions and rules made thereunder. As we have noted earlier sometimes rules may not be framed for quite sometime even after a law may have been passed. Is is necessary that rules should be framed, which should be exhaustive but in simple language, as soon as a law relating to transfer or partition of land is enacted. Where rules remain to be framed immediate action should be taken. Detailed guidelines should also be issued to ensure that the basic objective of the concerned law is communicated to the officers responsible for their implementation.

We have seen earlier that the progress of cases relating to tribal lands is not satisfactory. The proceedings in Civil Courts is far too tardy and formal-technical. The law relating to all aspects of tribal lands should be simplified with a view that it is possible to dispense justice to the tribal rather than being satisfied with completing the technical requirements of the law. The jurisdiction of Civil Courts should be barred. In those States where Revenue Courts do not exist, special machinery should be created for this purpose. The procedure for disposal of these cases should be streamlined to enable prompt disposal and early finality. The possibility of prolonging the proceedings by the interested parties should be removed by limiting the number of appeals and also the points in which intervention of higher authorities can be sought. The administration should not appear as an unconcerned on looker in this important matter. The determination to ensure justice in these cases should get reflected in the administrative system. The officers should not be content with technical disposal of cases, the real facts being treated as inadmissible pieces of evidence. The administration should forcefully appear on the side of the weak because the equations are heavily loaded against him in our present system. There should be a visual demonstration of the capability of law to undo injustice against the tribal. The orders of the revenue court for restoration must be implemented within a time limit, the responsibility for all necessary action in this regard being placed on the Project Administrator.

Continuous vigilance is needed all through, right from the points where the land changes hands to the final disposal of the dispute in the highest court. In case force is used against the tribal disturbing his possession or preventing him from taking back the fightful possession, administration must intervene, *suo moto* if necessary, and the other party suitably chestised. Occupation of tribal lands through deceit or use of force should be made a penal offence. Even when lands may have been restored legally, the tribal may still find it difficult to keep continued possession of the restored lands. The trial of cases relating to possession of lands restored should be tried by Executive Magistrates. Such cases should be made penal offence under the law. In case an individual does not vacate the land in pursuance of the law directions of decree of a court or reoccupies it, more stringent punishment should be provided.

Special legal assistance should be provided to the tribals in all cases relating to their land disputes. There may be instances, where the tribal himself may not come forward to seek this assistance, either because he is indifferent, or may be under threat. The Project Administrator should come in the picture and ensure that all cases are brought to court of law. In all tribal areas, standing counsels should be appointed who should take up, *inter alia,* all cases of land disputes in which tribal is a party. The number of Standing Counsels may be fixed on the basis of the work load in the District or the Project. A panel of Counsels may be prepared so that in case of sudden increase in work additional Counsels can be drawn from it. The remuneration of the Counsels should be fixed liberally so that leading lawyers can be attracted. A convention should also develop that service of lawyers as Standing Counsels for protection of tribal interests will be taken into account while making selection for Government Pleaders and other assignment in the Judiciary. The Special Counsel should be responsible for bringing to the notice of the Deputy Commissioner and the Project Administrator all cases of judgments in which the spirit of the law might not have been honoured so that immediate corrective measures can be taken. In all such cases, the Deputy Commissioner should be responsible for prompt appeals in higher Courts. There should be a constant review of the judicial pronouncements to ensure that no technical flaw is taken advantage of by the interested groups in these proceedings and the corrective measures are immediately taken. As we have discussed while reviewing the Constitutional provisions, wide discretion is available to the Executive. It is only when constant vigilance is exercised as suggested by us, that it can be said that the Executive has risen to the occasion and has deserved the trust reposed in them by the framers of the Constitution.

The measures suggested above should help in solving the problem of land alienation substantially. However, a discriminating approach may have to be adopted for better results and effectiveness. As we have observed earlier, the incidence of land alienation is not of the same order everywhere. It is very high where the areas are getting opened up, along the main roads, around the growing urban centres and mineral complexes. Here the economy of the average tribal has got disrupted all of a sudden. Therefore, in their case restoration of alienated lands will be crucial in any scheme and tribal development. While general measures for identification and restoration of alienated land may be taken throughout the tribal region, areas with possible high incidence of land alienation should be organised. Special teams comprising revenue officers and representatives of development administration should be constituted who may take up the task of identification and disposal of cases simultaneously. There should be a time-bound programme for identification of critical areas, assessment of the problem of land alienation and the final disposal of cases. A period of two years should be the outer limit for this programme in view of its crucial importance.

It may not be practical to reopen all cases of alienation irrespective of the time of their occurrence. The second generation of a settler group generally gains acceptability; considerable mutual adjustment and understanding develops over a long period. Therefore, long-standing relationships need not be disturbed. But effective measures should be taken in respect of alienation during a clearly specified period of which a conscious decision is taken and action within that time frame should not be allowed to be diluted. Taking all the above considerations into account, it would be necessary as also practical that all illegal and irregular transfer in the last forty years or less, i.e., after the year 1940, should be identified and necessary steps taken to restore them to their rightful owners. The law of limitation should be suitably amended for this purpose.

It is necessary that a determined effort is made to restore all those lands which have been alienated illegally or irregularly. But one of the basic tasks which should be undertaken concurrently is to be stabilise the present position in relation to land-ownership and ensure that the process of alienation is effectively stopped. One of the important reasons for the process continuing unabated is that while much has been talked about alienation and restoration not much attention has been paid to those basic reasons which are forcing the tribal to part with his land notwithstanding his deep attachment to the land and many a legal provision against alienation. The individual tribal is under continuous pressure of a variety of forces which ultimately result in the loss of his only capital-base, the agricultural land. He is neither interested nor in a position to comprehend the significance of individual transactions like transfer of land by him in the total socio-economic dynamics of the community and the areas. He is taken to solve his immediate problem somehow. Therefore, it is necessary that all those forces which individual tribals are facing incessantly are identified, understood and countered suitably, otherwise the legal measures taken by the States will continue to be inadequate and ineffective.

An individual tribal may be forced to transfer his land because he may already be indebted and under pressure from the money lender or a lending institution for its payment. Finding no way out, merely to avoid the continued botheration, to which he is not accustomed, he may prefer to sell all or a part of his land and seek alternative means of livelihood as a landless labourer or be content with a smaller holding. A Study on 'Problems of Land Alienation Among Tribals of Gujarat' conducted by the Tribal Research and Training Institute, Ahmedabad, has revealed that major part of the problems of alienation of tribal land is directly related to the indebtedness. It is also noteworthy that most of the land mortgages (68 per cent) are among the tribals themselves. This is a significant sociological phenomenon insofar as a class amongst the tribals themselves has emerged which is taking advantage of the economic vulnerability of weaker sections amongst them as also of the law which enables them to purchase tribal lands. A similar situation may be emeging in other States as well. Only about 28 per cent of the mortgages were by tribals to non-tribals and money lenders and 4 per cent with the cooperative Banks. Many of the mortgages are now continuing for a long period even though the amount of money borrowed is usually very low. In view of the new situation where alienation is now in favour of stronger sections amongst the tribal community, it will be necessary that the transfer of land as between members of the tribal community themselves is also regulated. Suitable law or regulation should be enacted for this purpose.

The persons who have lost their lands or mortgaged them are those who have already fallen victims of their circumstances. But many more are heading in that direction. They may have a personal or social obligation to discharge or be faced with a sudden economic problem and finding no other support may turn to the money lender or take the last resort of disposing of their lands. In the next category are those people whose lands may be marginal or the size of their holdings may have become too uneconomical for a variety of reasons, like continued alienation, partition, etc. The unit may not be viable to maintain even a pair of bullocks. The tribal, therefore, may prefer to work as a landless labourer. The critical point of relation to land alienation is the tribal's need for consumption credit and discharging his social obligation. A strategy has to be worked out so that he is not forced to borrow at various rates of interest from the money-lender who readily comes to his help since he can finally lay his hand on his land. We would discuss at length the urgent need for making the co-operative credit system through the LAMPS effective without any further delay. The consumption credit linked to marketing of minor forest produce and other economic programme should get the highest priority. It will also be necessary that all existing debts are assessed and sealed down following principles of *dam dupat*. In most of the cases the net liability of the tribal may be very small since the loans originally taken are themselves small, as is clear from the Gujarat study and he may have already paid substantial amounts. It is the tricky accounting of the moneylender which may be responsible for his continuing indebtedness. In many cases he may have mortgaged the land and the usufruct enjoyed by the money-lender from the land should be sufficient to wipe out his debt and restore the land unencumbered. In some states there are laws to this affect. We have already discussed earlier that it will be necessary to go behind all the documents relating to the original debt, repayments and any deals about lands. If the tribal have a liability, it should be taken over by the LAMPS so that the link between the money lender and the tribal is broken and a new relationship gets established with the Co-operative System. This should be the primary task of Tribal Development Project Authority and all manpower resources of the State should be mustered to complete this task within a period of a year or so. This operation should be organised on a campaign basis so that this issue is solved once for all.

While the above discussion relate to the people who are already on the precipice, substantial number are in the zone of instable viability for different reascns. Sub-division and the fragmentation of holdings with increasing pressure of population and limited lands is an important factor in some areas. We nave noted that much of the land in the tribal areas is marginal and is not able to provide even a reasonable substance. Therefore, each person is keen to have a share in better lands and the problem of fragmentation of limited good land is increasing. The migration of co-parceners in search of opportunities elsewhere with their share in the family holdings intact, may be another contributing factor in areas with growing contact with the outside world. The claim to a share in the net income from the land final disposal of their respective shares by these people may result in weakening of the local economy and pauperisation of the individual members. To some enterprising people land may be the only means of acquiring new forms of capital for a different vocation, and so on. Those who want to move to an alternative occupation may be suitably assisted as a part of the general tribal development programme. However, it should also be appreciated that the schemes for occupational mobility do not result in unregulated transfer of property guided merely by personal consideration adversely affecting the economy of the community particularly of the weaker sections amongst them.

It is necessary that the reduction of the size of holdings below viability level is prevented to stabilise the economy of the tribal at the margin both by positive measures of assistance and regulation of fragmentation. The benefits of new technology should be made available to the vulnerable groups and they should be enabled to put their land to optimum use according to its potential. Their programmes will also help in creating a climate for voluntary mutual adjustment of fragmented holdings with a view to take advantage of development programmes. Nevertheless it may not be possible to go far in working such adjustments purely on a voluntary basis. Therefore, law prohibiting fragmentation of land below viability level should be enacted. Viability levels should be determined keeping in view the quality of land, level of technology and the socio-economic situation in each area. Village committees may be constituted under this Law which should be made responsible for working out mutual adjustments of lands in cases of likely partition for any reason whatsoever. Provision should also be made for assistance for improvement of comparatively unfavourable lands so that those who accept the comparatively poorer lands can take up land improvement programmes simultaneously and are not rendered non-viable. The transfer of lands as between members of the tribal communities themselves should also be regulated with a view to prevent holdings from becoming non-viable. Thus, an element of compulsion will be introduced and the community will be forced to think about the problem which is arising in these areas in the new context.

A stage has also reached in many tribal areas where the adverse impact of transfer of capital through sale of land and investment in other sectors needs to be seriously considered. In case a member of the Scheduled Tribes proposes to dispose of his land, because he may wish to migrate from the village or move to an alternative occupation, the co-parceners and other eligible tribal landless labourers and marginal farmers should be given the right of pre-emption. In many a tribal community such a practice is already prevalent and has the sanction of tradition. It will also be necessary to work out a scheme for the temporary management of land on behalf of those persons who may be in distress. This needs to be reinforced in the wake of growing individualism and new opportunities which are becoming available to section of the people as a part of tribal development programmes. Then there may be some tribals who may not be able to cultivate tbeir lands for the time being on account of some problems, personal, social or economic. They should be suitably assisted to regain command of their lands after the obligation is discharged or when they are again in a position to manage their lands.

The above measures primarily aim at stabilising the tribal economy; they will be equally applicable to the poorer sections amongst the non-tribal population in the tribal areas. One of the major contributing factor to the alienation of tribal lands is the high preference amongst the stronger sections for landed property whose value continues to appreciate and which can be converted into cash with a large profit at any time. This tendency can be countered by regulating the transfer of land amongst the non-tribals also. The right of pre-emption in these cases should be given to the tribal landless and marginal cultivators. Here, an important question arises about a poor man's capacity to purchase land even at a moderate price. Agriculture is one occupation for which a landless person has the requisite skills and which can be confidently taken upon by him provided necessary investments are available. Unless some provision is made, advantage of pre-emption provisions may be taken by the stronger sections of the community. Therefore, there should be a scheme for financing purchase of land by landless and marginal tribal land holders, should they have an opportunity in pursuance of the above policy frame. The loan should be soft and returnable in 10 to 15 years depending on the quality of land and the general economic situation in each area. In case a tribal is required to sell his land for unavoidable reasons and no eligible tribal comes forward to purchase it, the state should purchase the land and assign it to other tribal on easy terms.

The continuing change in the land-use as also in the economic base of the people in an area are important factors which will have to be kept in view while planning for stabilising the tribal's economy; its strengthening and further development. In some regions, with the depletion of forest resources, the traditional sources of tribals' substances have been adversely affected. The individual is forced to fall back on his limited land holding or to extend cultivation to sub-marginal lands or to move to casual wage employment, collection of fire-wood, etc. In many states, substantial areas have been allotted for cultivation from deforested lands. In many cases, illegally occupied lands have also been settled in favour of encroachers. A cautious and pragmatic policy in this important matter will go a long way to help the tribal economy. All available land should be allotted exclusively to tribal landless labourers and marginal landholders. Only if no eligible tribal is available it should be allotted to other landless agricultural labourers. On no account should bigger land owners be allowed to acquire more lands from deforested lands since it would ultimately lead to transfer of land in some form at some other point. Thus, the last opportunity to provide a responsible economic base to some people at the margin, who may not be ready as yet for any other occupation, may be lost.

Much of the de-forested land may not be capable of being developed as good agricultural land. Nevertheless, now that appropriate technology is available which can enable an individual becoming viable almost on any piece of land of an acre or so, suitable programmes should be prepared based on specific economic activity like horticulture, tussar rearing or animal husbandry. In case the land is fit for agriculture, suitable assistance should be given for land development, improved agricultural practices, etc., soon after its allotment. It is, therefore, necessary that a scheme of land-use in each area is prepared depending on its equality, potential for alternative economic use, available technology and the socio-economic situation. Suitable support should also be provided to enable the members of tribal communities to adopt these practices and programmes. An integrated programme, aimed at stabilising the economy of tribals located at the margin should be prepared in each area. It should include debt redemption, taking over of liabilities already incurred, provision of credit for consumption and social purposes, wherever necessary. The credit should be a part of a specific production programme for each family so designed as to enable him to discharge the old and the current liability on time and make him economically viable in the long-run.

A reasonable success in this Plan of action pre-supposes that it will be possible for the community as a whole to be convinced about the urgent need to take action and the usefulness of the new approach. The tribal must come forward willingly to participate in the economic programme. Some of these schemes will be eligible for direct assistance from the State, but many of them will need support of credit by the financing institutions. Therefore, the individual cultivator will be increasingly required to deal with modern institutions when he takes to intensive agriculture with the supporting new technology, irrigation, water harvesting, etc., or horticulture, tussar and animal husbandry. This is a complex system. An important factor responsible for much of the legal but improper alienation of land has been the individual inability to understand the complexity of the modern system. Sometimes even special measures taken to help him may go against his interest because of the malfunctioning of the system. A cautious approach, therefore, should be adopted in the Planning of programmes for the vulnerable group. In the first instance, all schemes should be within an integrated planning frame which should be prepared at the block and project level. Secondly, high cost technology should be avoided in the initial stage. For example, lift irrigation schemes not only require co-ordinated action on the part of a number of organisations but the cost of these schemes is also very high. The tribal cultivator takes some time before he can fully adopt and get benefit from irrigated agriculture. The state should come in and assist these programmes in such a way, as has been done in Drought Prone Areas Programmes, that the liability on the tribal is not heavier than under flow irrigation schemes. Thus, it will be possible to save him initially from the hazards of possible lower returns compared to high investments. Thirdly, in all these programmes the forward and backward linkages as also co-ordination between the different departments should be worked out very carefully. If there is neglect on the part of any department the state or corporation, it should assume the responsibility for the consequent liability. The availability for payment of interest, etc., should accrue to the tribal only when the scheme has been implemented successfully and the tribal begins to get the desired benefit. For example, in the case of a lift irrigation scheme if water is not available because irrigation pump has not been installed or electricity connection has not been given and the interest charges in respect of the loans taken for construction of well, etc., becomes due the interest should be payable by the state government. Thus, once a carefully prepared development programme picks up and the individual begins to get the benefit, a new climate of confidence and hope will be engendered.

If the above approach is adopted the present phase in tribal economy where it has got delinked from the local resource-base will be over. The symbiosis between the tribals and the local resources including the forests will be re-established. The factors which are responsible for disturbing the system can be kept under check by making adequate provision for the consumption needs of the tribals and assisting him through provision of finance, technical support and extension services. This symbiosis will be at a higher level of technology and with a reasonable level of living above the present subsistence levels. This entire package of programme is so important that it should be taken up on the basis of a drive. A comprehensive land-use plan should be prepared immediately in all villages where land has been allotted in the recent past or is likely to be allotted in future. A programme of development of land for agriculture or its utilisation for other purpose like Horticulture, tussar, animal husbandry, etc., should be given to the individual as soon as the land is allotted so that he can become economically viable within a reasonable period. The Tribal Development Project Administration should take the lead and they should be supported by all the concerned departments, including Department of Revenue and Forest for accomplishing it. Thus, identification of alienated land, its restoration and establishment of a new economic frame should be taken up almost simultaneously. The legal framework should also be strengthened to provide a firm base for this action programme. The new economy has to be built on the basis of family-wise programmes. These families have to be organised in viable groups as has been envisaged in the growth centre and cluster approach suggested by us for general adoption for development of backward areas. There should be a continuous review of progress made in the execution of this programme at the Project and the State levels.

Tribal Agriculture

OPERATIONAL HOLDINGS

According to the agricultural census of operational holdings held in 1981, the operational holdings below 2 hectares have gone up over the years with devolution by inheritance as well as redistribution of land, but skewed distribution of land among different size classes of operational holdings still persists. The number of holdings below 2 hectares went up from 49.63 million in 1970-71 to 66.6 million in 1980-81. These constituted 74.5 per cent of the total holdings in 1980-81 against 69.9 per cent in 1970-71, but operated only 42.76 million hectares or 26.3 per cent of the total operated area in 1980-81 against 20.9 per cent in 1970-71. Against this, holdings above 10 hectares came down from 2.77 million in 1970-71 to 2.15 million in 1980-81. These constituted 2.4 per cent of the total holdings in 1980-81 against 3.9 per cent in 1970-71, but operated as much as 37.13 million hectares or 22.8 percent of the total operated area in 1980-81 against 30.9 per cent in 1970-71.

The total operated area among the Scheduled Castes, Scheduled Tribes and others during 1980-81 is given in the Table 2.1.

TABLE 2.1

Social groups population	*Percentage of hectares*	*Area in lakh*	*Percentage*
Scheduled Castes	15.46	115.22	7.0
Scheduled Tribes	7.85	167.04	10.2
Others	76.69	1355.71	82.8
Total	100.00	1637.97	100.00

The percentage distribution of operational holdings in major size groups among the Scheduled Castes, Scheduled Tribes and others is furnished in the following Table 2.2.

TABLE 2.2

Size groups	*Scheduled Castes*	*Scheduled Tribes*	*Others*	*Total*
Marginal (below 1 hectare)	13.8	5.4	80.8	100
Small (between 1 and 2 hectares)	10.2	9.7	80.1	100
Semi-medium (between 2 and 4 hectares)	7.6	11.3	81.1	100
Medium (between 4 and 10 hectares)	5.4	11.6	83.0	100
Large (10 hectares and above)	4.4	10.8	84.8	100
All size groups	11.3	7.7	81.0	100

It would be seen from the above table that among marginal holdings the share of the Scheduled Castes was 13.8 per cent and in the case of large holdings their share was merely 4.4 per cent while that of other communities was as high as 84.8 per cent. It may be further observed that whereas the proportion of the Scheduled Castes in the rural population in the country was 17.34 per cent their share in the total number of operational holdings was only 11.3 per cent. Similarly, the Scheduled Tribes had 7.7 per cent of the total number of holdings though their proportion in the rural population was 9.54 per cent.

The distribution of holdings among the Scheduled Castes and

Scheduled Tribes and others by major size groups has been given in the Table 2.3.

It would be seen from the Table 2.3 that bulk of the landholdings (68.9 per cent) of the Scheduled Castes are marginal, i.e., below one hectare, while in the case of the Scheduled Tribes this percentage is 39.8.

TABLE 2.3

Size groups	*Scheduled Castes*		*Scheduled Tribes*	
	No. in lakhs	*Percentage*	*No. in lakhs*	*Percentage*
1	2	3	4	5
Marginal	69.23	68.9	27.28	39.8
Small	16.44	16.3	15.51	22.6
Semi-medium	9.52	9.5	14.05	20.5
Medium	4.38	4.4	9.36	13.7
Large	0.95	0.9	2.34	3.4
All size groups	100.52	100.0	68.54	100.0

Size groups	*Others*		*All social groups*	
	No. in lakhs	*Percentage*	*No. in lakhs*	*Percentage*
1	6	7	8	9
Marginal	404.71	56.2	501.22	56.4
Small	128.77	17.9	160.72	18.1
Semi-medium	100.98	14.0	124.55	14.0
Medium	66.94	9.3	80.68	9.1
Large	18.37	2.6	21.66	2.4
All size groups	719.77	100.0	888.83	100.0

LAND REFORMS

The objectives of the national land reforms policy are: (i) abolition of intermediary tenures; (ii) tenancy reforms aimed at security of tenure, regulation of rent and conferment of ownership rights on tenants; (iii) ceiling on landholdings and distribution of surplus lands; (iv) consolidation of holdings; (v) compilation and updating of land records. The Sixth Plan provided that legislative measures to confer ownership rights on tenants would be enacted in all the States by 1981-82. The programme of taking over and distribution of ceiling surplus lands was to be completed by 1982-83. Compilation and updating of land records was to be completed by 1985 and the consolidation of holdings was to be taken up in all the States with the aim of completing it in ten years with priority being assigned to command areas of irrigation projects. According to the available information none of the Sixth Plan targets on land reform measures has been fully achieved. Although most of the intermediary tenures have been abolished, there are quite a few States where legislative provisions do not exist for conferment of ownership rights on tenants and share-croppers. In some States the rent payable to landlords is higher than the limits of 1/5th or 1/4th of the gross produce as laid down in the national policy. Oral and informal tenancies with cultivating possession continue to exist under the guise of 'personal cultivation.' Despite the law for imposition of ceilings on agricultural holdings having been enacted by most State Governments the programme of taking over possession and distribution of ceiling surplus lands is still far from complete. Consolidation operations were also reported not to have made much headway in many States due to fear of displacement among tenants and share-croppers, advantage of having land in fragmented parcels in the events of floods and other natural calamities, and apprehension that big farmers would get a better deal.

The Seventh Five Year Plan had given a new direction by integrating implementation of land reforms with poverty alleviation programmes. Though the distribution of land to the landless has always been an important part of the 20-Point Programme in the new strategy of development reflected in the revised 20 Points, a high priority has been assigned to this work. Enforcement of land reforms under point 5 of the 20-point list includes compilation of land records, implementation of agricultural land ceilings and distribution of surplus land to the landless. Besides sub-points (2) and (3) of point No. 11 relate to ensuring possession of allotted land to members of the Scheduled

Castes and Scheduled Tribes and revitalisation of the land allotment programme.

LAND RECORDS

Correct and up-to-date land records are an essential precondition for effective implementation of land reform measures, particularly for security of tenure and tenants and share-croppers and consolidation of holdings. Land and crop records are basic for various developmental activities, whether it be for identification of small and marginal farmers or location of wastelands for social forestry or compilation of cropped area and production statistics or operational holdings data, etc. for agricultural census or for free flow of agricultural credit. Various planning exercises related to agriculture and rural development schemes and their implementation depend on availability of reliable and up-to-date land records, which reflect the correct status of all interests in land, avoid disputes and litigation as well as the tension which result therefrom. According to the Union Department of Rural Development a review of the status of survey and settlement, land records and revenue machinery at lower levels was done in 1984. According to information available with that Department in March 1986 records were fairly up-to-date in Andhra Pradesh, Gujarat, Haryana, Jammu and Kashmir, Karnataka, Kerala, Maharashtra, Madhya Pradesh, Punjab, Rajasthan, Uttar Pradesh and West Bengal though mutation and sub-division cases were reported to be in arrears in many States. In most of the States records were updated through the Annual Crop Registers. Revisional survey and settlement operations were being carried out in Andhra Pradesh, Assam, Bihar, Gujarat, Himachal Pradesh, Kerala, Madhya Pradesh, Meghalaya, Orissa, Sikkim, Tripura and West Bengal. Under the new 20-Point Programme States were urged by the Union Department of Rural Development to take all measures for updating of land records with utmost urgency by adopting a time-bound programme. States were asked by that Department to observe 1985-86 as a land Records year to update the land records and also introduce a register of operational holdings for collation at Tahsil level. The Department proposed to introduce a Centrally Sponsored Scheme during the Seventh Plan for strengthening revenue administration and updating land records in the States concerned with emphasis on the States and Union Territories which had unsurveyed lands and did not have land and crop-based records.

The Conference of Revenue Ministers held in November 1986 suggested that wherever no land records were maintained at present early steps would be taken to complete survey and settlement work. The facilities provided by the Survey of India for training of staff in survey techniques would be availed of to the maximum advantage. Similarly, State Governments would consider deputing their officers to the National Remote Sensing Agency, etc. to familiarise themselves with the latest techniques for such future use as was considered necessary. Priority was to be given to 430 Blocks selected for the Eastern India Rice Programme, the North-Eastern States/UTs and other predominantly tribal areas in completing survey and settlement, building up system of maintaining land records, periodic updating thereof and Strengthening of revenue machinery.

ALLOTMENT OF CEILING SURPLUS LANDS TO SCHEDULED CASTES AND SCHEDULED TRIBES

The national land reforms policy envisages imposition of ceilings on individual landholding so that sufficient surplus land is available for redistribution among the rural landless. Laws on imposition of ceiling on agricultural holdings were enacted in several States during the 1950s and implemented with varying degrees of effectiveness in different States. The ceilings set by these laws were very high in many cases and exemptions granted from the operation of ceiling law too many. There were also many loopholes in the laws that rendered their implementation difficult. In order to bring a certain degree of uniformity in the ceilings imposed in the various parts of the country and to plug loopholes, the national guidelines on land ceilings were evolved in 1972 by the Conference of Chief Ministers. Laws were enacted in various States in conformity with the national guidelines. There were, however, no ceiling laws in Meghalaya, Nagaland and Mizoram where communal ownership of land predominates. There are also no ceiling laws in Andaman and Nicobar Islands, Goa, Daman and Diu and Lakshadweep. In view of the revelation made by the agricultural census data for 1980-81 that skewed distribution of landholdings still continued, the Union Department of Rural Development advised the State Governments to consider redetermining ceiling limits so as to expand the availability of surplus ceiling land. The position of ceiling limits in each State during 1986-87 as against the national guidelines of 1972 and the lower ceilings suggested by the Central Government may be seen at Annexure I.

A statement showing the area of land declared surplus due to implementation of land ceiling laws and the area allotted to the Scheduled Castes, Scheduled Tribes and other beneficiaries in various States/UTs since the inception of the scheme upto 31-3-87 may be seen at Annexure II. It would be seen therefrom that out of the total area of 76.33 lakh acres declared surplus an area of 59.54 lakh acres was taken possession of, constituting 78 per cent of the total area declared surplus. Against this, an area of 44.09 lakh acres was distributed, constituting 74.06 per cent of the area taken possession of and 57.76 per cent of the area declared surplus, thus still leaving about 26 per cent of the area taken possession of and 42.24 per cent of the area declared surplus to be distributed. Out of the total area distributed an area of 15.07 lakh acres (34.18 per cent) was distributed to the Scheduled Castes, 5.81 lakh acres (13.18 per cent) to the Scheduled Tribes and 23.21 lakh acres (52.64 per cent) to other beneficiaries. Out of the total number of 40.67 lakh beneficiaries the number of Scheduled Caste beneficiaries allotted land was 14.15 lakh (34.79 per cent), that of the Scheduled Tribes 5.63 lakh (13.83 per cent) and that of other beneficiaries 20.89 lakh (51.37 per cent).

The matter of distribution of ceiling surplus land was considered by the Conferences of Revenue Ministers held in May 1985 and November 1986. Some of the important recommendations made by the earlier conference are given below:

(a) (i) The implementation of existing ceiling laws, both pre-revised and revised, should be monitored vigorously by the States/UTs States may analyse and intimate the reasons as to why after so many years even the preliminary stage of scrutiny of returns has not been completed.

(ii) An analysis of the gaps between estimated surplus and declared surplus, between declared surplus and area taken possession of, and between area taken possession of and area distributed be done for taking remedial action. Disposal of returns, cases pending in various courts including the remanded and reopened ones, taking possession of area declared surplus and its distribution followed by prompt mutations, issue of certificates/pottos, physical demarcation on spot and handing over possession, etc., need special attention.

(iii) Details of number of SC/ST beneficiaries of land allotted separately under the pre-revised and revised ceiling laws upto March 1985 be intimated to the Union Department of Rural Development by 30-6-1985. Likewise details of land involved in litigation at various stages, land unfit for agriculture, that set apart for afforestation and other public purposes under the two Acts separately be also intimated.

(b) (i) Sizable areas in Andhra Pradesh, Bihar, Haryana, Punjab, Uttar Pradesh and West Bengal have gone out of the total quantum of surplus land as a result of court decisions. Even land already distributed had to be denotified in many cases causing considerable hardship to the assignees who had invested their resources. State Governments should scrutinise such cases and take steps including legislative amendments to ensure that there is no repetition of such decisions.

(ii) Creation of Tribunals under Article 323(8) of the Constitution and/or creation of special courts/branches in High Courts in consultation with the concerned High Courts for quick disposal of ceiling cases may be considered.

(iii) States may ensure that the posts of officials, revenue as well as judicial, concerned with the disposal of ceiling cases, do not remain vacant. The general feeling that posting for ceiling work was punitive needs to be dispelled as early as possible and experienced and competent officers need to be posted to man these posts.

(iv) Land which has been declared surplus and which is

not the subject matter of litigation should be taken over without any delay.

(v) Making of provision for taking over surplus land in anticipation of the completion of proceedings, where the parties are agreeable, may be considered by the States/UTs.

(vi) Legislative provisions, wherever non-existent, may be made for barring lawyers from representing parties in land ceiling cases.

(c) (i) A campaign to detect cases of evasion and review of the existing legislations may be undertaken by the State Governments/UT Administrations.

(ii) Evasion and avoidance of law need to be looked into seriously. Vigorous action to investigate and determine the types of *benami* transfers and circumventions of law has to be taken followed by concrete remedial measures, legislative and otherwise, as may be necessary.

(iii) Survey needs to be undertaken by the States to check whether the surplus land said to be unfit for cultivation was really so and also if it was a fact that there were no takers for such land.

(d) (i) Steps have also to be taken to ensure that the classification of land under the ceiling law and as in land records is similar.

(ii) Classification of land in land records, particularly in areas brought newly under irrigation needs to be suitably revised in land records first.

(iii) The review of application of ceiling laws in areas newly irrigated by projects and schemes financed by the public exchequer should be taken up to subject these areas to the appropriate ceilings.

(e) (i) Lowering of the ceiling limits may be attempted wherever this is possible.

(ii) Inclusion of major son in the definition of family at this juncture as suggested in the agenda of May 1985 Conference may be considered by the States.

(f) States may also consider bringing land with religious and charitable institutions within the purview of land ceiling laws.

(g) Firm legal provision to provide security to the surplus land assignees from eviction and for prompt restoration where already evicted be made.

(h) Legislative provisions as indicated above and others including those by way of amendments to the existing ceiling law, be made at the earliest.

(i) Legal provision be made by the States/UTs for giving joint *patta* in the name of the head of the household and the spouse whenever land is allotted by Government or the Gram Sabha.

The Conference of Revenue Ministers held in November 1986 reviewed the progress of distribution of ceiling surplus lands and observed that effective steps had not been taken by the States to implement most of the recommendations of the Revenue Ministers Conference held in May 1985 and suggested that all the recommendations of the earlier Conference mentioned above should be fully implemented by 31-3-1988.

FINANCIAL ASSISTANCE TO ASSIGNEES OF SURPLUS LAND

Since the beneficiaries of the allotment of ceiling surplus land are mostly poor and much of the surplus land is of poor quality, it needs development so as to render it cultivable. A Centrally Sponsored Scheme, viz., financial assistance to assignees of ceiling surplus land, is being implemented by the Land Reforms Division of the Union Department of Rural Development since 1975-76. Under this scheme financial assistance is provided to the States for distribution among allottees of ceiling surplus land. Assistance by way of grant is given @ Rs. 2500 per hectare for various purposes like land development, provision of inputs as well as immediate consumption needs. This amount is shared equally by the Centre and the States. An amount of Rs. 22.43 crores was released as grant since the inception of the scheme upto 1984-85. During the Sixth Plan an amount of Rs. 10.34 crores was released by the Central Government while an amount of Rs. 10.88 crores was utilised by the States. During 1985-86 an amount of Rs. 3.10 crores was released. An outlay of Rs. 15.60 crores was made for the Seventh Plan. The scheme has been recommended by the

Union Department of Rural Development to be integrated with other schemes of rural development like the IRDP, NREP, RLEGP, etc. by entrusting its implementation to DRDAs. It is contemplated that assignees of surplus land would be given priority in the enlistment of beneficiaries under the IRDP and they are to be eligible for a total subsidy upto Rs. 8000 per family from all sources. Assistance from the different programmes of rural development would be so channelised as to help the assignees of surplus land to develop their land for purposes of agriculture or allied activities and enable them to build around that land a variety of economic activities which could provide them a viable source of income round the year. In this connection the Seventh Plan Working Group on the Development of Scheduled Castes observed that ceiling surplus lands were generally of marginal and sub-marginal quality and that while allotting any land to the Scheduled Castes and Scheduled Tribes the amount needed for comprehensive land development should be granted simultaneously to the allottees. All necessary inputs like seeds, fertilizers and irrigation water should be made available to them. The Working Group further suggested that allotment should be made preferably in clusters to the Scheduled Castes so that they could take advantage of the community facilities which were not otherwise available. Such group allotment would help in having an organisation of the Scheduled Castes which would reduce the scope of leakages and malpractices.

TENANCY REFORMS

The objective of national policy of tenancy reforms is to make the tiller of the soil its owner. Legislative provisions had been made in many States conferring ownership rights on tenants. In some States this right is acquired on payment of a reasonable compensation to the landlord. Some States have acquired ownership rights from landlords and transferred these to tenants from whom compensation is realised. The States where ownership rights have been given to the general body of tenants are Andhra Pradesh (Telengana area), Assam, Gujarat, Himachal Pradesh, Jammu and Kashmir, Karnataka, Kerala, Madhya Pradesh, Maharashtra, Manipur, Orissa, Rajasthan, Tripura and Uttar Pradesh. About 77 lakh tenants had benefited upto 1985-86 and they had been conferred ownership rights over a total area of 56 lakh hectares. Since the bulk of share-croppers and tenants belong to the Scheduled Castes and Scheduled Tribes their formal recognition, official recording and conferment of legal rights and ownership on them would go a long way towards the economic development of these communities. There is no legislative provision to confer ownership rights on tenants and share-croppers in Andhra Pradesh (Andhra area), Bihar, Haryana, Punjab, Tamil Nadu and West Bengal though security of tenure to tenants or landlords has been made. Further leasing has been prohibited in Jammu and Kashmir, Karnataka, Kerala, Uttar Pradesh and Delhi. However, oral and informal tenancies with cultivating possession still exist without any record in many areas of the country under the guise of personal cultivation, etc. The Conference of Revenue Ministers held in November 1986. *Inter alia,* made the following recommendations in this regard:

(i) The drive to find out the extent and spread of informal or concealed tenancies as suggested earlier should be continued wherever already started and initiated on a crash basis wherever not yet started. It should be followed by conferment of ownership rights on all categories of tenants including share-croppers excepting the specifically exempted categories. However, names of tenants tilling land belonging to exempted categories also should be recorded in the record of rights and they should be provided security of tenure.

(ii) The results of this drive should be regularly and vigorously monitored at the highest level by the respective State Governments.

(iii) In order to prevent emergence of informal and oral tenancies States may take steps to provide for a stricter definition of personal cultivation, wherever, not already done.

(iv) The existing definition of persons under disability and privileged tenants and provisions regarding exemptions in respect of other exempted categories including religious institutions should be reviewed. Necessary steps should be taken to plug loopholes in order to bring the existing legal provisions in conformity with national policy guidelines.

(v) It was agreed to examine the possibility of debarring lawyers in proceedings relating to conferment of ownership rights on tenants. If there were certain inherent legal difficulties in the way of enacting such a provision, the State Governments should provide free legal aid to tenants so that they could defend their rights in the courts.

According to the national policy the exempted category of tenants are members of Defence Services, widows, unmarried women, minors and persons suffering from physical and mental disabilities who were permitted to lease out lands to tenants without loss of ownership. But in some States deities have been treated as perpetual minors. The Union Department of Rural Development has, therefore, suggested to the States concerned to review such provisions relating to religious institutions. It has been further suggested that conferment of ownership rights on their tenants may also be considered after providing for an annuity as source of reasonable income to compensate for possible loss of land through suitable legislation.

ALIENATION OF TRIBAL LANDS

In spite of legislative and executive measures taken by various State Governments to prohibit transfer of lands belonging to Scheduled Tribe persons to non-tribals, alienation of tribal lands still continued. Such provisions were made either in the revenue laws or in the Regulations made under the Fifth Schedule to the Constitution. The problem existed in varying degrees in the tribal areas of Andhra Pradesh, Assam, Bihar, Gujarat, Kerala, Madhya Pradesh, Maharashtra, Orissa, Rajasthan, Tripura, Uttar Pradesh and West Bengal. The State Governments concerned were requested to furnish data about the alienation of tribal lands and information about the measure taken by them to meet this problem. The data received from eight States are given in Table 2.4.

In Andhra Pradesh the transfer of lands belonging to members of the Scheduled Tribes to non-tribals in the Scheduled Areas of the State was prohibited under the Andhra Pradesh Land Transfer Regulation, 1959. However, the State Government issued

TABLE 2.4

Sl. No	*State*	*No. of cases pending at the end of 1985-86*	*Fresh cases registered during 1986-87*	*Total of Cols. 3 and 4*	*No. of cases disposed of during 1986-87*	*Land restored during 1986-87 (in acres)*	*No. of pending cases at the end of 1986-87*
1.	Andhra Pradesh	—	—	40414	35998	74120.78	4414
2.	Assam	N.A.	2756	2756	2554	2062.00	202
3.	Bihar	5261 (1984-85)	7482 (1985-86)	12743	8292 (1985-86)	7276.76 (1985-86)	4451 (1985-86)
4.	Gujarat	2012	2477	4489	1462	4476.00	3027
5.	Maharashtra	548	52	600	163	949.00	437
6.	Orissa	2918	1877	4795	1009	479.30	3786
7.	Tamil Nadu	76 (1984-85)	107 (1985-86)	183	63 (1985-86)	121.97 (1985-86)	120 (1985-86)
8.	Tripura	1345	1640	2985	1220	205.38	1765

an order in 1969 that in the case of Government lands in the Scheduled Areas already encroached upon by non-tribals, while persons other than landless poor persons should be straightaway evicted from the lands occupied by them, landless poor persons should not be evicted from the lands under their occupation upto a maximum extent of 2.5 acres of wet or 5 acres of dry land, including other lands, if any, already owned by them, unless and until such lands were needed for assignment to tribals. The State Government in another order issued in 1971 decided that non-Scheduled Tribe poor persons in the Scheduled Areas of the State should not be evicted from the lands in their occupation upto the limits specified above if they had been in occupation of such lands for a period of not less than ten years and that tribal applicants might be assigned other lands in the same village or in the neighbouring villages. In 1974, the State Government decided that in the case of landless poor Scheduled Caste persons the condition of the ten-year period was not to be insisted upon and they were not to be evicted if they had been in possession of such lands since 1969. In 1979 the State Government issued yet another order in partial modification of the earlier orders to the effect that non-tribal landless poor in occupation of lands in the Scheduled Areas upto 5 acres of wet land or 10 acres of dry land should not be evicted for the time being under the provisions of the above mentioned Regulation of 1959. This order was challenged in the State High Court and was quashed on 5-12-1984. Although the judgment of the High Court was circulated to all the Collectors in the Scheduled Areas for information on 7-2-1985, the order had not yet been formally withdrawn by the State Government. Thus even though that State Government order of 1979 had become inoperative, the fact that it had not yet been withdrawn created an impression that the issue of land alienation was not being taken seriously and that even if the field officers ignored the implementation of this important Regulation, the Government were not likely to take a serious note of this default. On 12-9-1987 I wrote to the Chief Minister of Andhra Pradesh requesting him that a formal notification should be issued by the State Government immediately withdrawing the Government order of 1979, in order to remove the above impression. A reply is awaited.

I Kerala the State Government had enacted the Kerala Scheduled Tribes (Restriction on Transfer of Lands and Restoration of Alienated Land) Act, 1975. But it received the assent of the President only in November 1985. The State Government informed that the Act had been brought into force retrospectively with effect from 1-1-1982 on the issue of the Government Notification in January 1986. Necessary Rules under the Act known as Kerala Scheduled Tribes (Restriction on Transfer of Lands and Restoration of Alienated Lands) Rules, 1986 came into force on the issue of the State Government's Notification on 18-10-1986.

In Maharashtra the Maharashtra Land Revenue Code and Tenancy Laws (Amendment) Act, 1974, provided for restoration to a Scheduled Tribe person of his agricultural land involved in illegal transfer to a non-tribal, effected any time before 6-7-1974. Similarly, the Maharashtra Restoration of Lands to Scheduled Tribes Act, 1974 provided for restoration to a Scheduled Tribe person, of his agricultural land lawfully transferred to a non-tribal by way of sale, mortgage, gift, etc., effected between 1-4-1957 and 6-7-1974. The State Government informed that representations were received by them from persons affected by implementation of the above laws, particularly the latter Act, stating that a large number of non-tribals were rendered landless in the process of restoration of lands to the tribals. It was also reported that some of these non-tribals, as a result, lost their means of livelihood. In order to give relief to the affected non-tribal persons the State Government issued a circular on 31-7-1986 to the effect that no fresh proceedings under the above two Acts should be taken up. However, the cases already initiated before the issue of these instructions were to continue. Since these instructions adversely affected the interests of the Scheduled Tribe persons whose lands had been alienated. I took up the matter with the State Government requesting them to withdraw the above circular containing these instructions. The State Government agreed to my request and withdrew the circular on 4-6-1987 and the implementation of the above mentioned two Acts was resumed forthwith. The Collectors were also directed to issue necessary instructions to the Revenue officers concerned to decide the cases under the two Acts expeditiously.

The issue of alienation of tribal lands was discussed in the Conferences of State Revenue Ministers in May 1985 and November 1986. In pursuance of the decisions taken in these conferences the Government of India advised the State Governments to plug loopholes in the existing legal provisions, to make adequate administrative arrangements for speedy and effective implementation thereof and to create sufficient awareness among the tribals to enable them to take advantage of these legal provisions. The following recommendations were made by the above conference held in May 1985:

(i) A scrutiny of the existing provisions regarding banning of transfer of land belonging to tribals to non-tribals and its implementation with particular reference to:

(a) *suo moto* action;
(b) extension of limitation period;
(c) raising plea at any stage in proceedings before courts;
(d) making State as a party in civil proceedings;
(e) bringing trespass within the ambit of law; and
(f) physical restoration of land free from encumbrances

be completed by 31-12-1985 and necessary legislation for these and to plug loopholes be enacted by 31-12-1986.

(ii) Survey may be undertaken to detect old cases which could be taken up under the law.

(iii) Continuous review of legislative and executive measures be undertaken.

(iv) Updating of land records of the Scheduled Areas be completed in a phased manner by the end of the Seventh Plan.

(v) Complete reports on the recommendations of the Commissioner for Scheduled Castes and Scheduled Tribes be sent by the concerned State Governments/UT Administrations so as to reach the Union Department of Rural Development by 30-6-1985.

The Revenue Ministers' Conference held in November 1986 made the following recommendations:

(i) Suggestions made in May 1985 in respect of giving protection to tribals concerning their rights on land should be implemented without delay, if not already done.

(ii) Administrative and judicial machinery should be suitably strengthened to detect cases of alienation under the existing laws and for speedy disposal of these cases respectively.

(iii) Effective arrangements including deterrent legal provision should be made for ensuring that tribals were not evicted from land restored to them. In the context of the concern expressed about growing alienation of tribal lands, in spite of the existence of protective provisions, sufficient awareness must be created among the tribals about their legal rights.

(iv) While taking action to restore land to tribals from which they have been dispossessed the law of limitation and any other law seeking to nullify protective provisions should not apply. Suitable legislative proposals must be undertaken by the States for such enabling provisions.

(v) All steps should be taken for speedy disposal of cases arising out of alienation of tribal lands so that such lands can be restored to them under the existing legal provisions and the possession of tribals over the restored lands can be effectively protected. Most of the States did not consider setting up of special courts necessary because the disposal of such cases is done by the Revenue Courts. However, where such arrangements do not exist and the cases are tribal by judicial courts, special courts may be set-up. Appellate and revisionary forums should be curtailed to ensure speedy implementation of protective laws in favour of tribals.

TREE PATTA SCHEME

In pursuance of the recommendation of the Revenue Ministers' Conference held in May 1985 a Group was set-up by the Union Department of Rural Development to evolve guidelines for a Tree *Patta* Scheme to give usufructuary rights in trees planted on unculturable wastelands belonging to Government. Panchayats and the community including land alongside roads and canals, in order to give a vested interest to individuals and provide an incentive to grow and protect trees, mainly of fuelwood, fruit and fodder species. The Report of the Group containing the guidelines, terms and conditions, model format and model form of legislation was sent by the Department to all the State Government/UT administrations recommending its adoption with such modification as might be considered necessary to suit the local situation.

The salient feature of the Tree *Patta* Scheme as per the guidelines issued by the Union Department of Rural Development are given below:

(1) The scheme shall be applicable to growing trees on Government, Panchayat or community wastelands in rural areas including Bhoodan land, surplus ceiling land which is lying in small scattered fragments and land along roads and canal embankments. It would not be applicable to growing trees on lands belonging to Government, Panchayat or community which have been leased out or on lands on which there is a title or interest of a private person.
(2) Culturable or productive agricultural lands should not be diverted for growing trees.
(3) In the case of lands belonging to the Central Government prior consent of the Central Government shall be obtained.
(4) The scheme will not apply to lands covered by the Forest (Conservation) Act, 1980.
(5) Beneficiaries shall include rural poor, i.e., as defined under the IRDP-landless agricultural labour, small and marginal farmers.
(6) Fifty per cent of the allottees shall be SCs and STs and 30 per cent allottees women.
(7) Block level committees will select beneficiaries on the recommendation of the village level committees.
(8) Units of not more than one hectare or 1 km. strip will be allotted to an individual beneficiary.
(9) Tree planting permit will be issued by the appropriate authority in favour of the beneficiary who should plant trees thereon within a period of two years and after verification of plants in the field, tree *pattas* will be granted for a period co-terminus with the silvicultural life of the tree.

(10) Breach of any condition of the tree planting permit or tree *pattas* will render the beneficiary liable for punishment, e.g., fine, simple imprisonment and eviction.

(11) *Pattadar* will have the right only to the usufruct of trees but no other right on the land itself.

(12) Trees can be hypothecated to a bank/financial institution for raising loan.

(13) To ensure proper implementation recommendations have been made to create the following nodal agencies at different levels:

(a) Department of Rural Development to be the nodal agency at the Government of India level;

(b) State level committees with Secretary, Rural Development, as Convener with Secretaries of Revenue, Forest and PWD Department as members;

(c) District level committee with Collector as the head with the Project Directors, DRDA/ITDP and representatives of other Government Departments as members;

(d) Block level committee with representatives from all Departments and Panchayat Raj institutions; and

(e) A Revenue official to be placed with the BDO to look after this scheme and depending on the workload, a Forest official can also be placed at the Block level.

According to the information furnished by the Ministry of Environment and Forests the schemes has been introduced in Bihar, Madhya Pradesh and Uttar Pradesh. In Tamil Nadu rights similar to tree *pattas* have been granted under the Revenue Code by introducing an amendment in June 1986. The Governments of Jammu and Kashmir, Kerala and West Bengal and the Administrations of Arunachal Pradesh, Delhi and Lakshadweep expressed their inability to adopt this scheme because of tenurial problems and non-availability of land.

MINIMUM WAGES FOR AGRICULTURAL LABOURERS

Agricultural labourers being in the unorganised sector and

scattered all over rural areas have very little bargaining power in the absence of a viable organisation. Most of them, therefore, depend on Government machinery for benefits in the shape of fixation of minimum wages, etc. According to the 1981 Census 48.2 per cent of the total Scheduled Caste workers and 32.6 per cent of the total Scheduled Tribe workers were agricultural labourers. The percentages of SC and ST agricultural labourers among the total number of agricultural labourers in the country were 32.88 per cent and 12.93 per cent respectively. Disputes over payment of minimum wages to Scheduled Caste and Scheduled Tribe agricultural labourers constitute one of the important causes of atrocities on members of these communities. Under the Minimum Wages Act, 1948 the State Governments concerned had to fix the minimum wages for labourers in their respective States. Under Section 3 of the Act the State Governments were required to review, at such intervals as they might think fit but not exceeding five years, the minimum rates of wages and revise these, if necessary. A table giving State-wise information regarding the minimum wages for unskilled workers as on 20-5-1987 as furnished by the Ministry of Labour may be seen at Annexure III.

The disparity in wages and the formulation of a national minimum wage/regional minimum wages were discussed in the past in various forums. In pursuance of the suggestion of the National Commission on Labour, 1969 that a uniform monetary rate of remuneration for the country as a whole was neither feasible nor desirable and that efforts should be made to fix regional minimum wages in different homogeneous regions in each State, the matter was later discussed in the 28th session of the Indian Labour Conference held in November 1985. It recommended that till such time as a national minimum wage was feasible, it would be desirable to have regional minimum wages for which the Central Government could lay down the guidelines. The matter was considered in the meetings of the State Labour Secretaries held in April 1987 and the Labour Ministers' Conference held in May 1987. The guidelines for the regional minimum wages were circulated by the Ministry of Labour in the light of the conclusions of the Labour Ministers' Conference. These, however, did not have any statutory backing as the Minimum Wages Act, 1948 did not provide for fixation of regional minimum wages. These guidelines are given below:

(a) There will be six Regional Minimum Wages Advisory Boards with the nodal States shown within brackets: Eastern Region (West Bengal), North-Eastern Region (Assam), Southern Region (Tamil Nadu), Northern Region (Haryana), Western Region (Maharashtra) and Central Region (Uttar Pradesh). The meetings of the Boards will be chaired by the Labour Secretaries of the States where they are held. The Board will comprise six representatives each of employers and workers, one representative from each State Government/UT Administration and the Director/Deputy Secretary concerned from the Government of India.

(b) Regional Minimum Wages may be fixed employment-wise for selected employments within a region. The Regional Minimum Wages Advisory Boards may select such employments which are spread over more than two States in a region or in which wide differential causes flight of industry/business from one State to another.

(c) After the initial fixation of the regional minimum wages the Boards may meet at least twice a year to review the situation.

(d) In fixing the regional minimum wages the boards should take into account the prevailing wage rates in the particular employment in different States of the region and the neighbouring regions, the capacity to pay, requirement of skill for the employment, hazards involved, etc.

(e) The Regional Boards may keep the concept of poverty line in mind while determining the minimum wages.

(f) The minimum wages so fixed may be related to a particular level of All India Consumer Price Index Number compiled by the Labour Bureau, Shimla. However, the States may raise the wage whenever there is a rise of 50 points in the price index. The fixation and revision of wages may be done by each State Government by following the usual procedure under the Minimum Wages Act, 1948 while keeping the recommendation of the Board in view.

The above Labour Ministers' Conference, *inter alia,* also

recommended that in order to raise the status of the unorganised labour it was essential to implement the labour laws which most closely concerned them. Among these were the Minimum Wages Act, 1948; Inter-State Migrant Workmen (Regulation of Employment and Conditions of Service) Act, 1979; the Contract Labour (Regulation and Abolition) Act, 1970; the Bonded Labour System (Abolition) Act, 1976; the Child Labour (Regulation and Abolition) Act, 1986; the Beedi and Cigar Workers (Conditions of Employment) Act, 1986. The following action by the Central and State Governments was recommended by the conference to remove the difficulties faced in the implementation of the Minimum wages Act:

(a) Removing the lack of awareness among labour as well as employers of the provisions of the Minimum Wages Act and other Acts affecting unorganised labour, through a sustained publicity campaign both by the Central and State Governments;
(b) Strengthening and upgrading enforcement machinery of the State Governments with assistance from the Central Government as may be required;
(c) Ensuring that inspection staff have the necessary mobility by giving them transport facility and extending to them security in the course of their work involving enforcement of the Minimum Wages Act and other legislation governing agricultural and other labour especially in rural areas. The Central Government may consider extending suitable assistance to the State Governments for this.
(d) The assistance of other Departments of the State Governments like the Revenue Department, Rural Development Department and Welfare Department should also be taken, depending upon the conditions obtaining in individual States/Union Territories for the effective enforcement and implementation of the laws above mentioned.

Atrocities on SCs and STs on Account of Agrarian Tension

The persistence of serious social and economic inequalities in rural areas has given rise to tensions between different classes.

Although legislative and executive measures have been taken by various States to check alienation of tribal lands to non-tribals and to restore alienated lands back to the Scheduled Tribes, they have to face many difficulties in obtaining the actual possession of the allotted lands, Scheduled Caste and Scheduled Tribe persons have thus to face many atrocities at the hands of the vested interests on account of these reasons as well as due to non-payment of the prescribed minimum wages. A large number of representations from the SC/ST victims of such atrocities were received in this organisation. Such cases were also reported in the press. An illustrative State-wise list of 58 cases is given in Annexure IV alongwith a brief account of each case.

ALLOTMENT OF HOUSE-SITES TO LANDLESS WORKERS

The National Housing Policy lays special emphasis on the provision of house-sites to the Scheduled Castes and Scheduled Tribes, freed bonded labourers and landless labourers including artisans and provision of financial assistance for house construction to them on suitable loan-*cum*-subsidy basis. Under the scheme of Allotment of House-Site-*cum*-Construction Assistance for landless workers an allocation of Rs. 576.90 crores was made for the Seventh Five Year Plan period. An expenditure of Rs. 245.10 crores was incurred under the scheme during the first two years of the Seventh Plan. A total of 148.47 lakh families were provided house-sites by various States/Union Territories upto the end of 1986-87. The number of SC/ST families provided house-sites during the years 1983-84 to 1985-86 and 1986-87 under the scheme in various States, in respect of which information is available, may be seen in the Table 2.5.

INDIRA AWAAS YOJANA

The scheme known as Indira Awaas Yojana was launched during the Seventh Plan as part of the Rural Landless Employment Guarantee Programme (RLEGP) for construction of houses for SCs and STs and freed bonded labourers in rural areas. It was envisaged to construct one million houses during the Seventh Plan under the scheme. During the first two years of the Plan an expenditure of Rs. 196.04 crores was incurred on the

TABLE 2.5

Sl. No.	State/UT	No. of SC and ST families provided house-sites during			
		1983-84 to 1985-86		1986-87	
		SC	ST	SC	ST
1.	Andhra Pradesh	259341	117206	60311	18138
2.	Assam	Nil	11733	N.A.	N.A.
3.	Bihar	37673	6035	6570	666
4.	Gujarat	7163	5727	6174	7427
5.	Haryana	36981	*	1290	*
6.	Himachal Pradesh	Nil	Nil	N.A.	N.A.
7.	Jammu and Kashmir	94	*	N.A.	*
8.	Karnataka	175021	Nil	N.A.	N.A.
9.	Kerala	6760	972	N.A.	N.A.
10.	Madhya Pradesh	47558	49127	3368	3708
11.	Maharashtra	5420	1950	N.A.	N.A.
12.	Orissa	34808	16864	16105	N.A.
13.	Punjab	Nil	*	Nil	*
14.	Rajasthan	36248	16836	21395	9227
15.	Tamil Nadu	195252	2803	113131	N.A.
16.	Tripura	N.A.	N.A.	N.A.	N.A.
17.	Uttar Pradesh	133038	4287	48988	53
18.	West Bengal	12115	5908	2795	788

*Not applicable.

scheme. Upto December 1986 about 3.50 lakh houses were sanctioned by the Government of India spread over various States/UTs. According to the guidelines issued by the Union Department of Rural Development the identification of beneficiaries should be based on their economic condition so that the poorest among the poor are selected for the scheme in open Gram Sabha meetings. As far as possible construction of houses is to be taken up by beneficiaries themselves under technical supervision provided by the State Government. In case it is not possible for beneficiaries to construct the houses, the construction can be taken up by the rural engineering organisation, etc. of the State Government. But even in such cases beneficiaries should be engaged as workers in the construction of houses to the maximum possible extent, In the implementation of the scheme the habitat concept is to be followed, which implies proper clustering and arrangement of the houses in space for economy of design and construction cost, keeping in mind ventilation, natural lighting, etc., and also other basic necessities such as rudimentary drainage, toilets, storage lofts, means of waste disposal and plantation of trees, all weather road link to the village from the main road, etc.

The type and design of the houses for each region are to be worked out by the State Governments. The Central Government provide funds upto a ceiling of Rs. 7200 per unit subject to the RLEGP guidelines for the maximum ceiling of non-wage expenditure of 50 per cent. However, the unit cost of assistance may be increased upto Rs. 9000 for housing in hill areas, difficult and remote areas, black cotton soil areas, etc., with the prior approval of the Central Committee on RLEGP. The above additional requirement of funds for housing or for non-wage component over 50 per cent, if any, is to be (net by the State Governments from their own funds, contribution of beneficiaries, loans from the HUDCO or other State Corporations responsible for rural housing. Infrastructural developments like land levelling, provision of drainage, site development, construction of internal roads, water supply, etc., are funded in addition to the unit cost of the house indicated above, to the extent of Rs. 3,000 or 50 per cent of the ceiling approved by the HUDCO for rural housing per unit, by the Central Government under the RLEGP, subject to the minimum wage expenditure of 50 per cent. The requirement that the wage expenditure will not be less than 50 per cent of the expenditure applies to the cost of house construction and infrastructural development taken together for the annual programme of a Block. The State projects are, thereof, prepared on the basis of Block-wise projections and taking into account the type/design for different regions. The unit cost, type, design, infrastructure, etc., are approved by the Central Committee on RLEGP as part of the RLEGP projects to be submitted by the States. The additional requirements of funds and the arrangements of funds by the States are also considered by the Central Committee.

The scheme is being implemented through the DRDAs in most of the States except a few States. In Andhra Pradesh it is being implemented by the Housing Corporation while in Uttar

Pradesh by the Rural Housing Board. In Karnataka the Land Development Department is implementing it. The working of the scheme was reviewed by the Union Department of Rural Development of the basis of reports submitted by the inspecting officers of the Department. The shortcomings observed by the Department on the basis of these reports were: (i) lack of planning, (ii) improper cluster lay-out, (iii) lack of infrastructure facility, (iv) lack of latrines/*chulhas*/storage facility, (v) in some latrines only one leach pit being provided instead of two, (vi) lack of soak pits for kitchen and bath, (vii) lack of ventilation, (viii) poor workmanship and quality, (ix) in a few clusters the new tile roofing already sagging and not set properly, (x) improper design of smokeless *chulhas*, (xi) lack of involvement of beneficiaries, (xii) inappropriate techniques of construction with excessive use of cement and steel, (xiii) bought-out approach instead of make-out approach resulting in use of high cost materials involving long distance transportation rather than use of low cost local materials, (xiv) deficiency in the employment aspect, and (xv) lack of development of micro-habitat with linkages to social forestry, fishery development, workshed facility, approach roads, etc.

ANNEXURE I

State-wise Land Ceiling Limits as Against the National Guidelines of 1972 and Lower Limits Suggested by the Government of India

	Irrigated with two crops	*Irrigated with one crop*	*Dry land*
Suggested in National Guidelines of 1972	4.05 to 7.28	10.93	21.85
Suggested lower ceilings	5.00	7.5	12
Actual Ceilings			
Andhra Pradesh	4.05 to 7.28	6.07 to 10.93	14.16 to 21.85
Assam	6.74	6.74	6.74
Bihar	6.07 to 7.28	10.12	12.14 to 18.21
Gujarat	4.05 to 7.29	6.07 to 10.93	8.09 to 21.85
Haryana	7.25	10.9	21.8
Himachal Pradesh	4.05	6.07	12.14 to 28.33
Jammu and Kashmir	3.6 to 5.06	—	5.95 to 9.20 In Ladakh 7.7 hec.
Karnataka	4.05 to 8.10	10.12 to 12.14	21.85
Kerala	4.86 to 6.07	4.86 to 6.07	4.86 to 6.07
Madhya Pradesh	7.28	10.93	21.85
Maharashtra	7.28	10.93	21.85
Manipur	5.00	5.00	6.00
Orissa	4.05	6.07	12.14 to 18.21
Punjab	4.00	11.0	20.50
Rajasthan	7.28	10.93	21.85 to 70.82
Tamil Nadu	4.86	12.14	24.28
Sikkim	5.06	—	20.23
Tripura	4.00	4.00	12.00
Uttar Pradesh	7.30	19.95	18.25
West Bengal	5.00	5.0	7.00

Notes: (1) The actual ceiling limits for lands having two crops and single crop respectively irrigated in Karnataka and Uttar Pradesh are marginally higher due to classification of land.

(2) The actual ceiling limits in respect of dry land in Himachal Pradesh and Rajasthan are higher due to hilly terrain and being desert also respectively.

(3) In West Bengal ceiling limits are not dependent upon crop potential. The ceiling is based on the size of family and is different for irrigated and non-irrigated land.

ANNEXURE II

Statement Showing the Areas of Land Declared Surplus due to Imposition of Ceiling Laws and the Area Allotted to Scheduled Castes and Scheduled Tribes and other Beneficiaries During the Period Ending 31-3-1987

(Compiled as on 22-7-1987)

(Area in acres)

State/UT	Area declared surplus			Area taken possession			Area distributed to individuals		
	Pre-revised	Revised	Total	Pre-revised	Revised	Total	Pre-revised	Revised	Total
1	2	3	4	5	6	7	8	9	10
Andhra Pradesh	N.A.	766531	766531	N.A.	482862	482862	N.A.	362180	362180
Assam	N.A.	604172	604172	N.A.	527023	527023	N.A.	389164	389164
Bihar	N.A.	448190	448190	N.A.	334371	334371	N.A.	216739	217739
Gujarat	45956	194021	239977	44699	100485	145184	44304	63363	107667
Haryana	351734	31698	383432	9218	21264	110482	89038	21273	110311
Himachal Pradesh	N.A.	284046	284046	N.A.	281454	281454	N.A.	3340	3340
Jammu and Kashmir	450000	6000	456000	N.A.	450000	450000	N.A.	450000	450000
Karnataka	N.A.	295950	295950	N.A.	152891	152891	N.A.	114695	114695
Kerala	N.A.	126241	126241	N.A.	88881	88881	N.A.	59383	59383
Madhya Pradesh	75062	223038	298090	66376	141985	208362	40787	95277	136854
Maharashtra	319193	389512	708705	272520	334964	607484	179520	328981	508501
Manipur	—	1652	1652	—	1632	1632	—	1632	1632

Orissa	N.A.	183504	183504	N.A.	155404	155404	N.A.	144270	144270
Punjab	246036	49670	295706	89130	14310	103440	86289	13330	99619
Rajasthan	363281	248458	611739	314363	228154	542517	229284	156378	395662
Tamil Nadu	68170	98587	166757	64621	92771	157392	N.A.	124975	124275
Tripura	—	2012	2012	—	1929	1929	—	1521	1521
Uttar Pradesh	198780	309304	508084	198392	284597	482989	141154	202898	344052
West Bengal	1048848	191039	1239887	965814	143771	1109585	740209	92982	833191
Dadra and Nagar Haveli	—	8953	8953	—	7524	7524	—	4952	4952
Delhi	377	776	1153	377	764	1141	210	102	312
Pondicherry	—	2553	2553	—	1195	1195	—	935	935
Total	3167437	4465697	7633134	2105510	3848232	5953742	1560795	2848670	4409465

(*Contd.*)

Note: In respect of Andhra Pradesh, Assam, Bihar, Himachal Pradesh, Karnataka, Kerala and Orissa, figures of area declared surplus under the old law have not been reported by the States concerned. Figures in acres have been worked out taking 37.1 acres equivalent to 1 standard holding in case of Andhra Pradesh.

ANNEXURE II (*Contd.*)

States/UT	*No. of beneficiaries*			*Scheduled Caste beneficiaries*					
	Pre-revised	*Revised*	*Total*	*Area (acres)*			*No. of beneficiaries*		
				Pre-revised	*Revised*	*Total*	*Pre-revised*	*Revised*	*Total*
1	*11*	*12*	*13*	*14*	*15*	*16*	*17*	*18*	*19*
Andhra Pradesh	N.A.	308756	308756	N.A.	171411	171411	N.A.	137348	137348
Assam	N.A.	358697	358697	N.A.	31527	31527	N.A.	31027	31027
Bihar	N.A.	243669	243669	N.A.	123881	123881	N.A.	145131	145131
Gujarat	14784	9935	24719	6313	54158	60471	1534	7878	9412
Haryana	30949	6059	37008	33186	9698	42884	11474	2832	14306
Himachal Pradesh	N.A.	4400	4400	N.A.	2305	2305	N.A.	2934	2934
Jammu and Kashmir	N.A.	450000	450000	N.A.	N.A.	N.A.	N.A.	N.A.	N.A.
Karnataka	N.A.	26437	26437	N.A.	59626	59629	N.A.	15258	15258
Kerala	N.A.	117034	117034	N.A.	23162	23162	N.A.	49196	49196
Madhya Pradesh	10830	37958	48788	9335	24038	33373	2979	11430	14409
Maharashtra	34635	91580	196215	36193	110634	146827	7494	29876	37370
Manipur	—	326	326	—	5	5	—	3	3
Orissa	—	120744	120744	—	46177	46177	—	41653	41653
Punjab	22134	3494	25628	34246	6618	40864	8134	1636	9770
Rajasthan	38649	33825	72474	77748	51531	129279	13839	12872	26711
Tamil Nadu	N.A.	97785	97785	—	47946	47946	N.A.	43324	43324

Tripura	—	1317	1317	—	211	211	—	241	241
Uttar Pradesh	70490	217102	287592	89635	145955	235690	43226	154687	197913
West Bengal	1429467	282122	1711589	N.A.	310505	310505	520477	117380	637857*
Dadara and Nagar Haveli	—	2282	2282	—	38	38	—	17	17
Delhi	364	290	654	202	80	232	253	242	495
Pondicherry	—	1134	1134	—	581	581	—	—	723
Total	1652302	2414946	4067248	286958	1220090	1507048	609410	805688	1415098

(Contd.)

* Area distributed to SC, ST and others in West Bengal not reported. It has been calculated on the basis of average area allotted to an individual in that State.

ANNEXURE II (*Contd.*)

State/UT	*Scheduled Tribe beneficiaries*					
	Area in acres			*No. of beneficiaries*		
	Pre-revised	*Revised*	*Total*	*Pre-revised*	*Revised*	*Total*
1	20	21	22	23	24	25
Andhra Pradesh	N.A.	63970	63970	N.A.	57609	57609
Assam	N.A.	42113	42113	N.A.	28624	28624
Bihar	N.A.	26590	26590	N.A.	26376	26376
Gujarat	19260	7644	26904	9940	1662	11602
Haryana	—	—	—	—	—	—
Himachal Pradesh	N.A.	139	139	N.A.	261	261
Jammu and Kashmir	N.A.	N.A.	N.A.	N.A.	N.A.	N.A.
Karnataka	N.A.	3860	3860	N.A.	940	940
Kerala	N.A.	4926	4926	N.A.	6629	6629
Madhya Pradesh	16454	44004	60458	3989	14987	18976
Maharashtra	26661	58835	85496	7021	18043	25064
Manipur	—	25	25	—	15	15
Orissa	—	60114	60113	—	44776	44776
Punjab	—	—	—	—	—	—
Rajasthan	21597	18130	39727	5415	4843	10258
Tamil Nadu	N.A.	127	127	—	84	84
Tripura	—	426	426	—	314	314

Uttar Pradesh	294	1749	2043	102	1409	1511
West Bengal	—	159376	159376	270037	57363	327400
Dadra and Nagar Haveli	—	4912	4912	—	2264	2264
Delhi	—	—	—	—	—	—
Pondicherry	—	—	—	—	—	—
Total	842266	496939	581205	296504	266199	562703

(Contd.)

ANNEXURE II (CONTD.)

State/UT	*Other beneficaries*					
	Area in acres			*No. of beneficiaries*		
	Pre-revised	*Revised*	*Total*	*Pre-revised*	*Revised*	*Total*
1	*26*	*27*	*28*	*29*	*30*	*31*
Andhra Pradesh	N.A.	126799	126799	N.A.	113799	113799
Assam	N.A.	315524	315524	N.A.	299046	299046
Bihar	N.A.	67268	67268	N.A.	72162	72162
Gujarat	18731	1561	20292	3310	395	3705
Haryana	55852	11575	67427	19475	3227	27702
Himachal Pradesh	N.A.	896	896	N.A.	1205	1205
Jammu and Kashmir	N.A.	450000	450000	N.A.	45000	450000*
Karnataka	N.A.	51206	51206	N.A.	10239	10239
Kerala	N.A.	31295	31295	N.A.	61209	61209
Madhya Pradesh	15144	27089	42233	3822	11581	15403
Maharashtra	116665	159513	276178	20120	43661	63781
Manipur	—	1602	1602	—	308	308
Orissa	—	37980	37980	N.A.	34315	34315
Punjab	52043	7612	58755	14000	1858	15858
Rajasthan	139939	86717	226656	19395	16110	35505
Tamil Nadu	—	76202	76202	N.A.	54377	54377
Tripura	—	884	884	—	762	762

Uttar Pradesh	51125	55194	106319	27162	61006	88168
West Bengal	268616	94694	363310	638958	107374	746332
Dadra and Nagar Haveli	—	2	2	—	1	1
Delhi	10	20	30	112	47	159
Pondicherry	—	354	324	—	411	411
Total	718125	163087	2321212	746354	1343093	2089447

(Contd.)

*In Jammu and Kashmir area distributed to beneficiaries has not been reported by the State and hence total area has been shown as distributed to others.

ANNEXURE II (*Contd.*)

(*Area in acres*)

State/UT	*Area declared surplus but not distributed (Col. 4 to Col. 10)*	*Area not available for distribution due to*				*Total area not available for distribution (Total Col. 33 of Col. 36)*	*Net area available for distribution (Col. 32 to Col. 37)*
		Area involved in litigation	*Area reserved for public purposes*	*Area unfit for cultivation*	*Area not available for mics. reasons*		
1	*32*	*33*	*34*	*35*	*36*	*37*	*38*
Andhra Pradesh	404351	300856	4773	65479	—	371100	33243
Assam	215008	76000	56397	18423	59630	210420	4588
Bihar	230451	150173	—	13345	51119	214637	15814
Gujarat	132310	94793	25524®	—	8993	129310	3000
Haryana	273121	8748	180	—	264193*	273121	Nil
Himachal Pradesh	280706	2591	50928	136220	16048	205787	74919
Jammu and Kashmir	6000	—	—	—	—	—	6000
Karnataka	181255	169744	10295	338	878	181255	Nil
Kerala	66858	28827	19900	—	16450	65185	1673
Madhya Pradesh	162026	93942	11719	26891	18127	150607	11419
Maharashtra	200204	53727	90204	26471	21022	192224	7990
Manipur	20	5	—	—	—	5	15
Orissa	39234 ′	20076	2675	2154	12662	37567	1667

Punjab	196087	36189	—	—	159308	195491	590
Rajasthan	216077	109012	46329	8744	5701	169786	46291
Tamil Nadu	42482	26804	14017	—	—	40821	1661
Tripura	491	64	269	45	18	396	95
Uttar Pradesh	164032	45256	113529	93	2758	161636	2396
West Bengal	406696	181195	44000	121000	1934	348129	50567
Dadara and Nagar Haveli	4001	1429	927	1225	—	3581	420
Delhi	841	169	123	—	481	773	68
Pondicherry	1418	1156	—	—	—	1156	262
Total	3223669	1400756	491789	420356	640100	2953001	270668

@Area reserved for Narmada Project.

*Area came under exemptions due to inheritance.

ANNEXURE III

Statement of Minimum Wages in Agriculture (for Unskilled Workers) as fixed by the Central Government and Reported by the State Governments/UT Administrations as on 20-5-1987

State	Date from which effective	Rates of wages	Remarks
1	2	3	4
1. Central Government	12-2-1985	Rs. 850 to Rs. 12.75 according to areas	
2. Andhra Pradesh	9-2-1987	Rs. 11.00 per day	80% for children from 15 to 18 years
3. Assam	22-2-1985	Rs. 12.50 per day	
4. Bihar	16-10-1985	Rs. 10.00 per day	
5. Gujarat	2-10-1982	Rs. 11.00 per day	Steps to revise the minimum wages are being taken
6. Haryana	23-4-1982	Rs. 19.25 per day	Minimum wages linked to Consumer Price Index
7. Himachal Pradesh	4-1-1987	Rs. 15.00 per day	Workers are entitled to $12^1/_2$% to 25% higher wages in certain areas.
8. Jammu and Kashmir	7-7-1984	Rs. 10.50 per day	
9. Karnataka	31-1-1985	Rs. 9.50 to Rs. 14.00 per day according to class of work and type of land	
10. Kerala	1-6-1984	Rs. 12.00 per day for light work and Rs. 15.00 per day for hard work	No separate D.A.

11.	Madhya Pradesh	1-1-1982	Rs. 10.49 per day	The rate of Special Allowance is 45 paise per month per point for every point rise in the average of CPI Number above 449 (1960=100)
12.	Maharashtra	1-2-1983	Rs. 6.00 per day	
13.	Manipur	2-3-1983	Rs. 13.00 to Rs. 10.50 per day according to areas	
14.	Meghalaya	1-4-1985	Rs. 11.00 per day	
15.	Nagaland	1-2-1984	Rs. 15.00 per day	
16.	Orissa	15-7-1986	Rs. 10.00 per day	
17.	Punjab	1-4-1987	Rs. 18.48 per day	
18.	Rajasthan	16-1-1985	Rs. 14.00 per day	
19.	Sikkim	1-4-1985	Rs. 11.00 per day	Minimum Wages Act, 1948 not yet extended to the State. The minimum wages fixed by executive orders.
20.	Tamil Nadu	5-4-1983	Rs. 12.00 per day	
21.	Tripura	12-3-1984	Rs. 12.00 per day	
22.	Uttar Pradesh	13-7-1983	Rs. 11-50 per day	
23.	West Bengal	31-10-1985	Rs. 16.34 per day	
24.	Andaman and Nicobar	15-8-1986	Rs. 19.00 per day Islands	
25.	Arunachal Pradesh	1-9-1986	Rs. 16.00 per day	
26.	Chandigarh	1-1-1986	Rs. 17.25 per day	
27.	Dadra & Nagar Haveli	3-9-1983	Rs. 9.00 per day	
28.	Delhi	10-16-1985	Rs. 18.90 per day	
29.	Goa, Daman & Diu	2-10-1983	Rs. 12.00 per day	
30.	Mizoram	There is no organised agricultural labour. Prevailing rate is Rs. 16.00 per day		
31.	Pondicherry	28-11-1985	Rs. 8.00 per day	

ANNEXURE IV

Brief Accounts of Some Cases of Atrocities on SCs and STs on Account of Land Related Problems

Andhra Pradesh

(1) A representation was received in March 1987 from some Scheduled Tribe residents of village Hothi 'K' Zaheerabad Mandal, District Medak, stating that some Government wasteland was allotted to them and recorded in their names in 1965. It was alleged that some non-tribal landlords who gave loans to these Scheduled Tribe persons on surety of this land later dispossessed them of the land by obtaining their signatures on blank papers fraudulently. The matter was referred to the Collector, Medak. A reply was awaited.

Bihar

(2) A representation was received in February 1986 from a Scheduled Caste resident of village Jailgarha, District Dhanbad, alleging that a piece of land which was allotted to him by the Gram Panchayat about 30 years ago had been forcibly encroached upon by a non-Schedule Caste landlord. The matter was referred to the Collector, Dhanbad. A reply was awaited.

(3) A representation was received in May 1986 from a Scheduled Caste resident of village Subhanipur, District Samastipur, in which it was stated that his uncle mortgaged two pieces of cultivable land to a landlord for Rs. 28 and Rs. 15 respectively. After expiry of the stipulated time they had been requesting the landlord to return their mortgaged land on repayment of the loan. But even after 30 to 35 years the land was not restored. The matter was referred to the Collector, Samastipur. A reply was awaited.

(4) A representation was received in June 1986 from some Scheduled Caste residents of village Patra, P.O. Bihta, District Patna, alleging that some villagers had encroached on some portions of their lands. They had requested to get the encroachment removed. The matter

was referred to the District Magistrate, Patna. A reply was awaited.

(5) A representation was received in August 1986 from a Scheduled Tribe resident of village Hinu, Doranda, Ranchi, that some land purchased by his father in 1946 and registered in his name in the revenue records had been illegally encroached on by a non-tribal. The matter was taken up with the Collector, Ranchi, who informed that the possession of the land had since been restored to the representationist.

Haryana

(6) A representation was received in July 1985 from some Scheduled Caste residents of village Kashipur, Tahsil Atarchata, District Faridabad, alleging that the agricultural land allotted to them was being forcibly cultivated by some dominant and moneyed villagers who were conspiring to sell the land. The matter was referred to the Deputy Commissioner, Faridabad. A reply was awaited.

(7) A representation was received in July 1985 from some Scheduled Caste residents of village Kherhar, Tahsil Bahadurgarh, District Rohtak, alleging that some non-Scheduled Caste persons had forcibly occupied their plots of land allotted to them under the 20-Point Programme. These persons were also threatening them. The matter was referred to the Deputy Commissioner, Rohtak, who informed that the matter was *sub judice* and final outcome was awaited.

(8) A representation was received in August 1985 from a Scheduled Caste resident of village Pailak, Tahsil Palwal, District Faridabad, alleging that he had been forcibly dispossessed of the land allotted to him under the 20-Point Programme by the local Sarpanch who had sold the land to some other non-Scheduled Caste persons. In spite of his complaints to the district authorities no action was alleged to have been taken. He had requested for the restoration of the land to him. The matter was referred to the Deputy Commissioner, Faridabad. A reply was awaited.

(9) A representation was received in August 1985 from a Scheduled Caste resident of village Bahadurgarh, District Rohtak, alleging that a non-Scheduled Caste person had forcibly occupied his land. He had complained many a time to the Tahsildar about this but in vain. The matter was referred to the Deputy Commissioner, Rohtak. A reply was awaited.

(10) A representation was received in October 1986 from some Scheduled Caste residents of village Daboda Khurd, District Rohtak, alleging that some lands allotted to them by the Gram Panchayat under the 20-Point Programme had been illegally encroached on by some non-Scheduled Caste persons of that village with the collusion of the Sarpanch. The matter was referred to the Deputy Commissioner, Rohtak. A reply was awaited.

(11) A representation was received in November 1986 from the President, Akhil Bharatiya Anusuchit Jati and Backward Classes Seva Dal, Nilokheri, District Karnal, alleging illegal encroachment on land allotted to the Scheduled Caste residents of village Shahpur Sirsi in Karnal District under the 20-Point Programme, by some non-Scheduled Caste persons of that village. The matter was taken up with the Deputy Commissioner, Karnal, who informed that the case was *sub judice* and the final outcome was awaited.

(12) A representation was received in January 1987 from a Scheduled Caste resident of village Ladhuvas Ahir, P.O. Saharanvas, Distrist Mahendragarh, alleging that 5 Bighas of surplus land allotted to him in 1979 had been forcibly encroached upon by a non-Scheduled Caste landlord. The matter was taken up with the Deputy Commissioner, Mahendragarh, who reported that the possession of the disputed land had since been restored to the representationist.

Madhya Pradesh

(13) A representation was received in February 1987 from a Scheduled Caste resident of village Mangrol, District Morena, alleging that some part of his ancestral land registered in his name in the revenue records had been

illegally encroached on by a non-Scheduled Caste person with the collusion of the village Patwari. The matter was referred to the Collector, Morena. A reply was awaited.

Orissa

(14) A representation was received in February 1987 from a Scheduled Tribe resident of village Siripur, District Keonjhar, alleging that a piece of recorded land measuring 4 acres located in Baniapat Mauza which was in the possession of her father since 1922 Settlement operations and the possession of which passed on to her and her sister after her father's death, was illegally encroached on by a non-tribal in May 1984. He also constructed a house on the land. The matter was referred to the Collector, Keonjhar. A reply was awaited.

Rajasthan

(15) A representation was received in May 1985 from a Scheduled Caste resident of village Dulapura, Tahsil Ramgarh, District Sikar, alleging that some non-Scheduled Caste persons had forcibly occupied his land. He had sent an application to the Gram Panchayat who had given a decision in his favour. But instead of accepting the decision these people had allegedly beaten him. The police also did not file any case against these persons. The matter was referred to the District Magistrate, Sikar. A reply was awaited.

(16) A representation was received from a Scheduled Caste resident of Barmer alleging that some non-Scheduled Caste persons had entered into his house at night on 17-9-85, beat him and his family members and also tribed to murder them. These persons had also occupied his land. He had requested for protection to him and his family members and for restoration of his land. The matter was referred to the District Magistrate, Barmer, who informed that all the culprits had been arrested and charge sheets served on them. The matter was *sub judice* and the final outcome was awaited.

(17) A representation was received in October 1985 from a

Scheduled Caste resident of village Kulama, Tahsil Kama, District Bharatpur, alleging that some non-Scheduled Caste residents of the village and encroached on a piece of the house site allotted to him. The matter was referred to the District Magistrate, Bharatpur, whose reply was awaited.

(18) A representation was received in January 1986 from a Scheduled Caste resident of village Ghuma, Tahsil Sapotra, District Sawaimadhopur, alleging that an ex-Sarpanch had forcibly occupied his land for which the court had already given judgment in his favour. He had requested for the restoration of his land to him. The matter was referred to the District Magistrate, Sawaimadhopur, who informed that the case was *sub judice* and the final outcome was awaited.

(19) A representation was received in March 1986 from Dr. Ambedkar Seva Samiti, Dhankiya, Jaipur, alleging forcible dispossession from the land allotted to a Scheduled Caste resident of village Sinvar, District Jaipur, in June 1965, by a non-Scheduled Caste person. The matter was referred to the District Magistrate, Jaipur, whose reply was awaited.

(20) A representation was received in December 1986 from a Scheduled Caste resident of village Patoos, District Pali, alleging that his land measuring 5 Bighas which was allotted to him by the State Government had been illegally encroached on by some non-Scheduled Caste persons. The matter was referred to the District Magistrate, Pali, whose reply was awaited.

Tamil Nadu

(21) It was reported in the press in November 1985 that large areas of land belonging to marginal tribal farmers were being purchased by non-tribal outsiders in Coimbatore District, as a result of which the tribal cultivators were being reduced to the position of agricultural labourers. The matter was taken up with the State Government and the Collector of Coimbatore District. A reply was awaited.

Uttar Pradesh

(22) A complaint was received in May 1985 from some Scheduled Caste residents of village Sihorwa, District Gorakhpur, alleging atrocities committed on them by some influential and powerful persons at the time of consolidation of holidings. It was alleged that the Scheduled Caste persons were threatened with dire consequences if they tried to get their names entered in the official land records. The case was referred to the Collector, Gorakhpur, whose reply was awaited.

(23) A representation was received in January 1986 from a Scheduled Caste resident of village Khalikpur Khurd, P.O. Mustafabad, District Rai Bareli, alleging that agricultural land allotted to him by the State Government had been grabbed by a non-Scheduled Caste person. He had requested for restoration of his land and protection of his life. The matter was referred to the District Magistrate, Rai Bareli, who replied that the case fell in the jurisdiction of the civil court and the applicant should file a case in the court. The applicant was informed accordingly.

(24) A representation was received in January 1986 from a Scheduled Caste resident of village Mazra Mohammad Ali, District Nainital, alleging that a non-Scheduled Caste person had occupied his land forcibly. He had also been threatening to murder him. He had requested for security of his life and restoration of his land. The matter was referred to the District Magistrate, Nainital, whose reply was awaited.

(25) A representation was received in February 1986 from a Scheduled Caste resident of village Haripura Harsan, Tahsil Bazpur, District Nainital, alleging that some portion of the land allotted to him had been forcibly occupied by some persons who had also been threatening to kill him. He had requested for the protection of his life and the restoration of his land. The matter was referred to the District Magistrate, Nainital, whose reply was awaited.

(26) A representation was received in February 1986 from a Scheduled Caste resident of village Pakri Buzurg,

District Azamgarh, alleging that his land had been grabbed forcibly by some persons of the same village. The matter was referred to the District Magistrate, Azamgarh, whose final reply was awaited.

(27) A representation was received in March 1986 from a Scheduled Caste resident of village Khambari, P.S. Bazpur, District Nainital, alleging that some persons had occupied his land after the death of his father and he had got its possession back with the help of the police. These persons had been allegedly trying to murder him and they had attacked him several times. He had requested for protection of his life. The matter was referred to the District Magistrate, Nainital, whose reply was awaited.

(28) A representation was received in March 1986 from a Scheduled Caste resident of village Serawal, District Allahabad, alleging that a non-Scheduled Caste person had occupied the land allotted to his father by the Gram Sabha. The applicant was also threatened that he would be murdered. The matter was referred to the District Magistrate, Allahabad, whose reply was awaited.

(29) A representation was received in March 1986 from some Scheduled Caste residents of village Logava, Tahsil Manjhanpur, District Allahabad, alleging that some rich landlords of the village had been forcing them to work in their fields on meagre wages. They had been threatening them that if they did not do so they would be kicked out of the village. The matter was referred to the District Magistrate, Allahabad, who informed that the case was *sub judice.*

(30) In March 1986 the General Secretary, All India Safai Mazdoor Congress, Delhi, represented to this office on behalf of some Scheduled Caste residents of village Pipli, Tahsil Khair, District Aligarh, that they were allotted some land under the 20-Point Programme in 1975 which was alleged to have been illegally encroached upon by caste Hindu landlords. The case was referred to the District Magistrate, Aligarh, whose reply was awaited.

(31) A representation was received in April 1986 from a

Scheduled Caste resident of village Padainia (Bhagat Tola), P.S. Gola Bazar, District Gorakhpur, alleging that some non-Scheduled Caste persons had forcibly occupied his land on which he had been living alongwith his three brothers for the last 15 years. These people had been threatening to demolish his house. He had requested for restoration of his land. The matter was referred to the District Magistrate, Gorakhpur, whose reply was awaited.

(32) A representation was received in April 1986 from two Scheduled Caste residents of village Haripura, Tahsil Bazpur, District Nainital, alleging that some persons had forcibly occupied their land, even though the court had given a decision in favour of one of the Scheduled Caste persons. They had requested for restoration of their land and also for free legal aid. The matter was referred to the District Magistrate, Nanital, who informed that the case was *sub judice* and the final outcome was awaited.

(33) A representation was received in May 1986 from a Scheduled Caste resident of village Rudragarh Nausi, District Gonda, alleging that a part of his ancestral land was forcibly encroached on by a non-Scheduled Caste person who also wanted to encroach on the remaining part of the land. The matter was referred to the District Magistrate, Gonda, who informed that the matter was *sub judice* and the final outcome was awaited.

(34) A representation was received in June 1986 from the Uttar Pradesh Anusuchit and Dalit Varga Kalyan Samiti, Bhagatpur Tanda, District Moradabad, alleging that the land allotted under the 20-Point Programme to Scheduled Caste residents of village Akka Fattu Hafizpur, District Moradabad, had been encroached on forcibly by some non-Scheduled Caste persons. The matter was taken up with the District Magistrate, Moradabad, whose reply was awaited.

(35) A representation was received in July 1986 from the Akhil Bharatiya Harijan and Shoshit Varga Utthan Samiti, Bazpur, District Nainital, alleging encroachment of agricultural land belonging to a Scheduled Caste resident of village Darhiyal in Rampur District by a non-

Scheduled Caste person. The matter was taken up with the District Magistrate, Rampur, who informed that the possession of the land had since been restored to the applicant.

(36) A representation was received in August 1986 from the Akhil Bharatiya Harijan and Shoshit Varga Utthan Samiti, Bazpur, District Nainital, alleging illegal encroachment by a caste Hindu on about 0.87 acre land allotted to a Scheduled Caste resident of village Rafatpur, Tahsil Bilaspur, District Rampur, under the 20-Point Programme. The matter was referred to the District Magistrate, Rampur, who informed that the possession of the disputed land had since been restored to the representationist.

(37) A representation was received in September 1986 from a Scheduled Caste resident of village Chhitona, Tappa Nikodi, District Gorakhpur, alleging that his land which was his ancestral property was forcibly occupied by some persons of the same village. They had also been threatening to murder him. He had requested for restoration of his land. The matter was referred to the District Magistrate, Gorakhpur. The final outcome was awaited.

(38) A representation was received in October 1986 from a Scheduled Caste resident of village Nagsar (Meer Rai), Tahsil Jamnia, District Ghazipur, alleging that 1.5 acres of his ancestral land was forcibly encroached upon by some non-Scheduled Caste persons. He filed a case in the Civil Court which gave the verdict in his favour but he could not get possession of the land. The matter was taken up with the district authorities whose reply was awaited.

(39) A representation was received in October 1986 from a Scheduled Caste resident of village Gurvalia Tola, Banjara Patti, District Deoria, alleging that 0.7 acre land purchased by him and registered in his name in revenue records was fraudulently got transferred by a non-Scheduled Caste person in his name in revenue records in collusion with the Patwari. Later the applicant was also dispossessed of the land. The matter was taken up

with the District Magistrate, Deoria, whose reply was awaited.

(40) A representation was received in October 1986 from some Scheduled Caste residents of village Dhindhala, District Meerut, alleging that some lands allotted to them and for which *pattas* were issued in their names were forcibly encroached on by some non-Scheduled Caste persons. The matter was taken up with the District Magistrate, Meerut, whose reply was awaited.

(41) Some Scheduled Caste residents of village Jitiapur, Tahsil Harraiya, District Basti, represented in December 1986 that a non-Scheduled Caste person was trying to dispossess them of their ancestral lands forcibly and illegally. The matter was referred to the District Magistrate, Basti, who informed that the matter was *sub judice* and the final outcome was awaited.

West Bengal

(42) A representation was received in April 1985 from 26 Scheduled Caste and 12 Scheduled Tribe residents of village Chiknamati, P.O. Hardigachh, District Darjeeling, alleging that the Government vested land in the village which they had been cultivating for about 30 years had been included in West Dinajpur District during the last settlement operations. They had submitted several petitions to West Dinajpur district authorities for issuing *pattas* in their favour, but no action has been taken so far. Some outsiders from Nepal, Bhutan, Bangladesh and Bihar who were now residing in their village were trying to get the *pattas* in their names and to deprive their legal claims and title on the land. The matter was referred to the Deputy Commissioner, Darjeeling, and the District Magistrate, West Dinajpur, whose replies were awaited.

(43) A representation was received in August 1985 from a Scheduled Tribe resident of village Atharo Khai, P.S. Siliguri, District Darjeeling, alleging that a non-tribal had been harassing him and his father and wanted to grab the land on which he was having leasehold rights for the last 50 years. The representationist was also

allegedly being implicated in false court cases. The matter was taken up with the Deputy Commissioner, Darjeeling, whose reply was awaited.

(44) A representation was received in October 1986 from some Scheduled Tribe residents of Thana Falakata/ Birpara, District Jalpaiguri, alleging that their lands had been occupied by some brick kiln owners. They requested that their lands should be restored to them. The matter was referred to the District Magistrate, Jalpaiguri, who informed that action had been taken against unauthorised brick fields and that the Scheduled Castes and Tribes Welfare Officer, Alipurduar, had been asked to take action regarding restoration of land u/s 14E of W.B.L.R. (Amendment) Act, 1986.

Pondicherry

(45) A representation was received in October 1986 from a Scheduled Caste resident of Padmini Nagar, Pondicherry, alleging that a piece of his ancestral land was illegally and forcibly encroached upon by a non-Scheduled Caste person with the collusion of the local police. The matter was reported by him to the Police but he could not get the possession of the land. The matter was taken up with the U.T. Administration who informed that the case was *sub judice* and the final outcome was awaited.

The Agriculture Scenario

GENERAL TRENDS

According to the 1951 population census the average area of cultivable land per head of population engaged in agriculture in Bihar was 0.61 acre. With the transfer of 3166 sq. miles of area of the State to West Bengal in 1956 this average area went down further.

In 1951 the net cultivated area formed 49.5 per cent of total area and the average size of holdings was 4.06 acres (against the all-India figure of 7.5 acres). Although the number of large holders was about 0.5 per cent yet their holdings covered 32 per cent of total land area. Since then large chunks of cultivated land have gone under the bed of the Damodar Valley Corporation and the Mayurakshi Reservoir and for the establishment of various industrial units in the State.

Our dependence on agriculture continuously increased since 1931. 78.7 per cent of our earners had pasture and agriculture as their principal occupation in 1931 and 87.3 percent of them had these as such in 1951.

In 1951 in some districts such as Saran 100 acres of sown area had to support as many as 230 persons belonging to the agricultural classes.

In 1951, 11.67 per cent of the cultivators and 11.77 percent of the agricultural labourers in the whole country lived in Bihar on 7.71 per cent of its total land area whereas in 1961, 10.41 per cent of the cultivators and 14.05 per cent of the agricultural labourers in the whole country lived in Bihar on 6.07 per cent of its total land area.

The area sown more than once in Bihar had increased from 26 per cent in the last decade of the 19th century to 31 per cent during 1945-48 whereas our culturable wastes other than current fallows had decreased from 13 per cent of the total land area to 8 per cent during the same period.

According to the 1951 census, the agricultural population in Bihar as percentage of the all-India figure was the highest, as shown by Table 3.1 given below.

TABLE 3.1

Area, Population and Agricultural Population as Percentage of All-India

States	*Area as percentage of all-India of different reorganised States (1956)*	*Population as percentage of all-India of different re-organised States (1951)*	*Agricultural population as percentage of all-India of different re-organised States (1951)*
Andhra Pradesh	8.34 (5)	8.65 (3)	8.45 (3)
Assam	6.32 (7)	2.50 (12)	2.66 (12)
Bombay	15.10 (1)	17.37 (1)	11.99 (2)
Bihar	5.30 (9)	10.74 (2)	13.39 (1)
Jammu & Kashmir	7.32 (6)	1.22 (13)	N.A.
Kerala	1.15 (14)	3.75 (10)	2.92 (11)
Madhya Pradesh	13.39 (2)	7.23 (5)	8.17 (4)
Madras	3.96 (11)	8.30 (4)	7.56 (5)
Mysore	5.85 (8)	5.37 (6)	5.55 (7)
Orissa	4.75 (10)	4.06 (9)	4.86 (8)
Punjab	3.74 (12)	4.47 (7)	4.26 (10)
Rajasthan	10.45 (3)	4.41 (8)	4.46 (9)
Uttar Pradesh	8.95 (4)	4.41 (8)	4.46 (9)
West Bengal	2.63 (13)	2.27 (11)	6.21 (6)
Union Territories	2.19	1.14	0.87

Note: Figures in brackets indicate ranks.

As would appear from Table 3.2, on the one hand, the availability of cultivable land per capita of the rural population was among the lowest in Bihar and, on the other, the percentage of working force occupied in agriculture to total rural population was fairly high. This had resulted in a heavy pressure of population on land.

TABLB 3.2

Per Capita Cultivable Land and Participation Rate in Rural Areas of Different States of India (1957)

States	*Per Capita Cultivable Land of Rural Population (Acres)*	*Participation Rate (percentage of working force in agriculture to total rural population)*
Assam	0.73 (15)	31.81 (11)
Bhopal	2.31 (1)	33.43 (8)
Bihar	0.72 (14)[a]	32.59 (9)
Bombay	1.72 (6)	37.83 (5)
Hyderabad	1.75 (4)	38.51 (4)
Madhya Bharat	1.73 (5)	37.20 (6)
Madhya Pradesh	1.78 (3)	50.73 (1)
Madras	0.79 (13)	23.72 (16)
Mysore	1.24 (9)	25.07 (15)
Orissa	1.07 (11)	30.03 (13)
Punjab	1.36 (10)	32.44 (10)
Rajasthan	1.96 (2)	45.59 (2)
Uttar Pradesh	0.90 (12)	37.03 (7)
Saurashtra & Kutch	1.44 (7)	31.36 (12)
Travancore-Cochin	0.42 (17)	20.84 (17)
Vindhya Pradesh	1.43 (8)	43.25 (3)
West Bengal	0.71 (16)	27.93 (14)

[a]In 1962-63 cultivable area per agricultural worker amounted to 1.81 acres.
Note: Figures in brackets indicate ranks.

LAND UTILIZATION

The extent of land utilization considerably varies from region to region according to the fertility of soil, rainfall, availability of irrigation facilities, cultivation practices, etc. The following Table 3.3 shows State-wise break-down of land utilization under different heads for the year 1956-57.

It is evident from the following Table 3.3 that the net sown area for all-India was only 44.7 per cent of the total area during 1956-57. At the State levels the percentage of net sown area was above the all-India average in Bihar, Madras, Kerala, Mysore, Bombay, Punjab, Uttar Pradesh and West Bengal, ranging from 45 (Madras) to 58.8 (West Bengal) in the ascending order. It was below 20 per cent of the total area only in Assam; it ranged between 35 and 42 in Madhya Pradesh, Orissa, Rajasthan and Andhra Pradesh in the ascending order.

Only 14.3 per cent of the net sown area of the country was under double cropping. Excepting Madhya Pradesh, Orissa, Andhra Pradesh, Bombay, Mysore and Rajasthan, the double-cropped area was above the all-India average in all other States.

It would appear that there is still scope for bringing more land under cultivation. It would seem that there is relatively greater scope for extension of cultivation particularly in Rajasthan, Madhya Pradesh, Bihar, Orissa, Andhra Pradesh, Madras and Mysore.

The next Table 3.4 contains subsequent information on the cropped area per 1000 population, net area irrigated as percentage to the net area sown, percentage distribution of foodgrain production, per capita gross value of agricultural production and value of forest produce per thousand population towards the end of the First Plan and the beginning of the Second Plan. The relative position of Bihar among the States seems to be inglorious.

LAND HOLDINGS

Insofar as any attempt to deal effectively with the question of land reform must be based on information regarding the distribution of land and the fragmentation of holdings, it would not be out of place to try to find out here how far this information is available in relation to Bihar.

A Sample Food Survey of Bihar was conducted in 1946 by Professor Gorakhnath Sinha. This survey was based on a sample of 1520 villages, i.e., 2.3 per cent of the total number of villages in Bihar. Although the purpose of the survey was the estimation of production and consumption of food, certain statistics of land-holdings were also collected. Information was collected from all the families living in the villages surveyed and the land held by

TABLE 3.3

Land Utilization in States

(In Percentage)

States	*Net area sown*	*Area under current fallows, fallow lands other than current fallows, other uncultivated land*	*Total area irrigated*	*Area sown more than once*	*Area now available for cultivation*
Andhra Pradesh	42.3 (9)	21.8 (6)	25.2 (5)	9.4 (10)	15.3 (7)
Assam	15.0 (13)	13.2 (12)	28.9 (3)	16.6 (7)	36.6 (1)
Bihar	44.8 (8)	20.2 (7)	22.9 (7)	30.3 (2)	12.4 (10)
Bombay	55.6 (4)	15.7 (8)	5.4 (12)	4.7 (11)	15.9 (6)
Kerala	48.1 (6)	15.2 (9)	18.3 (8)	20.8 (4)	10.6 (12)
Madhya Pradesh	35.6 (12)	22.5 (5)	5.3 (13)	13.6 (8)	10.7 (11)
Madras	45.0 (7)	23.8 (3)	38.3 (2)	19.0 (5)	17.4 (4)
Mysore	54.0 (5)	22.7 (4)	7.4 (11)	3.2 (13)	8.9 (13)
Orissa	36.1 (11)	24.7 (2)	17.4 (9)	8.0 (12)	16.3 (5)
Punjab	56.5 (3)	15.2 (9)	40.2 (1)	32.0 (1)	24.0 (2)
Rajasthan	36.3 (10)	41.9 (1)	11.4 (10)	10.4 (9)	17.6 (3)
Uttar Pradesh	57.6 (2)	15.1 (10)	27.3 (4)	26.2 (3)	15.1 (8)
West Bengal	58.5 (1)	14.6 (11)	23.5 (6)	16.8 (6)	15.0 (9)
All-India (Excluding islands)	44.7	21.7	17.3	14.3	16.1

Note: Figures in brackets indicate ranks.

TABLE 3.4

Agriculture, Irrigation and Forests

States	*Cropped area per 1000 population (1959-60) (Acres)*	*Net area irrigated as percentage to net area sown (1959-60)*	*Percentage distribution of foodgrain production in States (Average of 1958-59 to 1962-63)*	*Per capita gross value of agricultural production (1958-59)*	*Value of forest produce per thousand population (1960-61) (Rs.)*
Andhra Pradesh	841 (1)	27.1 (6)	8.45 (4)	111.1 (3)	920 (10)
Assam	575 (11)	28.1 (5)	2.14 (12)	145.5 (1)	1318 (7)
Bihar	604 (10)	22.6 (8)	9.15 (3)	82.6 (9)	391 (14)
Gujarat	1245 (3)	6.7 (13)	2.80 (12)	82.1 (10)	1425 (6)
Jammu & Kashmir	562 (12)	45.1 (1)	0.76 (15)	55.0 (14)	28216 (1)
Kerala	350 (15)	18.7 (9)	1.36 (14)	75.2 (11)	1729 (4)
Madhya Pradesh	1458 (2)	5.8 (14)	11.93 (2)	123.2 (2)	2885 (2)
Madras	525 (13)	38.6 (3)	6.83 (7)	93.3 (7)	597 (11)
Maharashtra	1218 (5)	5.7 (15)	8.32 (5)	82.1 (10)	1729 (4)
Mysore	1146 (6)	7.9 (12)	5.02 (10)	74.9 (12)	2124 (3)
Nagaland	—	—	0.09 (16)	—	—
Orissa	889 (7)	17.4 (10)	4.75 (11)	62.9 (13)	1622 (5)
Punjab	1231 (4)	40.1 (2)	7.94 (6)	104.3 (4)	591 (12)
Rajasthan	1859 (1)	10.9 (11)	6.44 (8)	90.0 (8)	1111 (9)

Uttar Pradesh	750 (9)	30.1 (4)	17.69 (1)	103.7 (5)	1159 (8)
West Bengal	454 (14)	25.8 (7)	6.33 (9)	99.5 (6)	422 (13)
All States	892	18.1	100.0	102.0	—

Notes: Col. (2) Cropped area: If different crops are raised in a year successively on a portion of land, the same area is counted more than once.

Col. (3) In computing the net area sown; Area sown more than once is counted only once and similarly in respect of the net area irrigated.

Col. (4) Foodgrains include: Cereals (rice, jowar, bajra, maize, ragi, small millets, wheat and barley) and pulses (gram, tur and other pulses).

Col. (5) Figures against Gujarat and Maharashtra relate to the old Bombay State.

Figures in brackets indicate ranks.

a family, whether situated inside or outside a village was recorded against that family. Besides, the land shown against a family was the land it cultivated, whether the family owned it or not.

While compiling the results of the survey, the families were divided into three classes according as they owned or cultivated lands up to five acres, between five to fifteen acres, and above fifteen acres. The percentage of distribution of these families was found to be as shown in the following Table 3.5

TABLE 3.5

Category of Family	*Description*	*Percentage of total number of families owning or cultivating land*
Class I	Families with lands above 15 acres	7.8
Class II	Families with lands between 5 and 15 acres	23.3
Class III	Families with lands up to 5 acres	68.9

Although no information was given as to the total area of land owned or cultivated by each of these classes of families, yet the foodgrains produced by each of these classes were estimated. Neglecting the foodgrains produced by the landless families, which amounted to 8.6 per cent of the total foodgrains grown in the surveyed villages, the information collected can be put in the form of a table, as given below:

TABLB 3.6

	Percentage of total number of families owning or cultivating	*Percentage of total foodgrain produced by the three classes of families*
Class I	7.8	31.9
Class II	23.3	32.4
Class III	68.9	35.7

Assuming that there is no material difference in the yield of the land held by the three classes and in the proportion between the cultivated and the uncultivated land held by each class, the conclusion which emerges is that about 8 per cent of the land owning families cultivated 32 per cent of the land whereas 23 per cent of them cultivated 32 per cent and 69 per cent of them cultivated 36 per cent of the land.

An Agricultural Labour Enquiry was undertaken in Bihar in 1950 by the Ministry of Labour of the Government of India. Bihar was divided into four homogeneous zones and a total of 80 villages were randomly selected from all the four zones in proportion to the number of villages and the population in each zone. As this was part of an all-India enquiry, the sample selected, although representative for an all-India point of view, could not necessarily be representative from the point of view of Bihar.

The eighty villages sampled covered a population of 52,471 persons and an area of 49,120 acres, that is, the size of the sample selected covered 9.109 per cent of the area, 0.141 per cent of the rural population and 0.112 per cent of the villages in Bihar.

Among others, information was collected during this enquiry regarding the distribution of the cultivators' holdings according to the size and category of family. Only the land inside the village held by the villagers was taken account of. The village lands held by outsiders were excluded. All lands in the village held by one family were shown as one holding even though they might have been registered under separate holdings. Only cultivated lands were shown in the size of the holdings. Thus, out of a total area of the villages surveyed of 49,120 acres, detailed classification in respect of the size of holdings is available in respect of 28,539 acres only. The result of the classification may be put in the form of a Table 3.7.

Nearly 77 per cent of the holdings in Bihar were less than 5 acres each and accounted for nearly 30 per cent of the total cultivated area. On the other hand, the number of holdings over 50 acres constituted only 0.5 per cent of the total area. The average size of the holdings worked out at 4.06 acres.

A rapid survey of agricultural holdings was conducted by the Department of Agricultural Statistics in April, 1952. One village from each of the 200 circles was selected for the survey except in the case of the Jehanabad circle where two villages were selected. Since the return from one village could not be collected, the size of the sample was 0.278 per cent of the total number of villages.

TABLE 3.7

(In Percentage)

Size	*Number*	*Area*
1. Below 1 acre	31.0	3.6
2. Between 1.1 and 2.5 acres	25.5	10.3
2. Between 2.6 and 5 acres	20.5	17.9
4. Between 5.1 and 10 acres	14.3	24.2
5. Between 10.1 and 25 acres	7.1	24.9
6. Between 25.1 and 50 acres	1.1	8.6
7. Over 50 acres	5.5	10.5
Total	100.0	100.0

Unlike the above-mentioned two surveys, this survey was based on the number of registered holdings rather than the amount of land owned or cultivated by a family. The land held by a villager put situated outside a village was excluded, while the land inside a village but held by the outsiders was included.

A comparison of the results reached by the Sample Food Survey with those reached by the Agricultural Statistics Department Survey shows:

TABLE 3.8

	Percentage of holdings up to 5 acres	*Percentage of holdings between 5 and 15 acres*	*Percentage of holdings over 15 acres*
Sample survey of the Agricultural Statistics Department	86.7	10.3	3.0
Sample Food Survey	68.9	23.3	7.8

It is easy to see why the figures of the percentage of holdings under 5 acres should have been less according to the Sample Food Survey than according to the Agricultural Statistics Department Survey, for, as we have already seen, the former survey combined into one holding lands held by a family although registered under two or more holdings and also included *batai* lands whereas the latter survey did not do so. A comparison of the results of the

Agricultural Labour Survey with those of the Agricultural Statistics Department Survey shows:

TABLE 3.9

	Percentage of holdings up to 5 acres	*Percentage of holdings between 5 and 10 acres*	*Percentage of holdings above 10 acres*
Sample Survey of the Agricultural Statistics Department	86.7	7.8	5.5
Sample Survey of the Agricultural Labour Enquiry	77.0	15.3	8.7

That the figures of the percentage of holdings under 5 acres as ascertained by the Agricultural Labour Enquiry should be smaller than those of the Agricultural Statistics Department Survey can only be accounted for on the assumption that the proportion of the cultivated land in small holdings was almost negligible.

But the reason why the Sample Food Survey figures were even lower than those of the Agricultural Labour Enquiry was perhaps that in the former lands owned by the villagers but situated outside the villages had also been included whilst in the other two surveys they had not been so included. An examination of the results of the surveys conducted by the Agricultural Labour Enquiry and the Agricultural Statistics Department of the proportion of land covered by the holdings of more than 50 acres brings out a material difference between them, which must be due to the high proportion of cultivated land in the case of the larger holdings.

According to the results of the Agricultural Labour Enquiry, the average size of all holdings of more than 50 acres was 77 acres. On the other hand, according to the survey of the Agricultural Statistics Department, it was 282 acres. According to the survey of the Agricultural Statistics Department, the total area of land in Bihar covered by the holdings of more than 50 acres each was estimated at 14.5 million acres out of a total geographical area of 45 million acres.

It is also of interest to note that although, according to the survey of the Agricultural Statistics Department, the proportion of cultivated area to uncultivated area was 100.60 for the entire area surveyed, yet it was as low as 100:505 for the area covered by the holdings exceeding 50 acres.

Therefore, if in a measure of land reform it were decided to put a ceiling on land holdings at 50 acres then, although an area of about 14 million acres might be available for distribution among about 2 million families of the landless agricultural labourers and *bataidars*, each such family would get about 7 acres of land, provided it could find the means to pay for the land and was prepared to move from the densely populated area of North Bihar to the distant districts of Chotanagpur division in order to cultivate the land there.

An examination of the position of the districts from this angle shows that in 1952 the proportion of the small holdings up to 5 acres varied almost directly with the average density of the population of a district, as Table 3.10 illustrates.

It was unfortunate that the survey undertaken by the Department of Agricultural Statistics was conducted in a hurry and the sample selected was not a perfectly random one. Moreover, the compilation left out an important piece of information, namely, the total area of land under each size of the holdings.

To put it in a nutshell, on the eve of the First Plan 31 per cent of the land holdings in Bihar were of the size of one acre or less; 77 per cent of them were of 5 acres or less; 92.3 per cent of them were of the size of 10 acres or less; and only 8.7 per cent of them were of a size of more than 10 acres. However, holdings of one acre or less comprised 3.6 per cent of the total area of all holdings; those of 5 acres or less 31.8 percent; those of 10 acres or less 56.0 per cent; and lastly, those of more than 10 acres formed 44.0 per cent of the total area.

By 1961 the average size of holdings in Bihar had further diminished to 3 acres fragmented into 12 plots. On the whole, 61 per cent of the total holdings were of not more than the size of one standard acre. 94 per cent of the owner and tenant families cultivated their entire holdings. The number of large holders was comparatively few, forming less than 0.5 per cent, though the area covered by their holdings was nearly 32 per cent of the total land area. This spoke of an unequal distribution of land, which added

TABLE 3.10

Districts	*Density of Population per sq. mile*	*Percentage of Holdings under 5 acres (Agricultural Statistics Survey)*
Patna	1219 (1)	91.6 (4)
Gaya	652 (8)	79.6 (14)
Shahabad	616 (10)	84.0 (10)
Saran	1172 (2)	95.0 (1)
Champaran	713 (6)	88.0 (8)
Muzaffarpur	1168 (3)	93.0 (2)
Darbhanga	1125 (4)	92.4 (3)
Monghyr	726 (5)	89.0 (5)
Bhagalpur	658 (7)	80.0 (3)
Saharsa	619 (9)	88.3 (6)
Purnea	514 (12)	88.1 (7)
Santhal Parganas	427 (13)	78.7 (15)
Hazaribagh	276 (15)	81.9 (11)
Ranchi	261 (16)	77.4 (16)
Palamau	192 (17)	77.1 (17)
Manbhum	556 (11)	84.8 (9)
Singhbhum	329 (14)	80.4 (12)

Note: Figures in brackets indicate ranks.

to the inefficiency of our agriculture. The percentage of uncultivated area was also as high as 78 in respect of the holdings above 50 acres. The Report on the Techno-Economic Survey by the National Council of Applied Economic Research conducted in 1956-57 suggested the levy of a surcharge on land revenue in respect of such uncultivated lands excepting those which were clearly uncultivable.

THE AGRICULTURISTS

The agricultural labour families constitute a substantial part of the rural labour force in Bihar. In 1951, they formed 39.9 per cent of all the rural families in Bihar as against the all-India average of 34.4 per cent (see Table 3.11).

TABLE 3.11

Proportion of Agricultural Labourers to Total Population in Different States of India (1951)

Census Zones	*Percentage of Agricultural Labour in Rural Population*		
	Total	*With Land*	*Without Land*
Central Zone	36.7	14.6	22.1
Hyderabad	42.1	19.5	22.6
Madhya Bharat	19.9	7.5	12.4
Madhya Pradesh	40.1	14.9	25.2
East India	32.7	19.0	13.7
Assam	10.7	6.7	4.0
Bihar	39.9	25.6	14.3
Orissa	43.0	23.8	19.2
West Bengal	23.8	10.5	13.2
North India	43.3	5.7	8.6
Uttar Pradesh	43.3	5.7	8.6
North West India	9.0	2.7	7.1
Jammu & Kashmir	3.4	2.7	0.7
PEPSU	13.2	0.6	12.6
Punjab	10.1	1.6	8.5
Rajasthan	9.3	3.7	5.6
South India	50.1	27.3	22.8
Madras	53.0	28.3	24.7
Mysore	42.0	27.4	14.6
Travancore-Cochin	39.5	20.8	18.7
West India	20.4	8.8	11.6
Bombay	20.4	9.6	17.8
Saurashtra	20.0	2.2	22.1
All-India (including Jammu & Kashmir)	34.4	15.2	15.2

Among the agricultural classes, the cultivators of land, wholly or mainly owned, formed in 1951 roughly 55.3 per cent of the total population of Bihar as against the all-India figure of nearly 47 per cent—the percentages of the cultivator's land, wholly or mainly unowned, and the cultivating labourers to the total population respectively were 8.3 and 8.9 in the case of India and 22 and 12.6 in that of Bihar. The cultivating labourers constitute the weakest link of the State's agricultural population.

The percentage of the landless agricultural labourers to total population was in 1951, 22 in Bihar, 20.3 in Madhya Pradesh, 12.5 in West Bengal, 10.2 in Madras and 5.7 in Bombay. 77 per cent of these in Bihar were casual workers and remained idle for the greater part of the year.

The proportion of the cultivating labourers to total population in 1951 was the highest in North Bihar where they numbered more than 54 lakhs and constituted 29.86 per cent of the total population and 32.2 per cent of the agricultural population. They were most numerous in Darbhanga district where they formed nearly 39 per cent of the total population and 44 per cent of the agricultural population. In South Bihar they formed 22.25 per cent of the total population and 28.2 per cent of the agricultural population. In Chotanagpur they formed only 7.79 per cent of the total population and 9.2 per cent of the agricultural population. The only district in Chotanagpur in which they formed more than 10 per cent of total population was Palamau. Less than 1 per cent of the total population in Bihar in 1951 constituted the non-cultivating owners and the rent receivers. Only 7 per cent of the self-supporting persons of the agricultural classes had some subsidiary source of livelihood.

Although the agricultural labourers and their families constituted 12.6 per cent of the total population of the Indian Union in 1951, and as much as 21.9 per cent of the total population in Bihar, yet a detailed study of their economic conditions, specially on a comparable all-India basis was lacking since 1928 when a Royal Commission on Agriculture reported. It was only in 1949 that the First Agricultural Labour Enquiry was undertaken by the Minister of Labour, Government of India.

The report of the First Agricultural Labour Enquiry, published in 1954, contained some useful information and made possible some inter-State comparisons. The enquiry was conducted in 806 villages of the Indian Union, selected on a stratified random sampling basis, leaving out only villages with a population of less than one hundred persons. Thus, 120 villages were selected from Uttar Pradesh, 84 from Madras, 80 from Bihar, and so on. The enquiry was conducted in two stages. In the first stage, each sampled village was surveyed in respect of its population, number and classification of families, and utilization and yield of crops livestock, and so on. In the second stage, about

50 per cent of the agricultural labour families, randomly selected, in each sampled village, was intensively surveyed in respect of certain other characteristics such as income, employment, consumption expenditure, indebtedness, and so on.

As stated earlier the enquiry was conducted in 80 villages of Bihar covering an area of 49,120 acres of (of which 7,171 acres were not taken note of as they were owned by persons residing outside the sampled villages) and a population of 52,471 persons comprised by 9556 families of which 1228 families of the agricultural labourers were intensively surveyed.

In the following Table 3.12 some of the averages computed from this enquiry are compared with those computed from the complete population census of 1951.

TABLE 3.12

	Bihar State	*Agricultural Labour Enquiry (1950-51)*	*Population Census (1951)*
(1)	Average area per village	614	626
(2)	Average population per village	656	526
(3)	Average density of population	684	537
(4)	Average number of persons per family	5.5	5.2[a]

[a]On the basis of 6883 sample households in the rural areas.

The pattern of land utilization in Bihar, as revealed by the Agricultural Labour Enquiry (A.L.E.), is given below for comparison with the figures published by the Superintendent of Agricultural Statistics (Supdt., A.S.), Bihar. It should, however, be noted that the comparison is somewhat vitiated by the fact that

TABLE 3.13

	As Percentage of total area	*A.L.E. (1950-51)*	*Supdt., A.S. (1951)*
1.	Net area sown	64.0	49.4
2.	Current fallow	3.8	12.1
3.	Forest	9.6	18.9
4.	Cultivable waste	10.3	7.2
5.	Area not available for cultivation including cultivable waste	12.3	12.4
6.	Area sown more than once	15.1	10.9
7.	Area irrigated	13.4	12.5

for 7171 acres of the village land which were owned by persons residing outside the sampled villages, no details of land utilization were collected. Both sets of figures are unreliable and the first set can in no case be taken as representative of the State as a whole. A comparison of the crop pattern of Bihar as given by the

TABLE 3.14

	Crops	*A.L.E. (1950-51) (Percentage of Net Sown Area)*	*Supdt., A.S. (1951) (Percentage of Net Sown Area)*
1.	Paddy	33.6	66.1
2.	Wheat	6.2	9.7
3.	Maize	8.1	7.0
4.	Gram	0.9	5.8
5.	Khesari	2.5	6.5
	Total for the five crops	51.3	92.1

TABLE 3.15

	Percentage of families
Non-cultivating owners	0.3
Wholly cultivating owners	3.3
Partly cultivating and partly non-cultivating owners	0.4
Total Owners	4.0
Non-cultivating tenants	1.2
Wholly cultivating tenants	37.3
Partly cultivating and partly non-cultivating tenants	0.6
Total Tenants	39.7
Agricultural labourers without land	14.7
Agricultural labourers with land	23.1
Total Agricultural Labourers	37.8
Total Agriculturists	81.1
Non-agricultural Labourers	2.4
Artisans	3.9
Traders	3.9
Others	8.7
Total Non-agriculturists	18.9

Agricultural Labour Enquiry with that given in the complete enumeration survey of the Superintendent of Agricultural Statistics gives the following results, which too are hard to rely upon.

An interesting information collected in the Agricultural Labour Enquiry was the occupational distribution of the 9556 families found in the 80 villages of Bihar. The following Table 3.15 shows the percentage distribution of the families among some significant classes.

An interesting feature brought out by the enquiry was that the size of the family depended roughly on its economic states. Thus in Bihar while the average size of the family among the landowners was found to be 6.8; among tenants it was 6.2; among the agricultural labourers with land 5.4; and among the agricultural labourers without land 4.3.

It is interesting to note further that an examination of the maternity data collected in some of the States of India at the time of the Population Census of 1951 led the Census Commissioner of India to come to very much the same conclusion as would appear from the following remarks of his. "It is something stated on the basis of mainly of European experience that the classes which are at the bottom of the social scale have more children and grow in number faster than others. There is a little doubt as to the place of the agricultural labourer in the social scale anywhere in India. The figure for the agricultural labourers' families in Travancore-Cochin do not show that this generalisation was true in that State. Not is it true of any of the three divisions of Madhya Pradesh."

The average size of holdings, which was found to be 7.5 acres for all-India, varied from 2.4 acres in Travancore-Cochin, 3.8 acres in Jammu & Kashmir, and 4.06 acres in Bihar to 29.6 acres in Saurashtra and 13.9 acres in Madhya Pradesh. The average size of the holdings in Bihar was the lowest among the Part-A States of India. Although the average over-all size of the holdings in Bihar worked out at 4.06 acres, it was 12.0 acres for the landowners' holdings. 5.6 acres for the tenants' holdings, 106 acres for the holdings of the agricultural labourers with land and 2.1 acres for the holdings of the non-agricultural families. The percentage distribution of the holdings in Bihar, according to their size, is shown in the following Table 3.16.

TABLE 3.16

(Percentage)

Size of Holdings	*Number*	*Area*
One acre and less	31.0	3.6
Above one acre but not above 2.5 acres	25.5	10.3
Above 2.5 acres but not above 5.0 acres	20.5	17.9
Above 5.0 acres but not above 10 acres	14.3	24.2
Above 10.0 acres but not above 25.0 acres	7.1	24.9
Above 25.0 acres but not above 50.0 acres	1.1	8.6
Above 50.0 acres	0.5	10.5

It has been estimated on the basis of data collected at the Agricultural Labour Enquiry (1950-51) that there were 4.9 million holdings in Bihar. To the extent to which it is possible to generalise on the basis of data collected from only 80 villages in Bihar, it appears that the total area of all the cultivated holdings of a size exceeding 25 acres each was about 3.84 million acres and of a size exceeding 50 acres each it was 2.11 million acres. More than 50 per cent of the holdings were of the size of 2.5 acres or less, while the large holdings of the size of 25 acres or more, although they constituted less than 2 per cent of the total holdings in number, yet in total area they comprised almost one-fifth of the entire area of the cultivated holdings. Not only was the average size of the holdings in Bihar almost the lowest among the Part-A States of India but also the inequality in the distribution of land in Bihar was amongst the highest in the country.

Data available for 1960 shows that the average size of land-holdings in Bihar is one of the lowest in the country, though there is proportionally less cultivable waste land in Bihar than in most other States in India (See Table 3.17).

CROPS AND THEIR OUT-TURN

Tables 3.18 and 3.19 give the ranking of the States according to the total area sown under all crops in different years. Although

TABLE 3.17

Size of Holdings and Cultivable Waste in different States of India (1960)

States	*Average size of Holdings (Acres)*	*Percentage of cultivable waste land to total*
Andhra Pradesh	4.5 (4)	13.4 (4)
Bihar	3.0 (5)	11.6 (5)
Kerala	N.A.	N.A.
Madhya Pradesh	8.5 (3)	22.2 (2)
Maharashtra	13.3 (2)	1.8 (6)
Rajasthan	16.2 (1)	39.0 (1)
Uttar Pradesh	2.5 (6)	13.9 (3)

Note: Figures in brackets indicate ranks.

TABLE 3.18

Total Area Sown Under All Crops

(In thousand acres)

States	*1950-51*[a]	*1956-57*	*1959-60*
Andhra Pradesh	17408 (6)	30750 (5)	26521 (6)
Assam	6313 (12)	6003 (13)	6436 (12)
Bihar	26997 (4)	25004 (7)	27010 (5)
Jammu & Kashmir	1600 (13)	1906 (14)	1973 (14)
Kerala	N.A.	5465 (12)	5698 (13)
Madhya Pradesh	31172 (3)	43573 (3)	44932 (3)
Madras	17080 (7)	17145 (9)	17403 (9)
Maharashtra[b]	42603 (2)	70361 (1)	70977 (1)
Mysore	8496 (11)	25699 (6)	26182 (7)
Orissa	14804 (8)	14958 (11)	14958 (11)
Punjab	14646 (9)	23786 (8)	23997 (8)
Rajasthan	24792 (5)	33881 (5)	35748 (4)
Uttar Pradesh	49322 (1)	52766 (2)	53805 (2)
West Bengal	13234 (10)	14977 (10)	15055 (10)
All-India	325904	368461	375838

Note: Figures in brackets indicate ranks.

a. Indicating figures before the reorganisation of the States.

b. Indicating Gujarat.

TABLE 3.19

States	*Percentage distribution of gross area under crops*	*Percentage distribution of net value of agricultural output*	*Value of output per acre (Rs.)*	*Net value of output per acre (Rs.)*	*Input as percentage of gross output*	*Net output per worker (Rs.)*
1	2	3	4	5	6	7
Andhra Pradesh	7.7 (5)	7.7 (6)	188.23 (8)	156.65 (10)	16.8 (2)	365 (13)
Assam	1.6 (13)	3.5 (14)	370.87 (2)	347.78 (2)	6.2 (15)	620 (5)
Bihar	7.1 (6)	7.2 (1)	186.83[a] (10)	161.53 (8)	13.5 (8)	302[b] (16)
Gujarat	6.3 (9)	5.4 (10)	153.10 (16)	136.77 (13)	10.7 (13)	578 (6)
Jammu & Kashmir	0.5 (15)	0.7 (15)	261.82 (5)	231.11 (5)	11.7 (11)	395 (12)
Kerala	1.4 (14)	4.0 (13)	521.56 (1)	445.44 (1)	14.6 (7)	1159 (1)
Madhya Pradesh	11.8 (3)	7.8 (5)	125.29 (16)	106.10 (6)	15.3 (6)	360 (14)
Madras	4.5 (10)	7.9 (4)	338.92 (4)	282.87 (4)	16.5 (3)	530 (7)
Maharashtra	12.1 (2)	10.0 (2)	152.24 (15)	132.08 (15)	13.2 (9)	467 (1)
Mysore	6.7 (7)	5.8 (9)	167.41 (12)	137.94 (12)	17.1 (1)	476 (10)
Orissa	3.9 (12)	4.4 (11)	208.21 (6)	180.80 (6)	13.2 (9)	488 (8)
Punjab	6.5 (8)	6.3 (8)	175.83 (11)	155.55 (11)	11.5 (12)	861 (2)
Rajasthan	9.2 (4)	4.1 (12)	84.41 (17)	71.34 (17)	15.5 (5)	353 (15)

(Contd.)

TABLE 3.19 (*Contd.*)

1	2	3	4	5	6	7
Uttar Pradesh	16.1 (1)	16.8 (1)	199.88 (7)	167.09 (7)	16.4 (4)	479 (9)
West Bengal	4.2 (11)	8.3 (3)	348.84 (3)	313.21 (3)	10.2 (14)	824 (3)
Delhi	0.1 (17)	0.1 (17)	187.05 (9)	164.73 (9)	11.9 (10)	800 (4)
Himachal Pradesh	0.3 (16)	0.2 (16)	164.13 (12)	136.04 (14)	17.1 (1)	214 (17)
All States	100.0	100.0	187.21	160.61	14.2	477

Note: Figures in brackets indicate ranks.

a. In 1962-63, gross agricultural income per acre of net area sown in Bihar was Rs. 207.

b. In 1962-63, gross agricultural income per worker in Bihar was Rs. 282.20. The value of gross agricultural output per capita of the rural population was Rs. 136.39 (being the average for the years 1960-61 to 1962-63),

Bihar occupied in 1960-61 the sixth position among the Indian States in respect of the percentage distribution of the gross area under crops, yet in respect of the percentage distribution of the net value of the agricultural output it occupied the seventh position. In respect of the gross value of output and the net value of output per acre and the input as percentage of gross output and the net output per worker its position was tenth, eighth, ninth and sixteenth respectively. This is indicative of either low prices or inferior quality of crops, low investment in agriculture and low productivity of the agricultural workers.

The average annual production of rice and wheat during 1945-60 is believed to have consistently declined in all the four civil divisions of the State. The magnitude of the decline can be judged from the fact that the share of rice production to total agricultural production had come down from 44 per cent to 27 per cent and that of wheat from 28 per cent to 18 per cent during this period.

Rice is Bihar's most important crop. In 1955 it alone accounted for more than 45 per cent of the State's total sown area and its out-turn constituted 72 per cent of the total out-turn of the five staple foodgrains, viz., rice, wheat, gram, maize and barley, grown in the State. Bihar's potato crop is large but it concentrated mostly in Patna district. Bihar grows more jute than its three jute mills can consume. Hence, the surplus jute has to be sold outside the State.

Till Independence one fails to come across any distinct correlation between price fluctuations and volumes of agricultural production in Bihar. The steep and continuous rise in the general price-level from 1939 onwards did not by itself affect agricultural production in any way. Movements in the relative prices of some agricultural commodities might have affected their acreage and production but even in their case there was no stable correlation.

The general trend in Bihar was rather a steady figure of area sown inspite of the rise in the prices of the agricultural commodities and increase in population. In course of the period between 1917-18 and 1943-44 the percentage of current fallow recorded an increase from 3.6 per cent in the 1920's to 16.16 per cent in 1943-44, causing a dimunition in the area sown from 23.7 million acres in the 1920's to approximately 17.8 million acres in 1943-44. The acreage distribution among the different crops

TABLE 3.20

Area and Production of Foodgrains

(In thousand acres/tons)

States	*Area*				*Production*	
	1950-51[a]	*1956-57*	*1961-62*	*1962-63*	*1961-62*	*1962-63*
Andhra Pradesh	11982 (6)	22081 (6)	23013 (6)	22078 (6)	6765 (4)	6361 (6)
Assam	3326 (11)	4550 (13)	4609 (14)	4711 (14)	1688 (13)	1546 (13)
Bihar	24292 (3)	22980 (5)	24046 (5)	24188 (5)	7288 (3)	7233 (4)
Gujarat	N.A.	12515 (11)	11273 (12)	11222 (7)	2362 (12)	2258 (12)
Jammu & Kashmir	1394 (12)	1383 (15)	1822 (15)	1881 (15)	608 (15)	650 (15)
Kerala	N.A.	2058 (14)	2003 (13)	2093 (13)	1015 (14)	1116 (14)
Madhya Pradesh	24851 (2)	36197 (2)	38056 (2)	37714 (2)	9167 (2)	8360 (3)
Madras	11474 (7)	12282 (10)	12549 (10)	12625 (1)	5587 (7	) 5553 (8)
Maharashtra[b]	24292 (3)	30241 (3)	30386 (3)	30675 (3)	5974 (6)	6286 (7)
Mysore	5849 (10)	16190 (8)	18006 (7)	17952 (8)	3808 (11)	4078 (11)
Orissa	12332 (5)	11226 (12)	11720 (11)	12633 (12)	3970 (10)	3915 (5)
Punjab	11074 (9)	17197 (7)	17496 (8)	17443 (9)	6239 (5)	6390 (2)
Rajasthan	18895 (4)	26642 (4)	28883 (4)	27483 (8)	5480 (8)	4987 (9)
Uttar Pradesh	42616 (1)	44818 (1)	45442 (1)	44266 (1)	13854 (1)	13247 (1)
West Bengal	11456 (8)	12260 (9)	13256 (9)	13218 (10)	5171 (9)	4791 (10)
All-India	250061	274727	284816	283130	79757	77507

Note: Figures in brackets indicate ranks.

a. Indicates the figures before the reorganisation of the States.

b. Including Gujarat.

depended on the climatic conditions and rainfall rather than on their relative prices.

Table 3.20 gives the area and production of foodgrains in the major States of India. It shows that after the reorganisation of States in India, Bihar's position in respect of the land area devoted to foodgrains fell from being the third to the fifth. On the other hand, in respect of the total production of foodgrains its position fluctuated between the third and the fourth. In 1964-65, Bihar produced 9 per cent of the total out-turn of foodgrains in the country and occupied the third position among the Indian States. It produced 14 per cent of rice, 20 per cent of maize and 4 per cent of wheat in all States taken together. Winter rice accounted roughly for 95 per cent to the total rice produced in Bihar. Autumn maize accounted for 95 per cent of the total maize produced in the State.

Table 3.21 gives State-wise particulars of area and production of rice based on 1962-63 final forecast estimates.

TABLE 3.21

State-wise Area and Out-turn of Rice (1962-63 Final Estimates)

States	*'000 acres*	*Per cent of total*	*'000 tons*	*Per cent of total*
Andhra Pradesh	7532 (6)	8.8 (5)	3605 (4)	11.4 (4)
Assam	4449 (8)	5.2 (7)	1501 (8)	4.8 (8)
Bihar	12843 (1)	14.9 (1)	4213 (2)	13.4 (2)
Gujarat	1303 (12)	1.5 01)	372 (14)	1.2 (13)
Jammu & Kashmir	563 (15)	0.6 (14)	242 (15)	0.8 (15)
Kerala	1947 (11)	2.3 (10)	1088 (11)	3.5 (11)
Madhya Pradesh	10341 (5)	12.0 (4)	2276 (7)	7.2 (7)
Madras	6340 (7)	7.4 (6)	3800 (3)	12.1 (3)
Maharashtra	3179 (9)	3.7 (8)	1116 (10)	3.5 (10)
Mysore	2473 (10)	2.9 (9)	1350 (2)	4.3 (9)
Orissa	10970 (3)	12.8 (2)	3593 (5)	11.4 (5)
Punjab	1163 (13)	1.3 (12)	454 (12)	1.4 (12)
Rajasthan	280 (16)	0.3 (15)	99 (16)	0.3 (16)
Uttar Pradesh	10449 (4)	12.2 (3)	3071 (6)	9.8 (6)
West Bengal	10894 (2)	12.8 (2)	4340 (1)	13.8 (1)
Other Territories	1145 (14)	1.3 (13)	392 (13)	1.1 (14)

Note: Figures in brackets indicate ranks.

India has never been self-sufficient in its requirements of rice. Since 1949-50 production of rice has been increasing at the rate of 2.28 per cent per annum, almost at about the same rate at which population has been increasing. But this is not the only point to consider. There is the additional point that the demand for rice has also been increasing because of increase in per capita income and improvement in the standard of living of the people and their changing habits, e.g., their preference for superior foodgrains like rice instead of coarse foodgrains. This accounts for a persistent shortage of rice. Per capita consumption of rice varies from State to State and depends largely on the pattern of production and the availability of rice in the region. Predominantly rice-consuming States are Andhra Pradesh, Madras, Kerala, Orissa, West Bengal and Assam. Rice is consumed in considerable quantities also in parts of Bihar, Maharashtra, Gujarat, Uttar Pradesh, Madhya Pradesh and Mysore, Gujarat, Maharashtra, West Bengal and Kerala generally have a deficit of rice while Madhya Pradesh, Orissa, Andhra Pradesh and Madras have some surplus available for export to deficit regions. Gujarat and Maharashtra depend on Madhya Pradesh for their additional requirements. West Bengal obtains part of its requirements from Orissa while Kerala depends on the neighbouring States to meet its small deficit of rice. Supplies from the Central stock are also made to meet the rice needs of people in these deficit areas.

In a normal year the marketable surplus of the rice producing farmers in the country is estimated to be about one-third of total production, the rest being retained by the farmers themselves for domestic consumption, seed, payment in kind to labour and for payment of rent for land. This quantity of the marketable surplus is not sufficient to meet the requirements of the masses in the urban areas and for those farmers who do not produce rice. The country, as a whole, therefore, goes short of rice and has to import it from year to year, its actual volume depending on production every year.

Table 3.22 prepared on the basis of 1962-63 final estimates gives a general idea about the seasonal pattern of rice cropping in different States. The winter crop accounts for the major share in Bihar as well as in Uttar Pradesh, West Bengal, Orissa and Assam.

TABLE 3.22

Seasonal Harvest as Per Cent of Total Out-turn of each State

States	*Autumn crop*		*Winter crop*		*Summer crop*	
Andhra Pradesh	9.2	(10)	77.9	(7)	12.9	(1)
Assam	14.8	(8)	84.4	(6)	0.8	(6)
Bihar	4.5	(11)	95.4	(4)	0.1	(9)
Gujarat	100.0	(1)	—		—	
Jammu & Kashmir			100.0	(1)		
Kerala	44.8	(6)	44.0	(10)	11.2	(2)
Madhya Pradesh	100.0	(1)	—		—	
Madras	75.3	(4)	22.8	(11)		
Maharashtra	99.3	(2)	—		0.7	(7)
Mysore	52.4	(5)	45.2	(9)	2.4	(3)
Orissa	3.1	(12)	96.0	(3)	0.9	(5)
Punjab	100.0	(1)	—		—	
Rajasthan	100.0	(1)	—		—	
Uttar Pradesh			99.9	(2)	0.1	(9)
West Bengal	9.3	(9)	90.1	(5)	0.6	(8)
Delhi	100.0	(1)	—		—	
Himachal Pradesh	100.0	(1)	—		—	
Manipur	100.0	(1)	—		—	
Tripura	32.2	(7)	66.6	(8)	1.2	(4)
Andaman & Nicobar	100.0	0)				
Nagaland	78.1	(3)	21.3	(12)	—	
Average	31.4		66.2		2.4	

Note: Figures in brackets indicate ranks.

Table 3.23 shows that from the standpoint of the area of land utilized in the production of oilseeds and their aggregate output Bihar's position among the major States of India cannot be said to be available.

Table 3.24 contains figures of the area and production of sugar-cane and chillies. It shows that both the area and production of sugar-cane in Bihar are dwindling whereas those of chillies are more or less stable.

The following tables contain data on the area and production of jute and tobacco separately. In 1964-65, Bihar and Assam together accounted for 36 per cent of the all-India jute acreage but they together consumed only about 17 per cent of the total

TABLE 3.23

Area and Production of Oilseeds

(In thousand acres)

States	Area in Oilseeds				Production of Oilseeds	
	1950-51[a]	1956-57	1961-62	1962-63	1961-62	1962-63
1	2	3	4	5	6	7
Andhra Pradesh	2949 (2)	4890 (2)	3507 (4)	3427 (5)	679 (5)	765 (5)
Assam	346 (11)	312 (13)	298 (11)	323 (13)	41 (13)	48 (12)
Bihar	856 (8)	390 (11)	650 (10)	615 (10)	91 (10)	96 (10)
Gujarat	N.A.	2878 (5)	5129 (2)	5557 (2)	1297 (2)	1092 (2)
Jammu & Kashmir	91 (13)	68 (15)	75 (15)	75 (14)	17 (14)	16 (14)
Kerala	N.A.	82 (14)	70 (14)	69 (15)	17 (14)	19 (13)
Madhya Pradesh	2529 (4)	3737 (3)	3876 (3)	3765 (3)	514 (6)	477 (6)
Madras	2935 (3)	2141 (8)	2407 (8)	2415 (8)	1043 (3)	1043 (3)
Maharashtra	3954[b] (1)	3513 (4)	3499 (5)	3417 (4)	795 (4)	778 (4)
Mysore	1023 (6)	2634 (6)	2475 (6)	2472 (7)	436 (7)	469 (7)
Orissa	847 (9)	515 (10)	493 (12)	497 (11)	71 (11)	72 (11)
Punjab	568 (10)	945 (9)	985 (9)	1216 (8)	240 (9)	301 (9)
Rajasthan	1980 (5)	2389 (7)	2450 (7)	3044 (5)	256 (8)	322 (8)
Uttar Pradesh	895 (7)	6013 (1)	8762 (1)	8589 (1)	1302 (1)	1214 (1)
West Bengal	326 (12)	333 (12)	422 (13)	360 (12)	44 (12)	48 (12)
All-India	27102	30875	35123	35875	6848	6766

Note: Figures in brackets indicate ranks.

a. Indicates the figures before the reorganisation of the States.

b. Including Gujarat.

TABLE 3.24

Area and Prodaction of Sugar-cane and Chillies

States	*I: Sugar-cane*					
	Area (in thousand acres)				*Production (in thousand tons)*	
	1950-51[a]	*1956-57*	*1961-62*	*1962-63*	*1961-62*	*1962-63*
1	2	3	4	5	6	7
Andhra Pradesh	124 (6)	190 (5)	228 (5)	233 (5)	750 (3)	837 (4)
Assam	58 (8)	63 (10)	67 (11)	70 (11)	107 (11)	98 (11)
Bihar	410 (2)	403 (3)	487 (3)	400 (3)	623 (6)	480 (7)
Gujarat	N.A.	30 (13)	52 (13)	50 (13)	110 (10)	103 (10)
Jammu & Kashmir	2 (12)	3 (15)	5 (15)	3 (15)	2 (15)	2 (15)
Kerala	N.A.	19 (14)	23 (14)	23 (14)	37 (14)	41 (14)
Madhya Pradesh	45 (10)	131 (6)	136 (8)	135 (8)	140 (9)	140 (8)
Madras	132 (5)	115 (8)	187 (6)	180 (6)	627 (5)	613 (5)
Maharashtra	206[b] (4)	214 (4)	349 (4)	370 (4)	646 (4)	891 (3)
Mysore	58 (8)	124 (7)	163 (7)	168 (7)	479 (7)	565 (6)
Orissa	72 (7)	58 (12)	62 (13)	63 (12)	74 (13)	75 (13)
Punjab	306 (3)	487 (2)	668 (2)	644 (2)	870 (2)	1003 (2)
Rajasthan	43 (11)	83 (9)	84 (10)	80 (9)	78 (12)	81 (12)
Uttar Pradesh	2505 (1)	3066 (1)	3367 (1)	3144 (1)	5045 (1)	4320 (1)
West Bengal	53 (9)	60 (11)	85 (9)	77 (10)	179 (8)	133 (8)
All-India	4258	5066	9984	9223	9984	9223

(Contd.)

TABLE 3.24 (*Contd.*)

States	*II: Chillies*				
	Area (in thousand acres)			*Production (in thousand tons)*	
	1957-58	*1961-62*	*1962-63*	*1961-62*	*1962-63*
1	*8*	*9*	*10*	*11*	*12*
Andhra Pradesh	411 (1)	280 (2)	288 (2)	80 (2)	85 (2)
Assam	8 (12)	17 (10)	18 (11)	4 (12)	4 (11)
Bihar	102 (5)	79 (6)	80 (6)	14 (8)	19 (7)
Gujarat	19 (10)	56 (8)	46 (9)	15 (7)	12 (9)
Jammu & Kashmir	—	3 (14)	3 (14)	2 (13)	2 (12)
Kerala	8 (12)	8 (13)	8 (13)	2 (13)	2 (12)
Madhya Pradesh	105 (5)	92 (5)	93 (5)	12 (9)	13 (8)
Madras	156 (4)	179 (4)	179 (4)	94 (1)	94 (1)
Maharashtra	321 (2)	338 (1)	349 (1)	60 (3)	61 (3)
Mysore	260 (3)	265 (3)	265 (3)	28 (4)	28 (4)
Orissa	16 (11)	18 (11)	18 (11)	2 (13)	2 (12)
Punjab	66 (7)	67 (7)	79 (7)	22 (5)	26 (5)
Rajasthan	57 (8)	55 (9)	59 (8)	21 (6)	21 (5)
Uttar Pradesh	8 (12)	36 (10)	35 (10)	5 (11)	5 (10)
West Bengal	18 (9)	18 (11)	10 (12)	8 (10)	4 (11)
All-India	1575	1516	1540	370	383

Note: Figures in brackets indicate ranks.

a. Before the reorganisation of the States. b. Including Gujarat.

TABLE 3.25

Area and Production of Jute

States	*Area (in '000 acres)*				*Production (in '000 tons)*	
	1950-51	*1956-57*	*1961-62*	*1962-63*	*1961-62*	*1962-63*
Assam	249 (3)	355 (3)	363 (3)	265 (3)	1131 (3)	696 (3)
Bihar	314 (2)	665 (2)	565 (2)	490 (2)	1263 (2)	1024 (2)
Orissa	117 (4)	91 (4)	114 (4)	114 (4)	304 (4)	293 (4)
Uttar Pradesh	17 (4)	56 (4)	59 (4)	52 (4)	114 (4)	92 (4)
West Bengal	651 (1)	665 (1)	1114 (1)	1074 (1)	3352 (1)	3113 (1)
All-India	1387	1908	2280	2095	6347	5367

Note: Figures in brackets indicate ranks.

TABLE 3.26

Area and Production of Tabacco

States	*Area (in '000 acres)*			*Production (in '000 tons)*	
	1956-57	*1961-62*	*1962-63*	*1961-62*	*1962-63*
Andhra Pradesh	396 (1)	400 (1)	405 (1)	129 (1)	134 (1)
Assam	23 (9)	24 (8)	26 (9)	7 (10)	8 (8)
Bihar	41 (7)	43 (6)	42 (6)	14 (6)	15 (5)
Gujarat	175 (2)	229 (2)	229 (2)	83 (2)	95 (2)
Jammu & Kashmir	—	1 (15)	N.A.	N.A.	N.A.
Kerala	1 (14)	2 (14)	3 (13)	1 (13)	1 (11)
Madhya Pradesh	16 (11)	10 (12)	10 (10)	2 (12)	2 (11)
Madras	48 (5)	49 (5)	47 (5)	29 (3)	28 (3)
Maharashtra	71 (4)	62 (4)	63 (4)	15 (5)	15 (5)
Mysore	135 (3)	97 (3)	95 (3)	23 (4)	23 (4)
Orissa	11 (12)	18 (9)	38 (8)	9 (9)	11 (7)
Punjab	5 (13)	4 (13)	4 (12)	1 (13)	1 (11)
Rajasthan	22 (10)	15 (10)	12 (10)	4 (11)	4 (9)
Uttar Pradesh	46 (6)	40 (7)	40 (7)	12 (8)	13 (6)
West Bengal	40 (10)	11 (11)	38 (8)	13 (7)	13 (6)
All-India	1035	1014	1062	343	361

Note: Figures in brackets indicate ranks.

quantity of fertilizers distributed while Orissa with 6.5 per cent of the acreage utilized more than 27 per cent of the fertilizers applied to jute in the country. The share of Bihar in line sowing was not commensurate with the average under jute.

Table 3.27, giving the average per acre out-turn of crops in different States of India, shows that in this respect several States are decidedly superior to Bihar. In the production of rice ten States out of fifteen, in that of wheat eight States and in that of maize and gram four States have a lead over Bihar. In the production of sugar-cane nine States have an advantage over Bihar.

Bihar held the fourth position in the total production of rice, third position in that of potato, and second position in that of sugar in India exactly a decade ago (See Table 3.28)

In Bihar the dependence of the agriculturists is the heaviest on the *aghani* crops (53 per cent). Next in importance is *rabi* (27 per cent). *Bhadai* claims 17 per cent and *baisakha-jethua* 3 per cent only.

About a decade ago a look at the figures of acreage under different crops in Bihar would have revealed the following characteristics: (1) Deficiency in the acreage under oilseeds and nuts. Our food continued to be deficient in fats. Oilseeds were regarded as cash crops by the average cultivator. (2) Deficiency in the acreage under sugar-cane. (3) Deficiency in the acreage under vegetables. (4) Very low acreage under cotton. Within the memory of people still living, cotton was grown in Bihar on a fairly wide scale and was considered to be a recuperative crop for land. As was normal, the cash crops competed with the food crops so far as their relative shares in the total acreage were concerned.

The economic laws have failed to force our subsistence type, uncommercialised agrarian economy to work towards the restructuring of the existing pattern of agricultural production so that a better nutritional balance is achieved. The re-structuring will be necessary as productive efficiency and yield per acre increase. A re-organisation of self-employment by a large percentage of the agricultural population by promoting the labour-intensive methods such as arable animal farming is imperative in view of our huge population. Dairying and animal husbandry will continue to be household occupations based chiefly on stall-feeding instead of pasturing owing to our climatic conditions.

TABLE 3.27

Average Out-turn Per Acre of Crops in different States of India (1960-61)

Crops	*Bihar*	*Andhra Pradesh*	*Assam*	*Gujarat*	*Jammu & Kashmir*	*Kerala*	*Madhya Pradesh*	*Madras*
1	2	3	4	5	6	7	8	9
Rice (ton)	0.345 (11)	0.510 (4)	0.379 (10)	0.209 (15)	0.418 (6)	0.533 (2)	0.332 (12)	0.600 (1)
Jowar	0.142 (10)	0.225 (6)	—	0.074 (12)	—	0.250 (4)	0.278 (2)	0.311 (1)
Bajra	0.187 (3)	0.177 (5)	—	0.126 (8)	0.181 (4)	—	0.261 (1)	0.253 (2)
Maize	0.406 (5)	0.327 (6)	0.171 (13)	0.487 (1)	0.372 (8)	—	0.450 (3)	0.455 (2)
Ragi	0.198 (7)	0.226 (5)	—	0.350 (3)	—	0.571 (1)	0.102 (12)	0.390 (2)
Wheat	0.270 (8)	0.111 (13)	0.333 (4)	0.291 (5)	0.241 (10)	—	0.251 (9)	0.333 (4)
Barley	0.206 (7)	—	—	0.235 (5)	0.280 (4)	—	0.356 (3)	—
Small millets	0.151 (10)	0.156 (9)	0.214 (5)	0.308 (2)	0.241 (3)	0.241 (5)	0.094 (13)	0.318 (1)
Gram	0.238 (6)	0.114 (13)	0.250 (5)	0.133 (11)	0.142 (10)	—	0.229 (8)	0.333 (1)
Tur	0.236 (4)	0.154 (10)	0.200 (7)	0.209 (6)	—	0.181 (8)	0.345 (3)	0.142 (11)
Masur	0.204 (3)	—	0.181 (4)	—	—	—	0.171 (5)	—
Khesari	0.199 (2)	—	0.166 (4)	—	—	—	0.184 (3)	—
Peas	0.188 (4)	—	0.142 (6)	—	—	0.130 (7)	—	—
Other Pulses	0.159 (3)	0.066 (12)	—	0.105 (9)	—	0.155 (4)	0.121 (7)	0.086 (11)
Seasamum	0.094 (8)	0.066 (12)	0.210 (2)	0.067 (11)	—	0.100 (6)	0.046 (14)	0.128 (4)
Rape and Mustard	0.142 (9)	—	0.152 (7)	0.067 (12)	0.256 (1)	—	0.155 (6)	—
Linseed	0.115 (4)	0.056 (10)	—	—	0.269 (1)	—	0.088 (6)	—

Castor Seed	0.280 (2)	0.059 (11)	0.200 (3)	0.135 (6)	—	—	0.111 (7)	0.161 (5)
Sugar-cane	1.513 (9)	3.415 (1)	1.403 (11)	2.022 (6)	0.250 (15)	1.686 (7)	1.080 (13)	3.381 (2)
Cotton (bales of 392 lbs.)	0.200 (9)	0.159 (11)	0.187 (10)	0.330 (5)	0.500 (2)	0.458 (3)	0.239 (8)	0.378 (4)
Jute (bales of 400 lbs.)	2.348 (5)	—	2.722 (3)	—	—	—	—	—
Mesta	1.322 (5)	1.937 (3)	1.727 (4)	0.666 (9)	—	—	0.750 (8)	—
Sann hemp (ton)	0.185 (4)	0.111 (9)	—	—	—	—	0.136 (7)	—
Dry chillies	0.189 (9)	0.279 (5)	0.200 (8)	0.322 (3)	—	0.250 (7)	0.151 (11)	0.528 (1)
Turmeric	0.500 (11)	1.107 (6)	—	—	—	0.363 (10)	—	1.363 (5)
Potatoes	3.122 (6)	2.000 (10)	1.894 (11)	7.800 (2)	—	—	3.500 (5)	3.714 (4)
Sweet Potatoes	2.527 (7)	1.187 (10)	1.187 (10)	5.000 (1)	—	3.000 (5)	2.470 (8)	3.846 (2)
Tobacco	0.307 (6)	0.326 (4)	0.291 (7)	0.273 (8)	—	0.500 (2)	0.200 (11)	0.583 (1)
Tea (lbs.)	.322 (1)	—	4.121 (2)	—	—	4.107 (3)	—	4.569 (1)

(*Contd.*)

TABLE 3.27 *(Contd.)*

Crops	*Maharashtra*	*Mysore*	*Orissa*	*Punjab*	*Rajasthan*	*Uttar Pradesh*	*West Bengal*
1	*10*	*11*	*12*	*13*	*14*	*15*	*16*
Rice (ton)	0.414 (7)	0.522 (3)	0.392 (8)	0.391 (9)	0.264 (14)	0.299 (13)	0.471 (5)
Jowar	0.267 (3)	0.155 (9)	0.235 (5)	0.068 (13)	0.113 (11)	0.220 (7)	0.200 (8)
Bajra	0.119 (9)	0.102 (10)	0.166 (6)	0.126 (8)	0.064 (11)	0.156 (7)	—
Maize	0.200 (12)	0.391 (7)	0.163 (14)	0.428 (4)	0.397 (9)	0.236 (11)	0.251 (10)
Ragi	0.283 (6)	0.300 (4)	0.169 (9)	0.142 (10)	—	0.184 (8)	0.111 (11)
Wheat	0.161 (12)	0.300 (5)	0.235 (11)	0.481 (1)	0.376 (3)	0.398 (2)	0.290 (7)
Barley	0.222 (6)	0.200 (8)		0.364 (2)	0.461 (1)	0.364 (2)	0.190 (9)
Small millets	0.182 (6)	0.116 (11)	0.156 (9)	0.106 (12)	0.180 (7)	0.163 (8)	0.227 (4)
Gram	0.133 (11)	0.147 (9)	0.120 (12)	0.328 (2)	0.265 14)	0.285 (3)	0.230 (7)
Tur	0.374 (2)	0.124 (12)	0.171 (9)	0.171 (9)	0.112 (13)	0.540 (1)	0.247 (5)
Masur	—	0.250 (1)	—	0.233 (2)	0.250 (1)	0.165 (6)	0.147 (7)
Khesari	0.106 (5)	—	—	—	—	—	0.697 (1)
Peas	0.142 (6)	—	—	0.173 (5)	0.250 (3)	0.397 (1)	0.281 (2)
Other pulses	0.114 (8)	0.098 (10)	0.170 (2)	0.129 (6)	0.058 (13)	0.135 (5)	0.178 (1)
Seasamum	0.099 (7)	0.070 (10)	0.083 (9)	0.127 (5)	0.241 (1)	0.050 (13)	0.200 (3)
Rape and Mustard	0.125 (10)	0.100 (11)	0.168 (4)	0.209 (2)	0.146 (8)	0.198 (3)	0.164 (3)
Linseed	0.090 (5)	0.082 (8)	0.148 (2)	0.080 (9)	0.119 (3)	0.083 (7)	0.011 (15)
Castor seed	0.066 (10)	0.098 (8)	0.096 (9)		0.333 (1)	0.166 (4)	
Sugar-cane	2.980 (3)	2.889 (4)	1.169 (12)	1.510 (10)	0.970 (14)	1.633 (8)	2.049 (5)

Cotton (bales of 392 lbs.)	—	0.157 (12)	0.105 (13)	0.599 (1)	0.296 (6)	0.253 (7)	—
Jute (bales of 400 lbs.)	—	—	2.369 (4)	—	—	2.875 (1)	2.759 (2)
Mesta	1.159 (6)	0.966 (7)	2.000 (2)	2.000 (2)	—	—	2.219 (1)
Sann hemp (ton)	0.193 (3)	0.099 (10)	0.250 (1)	0.130 (8)	0.142 (6)	0.154 (5)	0.230 (2)
Dry chillies	0.172 (10)	0.105 (13)	0.117 (12)	0.298 (4)	0.258 (6)	0.200 (8)	0.388 (2)
Turmeric	1.454 (4)	1.000 (7)	0.684 (9)	—	0.750 (8)	2.801 (2)	3.931 (1)
Potatoes	2.566 (8)	2.555 (9)	1.074 (12)	6.321 (1)	0.750 (13)	2.801 (7)	3.931 (1)
Sweet Potatoes	5.000 (1)	1.833 (9)	0.655 (12)	3.500 (3)	1.000 (11)	2.683 (6)	3.333 (4)
Tobacco	0.184 (12)	0.247 (10)	0.500 (2)	0.250 (9)	0.333 (3)	0.333 (3)	0.325 (5)
Tea (lbs.)	—	3.942 (5)	—	933 (9)	—	1.570	4.079 (4)

Note: Figures in brackets indicate ranks.

TABLE 3.28

Production of Rice, Potato and Sugar in different States of India

States/Union Territories	*Production of rice as percentage of all-India in different States in 1955-56*	*Production of Potato as percentage of all-India in different States in 1954-55*	*Quantity of Sugar produced as percentage of all-India in different States 1954-55*
Andhra Pradesh	11.56 (2)	0.06 (12)	4.09 (4)
Assam	6.40 (8)	7.83 (4)	
Bhopal			0.25 (12)
Bihar	10.02 (4)	13.45 (3)	14.15 (2)
Bombay	5.50 (9)	6.24 (5)	10.94 (3)
Hyderabad			2.96 (6)
Jammu & Kashmir	0.84 (12)		
Kerala	3.64 (11)		
Madhya Pradesh	11.23 (3)	2.50 (8)	0.69 (9)
Madras	9.91 (5)	3.18 (7)	3.52 (5)
Mysore	4.25 (10)	0.68 (10)	2.39 (7)
Orissa	8.36 (7)	1.08 (9)	0.19 (11)
PEPSU	—		0.57 (10)
Punjab	0.79 (13)	5.22 (6)	1.26 (8)
Rajasthan	0.34 (14)	0.34 (11)	0.69 (9)
Travancore-Cochin			0.31 (11)
Uttar Pradesh	9.55 (6)	37.06 (1)	56.79 (1)
West Bengal	16.27 (1)	21.23 (2)	0.57 (10)
Union Territories	1.32	1.14	

Note: Figures in brackets indicate ranks.

Individual cultivators seek to ensure themselves against the vagaries of rainfall and climate by the practice of mixed cropping. It is common practice in some parts of Bihar, liable to inundation or drought, to sow broadcast some assortment of the following food crops—paddy, maize, arhar, urad, sesamum, mung, and so on.

In Bihar the high pressure of population has not resulted in an urge towards an intensive pattern of land utilization as it has done in Kerala. The Kerala peasantry is highly enlightened as is evident from the advanced agricultural techniques employed and the high level of consumption of organic manures. Although Kerala's soil is basically infertile yet because of these factors the physical yields of different crops compare quite favourably with the all-India standards.

It is no doubt true that the fallow land area that can still be brought under cultivation is not very large in Bihar but it is possible to bring under irrigation a much large proportion of the cultivated area and to increase the yields of crops further by intensive methods like the use of fertilizers and adoption of other improved agricultural practices.

Field experiments have demonstrated that by the mere use of fertilizers agricultural production can be increased fairly enough. The table below bears this out.

TABLE 3.29

Crops	*Average Yield Per Acre (Mds.)*	*Average Yield*[a] *with Fertilizer (Mds.)*
Paddy	12	22.0
Wheat	6.8	14.0
Barley	5.7	12.0
Maize	10.9	15.0
Gram	6.5	9.0
Sugarcane	250.0	650.0

a. Based on field experiments.

But all attempts to reorganise the pattern of land utilization and cropping will depend for their success on the basic structural reforms in tenure and tenancy to provide security to the cultivators and on organisational adjustment to secure credit and other facilities for improving farm efficiency.

LOW AGRICULTURAL PRODUCTIVITY

Agricultural productivity in Bihar has been low. One of the important reasons for this is the uneconomic nature of the average holding.

The figures of the acreage under cultivation and the double-cropped area during the period 1921 to 1951 have been taken by the planners as a broad index of agricultural productivity for want of precise statistics of the yields of various crops. The net area cultivated increased from 21.17 million acres in 1921 to 22.19 million acres in 1951, i.e., a rise of only about 4.8 per cent as against an increase in population of nearly 38 per cent.

However, some increase was evident in tbe double-cropped area indicating the adoption of intensive methods. The double-cropped area is estimated to have been 56.61 lakh acres in 1921 and 63.68 lakh acres in 1951, thus giving a rise of about 12.5 per cent over the three decades.

Another important factor that has contributed to low agricultural productivity in Bihar is inadequate irrigation. The net area irrigated increased from 41.05 lakh acres in 1921 to 51.74 lakh acres in 1951. Irrigation facilities were available from the Government canals and tube-wells to only 10.37 lakh acres till 1951. The minor irrigation schemes irrigated small areas from the local run-off water in a year of adequate rainfall. These figures include the large area under the command of various minor irrigation works, required to be maintained by the Zamindars, according to the Survey and Settlement records. These had actually gone into disrepair and were not available for storage or diversion even of the local rain water in years of normal rainfall. In the complete absence of any revenue administration below the district level, which was more or less the picture till 1956, no accurate or complete information about the area really benefiting from the old or new minor irrigation works could be obtained. Even according to the above figures, which suffer from serious limitations, it could be seen that (on a per capita basis) there was a decline in the net area cultivated, the net area irrigated, and also in the double-cropped area during the period 1921 to 1951, as shown under:

TABLE 3.30

(Figures in cents of an acre)

	1921	*1951*
Per Capita net area cultivated	73	55
Per Capita net area irrigated	14	13
Per Capita double-cropped area	19	16

The inadequacy or irrigation facilities in Bihar throws into bold relief the dependence of the agricultural sector on the monsoon. The result of this has been that agricultural production has always suffered violent fluctuations and depended on the adequate distribution or otherwise of the monsoon rains. The main crop in Bihar in winter paddy and this crop not merely requires rainfall in adequate quantity but also demands that the rainfall should be distributed evenly over the season of the crop. When rainfall is heavy, there are floods, specially in North Bihar, this serves as a further deterring influence against improvement in the agricultural sector. Floods and droughts have contributed mostly to the backwardness of the agricultural sector and also to the distress migration of people over all these years.

While there has been some absorption of population in industries allied to agriculture such as the sugar industry, the average rate of increase in population has been much ahead of the absorptive capacity of either agriculture or industry or other occupations. On the one side is the fact that in Bihar the working population carries on its shoulders a much heavier burden on dependence than is the average for the country as a whole. On the other side is the fact that between 1931 and 1951 the percentage of the actually working population to the total population in Bihar had declined from 41.54 to 36.60. This decline was noticeable particularly in the plains of North Bihar and South Bihar, i.e., the regions which depended primarily on agriculture, and not in the plateau of Chotanagpur where mines provided some alternative occupations.

The central weakness of Bihar's economy lies in its poor agricultural base, which produces neither enough food for its growing population nor raw materials for its industry. Lack of proper flood control and adequate irrigation measures bring great instability to the economy. Due to historical reasons such as the prevalence of a Zamindar class in society for hundreds of years numbering over 4.5 lakhs on the eve of Independence, a strong middle class had failed to emerge and develop. The inequities of the Zamindari system had resulted in conspicuous consumption rather than in capital formation. It had encouraged and perpetuated attachment to land. This had acted as a disincentive to industrial expansion, in general, and to entrepreneurial development, in particular. As the Techno-Economic Survey

Report puts it, the absence of a healthy middle class in Bihar has arrested its economic development, affected the saving potential, and almost polarised society into two distinguishable high-income and low-income groups, the latter left with little urge to raise its material standard of life.

Bihar is an outstanding example of a State which despite rich endowments of natural resources has remained extremely backward. Agriculture, which is the predominant sector of the State's economy, has remained highly depressed. The prevailing techniques of cultivation yield a much smaller output than is possible. Inadequate transport and marketing facilities depress the prices which the farmer can get for his produce. The agricultural base of the Bihar economy is thus extremely shaky with inadequate food production, widely fluctuating production trends, growing deficits and insufficient raw materials for the industrial projects. No industrial structure can be firmly built on such a weak foundation.

This may be contrasted with the state of agriculture in Punjab. Punjab has progressed rather quickly in the provision of irrigation facilities, improved seeds and fertilizers. The Punjab farmer is known for his hard work, coupled with a progressive bent of mind. He is quick to adopt improved agricultural practices. Agriculture in Punjab plays a plural role. It caters to the basic food requirements of the State. It aims at an export surplus. It provides a strong base of raw materials for the growth of industries since metallic minerals and coal are non-existent in the State. The percentage of land irrigated in Punjab is higher than in other States. Punjab has a well-developed animal husbandry sector. This ensures the development of a chain of milk-processing industries.

CAPITAL FORMATION

One aspect of the development of the co-operative movement in the agricultural sector of India is that as between the States its progress has not been even during the Plan periods. The impact of this uneven growth of the co-operative movement on capital formation can be seen easily. So far as we know only two surveys on this have been conducted on an all-India level: one by the National Sample Survey (N.S.S.) in its fifth round (Socio-Economic Survey) in July, 1959—June, 1960, and the other by the Reserve

Bank of India (All-India Rural Debt and Investment Survey, 1961-62). Some information on the capital formation obtained from these two surveys has been given in Table 3.31. The data contained in columns (2) to (8) in this table do not give us a clear idea of the extent of capital formation in agriculture because the N.S.S. estimates were based on the rural households. But the data in columns (2), (3) and (4) largely relate to farm investment. The data given in columns (9) and (10) relate to expenditures made exclusively for farm business. The estimates of the two surveys are not comparable, yet we shall use both sets of the estimates to rank the States in order to per household expenditure on each item of capital formation.

According to the All-India Rural Debt and Investment Survey conducted by the Reserve Bank in 1961-62 the average value of recorded assets per rural household ranged from Rs. 3135 in Assam to Rs. 10,482 in Punjab, the All-India average being Rs. 5358 per rural household. In Orissa, the value of assets per household was Rs. 3461. In West Bengal and Madhya Pradesh it was around Rs. 4000. In Bihar it was Rs. 5586. In other States it ranged between Rs. 5000 and Rs. 7,000 per rural household. The average value of assets owned by the non-cultivators (Rs. 1678 per household for all-India) was much lower than that of the cultivators (Rs. 6696 per household for all-India) insofar as the artisans and other low-income groups formed a large proportion of the non-cultivating households. This disparity was particularly marked in Kerala and Maharashtra (See Table 3.32). The Survey further revealed that quite a large percentage (nearly 62 per cent) of the rural households reported outstanding loans at the end of June, 1962. The proportion of households reporting outstanding loans was more than 50 per cent in all the States except Assam and Orissa. In Mysore, Rajasthan, Madras and Punjab the proportion exceeded 70 per cent. In Bihar it stood at 62.9 per cent. The proportion was higher among the cultivators than among the non-cultivators in all the States.

An examination of the outstanding debt of the cultivators in relation to their cultivated holdings disclosed that the incidence of debt per acre was the highest in Madras followed by Kerala, Andhra Pradesh and Bihar. In all these States debt per acre of the cultivated holdings exceeded Rs. 100. At the other extreme, debt per acre of the cultivated holdings was very low in Madhya

TABLE 3.31

Per Household Capital Formation Per Year

States	Estimates Based on NSS Data							Estimates of fixed capital formation in farm business during July 1961 to June RBI Survey*	
	Expenditure on								
	Land and Building	*Tools and implements*	*Vehicles*	*Power driven equipment*	*Durable goods*	*Live-stock*	*Total*	*All Rural households*	*Culti-vators*
Andhra Pradesh	142.00 (5)	17.98 (6)	9.08 (6)	2.26 (8)	0.21 (12)	90.50 (8)	262.63 (8)	29 (5)	43 (6)
Assam	106.12 (9)	5.37 (13)	1.09 (13)	—	1.21 (4)	50.77 (11)	164.56 (10)	18 (8)	22 (10)
Bihar	90.02 (13)	7.18 (10)	1.02 (14)	0.05 (9)	0.69 (8)	57.10 (10)	156.02 (11)	6 (11)	8 (13)
Gujarat	139.72 (6)	23.53 (3)	47.56 (1)	28.26 (3)	1.39 (3)	103.48 (6)	343.96 (3)	52 (2)	77 (2)
Kerala	93.36 (11)	3.66 (14)	1.11 (12)	—	0.29 (11)	47.91 (12)	146.33 (13)	19 (7)	23 (9)
Madhya Pradesh	98.08 (10)	12.42 (8)	8.95 (7)	—	0.90 (6)	86.97 (9)	207.32 (9)	12 (10)	15 (12)
Madras	143.07 (4)	16.04 (7)	7.92 (8)	32.38 (2)	4.34 (1)	119.21 (4)	322.96 (4)	40 (3)	62 (3)
Maharashtra	164.46 (3)	29.78 (1)	6.88 (9)	15.54 (4)	0.55 (10)	99.04 (7)	316.25 (5)	36 (4)	55 (4)
Mysore	236.40 (2)	18.42 (5)	23.44 (2)	10.40 (5)	0.56 (9)	124.10 (3)	413.32 (2)	61 (1)	82 (1)
Orissa	66.70 (14)	7.17 (11)	1.18 (11)	—	0.04 (13)	30.84 (13)	105.93 (14)	17 (9)	24 (8)
Punjab	259.96 (1)	21.91 (4)	15.42 (3)	49.81 (1)	3.74 (2)	115.76 (5)	466.60 (1)	29 (5)	48 (5)
Rajasthan	118.55 (7)	23.98 (2)	11.26 (4)	6.71 (6)	0.75 (7)	125.40 (2)	283.65 (6)	23 (6)	26 (7)
Uttar Pradesh	90.82 (12)	9.66 (9)	9.48 (5)	2.52 (7)	1.13 (5)	157.37 (1)	270.98 (7)	17 (9)	20 (11)
West Bengal	112.62 (8)	5.48 (12)	2.26 (10)	—	—	26.48 (14)	146.84 (12)	5 (12)	8 (13)

**Reserve Bank of India Bulletin*, Vol. XVII, No. 12, December, 1963.

Note: Figures in brackets indicate ranks.

TABLE 3.32

(Averages in Rs.)

States	*Value of Assets as on 31st December, 1961*			*Net outstanding debt as on 30th June, 1962*		
	Proportion of house-holds report-ing (per cent)	*Average per reporting household*	*Average per household*	*Proportion of house-holds report-ing (per cent)*	*Average per reporting household*	*Average per household*
1	2	3	4	5	6	7
Andhra Pradesh	100.0 (1)	5730 (5)	5730 (5)	69.5 (5)	757 (6)	526 (6)
Assam	99.9 (2)	3118 (14)	3115 (14)	39.5 (14)	346 (15)	137 (14)
Bihar	100.0 (1)	5586 (6)	5586 (8)	62.9 (8)	549 (9)	345 (8)
Gujarat	99.9 (2)	6592 (3)	6585 (3)	67.0 (7)	810 (5)	542 (5)
Jammu & Kashmir	100.0 (1)	6118 (4)	6118 (4)	60.7 (9)	393 (11)	239 (12)
Kerala	99.6 (5)	5253 (8)	5224 (8)	67.5 (6)	368 (14)	249 (11)
Madhya Pradesh	99.9 (2)	4111 (13)	4109 (1U	57.8 (11)	615 (7)	356 (7)
Madras & Pondichery	99.6 (5)	5241 (9)	5221 (9)	72.3 (4)	869 (4)	629 (4)
Maharashtra	99.7 (4)	5113 (11)	5098 (10)	54.4 (13)	610 (8)	332 (9)
Mysore	99.4 (6)	7072 (2)	7026 (2)	79.1 (1)	871 (3)	689 (3)
Orissa	100.0 (1)	3461 (13)	3461 (13)	28.7 (15)	374 (13)	107 (15)
Punjab	100.0 (1)	10482 (1)	10482 (1)	73.2 (3)	1096 (1)	803 (1)
Rajasthan	100.0 (1)	5489 (7)	5489 (7)	76.9 (2)	1039 (2)	797 (2)
Uttar Pradesh	100.0 (1)	5221 (10)	5221 (9)	60.3 (10)	462 (10)	279 (10)
West Bengal	99.8 (3)	3984 (12)	3977 (12)	56.8 (12)	378 (12)	215 (13)
All-India*	99.9	5362	5358	62.1	654	406

(Contd.)

TABLB 3.32 (*Contd.*)

States	*All Rural Households Borrowing during 1st July, 1961—30th June, 1962*			*All Rural Households Repayments during 1st July, 1961—30th June, 1962*		
	Proportion of households reporting (per cent)	*Average per reporting household*	*Average per household*	*Proportion of households reporting (per cent)*	*Average per reporting household*	*Average per household*
1	*8*	*9*	*10*	*11*	*12*	*13*
Andhra Pradesh	51.4 (8)	398 (6)	204 (6)	30.9 (8)	266 (5)	82 (8)
Assam	20.1 (14)	163 (15)	33 (14)	20.2 (13)	131 (14)	26 (15)
Bihar	40.4 (8)	230 (14)	93 (12)	22.0 (12)	198 (12)	44 (12)
Gujarat	55.0 (5)	555 (1)	305 (3)	38.7 (6)	460 (1)	178 (2)
Jammu & Kashmir	50.7 (10)	293 (10)	148 (10)	15.5 (14)	185 (13)	29 (13)
Kerala	61.3 (2)	289 (11)	177 (7)	49.8 (2)	259 (7)	129 (4)
Madhya Pradesh	50.0 (11)	296 (9)	141 (10)	27.7 (10)	242 (9)	67 (11)
Madras & Pondichery	52.9 (6)	440 (5)	233 (5)	45.9 (4)	262 (6)	121 (6)
Maharashtra	43.4 (12)	383 (7)	166 (8)	25.4 (11)	293 (4)	74 (2)
Mysore	59.2 (4)	463 (4)	274 (4)	47.8 (3)	262 (2)	125 (5)
Orissa	18.8 (15)	248 (13)	47 (13)	12.8 (15)	213 (11)	27 (14)
Punjab	59.6 (3)	517 (3)	308 (2)	38.9 (5)	359 (3)	140 (3)
Rajasthan	71.4 (1)	547 (2)	390 (1)	53.1 (1)	384 (2)	204 (1)
Uttar Pradesh	50.8 (9)	307 (8)	156 (9)	35.3 (7)	234 (10)	83 (7)
West Bengal	52.8 (7)	255 (12)	134 (11)	28.3 (9)	251 (8)	71 (10)
All-India	49.1	365	180	32.8	275	90

(*Contd.*)

TABLB 3.32 (*Contd.*)

States	*Fixed capital formation inform business during 1st July, 1961—30th June, 1962*			*Fixed capital formation in non-farm business during 1st July, 1961—30th June, 1962*		
	Proportion of house-holds report-ing (per cent)	*Average per reporting household*	*Average per household*	*Proportion of house-holds report-ing (per cent)*	*Average per reporting household*	*Average per household*
1	*14*	*15*	*16*	*17*	*18*	*19*
Andhra Pradesh	11.9 (14)	246 (5)	29 (5)	1.5 (10)	99 (12)	2 (7)
Assam	20.4 (6)	87 (9)	18 (9)	1.2 (11)	119 (10)	1 (8)
Bihar	12.6 (12)	49 (14)	6 (12)	2.1 (7)	143 (8)	4 (6)
Gujarat	16.0 (8)	327 (1)	52 (2)	2.3 (6)	217 (5)	5 (4)
Jammu & Kashmir	8.9 (15)	249 (3)	22 (7)	1.2 (11)	268 (2)	3 (6)
Kerala	24.1 (4)	77 (11)	19 (8)	5.8 (1)	159 (7)	9 (1)
Madhya Pradesh	18.1 (7)	66 (12)	12 (11)	0.8 (13)	91 (13)	1 (8)
Madras & Pondichery	15.1 (10)	263 (2)	40 (3)	3.0 (4)	215 (4)	6 (3)
Maharashtra	15.3 (9)	248 (4)	38 (4)	1.7 (9)	366 (1)	6 (3)
Mysore	28.3 (1)	216 (6)	61 (1)	2.0 (8)	245 (3)	5 (4)
Orissa	28.1 (2)	62 (13)	17 (10)	1.0 (12)	29 (14)	0.3 (9)
Punjab	27.6 (3)	106 (8)	29 (5)	5.4 (2)	124 (9)	1 (2)
Rajasthan	14.1 (11)	163 (7)	23 (6)	2.1 (7)	195 (6)	4 (5)
Uttar Pradesh	20.8 (5)	80 (10)	17 (10)	2.9 (5)	219 (4)	6 (3)
West Bengal	12.0 (13)	45 (15)	5 (13)	3.2 (3)	116 (11)	4 (5)
All-India*	18.0	132	24	2.4	180	4

(*Contd.*)

TABLB 3.32 (*Contd.*)

States	*Major alterations, additions and new constructions of residential houses during 1st July, 1961—30th June, 1962*		
	Proportion of households reporting (per cent)	*Average per reporting household*	*Average per household*
1	*20*	*21*	*22*
Andhra Pradesh	3.0 (10)	630 (7)	19 (8)
Assam	3.7 (8)	187 (15)	7 (13)
Bihar	4.6 (5)	456 (10)	21 (7)
Gujarat	3.2 (9)	867 (3)	28 (5)
Jammu & Kashmir	5.0 (4)	944 (2)	48 (1)
Kerala	6.2 (2)	535 (8)	33 (4)
Madhya Pradesh	3.8 (7)	434 (12)	17 (10)
Madras & Pondichery	2.4 (12)	789 (4)	19 (8)
Maharashtra	2.8 (11)	647 (6)	18 (9)
Mysore	1.9 (13)	1479 (1)	28 (5)
Orissa	3.7 (8)	232 (14)	9 (12)
Punjab	5.3 (3)	779 (5)	41 (3)
Rajasthan	7.8 (1)	534 (9)	42 (2)
Uttar Pradesh	5.1 (4)	450 (11)	23 (6)
West Bengal	4.0 (6)	398 (13)	16 (11)
All-India*	4.1	.537	22

*Exclusive of Delhi, Himachal Pradesh, Manipur and Tripura. Estimates are provisional.

Pradesh, Rajasthan, Maharashtra, Orissa and Assam. The incidence of the outstanding debt, measured in relation to the value of recorded assets, was less than 5 per cent of the assets in Assam, Orissa, Jammu and Kashmir and Kerala. In Madras, Rajasthan, Mysore and Andhra Pradesh the proportion of the outstanding debt to the value of recorded assets exceeded 9 per cent thereby indicating the comparatively high incidence of debt in these States.

The State-wise data of per member loans advanced by the primary agricultural credit and the multi-purpose co-operative societies and loans per acre of cropped area are given in the Table 3.33 below.

TABLE 3.33

Co-operatire Loans Advanced Per Member and Per Acre of Cropped Area (1959-60)

States	*Loans per acre of cropped area Amount (in Rs.)*	*Loans per member Amount (in Rs.)*
Andhra Pradesh	5.86 (5)	138.67 (4)
Assam	1.11 (13)	32.79 (13)
Bihar	0.47 (14)	20.81 (14)
Gujarat	9.02 (2)	283.47 (1)
Kerala	7.39 (3)	54.10 (11)
Madhya Pradesh	2.97 (9)	164.89 (3)
Madras	10.16 (1)	109.66 (6)
Maharashtra	6.41 (4)	191.84 (2)
Mysore	4.62 (7)	114.14 (5)
Orissa	1.57 (11)	63.69 (10)
Punjab	11.60 (8)	100.27 (9)
Uttar Pradesh	5.43 (6)	101.35 (8)
Rajasthan	1.39 (10)	105.07 (7)
West Bengal	1.51 (12)	39.75 (12)

Note: Figures in brackets indicate ranks.

The investment in the agricultural sector of Bihar and the resulting capital formation in it need to be studied in the background of the agro-economic status of its cultivators. The scope of investment in agriculture through private investment is limited to three-fifths of the total agricultural labour households possessing land. The remaining two-fifths of the total agricultural labour households do not directly contribute to capital formation.

Nearly 78.2 per cent of the total owned holdings are of size less than 5 acres having nearly 34.6 per cent of the total cultivated area. The remaining farm holdings with more than 5 acres in size (21.8 per cent) possess nearly 65.4 percent of the total cultivated area and offer scope for making savings after meeting the labour and material charges. These may be expected to contribute to capital formation.

During the First Plan the total outlay on agriculture and community development in Bihar was Rs. 16.04 crores, that is, an average annual outlay of Rs. 3.21 crores during the quinquennium. During the Second Plan the total outlay in this sector was estimated to be Rs. 54.87 crores, that is, an average annual outlay of Rs. 10.97 crores during the quinquennium. The total outlay during the Third Plan was anticipated to be Rs. 82.49 crores, that is, an average annual outlay of Rs. 16.50 crores during the quinquennium.

But the outlay in any plan includes also the salary and other such expenditures along with the current expenditure on development. Valid information for working out the investment component of this total outlay is lacking. However, during the Second Plan the investment component of this total outlay in agricultural development was approximately estimated to be 60 per cent of the total outlay. On the basis of this yard-stick the public sector investment components were estimated to be Rs. 9.65 crores, Rs. 32.90 crores and Rs. 49.49 crores during the First, Second and Third Plan periods respectively. The average annual investment in the public sector during these periods thus worked out to Rs. 1.93 crores, Rs. 6.58 crores and Rs. 9.90 crores respectively.

While discussing the investment pattern during the Second Plan and the Third Plan periods, the Reserve Bank of India estimated that investments in agriculture and community development for the country as a whole during the Second Plan were Rs. 160 crores in the public sector and Rs. 675 crores in the private sector. This meant that the investment of the private sector was a little more than four times that of the public sector. This yard-stick of the ratio between the public and the private sector investments could also be applied for Bihar and on this basis the public sector investment in the Second Plan might be taken as one-fourth of that of the private sector. The private investment thus worked out to Rs. 131.60 crores approximately during the Second Plan.

The average gross area sown in Bihar was 248 lakh acres during the First Plan period and 251 lakh acres during the Second Plan period and was expected to be 275 lakh acres during the Third Plan period. The private sector investment per acre worked out to Rs. 10.5 only during the Second plan period. There was a heavy dependence of the population on the cultivated area of land in the State, the per capita figure being nearly Rs. 2.5 per acre. The strain that the agricultural sector had to bear was tremendous. Against this background it is quite probable that the private sector investment might be low, being only Rs. 10.5 during the Second Plan period. The monetary changes in the price-level were also taken into account. The general rise in the price-level during the Second Plan was approximately 30 per cent over the First Plan and during the Third Plan it was anticipated to be 25 per cent more over the Second Plan, neglecting the sudden rises in the price-level recently.

On this basis the average per acre investment during the First and the Third Plan periods worked out to Rs. 8.1 and Rs. 13.1 respectively. Thus, the annual rate of investment during the First, Second and Third Plan periods worked out to Rs. 20.09 crores, Rs. 26.32 crores and Rs. 36 crores respectively. The total investment in the private sector in agriculture during the three Plan quinquennia was estimated to be nearly Rs. 100.45 crores, Rs. 131.60 crores and Rs. 180 crores respectively at constant prices.

It is now possible to frame an idea about the over-all investment in both the public and the private sectors. The total investment in the First Plan worked out to Rs. 110.10 crores or Rs. 22.02 crores per annum. The total investment during the Second and the Third Plan periods worked out to Rs. 164.50 crores and Rs. 229.49 crores, the average annual investment being Rs. 32.90 crores and Rs. 45.50 crores respectively.

The average annual investment in Bihar during the First and the Second Plan periods was nearly 7 per cent of the total gross value of output in agriculture. The capital formation created or expected to be created during the different plan periods through the execution of such programmes as land reclamation and soil conservation, construction of farm buildings, roads and fencing, distribution of agricultural implements, utilization of irrigation water, etc. could be estimated as they belonged to the public sector. The estimate of investment for the private sector is not available. As the majority of the farmers in Bihar had holdings below the average size, there was hardly any surplus of farm receipts left for further investment towards capital formation after the payment of labour (including family labour) and raw material charges for the maintenance of the farmers at the subsistence level, at least after incurring the minimum input costs. It has been assumed here that the capital formation through investment in the private sector is not appreciable. The investment of the public sector under different items during the three Plan periods is shown in the following Table 3.34.

TABLE 3.34

Distribution of Capital Formation during different Plan Periods

(In Lakh Rupees)

	Items	*First Plan*	*Second Plan*	*Third Plan*
1.	Land reclamation and soil conservation	15.0	153.0	150.0
2.	Farm buildings, roads and fencing and agricultural implements and equipments	33.5	416.0	680.6
3.	Irrigation (major and minor)	1218.0	2336.0	4198.0
	Total	1266.5	2905.0	5028.6
	Average annual	253.3	581.0	1005.7

It will be seen from this table that the percentage contributed towards capital formation through irrigation was very large. The average annual capital formation was Rs. 2.54 crores, Rs. 5.81 crores and Rs. 10.66 crores respectively during the First, Second and Third Plan quinquennia. An estimate of capital formation for the year 1953-54 was worked out by the National Council of Applied Economic Research in the Techno-Economic Survey of Bihar. The average estimated figure of capital formation during the First Plan and that given in Techno-Economic Survey are more or less of the same order. The proportion of annual capital formation was only 1.0 per cent of the total gross income from the agricultural sector in 1955-56 and 1.6 per cent during 1960-61.

The per capita income of Bihar was lower than that of other States. It was estimated at Rs. 156 in 1955-56 and Rs. 189 in 1960-61 at 1948-49 prices, the corresponding per capita income for all-India being Rs. 268 and Rs. 293 respectively. The annual gross value of output per acre from agriculture proper was also very low and worked out to Rs. 109 in 1950-51, Rs. 138 in 1955-56 and Rs. 162 in 1960-61 at constant prices.

Thus the over-all investment per acre in Bihar constituted 7 per cent of the gross value of output per acre at the end of the First Plan and 7.4 per cent at that of the Second Plan. During the Third Plan also it was expected that the proportion between investment per acre and the estimated gross value of output per acre would be more or less the same. The rate of investment per acre appeared to be too low to increase the rate of productivity in agriculture. Again, the proportion between capital formation and investment during the three Plan periods worked out to 11.5 per cent, 17.6 per cent and 21.6 per cent respectively. Unless the saving through private investment in the rural sector was increased considerably any addition of investment in the public sector alone would hardly be able to increase output considerably.

Mr. C.P. Sastri, Agricultural Economist, Directorate of Agriculture, Government of Bihar, has studied the problem of capital formation in relation to agriculture in Bihar in a paper entitled *"Investment in Farm and Capital Formation in Agriculture with particular reference to Bihar,"* published in the *Indian Journal of Agricultural Economics*, January-March, 1965. The basic data for this study were obtained on the basis of an investigation conducted during the agriculture year 1963-64 in six villages of Bihar, namely, (1) Damodarpur and Bithouli in the district of Muzaffarpur (North Bihar), (2) Mainpura and Deepnagar in the district of Patna (South Bihar), and (3) Hemantpur and Vishnugarh in the district of Hazaribagh (Chotanagpur). The basic information was obtained from 18 holdings in each village, making a total of 108 holdings.

An attempt was made by Mr. Sastri to throw light on the following aspects: (i) determination of the pattern of investment in farm, (ii) sources of farm investment, and (iii) methods of increasing farm investment.

The investment per farm included the purchase of land, purchase of live-stock, purchase of implements, machinery and equipment, construction and repair of the farm house, buildings and other land improvement activities including land reclamation, development of irrigation resources, etc. Table 3.35 shows the investment per farm.

TABLE 3.35

Investment Per Farm by Size of Holdings

Size groups (in acres)	*Average size of holdings (in acres)*	*Investment (Rs.)*	*Disinvest-ment (Rs.)*	*Net Invest-ment (Rs.)*
Below 2	1.42	178	101	77
2 to 5	3.44	207	92	115
5 and above	10.39	550	157	393
All holdings	5.09	311	116	199

The farmers in the large size-group of the holdings made a larger investment but the increase in investment was not proportional to the increase in the size of the holdings. The total investment varied between Rs. 178 and Rs. 530, the average investment per farm being Rs. 311. The investment per holding in the large size group of the holdings was about three times more than that in the small size group of the holdings, while the increase in investment in the medium size-group of the holdings was only 12 per cent, when compared to the small size-group of the holdings.

Table 3.36 gives data regarding per acre investment in the selected holdings.

TABLE 3.36

Size groups (in acres)	*Average size of holdings (in acres)*	*Investment (Rs.)*	*Disinvest-ment (Rs.)*	*Net Invest-ment (Rs.)*
Below 2	1.42	125	71	54
2 to 5	3.44	60	27	33
5 and above	10.59	50	14	36
All holdings	5.09	61	23	38

Investment per acre tended to decrease with increase in the size of the holdings. It ranged from Rs. 50 to Rs. 125. On an average, it was Rs. 61 per acre. A similar tendency was exhibited by disinvestment which varied between Rs. 14 and Rs. 71, the average disinvestment per acre being Rs. 23. Consequently, the net investment was the highest being Rs. 54 per acre in the small size-group of the holdings. The main reason of per acre net investment being higher in the small-size group than in other two size-groups of the holdings to be the very high investment, being about twice, in construction and repair of the farm house.

Table 3.37 shows the distribution of investment under different heads.

It will be observed from the Table 3.37 that in the case of the small size-group of holdings, construction and repair of the farm house was responsible for the largest investment and accounted for 43.2 per cent of the total investment. It was followed by investment in land and live-stock, accounting for 27 and 19.2 per cent respectively.

In the case of the holdings in the medium size-group, livestock alone accounted for about two-thirds of the total investment, followed by investment in construction and repair of the farm houses and on land, accounting for 17.9 and 11.3 per cent respectively. In the case of the holdings in the highest size-group, investment in live-stock and land along accounted for more than four-fifths of the total investments.

The Table 3.38 shows the per holding investment in different regions of the State.

It will be seen from the Table 3.38 that investment per holding was more than twice in North Bihar as compared to that in Chotanagpur, while it was 28 per cent highest in North Bihar than in South Bihar. In North Bihar purchase of live-stock alone was responsible for 56 per cent of the total investment. Construction and repair of the farm house, purchase of land and purchase of implements were the other items of investment in North Bihar, accounting for 21.1 per cent, 20.3 per cent and 2.6 per cent respectively of the total investment in the region. In South Bihar, purchase of land and purchase of live-stock each accounted for 42.2 per cent of the total investment. Construction and repair of the farm house accounted for 10.3 per cent of the total investment.

TABLE 3.37

Distribution of Investment Under Different Heads by Size of Holdings

(Investment in Rupees) (Size groups in acres)

Items	*Below 2*		*2 to 5*		*5 and above*		*All Holdings*	
	Invest-ment	*Per cent to total*	*Invest-ment*	*Per cent to total*	*Invest-ment*	*Per cent to total*	*Invest-ment*	*Per cent to total*
Purchase of land	48	27.0	24	11.3	214	39.0	95	30.6
Purchase of live-stock	34	19.2	134	64.8	241	43.9	136	43.6
Purchase of implements, machinery and equipment	5	2.8	8	3.8	10	1.8	8	2.6
Construction and repair of farm-house	77	43.2	37	17.9	44	8.0	52	16.7
Building and other land improvements including land reclamation	14	7.8	1	0.5	27	4.9	14	4.5
Development of irrigation Sources	—	—	3	1.7	6	1.1	3	1.0
Laying of orchards and plantation	—	—	—	+	8	1.3	3	1.0
Total	178	100.0	207	100.0	550	100.0	311	100.0

+Less than one.

TABLE 3.38

Distribution of Investment Per Farm under Various Heads in Different Regions of Bihar

(Investment in Rs.)

Items	*North Bihar*		*South Bihar*		*Chotanagpur*		*Average*	
	Invest-ment	*Per cent to total*	*Invest-ment*	*Per cent to total*	*Invest-ment*	*Per cent to total*	*Invest-ment*	*Per cent to total*
Purchase of land	86	20.3	139	42.2	61	33.5	95	30.6
Purchase of live-stock	237	56.0	139	42.2	32	17.6	136	43.6
Purchase of implements etc.	11	2.6	7	2.2	4	2.2	8	2.6
Construction and Repair of farm-house	89	21.1	34	10.3	35	19.2	52	16.7
Bunding and other land improvements including land reclamation	—	—	7	2.2	35	19.2	14	4.5
Development of irrigation sources	—	—	—	—	9	5.0	3	1.0
Laying of orchards and plantation	+	—	3	0.9	6	3.3	3	1.0
Total	423	100.0	329	100.0	182	100.0	311	100.0

+Less than one.

The sale of live-stock was the major item of disinvestment as is evident from the Table 3.39.

Land was sold in two cases only—in one case to repay the old debt while in another to repurchase the land in Deepnagar village of South Bihar. Besides, the only disinvestment was due to the sale of live-stock.

The sources of obtaining the necessary amount for investment included the following:

(A) Owned—readily available sources: (i) Past savings, and (ii) Current income.

(B) Sale of assets.

(C) Borrowing: (i) Government agencies, (ii) Co-operative agencies, and (iii) Private agencies.

(D) Other Sources: These included gifts, prizes, etc.

The following Table 3.40 shows the percentage contribution by these different sources to the total investment:

TABLE 3.40

Percentage Contribution of Different Sources to Total Investment by Size of Holdings

Sources	*Size-groups (in acres)*			
	Below 2	*2 to 5*	*5 and above*	*Average*
A. Owned readily available sources				
(i) Past savings	17.1	17.1	33.8	27.1
(ii) Current Income	46.3	53.7	26.5	35.9
Total	63.4	70.8	60.3	63.0
B. Sale of Assets	29.7	29.2	26.5	27.8
C. Borrowings	6.9	—	13.2	9.2
Total	100.0	100.0	100.0	100.0

It is evident from the above table that past savings and current income were responsible for financing the major portion of investment, amounting to about two-thirds of the total investment. The contribution by current income alone was 53.7

TABLE 3.39

Distribution of Disinvestment Per Farm under Various Heads in Different Regions of Bihar

(Investment in Rs.)

Items	*North Bihar*		*South Bihar*		*Chotanagpur*		*Average*	
	Amount	*Per cent to total*	*Amount*	*Per cent to total*	*Amount*	*Per cent to total*	*Amount*	*Per cent to total*
Sale of land	—	—	58	41.7	—	—	19	16.4
Sale of Live-Stock	180	100.0	81	58.3	31	100.0	97	83.6
Total	180	100.0	139	100.0	31	100.0	116	100.0

and 46.3 per cent in the medium and the small size-groups of the holdings respectively, while it was only 26.5 per cent in the holdings in the large size-group.

The following measures are suggested for augmenting the farm investment:

(1) *To improve employment situation*: Labour input is in excess in the rural areas. This unproductive surplus labour may be utilized for productive purposes through the construction of irrigation channels, excavation of tanks, etc., and by setting up industries in the rural areas.

(2) *To increase savings*: In fact, savings depend partly on the desire of the people to improve their economic conditions. It is, therefore, essential that the outlook of the people for improvement should be re-oriented which, in turn, will create savings. The creation of surplus through increased output provides the pool for savings and also the incentive to investment.

(3) *To make larger funds available*: (i) Co-operative credit must be enlarged and linked with productive investment. Some capital forming activities should be undertaken by the co-operative institutions, (ii) Some constructional works, e.g., reclamation and levelling of wide tracts of land, excavation of tanks, sinking of tube-wells and installation of small plants or machinery should be undertaken by the development authorities at least in the initial stages, (iii) The Central and State Governments should provide some funds and channelise them through the establishment of industries, construction of storage houses or godowns and provision of transport facilities in the rural areas.

FIVE-YEAR PLANS: THEIR ACHIEVEMENTS AND FAILURES

Our agricultural statistics show that the acreage under the five important food crops, viz., rice, wheat, barley, gram and maize, which account for more than two-thirds of the total sown area in our State, decreased from an average of 19,784 thousand acres during the quinquennium ending 1950-51 to an average of

18,435 thousand acres during the quinquennium ending 1955-56, while the out-turn of the same crops decreased from 4917 thousand tons in the former quinquennium to 4500 thousand tons in the latter quinquennium.

This appears somewhat queer in the light of the fact that, according to the statements issued by the Government of India, both the average of all-India acreage under cereals and the yield rate increased by about 13 per cent between the quinquennium ending 1951-52 and the quinquennium ending 1956-57. It is no doubt true that Bihar had experienced a succession of bad harvests beginning from 1950-51 and from that year on to 1956-57 only two years, viz., 1952-53 and 1953-54, had witnessed normal harvests comparable to the harvest in 1949-50. In consequence, while our net imports of foodgrains by rail and river averaged 135 thousand tons per year during the quinquennium ending 1949-50, they averaged 351 thousand tons per year during the next quinquennium. Similarly, the expenditure on famine relief and the advances under the National Calamities and Agriculturists' Loans Acts, which had averaged Rs. 16.3 lakhs and 30.4 lakhs per annum respectively in the quinquennium ending 1950-51, rose to Rs. 239.0 lakhs and 343.5 lakhs respectively per annum in the quinquennium ending 1955-56.

Part of this can be explained by the inaccuracy of our agricultural statistics. Take the case of sugarcane statistics. They show the total production of sugar-cane in Bihar in 1952-53 to be actually less than the quantity of sugar-cane crushed by the sugar factories in the State by 54 lakh maunds, which amounts to 8 per cent of the estimated production. Take our linseed statistics. According to them, the quantity of linseed exported from Bihar by rail and river in 1950-51 exceeded its estimated production. Or, take our jute statistics, which show that the export of raw jute in 1949-50 (37 lakh maunds) exceeded its estimated production (21 lakh maunds) by 16 lakh maunds, which discrepancy is hard to account for even if the exports of jute had included mesta and some sunn hemp. Similarly, the area and production of tobacco, as published in the Season and Crop Report, different markedly from the data collected by the staff of the Central Excise Department for the levy of excise duty on tobacco.

Our land utilization statistics too are no better, as would appear from the Table 3.41.

TABLE 3.41

(In Lakh Acres)

Land Area		*Area of cultivable waste including fallow lands*	*Area not available for cultivation including forests*	*Net area sown*
1. According to Village Papers S.C.R.	447.9	92.0	144.0	211.9
2. According to Survey and Settlement Operations	424.3	88.8	98.4	237.1
3. Difference	+23.6	+3.2	+45.6	—25.2

The Table 3.41 shows that our total land area, according to the Village Papers which from the basis of the Season and Crop Report exceeded in 1952-53 that, according to the Survey and Settlement Operations (1892-1938) whereas the net area sown, according to the former, fell short of that, according to the latter. This ambiguity is accounted for by an enormous increase in the area not available for cultivation including forests. In fact, the forest areas in 1952-53 exceeded the forest area shown in the Survey and Settlement Report by as much as 40 lakh acres.

A further break-down of these figures by districts shows that out of an increase of 45.6 lakh acres in the areas not available for cultivation including forests about 28 lakh acres were accounted for by an increase in the area covered by forests in the districts of Hazaribagh, Ranchi, Palamau and Singhbhum over the jungle area in these districts, as shown in the Survey and Settlement Report. The gross area sown in 1952-53 showed a decrease of 20 lakh acres from the gross sown area found at the time of the Survey and Settlement Operations. This decrease was largely the result of a reduction in the area under oilseeds, pulses, and minor cereals. In the same manner, the gross area under cereals and pulses decreased by 8.2 lakh acres and that under oilseeds by 12.7 lakh acres whereas the area under sugar-cane increased by 1.1 lakh acres, that by 3.4 lakh acres, and that under fruits and vegetables by 2.7 lakh acres. Of the gross sown area, the percentage of area under cereals and pulses increased from 86.2 per cent in the

Survey year (1892-1938) to 89.4 per cent in 1952-53, that under fruits and vegetables from 1.6 per cent to 2.7 per cent whereas the percentage of area under oilseeds had decreased from 7.6 per cent to 3.6 per cent. Coming to cereals and pulses, we find that although the total area decreased by 8.2 lakh acres, the area under rice showed an increase of 9 lakh acres; of wheat an increase of 3.5 lakh acres; and of maize an increase of 2 lakh acres. The gain in area by wheat was almost exactly offset by the loss of area by barley. Gram decreased by 3.5 lakh acres; marua by 3.3 lakh acres; and other cereals and pulses by 13 lakh acres. People were perhaps taking to finer cereals for consumption in place of coarser ones.

It follows from the foregoing that most of the areas left unsurveyed at the time of the Survey and Settlement Operations, for which Village Papers were prepared subsequently, were forest areas. Moreover, as the Survey and Settlement Report pointed out, a good proportion of the areas in Chotanagpur uplands, which had been shown as cropped area, was also jungle land. What, however, is difficult to account for is that about 12 to 15 lakh acres of cropped area shown as such at the time of the Operations should have turned into cultivable waste and fallow land. On the country, there is every reason for maintaining that a reduction had occurred in the area of cultivable waste. In fact, calculating from the mid-point of the Survey and Settlement Operations period, i.e., 1915, we find that the population of Bihar had increased by not less than 100 lakhs during 1915-51. To support the increased population of 100 lakhs in 1951 the net sown area should have increased at least by 77 lakh acres, if the proportion of the double-cropped area had not increased, or the yield rate per acre had not risen, or if we had not been depending to a larger extent on imports from outside than before. A reduction in the net cropped area, apart from the vicissitudes of the weather in particular years, would thus appear to be almost inexplicable.

This examination affirms our suspicion that both the cropped area and the rates of yield of crops had been under-estimated. To remedy this, there is an urgent need for ensuring that the coverage of area surveyed is increased and that our crop-cutting experiments are conducted properly and extended to the more important crops such as maize, sugar-cane, jute, and so on, which are not covered by them. More stringent supervision than has hitherto been exercised is also essential.

The various "Grow More Food" schemes executed during the Bihar's First Plan provided for an additional production *potential* (which word should be noted carefully) of 7.22 lakh tons of cereals and pulses.

On the basis of the approved yardsticks of additional production proposed to be attained by the various kinds of "Grow More Food" schemes included in the First Plan it was estimated at the end of the Plan that the target was fulfilled, though no attempt was made by the planners to explain what these yardsticks were and how they had been applied.

RATE OF GROWTH: AN INTER-STATE COMPARISON

The following table shows that during the First Plan period the linear rates of growth of the under crops, agricultural production and agricultural productivity in Bihar, as compared to those in a number of other States were not very reassuring.

In 1961 an official committee of experts in its report on the working of the Agriculture Department of the Bihar Government recorded its opinion that the department had failed utterly to attain the desired targets in the field of production and that a streamlined agricultural administration was an urgent necessity to ease the food situation in the State.

The average annual production of foodgrains during the Second Plan was estimated at 59.15 lakh tons. The Planning Commission estimated the production in 1965-66 in Bihar at 82.89 lakh tons, taking the 1960 production of 62.62 lakh tons as the base. This target of 82.89 lakh tons was not enough to provide sufficient cattle feed, which is usually calculated at 10 per cent of the food requirements of the human population. It assumed per day per adult consumption of 17.5 ounces of foodgrains, the accepted standard for the nation. Even this was not likely to meet total requirements of about 51.2 million people in Bihar by 1965-66 and their cattle. The total foodgrains requirements were expected to exceed 86 lakh tons.

There were during 1952-53 to 1961-62 significant differences in the rates of growth of agricultural output in different States in India. The growth rate was high as 5.6 per cent per annum in the case of Punjab, 4.9 per cent in the case of Madras and only around 1 per cent for the three eastern States of Assam, Orissa and

TABLE 3.42

All-India and State Linear Rates of Growth of Area under Crops, Agricultural Production and Productivity during 1952-53 to 1961-62

All Crops (Average: 1952-53 to 1954-55=100)

(Per cent)

All-India/States	*Production*	*Area*	*Productivity*
(i) Foodgrains	2.66	1.10	1.45
(ii) Non-foodgrains	4.40	2.38	1.74
Punjab	5.62 (1)	2.56 (2)	2.55 (4)
Madras	4.93 (2)	0.74 (10)	3.98 (1)
Himachal Pradesh	3.83 (3)	0.84 (9)	2.82 (3)
Madhya Pradesh	3.64 (4)	1.37 (4)	2.05 (7)
Mysore	3.56 (5)	1.25 (5)	2.12 (6)
Maharashtra	3.53 (6)	0.49 (13)	2.89 (2)
Bihar	3.40 (7)	1.08 (7)	2.16 (5)
All-India (All crops)	3.23	1.31	1.76
Rajasthan	2.92 (8)	3.90 (1)	(–) 0.76 (15)
Kerala	2.44 (9)	1.15 (6)	1.18 (10)
Gujarat*	2.22 (10)	0.68 (11)	1.50 (9)
	(2.57)	(0.27)	(2.30)
Uttar Pradesh	2.06 (11)	0.85 (8)	1.13 (11)
Andhra Pradesh	1.91 (12)	(–) 0.07 (15)	1.99 (8)
Assam	1.34 (13)	1.55 (3)	(–) 0.20 (14)
Orissa	1.18 (14)	0.52 (12)	0.66 (12)
West Bengal	0.89 (15)	0.18 (14)	0.51 (13)
	(3.13)	(0.71)	(2.04)

* In the case of Gujarat and West Bengal, the first two years of the period under consideration were somewhat abnormal; leaving out these two years, the growth rates for the period 1954-55 to 1961-62 with the average of 1954-55 to 1956-57 as 100 are given in the brackets.

Note: Figures in brackets indicate ranks.

West Bengal. The inter-State disparities in the growth rates raised an important question as to why the States' performance varied so widely. In particular, it would be worthwhile to make a detailed enquiry into the sources of growth of agriculture in States like Punjab which have done very well compared to several other States.

With vast differences in soil, topography, climate, irrigational facilities, cropping pattern, etc., between different States the progress of agricultural production was not obviously uniform among the various States. State-wise linear growth rates of agricultural production, area under crops and agricultural productivity during 1952-53 to 1961-62 are given in Table 3.36. Seven States, viz., Punjab, Madras, Himachal Pradesh, Madhya Pradesh, Mysore, Maharashtra and Bihar showed rates of growth of agricultural production during this period higher than the all-India rate. The States of Rajasthan, Kerala, Gujarat, Uttar Pradesh and Andhra Pradesh showed moderate rates of growth, but lower than the all-India rate. The eastern States of Assam, Orissa and West Bengal showed very low rates of growth. West Bengal was at the lowest rung of the ladder of agricultural development in the country, while Punjab was at the top. The highest growth rates of agricultural production in the country was roughly six times the lowest growth rate.

Usually States with high rates of growth of agricultural production showed bigh rates of growth of productivity as well. In the case of Punjab, area and productivity contributed equally to the growth of agricultural production. In other States, except Rajasthan and Assam, contribution of productivity was relatively more than that of area. In Maharashtra, the rate of growth of productivity was about six times that of area and in Madras five times. In the case of Himachal Pradesh, Bihar, Madhya Pradesh and Mysore the ratio of growth rate of productivity to that of area was 3.4, 2.0, 1.5 and 1.7 respectively. Among the eight States of the lower group, Rajasthan showed a high rate of growth of area, highest in the country, but a negative growth rate of productivity resulting in a moderate growth rate of over-all agricultural production. Both the area and the productivity growth rates were moderate for Kerala, Andhra Pradesh showed a rate of growth of productivity higher than the all-India, but a negative rate of growth of area with the result that its rate of growth of over-all production was considerably depressed. In the case of Assam, on the one hand, while the growth rate of area like Rajasthan was higher than all-India, productivity actually declined. For Gujarat, Uttar Pradesh, Orissa and West Bengal, both area and productivity rates were low.

In the background of the above pattern of State growth rates of area under crops, agricultural production and agricultural productivity it will be interesting to study the growth rates for the two major groups of crops, viz., foodgrains and non-foodgrains in different States. As in the case of all crops, there were considerable variations in the growth rates of the two major groups of crops, viz., foodgrains and non-foodgrains, from State to State. Even within the same State, performances of the two groups were quite divergent in some cases. For example, in Gujarat, the rate of growth of foodgrains production was negative while that of non-foodgrains was high at 5.4 per cent per annum. Similarly, in West Bengal, the rate of growth of foodgrains production was negative, while in the case of non-foodgrains, it was positive. For foodgrains the growth rates were negative for Gujarat and West Bengal and varied, for the rest of the States, between 0.6 per cent per annum in Assam to 4.6 per cent per annum in Madras. For non-foodgrains'Andhra Pradesh and Orissa registered negative growth rates and for the rest of the States, the range was from 0.95 per cent per annum in Himachal Pradesh to 9.15 per cent in Punjab. Thus, considering the positive growth rates only, both the lower and the upper limits of the range were higher in the case of non-foodgrains as compared with them in the case of foodgrains.

The States of Punjab, Madras, Madhya Pradesh and Mysore did well in both foodgrains and non-foodgrains with growth rates higher than the all-India. Punjab with a growth rate of 5.6 per cent per annum for all crops, occupied the first place for non-foodgrains and second for foodgrains. Madras with an over-all growth rate of 4.9 per cent per annum got the first place for foodgrains and the third for non-foodgrains. Madhya Pradesh, which ranked fourth for all crops, had the fifth place for foodgrains and the seventh for non-foodgrains. Mysore with an over-all rate of growth of 3.6 per cent, which was just a shade lower than Madhya Pradesh, occupied the eighth place for foodgrains and the fifth for non-foodgrains. Thus, even among these four States Punjab and Madras only could be considered to have achieved a high balanced growth in respect of production of both foodgrains and non-foodgrains.

The States of Himachal Pradesh, Kerala, Bihar and Andhra Pradesh did well in foodgrains, but not so well in non-foodgrains. While there is need for accelerating the rate of growth of food-grains production in all States, these States will have to devote greater attention to non-foodgrains in the future agricultural programmes, Maharashtra, Gujarat, Uttar Pradesh and Rajasthan did well in non-foodgrains, but not so well in foodgrains. The remaining three States of Assam, Orissa and West Bengal showed low growth rates for both foodgrains and non-foodgrains.

Rice occupied the foremost position among the foodgrains which together occupied nearly four-fifths of the total cultivated area in the country. Against the all-India rate of rice production of 3.29 per cent per annum, the relatively minor rice growing States of Punjab and Himachal Pradesh showed very high growth rates of 12.0 per cent and 7.9 per cent respectively. On the other hand, the State with the highest proportion of all-India rice production, viz., West Bengal showed the lowest rate of growth of production. In the case of jowar high-growth rate of productivity was a major factor contributing to the increase in production during the period under review. The most important jowar-producing State, viz., Maharashtra, which alone accounted for 37 per cent of the all-India production of jowar, showed a high rate of growth of over 4 per cent per annum. Madras has the highest growth rate of productivity of jowar of about 6 per cent.

From the point of view of production, wheat came next to rice among cereals. The most important wheat-growing State, viz., Uttar Pradesh, which accounted for about one-third of all-India wheat production, showed a low growth rate of 4.74 per cent. Punjab, which came next to Uttar Pradesh from the point of view of wheat production, showed a high rate of growth of 5.49 per cent per annum due to a high rate of growth of area under the crop.

Among the non-foodgrains cotton was an important commodity in whose case the expansion in area was due to diversion from other dry crops like bajra and jowar. Gujarat which showed a growth rate of 2.13 per cent per annum, only marginally higher than the all-India growth rate. The relatively lesser important States of Punjab and Madras, on the other hand, showed very high rates of growth of cotton production. In the case of jute, West Bengal, the premier jute-growing State, showed a good rate of growth.

For sugar-cane, against the all-India growth rate of 6.56 per cent per annum, the States of Punjab, Maharashtra, Madras, Mysore and Gujarat had growth rates of production of sugar-cane ranging from 11.15 per cent to 13.87 per cent. All these States had very high rates of growth of area under sugar-cane. Except for Punjab and Mysore, the growth rate of productivity of sugar-cane was very low in all the remaining States.

The growth of agricultural output in the various States varied widely during this period. The first seven States whose rates of growth of agriculture production were higher than all-India accounted for a gross sown area of 190 million acres in 1961-62, which constituted about 50 per cent of the gross area sown in the fifteen States under study. In Punjab and Madras, which had a high percentage of irrigated area to gross sown area, substantial increases were recorded in gross irrigated area, which went up by about 22.7 and 35.9 per cent respectively, during this period. The impressive increase in gross irrigated area in Madras pushed up the percentage of gross irrigated area to gross sown area from 37.8 per cent in 1952-53 to 43.6 per cent in 1961-62, the highest in the country. This helped the State in achieving the highest rate of growth of agricultural productivity in the country. In the case of other States like Maharashtra, Madhya Pradesh, Mysore and Bihar also, the increase in irrigated area helped to achieved a high rate of growth of agricultural productivity. On the other hand, among the States in the lower group, viz., Rajasthan, Assam, Kerala, Gujarat, Uttar Pradesh and Andhra Pradesh, the rates of growth of agricultural output was less, mainly because of no increase in the irrigated area. In the remaining States of Orissa and West Bengal also not much progress had been witnessed in the irrigated area during the period under review.

The various "Grow More Food" schemes provided for in Bihar's Second Plan were originally estimated to secure an additional production potential of 15 lakh tons of foodgrains. The anticipated achievement at the end of the Second Plan was, however, likely to have been of the order of 11.75 lakh tons only, particularly because of the short supply of chemical fertilizers, delay in the establishment of seed multiplication farms and lack of a suitable agency to ensure exchange of improved seeds among the different classes of the registered growers.

Bihar's Third Plan proposed to increase the production of non-food crops by about 6 lakh tons and that of foodgrains by 20.27 lakh tons. This was based on the following assumptions:

(1) That irrigation schemes, both major and minor, would

build up an additional potential of 5.03 lakh tons of foodgrains and 2.10 lakh tons of non-foodcrops.

(2) That the farmers could be induced to make an intensive use of manures and fertilizers, which were expected to increase the production of food crops by 8.64 lakh tons and of non-food crops by 3.13 lakh tons. About 40 per cent of the increase in the production of foodgrains and about 50 per cent of the increase in that of non-food crops would depend on this.

(3) That through the multiplication and distribution of improved seeds, the production of foodgrains would be raised by 4.37 lakh tons and that of non-foodcrops by 0.22 lakh tons.

(4) That the land development and soil conservation measures would increase food production by 0.39 lakh tons.

(5) That the adoption of improved agricultural practices including the use of improved implements would increase the production of food crops by 1.84 lakh tons and that of non-food crops by 0.55 lakh tons.

(6) That the Package Programme would lead to an estimated production of about 2.14 lakh tons of foodgrains.

According to an estimate, which is available, by the end of the Third Plan improved seeds of foodgrains would have been sown over a gross area of 138 lakh acres.

In Bihar the "A" Class registered growers of paddy are entitled to a premium at the rate of Re. 1 per maund on each maund of "A" Class seeds produced from the "pedigree" seed received annually from the Agriculture Department and sold to or exchanged with those of the cultivators. No subsidy is admissible on the seeds produced with the seeds available with the "A" Class registered growers from the previous harvest.

In Bihar 25 per cent subsidy on the sale of pesticides and 50 per cent subsidy on the sale of plant protection tools and equipment are provided. The Plan Protection Organisation of the State purchases the pesticides and equipments and sells them to the individual cultivators at subsidised rates. When the Plant Protection Organisation renders plant protection service to the farmers only 75 per cent of the cost of pesticides is recovered from the beneficiaries.

An important constituent of the Third Plan agricultural programme was the Package Programme, i.e., the Intensive Agricultural District Programme, which sought to intensify the efforts of the community development and co-operative agencies in areas in which irrigation facilities were available. This programme was initiated in Shahabad district.

The essence of this programme was extension work on an integrated basis by combining all essential elements (for developing full food production potential) into one integrated food production programme. Its object was to provide for adequate and timely supplies of fertilizers, implements, pesticides, marketing, transportation and godowns. This programme was to be worked in districts which had the maximum of irrigation facilities and the minimum of natural hazards and was expected to set a pattern for extending such a programme to other similar areas. This intensive effort was to reach all farmers through panchayats and co-operatives and to formulate village and farm production plans, which would progressively involve all farm families. The programme was to be based on the developmental effort at the village level. Unlike the community development programme, which was a generalised statement of aspirations, this was a real programme for specific action in particular communities, having sufficient concern for human motivation, involving people in planning and paying due heed to the social setting of the farmer. But the experience of the past few years of this programme is already indicative of its inability to solve any problems of our rural economy.

An investigation into the working of the intensive agricultural district programme in the Udwantnagar block of Shahabad district conducted recently by the Agro-Economic Research Centre of the Visva-Bharati University revealed that the programme resulted in increased production and yield per acre following increased use of fertilizers and improved seeds and introduction of new crops. But inspite of a good deal of emphasis on fertilizers they were used without proper testing of soil and without proper response from the farmers. The programme caused progressive changes in the cropping pattern, namely, replacement of khesari by wheat. But it was felt that steps should be taken to

TABLE 3.43

Areas Recommended for Reclamation by the Uppal Committee

States	*Total area recom-mended for rec-lamation (Acres)*	*Total cost involved in recla-motion (Rs. in laks)*	*Total additional food pro-duction (Annual) (Mds.)*	*Priority Accorded for Different Categories*			
				Classification of land and class of (Priority)	*Area priority (Acres)*	*Cost involved (Rs. in lakhs)*	*Additional production (Mds.)*
1	2	3	4	5	6	7	8
Punjab	316650	543.31	3709000	I—Lands overgrown with jungles and shrubs	41850	58.59	837000
				II—Eroded lands	125000	75.00	625000
				III—Saline and alkaline lands	50000	240.00	750000
				IV—Riverine lands	99800	169.72	1497000
Madhya Pradesh	201625	251.000	1268904	I—Lands overgrown with jungles, shrubs and bushes	189037	238.35	1221327
				II— -do-	-do-	9066 5.13	28938
				III— -do-	-do-	3522 6.61	9644
Andhra Pradesh	137710	173.81	1182880	I—Saline lands	32571	62.44	651420
				II—Dry lands, lands overgrown	99874	98.46	496870
				III—Jungles, shrubs and bushes	5765	12.90	34590
West Bengal	113640	131.95	1171036	I—Eroded lands	85379	102.61	683032
				II—"Char" lands	12594	12.59	377720
				III—Saline lands	1798	2.88	28970
				IV—Terai lands	13869	13.87	83214

Bihar	72196	106.63	555376	I—Terai	14800	14.80	222000
				II—Eroded lands	57396	91.83	344376
Mysore	68820	165.18	560795	I—Khar (Saline) lands	7832	9.38	93984
				II—Lands infested with thick growth of jungle, shrubs and bushes	53957	114.07	431656
				III—Eroded lands	7031	11.73	35155
Uttar Pradesh	61018	173.60	697465	I—Usar Lands	50000	162.50	600000
				II—Jungle lands	11018	11.10	97465
Gujarat	44638	48.55	252014	I—Dry lands	7907	4.48	31628
				II—Khar lands	36731	44.07	220386
Maharashtra	35584	38.21	173324	I—Dry lands	29586	27.95	118384
				II—Lands infested with thick growth of bushes and jungle	5998	10.28	59980
Madras	25646	30.31	195186	I—Dry lands	24446	27.30	195186
				II—Lands infested with thick growth of bushes and jungle	1200	3.00	Commercial crops
Kerala	4823	20.81	37500	I—Hilly lands covered with forests	1000	2.50	30000
			(Paddy) 187765	II—Lands infested with weeds and shrubs	3323	8.31	182765
			(Tapioca)	III—Lands infested with bushes and shrubs	500	10.00	7500
Jammu & Kashmir	1340	1.07	10720	I—Lands infested with bushes and small babul trees	1340	1.07	10720
Total	1083690	1684.43					

remove the peasants' fears that additional crops would deplete soil fertility and to educate them in the use of pesticides and other details of farming.

Shortfalls in the financial outlay of the Third Plan resulted in shortfalls in the physical targets as well. For example, the additional agricultural production potential at the end of the Third Plan was about 14 lakh tons as against the original target of 20.27 lakh tons. Doubts were expressed as to whether the target proposed for chemical fertilizers for the Third Plan was realistic. Doubts were raised if the State Co-operative marketing Union with the existing arrangements would be able to distribute large quantities of chemical fertilizers.

The main reason for the shortfall in sugar-cane production was that in 1961 it had been decided to impose a 10 per cent cut on the production of sugar, and naturally the production of sugarcane suffered thereafter, though later on it was decided that the original production of sugar-cane be revived. The main reason for the shortfall in the production of jute was the uncertainty of jute price. However, with the announcement of the floor price in advance of the sowing season, its production was getting stabilised gradually. The jute-growers are, however, notorious for the unscientific and improper retting undertaken by them, resulting in poor quality jute.

By the end of Bihar's Third Plan the target of 75 lakh tons of foodgrains had not been reached. Improved seeds of foodgrains had not been sown over the proposed gross area of 138 lakh acres. 73 lakh tons of sugarcane had not been produced. 12.81 lakh bales of jute had not been produced. It was not possible to achieve the target of 1.26 lakh tons of oilseeds and all that could be achieved was 1.00 lakh tons. The effect of the nucleus oilseeds development scheme was not tangible by the end of the Third Plan. The following Table 3.44 gives an account of these shortfalls.

The yardsticks of the additional production are described in the following Table 3.45.

In 1963-64 there was a drought at the beginning of the monsoon and during the later part of October, 1963 there was a hail-storm in certain parts of Bihar. These factors affected agricultural production. During 1964-65 there was continuous rain in the month of July, 1964 whilst large areas of North Bihar were affected by floods. Further, there was failure of the winter rain also and this affected the crops.

TABLE 3.44

(Lakh Tons)

	Targets for 1965-66	*Actual production*
Sugar-cane	73 lakh tons per year	69 in 1960-61
		62.30 in 1961-62
		48.50 in 1962-63
		50.93 in 1963-64
Jute	12.81 lakh bales	12.63 (lakh bales) in 1961-62
		10.44 (lakh bales) in 1962-83
		9.42 (lakh bales) in 1963-64
Oilseeds	1.26 lakh tons	0.93 (lakh tons) in 1961-62
		0.97 (lakh tons) in 1962-63
		1.00 (lakh tons) in 1963-64

TABLE 3.45

	Item	*Yardstick*
1.	Irrigation	0.5 ton per acre
2.	Fertilizers	
	(a) Nitrogenous (S/A)	2 tons per ton
	(b) Phosphatic (S.S.P.)	1 ton per ton
	(c) Town compost	1 ton per ton
3.	Improved seeds	1/27 ton per acre
4.	Double cropping	
	(a) Cultivated	0.2 ton per acre
	(b) Paira crop	0.1 ton per acre
5.	Improved cultural practices	10 per cent of other inputs

The extent by which we are successful in eliminating the fluctuations in our total agricultural production will be a real measure of our success on the agricultural front. Progress is to be measured, not by the schemes proposed or sanctioned, but by the success achieved in the implementation of those schemes.

The Third Plan proposed that private trade should be allowed to manufacture and distribute fertilizers in a number of districts side by side with the Co-operative Marketing Union doing the same work in other districts. This was expected to infuse a spirit of healthy competition into the Union and private trade. If necessary, distribution of the various fertilizers was also to be entrusted to private trade in selected districts so that the competitive distribution arrangements could cope with the work in this field of activity. This was considered to be the simplest and cheapest way of attaining self-sufficiency in foodgrains. The proportion of shortfall in attaining the foodgrains target was equated with that of shortfall in the supply of fertilizers. But huge stocks of fertilizers were reported to be rotting during the Third Plan.

PROBLEMS AND REMEDIES

The Bihar Unemployment Committee (1954) found that the system of payment of subsidies for land reclamation and conversion of uplands into paddy fields was not operating in favour of the small man who ought to have been encouraged to take up these operations by manual labour. It suggested that the subsidies be paid to them in instalments as the work progressed as if wages were being paid for their labour.

In most parts of Bihar the entire countryside is turned into grazing ground after the harvesting of paddy with the result that even if a cultivator is enterprising enough to attempt to grow some broadcast catch-crop or to take up regular arable cultivation of his isolated field, he cannot do it when the fields all around are open to grazing. Again, in most districts outside Chotanagpur and Santhal Parganas cladenstine grazing of cattle of standing crops for profit or out of enemity is not uncommon in the villages. To this has to be added the depredations of the stray animals and of the old and useless animals let loose, and of the wild animals like monkeys, boars, neelgaos and deer and of squirrels, rats, locusts, fungi aad microbes.

The fruits ot agricultural research do not reach the peasant. He does not get fertilizers, improved seeds and credit facilities in time. As was put in a section of local press, had the Agricultural Department officials posted in the different districts of Bihar tried to maintain contact with the farmers instead of attending to the kitchen gardens of offices at the district headquarters and playing host to the visiting supervisory staff, agricultural production would have increased considerably. In many districts the farmers are not even aware that there are soil-testing and experimental farms, nay, that there is such a thing as the Agricultural Department. The Bihar Government has itself admitted that the experimental farms have shown no improvement in food production and have suffered heavy losses.

The frequency of serious droughts and floods in Bihar during the last twelve years has certainly been excessively high. These have probably been the worst twelve years in this respect in the present century. Floods subject vast areas of Bihar to perpetual insecurity and instability.

The poverty of the people of Bihar can be traced largely to the low productivity of its agricultural sector. No attempt to raise the standard of living of the people would succeed unless the productivity of this sector were raised appreciably. It must, however, be pointed out that in a region, where agriculture is as poor as in Bihar, the farmers cannot be expected to make any marked improvement in their techniques of cultivation and farming practices unless they are assured of reasonable prices for at least their major crops. One way of helping them to get better prices will be to improve transport, warehousing and marketing facilities. Development of transport facilities will make it possible for the farmers in surplus areas to take advantage of better prices even in distant markets. However, full benefits of improved transport facilities will accrue to the farmers only if a sufficiently large number of markets with warehousing facilities are organised under the supervision of the State and the growth of marketing and service co-operatives is encouraged. While the improvements suggested above will undoubtedly help in giving better prices to the farmers, uniformly good prices cannot be guaranteed unless the State Government impresses on the Central Government the needs for fixing floor and ceiling prices for the principal food-grains such as rice and wheat well in advance of the sowing season and for the Government programme of buying rice and wheat when prices touch the floor and of selling them when they exceed the ceiling.

The Government is trying to induce and persuade even the small cultivator to invest more money in land improvement, better implements, sturdier bullocks, superior milkers, better seeds, fertilizers, and so on, as well as to put in more labour. The rural credit facilities are being expanded and reorganised. But unless the uncertainties of agricultural production are tackled side by side, any adventure into the field of progressive farming by him may as much throw him into debt as bring him more produce and more income. The incentive of the cultivator has got to be fortified by fostering conditions under which he can appraise a proper correlation between his efforts and their fruits. This alone will generate self-confidence and a spirit of enterprise.

The success of the proposed programmes will turn on the responsiveness of the farmers. The Government can only render assistance in a number of ways but it can have no direct control over their decisions. To obtain the desired results, a few measures need to be carried out in regard to: (a) technical personnel, (b) agricultural credit, (c) agricultural marketing, (d) land ownership and size of holdings, and (e) availability and distribution of important farm inputs such as fertilizers, better seeds, etc. Much will depend on removing the instability of agriculture though considerable investment in the provision of irrigation facilities and on the control of floods and the vagaries of nature.

There is need for soil conservation in South Bihar and Chotanagpur. The Chotanagpur plateau region of the State and the escarpment zone and the sloping lands of South Bihar, lying between the plateau and the plain, are among the worst eroded areas in the country. The catchment areas of the southern rivers, which flow into the Ganges or flow out of Bihar into West Bengal or Orissa, lie largely in the Chotanagpur plateau region and the adjoining areas. The problem of soil erosion in these catchments falling in Chotanagpur and South Bihar is enormous. There are vast stretches of sloping uplands under intermittent cultivation, deep gullied lands and denuded forest lands which contribute heavily towards peak floods and high silt load in the rivers. Soil erosion from the sloping uplands as well as from forest lands has been going on for centuries, resulting in depleted fertility and consequent loss of yield from agriculture as well as forest crops. There is, therefore, immediate need for undertaking intensive soil conservation measures on agricultural lands, waste lands and forest lands in South Bihar and Chotanagpur both as a measure of flood protection and as a means of increasing production from these lands. A number of river valley projects have been executed in Chotanagpur, e.g., the Damodar Valley Corporation and the Mayurakshi Project. In addition, a large number of medium irrigation projects have been executed by the State Irrigation Department. The catchment areas of all these projects suffer seriously from soil erosion. It has been roughly estimated that about 58 lakh acres (representing about 14 per cent of the total area of the State) suffer seriously from soil-erosion and call for soil and water conservation measures.

Tables 3.46, 3.47 and 3.48, which follow, give a rough idea of the measures taken by the Government during the plan period in fields like soil conservation, afforestation, pasture development, reclamation of saline and alkali soils and ravines, contour bunding and terracing.

TABLE 3.46

Progress of Soil Conservation in the Second Five-Year Flan

States	*Physical Achievement (Area in '000 Acres)*	
	Agricultural Land	*Afforestation and Pasture Development*
Andhra Pradesh	71.50 (7)	15.70 (10)
Assam	0.60 (15)	4.40 (13)
Bihar	78.70 (5)	67.00 (2)
Maharashtra	1308.30 (1)	10.80 (11)
Gujarat	369.40 (2)	37.20 (7)
Kerala	11.50 (11)	—
Madhya Pradesh	51.10 (9)	21.10 (8)
Madras	131.30 (4)	76.40 (1)
Mysore	274.00 (3)	46.80 (5)
Orissa	59.50 (8)	19.90 (9)
Punjab	8.50 (13)	46.50 (6)
Rajasthan	13.00 (10)	10.90+44$^{1}/_{2}$ miles (3)
Uttar Pradesh	76.40 (6)	10.30 (12)
West Bengal	5.80 (14)	0.50 (15)
Jammu & Kashmir	—	54.90 (4)
Himachal Pradesh	0.6 (16)	10.80 (11)
D.V.C.	10.50 (12)	4.30 (14)

Note: Figures in brackets indicate ranks.

The distribution of the live-stock population between the different regions of Bihar is unfavourable. Notwithstanding its

TABLE 3.47

Progress of Contour Bunding and Terracing Programmes in the Third Five-Year Plan

(Area in Lakh Acres)

State	*Revised Plan targets*	*Actual achievement for 1961-63*	*Anticipated achievement for 1963-64**	*Anticipated achievement for first three years 1961-64 (Percentage in brackets)*	*Proposed targets for 1964-65*
Andhra Pradesh	4.00 (8)	0.58 (8)	0.39 (March '64) (7)	0.97 (24.36) (7)	0.73 (8)
Assam	0.29 (14)	—	0.01 (March '64) (14)	0.01 (3.7) (14)	(Negligible)
Bihar	4.05 (7)	0.71 (6)	0.46 (6)	1.17 (28.86) (6)	1.06 (6)
Gujarat	11.72 (3)	2.65 (2)	2.00 (3)	4.65 (39.0) (3)	2.92 (1)
Kerala	0.76 (13)	0.03 (11)	0.06 (13)	0.09 (10.65) (13)	0.06 (12)
Maharashtra	52.50 (1)	12.02 (1)	8.27 (1)	21.19 (40.36) (1)	12.97 (1)
Madhya Pradesh	14.45 (2)	2.31 (3)	3.66 (March '64) (2)	5.97 (41.33) (2)	4.44 (2)
Madras	4.30 (6)	1.11 (5)	0.52 (5)	1.63 (38.0) (5)	0.35 (7)
Mysore	6.50 (5)	0.65 (7)	0.27 (March '64) (10)	0.92 (14.02) (9)	1.43 (5)
Orissa	3.00 (9)	0.58 (9)	0.35 (8)	0.93 (31.00) (8)	0.50 (9)
Punjab	1.25 (11)	0.01 (12)	0.19 (March '64) (11)	0.20 (16.07) (11)	0.40 (10)
Rajasthan	1.78 (10)	0.43 (10)	0.31 (9)	0.74 (41.77) (10)	0.50 (9)
Uttar Pradesh	10.85 (4)	1.16 (4)	0.97 (March '64) (4)	2.13 (19.6) (4)	2.41 (4)
West Bengal	1.14 (12)	—	0.18 (12)	0.18 (15.78) (12)	0.32 (10)

*Figures are based on actual progress wherever reports are received upto March, and the targets for other cases for the year.

TABLE 3.48

Progress of Afforestation, Pasture Development, Reclamation of Saline and Alkali Soils and Ravines

(Area in '000 acres)

States	*Afforestation and Pasture Development*		
	Plan Targets	*Actual achievement for 1961-63*	*Anticipated achievement*
1	2	3	4
Andhra Pradesh	19.6 (9)	6.60 (9)	4.70 (7)
Assam	107.0 (5)	0.63 (12)	1.31 (9)
Bihar	64.0 (8)	22.50 (6)	12.0 (5)
Gujarat	—	—	—
Jammu & Kashmir	76.0 (6)	23.00 (5)	12.90 (4)
Kerala	—	—	—
Maharashtra	—	—	—
Madhya Pradesh	13.50 (10)	3.29 (10)	0.70 (10)
Madras	57.00 (9)	18.60 (7)	3.44 (5)
Mysore	65.00+500 miles L.H. (2)	23.00+107 miles L.H. (2)	25.00+89 miles L.H. (2)
Orissa	4.00 (11)	2.80 (11)	0.10 (11)
Punjab	9.00+250 miles Chos, 800 miles W.B. (1)	3.40+55 miles Chos, 331 miles W.B. (1)	1.40+22 miles Chos, 126 miles W.B. (1)
Rajasthan	13.00+100 miles S.B. (2)	2.00+34 miles S.B. (4)	2.85+34 miles S.B. (3)
Uttar Pradesh	50.00+50 miles R.S. (4)	12.60 (8)	7.90 (6)
West Bengal	100.00 (4)	53.70 (3)	N.A.

(Contd.)

TABLE 3.48 (*Contd.*)

States	*Reclamation of Saline and Alkali Soils*			*Reclamation of Ravine Lands*		
	Plan Targets	*Actual achievement for 1961-63*	*Anticipated achievement for 1963-64*	*Plan Targets*	*Actual achievement for 1961-63*	*Anticipated achievement for 1963-64*
1	*5*	*6*	*7*	*8*	*9*	*10*
Andhra Pradesh	—	—	—	—	—	—
Assam	—	—	—	—	—	—
Bihar	—	—	—	—	—	—
Jammu & Kashmir	45.00 (2)	N.A.	N.A.	12.00 (1)	0.70 (3)	2.30 (1)
	—	—	5.00 (4)	0.20 (4)	—	—
Kerala	—	—	—	—	—	—
Maharashtra	37.60 (4)	N.A.	17.00 (2)	—	—	—
Madhya Pradesh	0.40 (8)	Not started	—	2.00 (5)	1.40 (2)	0.40 (3)
Madras	1.00 (7)	Not started	—	—	—	—
Mysore	38.00 (3)	Not started	—	—	—	—
Orissa	8.00 (6)	Not started	—	—	—	—
Punjab	50.00 (1)	19.00 (1)	—	—	—	—
Rajasthan	10.00 (5)	1.65 (2)	0.50 (4)	6.00 (3)	1.80 (1)	1.35 (2)
Uttar Pradesh	10.00 (5)	1.60 (3)	1.62 (3)	10.00 (2)	—	—
West Bengal	—	—	—	—	—	—

*Includes achievements for 1961-62 and 1962-63. L.H.—Live Hedges, W.B.—Wind Breaks, S.B.—Shelter Belts and R.S.—Roadside Plantation.

advantages in pasture lands, Chotanagpur is the most backward region in this respect. The proportion of useless and decrepit animals is high in Chotanagpur and the practice of putting cows and buffaloes to the plough and working them as pack animals is widely common. Bihar is deficient in feeds and fodder. There are in Bihar about 2.83 acres of land under fodder per 100 bovine stock compared to 32 acres in Punjab. Less than necessary attention is paid to the conservation of grasses and fodder available during the monsoon and there is much wastage in the process of hay-making. The authors of the Report on the Techno-Economic Survey suggested the creation of a fodder reserve in every block and construction of silopits in all villages. Chotanagpur is suited for mixed farming. The hilly tracts and the jungle fringes can be turned into pasture lands with proper fencing and controlled grazing of milch animals. Besides, these tracts can be tapped for good quality hay. There is much room there for sheep-rearing.

If the fodder and hay section of the Animal Husbandry Department and the Forest Department co-operate better, the problem of fodder supply and soil conservation in Chotanagpur can be solved more efficiently and facilities provided for a prosperous stall-fed dairy industry there. In this way the problem of soil-building, prevention of unrestricted grazing, supply of milk and rural employment can be tackled all at once. Improvements of animal husbandry should be also in two other directions, namely, breeding and disease control. Throughout Bihar there is glaring want of good, scientific breeding centres for the cattle. The by-products of the animal slaughter houses, e.g., hides, skins, wool, bones, etc., are much wasted.

The Bihar State Board of Statistics and Evaluation at its meeting held on the 17th September, 1964 decided to undertake a survey for estimating the extent of adoption of improved agricultural practices in four blocks, namely, Sarath (Santhal Parganas), Dumraon (Shahabad), Patepur (Muzaffarpur) and Mandar (Ranchi), representing different geographical features of the State and belonging to its four divisions. The object of the survey was to assess the adoption of improved agricultural practices.

There are two aspects of the problem. First, what percentage of farmers have adopted improved agricultural practices? Second, what percentage of area has been brought under improved agricultural practices? Both aspects are relevant for the evaluation of programmes launched to step up agricultural production. While the first aspect relates to the acceptance of the programmes by the people, the second aspect seeks to assess the progress already made.

The schedules were designed to collect information as to whether a farmer's family in the villages selected for the survey did or did not adopt improved agricultural practices and if it adopted them, what percentage of his entire holding was covered by them, what quantities of improved seeds, fertilizers and pesticides were used by him, whether he adopted any new method of cultivation and employed modern implements, what percentage of area received irrigation and what crops were grown under these practices.

The survey showed that improved agricultural practices, had been adopted by about 86 per cent of the farmers in Dumraon, a block in the Package Programme area of Shahabad. Relatively smaller percentages of farmers had adopted improved agricultural practices in the remaining three blocks. One reason was that whereas facilities for adoption of improved agricultural practices existed in Dumraon, they were either meagre or negligible in other blocks. The second reason was that the farmers in Dumaraon had been educated about the use and benefits of improved agricultural practices due to the intensive agricultural programme operating in the area. Given facilities and proper education, the farmers in other area too may not lag behind.

Bihar produces compost and uses fertilizers and green manuring only in moderate doses as shown by Tables 3.49 and 3.50. A field study undertaken by the NCAER (see *Factors Affecting Fertilizer Consumption: Problems and Policies*, New Delhi, 1964) disclosed that the price policy now followed for fertilizers does not take into account the important fact that the use of fertilizers is a new experiment for most farmers and involves some real risks. Accordingly, in the interests of our crucial national objectives there is a great need to provide farmers with substantial incentives for the use of fertilizers. The Indian farmer will not use fertilizers unless he can clearly find a very favourable relation between the cost of this input and the additional returns attributable to

TABLE 3.49

Statistics of Rural Compost Production and Area Green Manured during 1961-62 and 1962-63

States/Union Territories	*Rural Compost (Lakh tons)*		*Green Manuring (Lakh acres)*	
	1961-62	*1962-63* (Tentative)*	*1961-62*	*1962-63** (Tentative)*
1	2	3	4	5
Andhra Pradesh	138.02 (2)	124.07 (2)	34.60 (1)	37.20 (2)
Assam	0.85 (17)	1.00 (16)	0.35 (14)	1.00 (13)
Bihar	10.19 (8)	19.50 (7)	7.42 (5)	7.33 (5)
Gujarat	2.32 (12)	3.46 (12)	0.80 (12)	1.17 (12)
Jammu & Kashmir	0.93 (16)	1.00 (16)	0.009 (18)	0.03 (17)
Kerala	1.49 (14)	2.22 (14)	2.59 (9)	5.12 (8)
Madhya Pradesh	7.09 (9)	14.29 (8)	1.81 (10)	3.28 (9)
Maharashtra	6.44 (10)	7.50 (11)	0.47 (13)	0.46 (14)
Madras	28.42 (5)	28.40 (6)	32.90 (2)	41.88 (1)
Mysore	30.62 (6)	36.43 (4)	3.81 (7)	6.00 (7)
Orissa	26.42 (6)	35.09 (5)	14.71 (4)	30.00 (3)
Punjab	77.42 (3)	99.22 (3)	4.50 (6)	6.75 (6)
Rajasthan	11.07 (7)	13.00 (9)	1.20 (11)	2.28 (11)
Uttar Pradesh	425.72 (1)	441.37 (1)	15.09 (3)	19.75 (4)
West Bengal	4.50 (11)	8.00 (10)	3.76 (8)	2.50 (10)
Delhi	0.06 (19)	0.30 (18)	0.006 (19)	0.019 (14)
Himachal Pradesh	1.94 (13)	2.50 (13)	0.35 (14)	0.36 (15)
Manipur	0.43 (18)	0.65 (17)	0.006 (19)	0.012 (21)
Tripura	1.10 (15)	1.36 (15)	0.018 (6)	0.028 (18)
Pondicherry	0.009 (20)	0.28 (19)	0.18 (15)	0.22 (16)
N.E.F.A.			0.006 (19)	N.A.
N.H.T.A.				—
Andamans & Nicobar	0.003 (21)	0.039 (20)	0.015 (17)	0.016 (20)
Laccadives & Minicoy	—	—	—	—
Total	775.052 or say 77.50* million tons	839.669 or say 84.00** million tons	124.600 or say 12.50 million acres	165.405 or say 17.00 Million Acres

Note: Figures in brackets indicate ranks.

*Subject to revision.

**In addition to this, farm yard manure produced in the country is roughly estimated at 216.00 million tons annually.

TABLE 3.50

Consumption of Fertilizers Per Unit Area of Agricultural Land (1962-63)

States /Union Territories	*Consumption in Lb. per Acre*			
	N	*P 205*	*K 20*	*Total*
1	2	3	4	5
Andhra Pradesh	6.05 (2)	1.60 (1)	0.03 (8)	7.68 (3)
Assam	0.10 (16)	0.07 (14)	0.11 (5)	0.28 (16)
Bihar	1.80 (7)	0.27 (7)	0.10 (6)	2.17 (8)
Gujarat & Maharashtra+	1.33 (9)	0.59 (5)	0.09 (7)	2.01 (9)
Jammu &			—	
Kashmir	1.18 (10)	0.01 (15)	—	1.19 (11)
Kerala	3.51 (3)	0.75 (4)	4.10 (1)	8.36 (2)
Madhya Pradesh	0.62 (12)	0.14 (10)	—	0.76 (13)
Madras	7.71 (1)	1.03 (2)	1.04 (2)	9.78 (1)
Mysore	1.84 (6)	0.53 (6)	0.36 (4)	2.73 (6)
Orissa	0.72 (11)	0.13 (11)	0.02 (9)	0.87 (12)
Punjab	2.79 (4)	0.21 (8)	0.01 (10)	3.01 (4)
Rajasthan	0.35 (14)	0.08 (13)	—	0.43 (14)
Uttar Pradesh	1.80 (7)	0.17 (9)	—	1.97 (10)
West Bengal	1.74 (8)	0.76 (3)	0.48 (3)	2.98 (5)
Delhi	2.30 (5)	0.14 (10)	—	2.44 (7)
Himachal Pradesh	0.22 (15)	0.21 (8)	—	0 43 (15)
Manipur	0.18 (16)	0.09 (12)	—	0.27 (17)
Tripura	0.02 (17)	—	—	0.02 (17)
Pondicherry	—	—	—	—
Goa	—	—	—	—
Andamans & Nicobar	0.48 (13)	—	—	0.48 (14)
Laccadives	—	—	—	—
All-India	2.24	0.49	0.19	2.92

+Separate figures of agricultural area in the two States are not available.

Notes: (1) Calculated on the basis of distribution figures.

(2) Figures in brackets indicate ranks.

fertilizers. The present price of fertilizers is proving to be a great impediment to their consumption. About half the farmers and almost all village level workers interviewed in the survey (which included from Bihar Shahabad and Bhagalpur districts) mentioned high prices as a great disincentive. Prices of fertilizers need to be reduced. If necessary, subsidies ought to be granted for this purpose. There is already a subsidy of up to 25 per cent of the price of superphosphate to the farmer. If prices of nitrogenous fertilizers now fixed by the central pool cannot be reduced, a subsidy should be extended to these fertilizers. The principle of subsidy for fertilizers is well organised even in the advanced countries where agriculture is a business and is not exposed to as serious risks as those characterising Indian agriculture. The use of fertilizers is not only a means of increasing the yields of lands, it is also important for its social benefit, namely, its long-term effect on soil fertility. By replenishing and maintaining the balance of plant nutrients in the soil, the country receives benefits over many years.

The survey further revealed that the co-operative societies were not able to provide for an adequate number of sale points. There was excessive and frequent accumulation of stocks. Marked irrationalities characterised the distribution of supplies between areas and over different periods of time. Accumulation was partly attributable to the inability of administration to arrange supply in time. The NCAER report suggested that the manufacturers of fertilizers themselves should be allowed to establish their own sales organisations. Inadequate credit was another major impediment to the use of fertilizers. The existing terms of credit, both the rate of interest and the repayment procedures, did not take into account the special types of risks incurred by the fertilizer user. The most common complaint was about the inflexible nature of the period of the repayment of the loans. Even when the harvest was poor, repayments were insisted on by the credit agencies.

The survey made it evident that fertilizer consumption was also a matter of basic motivations and concerned the attitudes of farmers towards farming as a business. Although a number of farmers had actually positive experience with fertilizers, they were not fully convinced about the efficacy of their continued use. The existing information and the promotional agencies had thus not succeeded in bringing about any basic change in the attitudes of most farmers. Demonstration on local places proved to be the most effective method of propagating knowledge about the advantages of fertilizers. The slowness of the Government in implementing land reforms was another institutional impediment to the use of fertilizers by most farmers.

Fertilizers will be misused, ineffective or wasted without careful soil analysis, improved seeds and pesticides. Like irrigation the use of fertilizers presumes a package of practices.

In many cases where the co-operatives are weak or exist merely to fulfil a target, fertilizer distribution is not as effective or widespread or timely as it should be. The co-operatives enjoy a monopoly and have little incentive to sell fertilizers.

The Central Team on Agricultural Programme, which visited Bihar in July, 1965, made the following recommendations to the Planning Commission:

(1) The Cabinet sub-committee on agriculture production should meet regularly.
(2) The districts of Bihar should be split up into viable agricultural districts with viable agricultural sub-divisions. The number of blocks in each district should be limited to 15 and each district should comprise three sub-divisions.
(3) Separate officers should be appointed for development and revenue work in all blocks and the posts of the Block Development Officers should be manned by technical officers of the Agriculture Department.
(4) Large-size seed farms for the production of wheat seeds should be established immediately.
(5) Prophylactic treatment should be taken up on a campaign basis in the TADP and IAA blocks and the proposal for short-term loan of Rs. 40 lakh should be sent to the Ministry or Food and Agriculture early.
(6) Immediate steps should be taken to appoint a Joint Director of Agriculture for looking after the IADP and IAA programmes at the State headquarters.
(7) The time-schedule for the construction of godowns should be strictly adhered to.
(8) A definite programme for speedy utilization of 4000

cusecs of water available from the Sone Project should be worked out.

(9) All the 17 agricultural schools should immediately take up integrated extension training programme. These training centres should have separate wings for farmers' training, farmers' sons' training, village artisans' training and in-service training of Gram Sevaks. This should be done immediately and necessary steps should be taken to upgrade all the training centres during the Fourth Plan period after integration had been effected.

(10) Steps should be taken to finalise proposals for the Fourth Plan in respect of training programmes as suggested by the Ministry of Food and Agriculture.

As regards minor irrigation the Team made the following recommendations:

(1) The State Government should complete ground water survey as early as possible.

(2) It should submit immediately proposals for urgent lift irrigation schemes drawn up in the light of guidelines prepared and sent from the Ministry of Food and Agriculture.

(3) There should be close co-ordination between the Agriculture Department and the Electricity Department, and rural electrification works should be taken up in those areas where there is scope for energising a large number of pump sets.

(4) The decision taken by the State Government for the maintenance of community works should be given effect to immediately.

(5) The State Government should chalk out a programme for renovation of ahars and pynes in a phased manner during the Fourth Plan and water-rates should be realised from the beneficiaries of these renovated works.

(6) The scheme for utilization of water from the eastern Kosi Canal system, as formulated by the State Government, should be implemented soon in consultation with the Ministry of Food and Agriculture.

(7) The detailed scheme for utilization of the water of the

Sone river, which flows down the Rehand Dam during the rabi season, should be sent to the Central Government and the scheme implemented as early as possible.

In respect of soil conservation the Team recommended the following:

(1) There is need for expediting establishment of integrated organisation for soil conservation,
(2) It should be the responsibility of the integrated organisation on soil conservation, when set-up, to carry out land capabilities surveys, formulate schemes on water-shed basis, carry out research and arrange for training of personnel.
(3) Steps should be taken to get soil conservation legislation enacted at an early date.

The Team made the following recommendations for the improvement of animal husbandry in Bihar:

(1) Insofar as the implementation of most of the schemes has been held up due to non-appointment of essential staff and the appointment of the staff through normal procedure will take time, *ad hoc* arrangements should be made.
(2) Since the progress of work under construction of buildings is very slow an engineering cell should be created in the Animal Husbandry Department.
(3) There is urgent need for reorganising the existing milk co-operatives on proper lines. For this purpose it is desirable to make the Director of Animal Husbandry *ex-officio* Registrar of Co-operation.

For agricultural marketing the recommendations made by the Team were the following:

(1) Raising the status of the Head of the Agricultural Marketing Organisation in the State should be considered.

(2) The fruit preservation industry in the State is undeveloped, though plenty of fruits are available. The possibilities of developing this industry should be explored on a priority basis.
(3) As much as half of the storage capacity of the warehouses run by the State Warehousing Corporation remains unutilized. A working group should be set-up to look into this problem and make suitable recommendations to improve the position.

For developing fishery the Team made the following recommendations:

(1) The tanks owned by the Revenue and other Departments, which could be exclusively used for cultivating fish, should be transferred to the Department of Fisheries.
(2) The Fisheries Department should also be given the right to collect fish spawn from the rivers for better utilization of the fish seed resources.
(3) The principle of introducing mechanised reservoirs should be accepted by the Government for rapid development of fisheries resources and exploitation of fisheries.
(4) The Fisheries Laboratory at Patna should be given at least 15 acres out of 100 acres owned by the Agricultural Research Institute.
(5) The Director of Fisheries should be empowered to incur an expenditure of at least Rs. 20,000 on the reclamation of tanks.
(6) The control of the fisheries co-operatives should be transferred to the Directorate of Fisheries. The Director of Fisheries, who would be *ex-officio* Registrar of the fisheries co-operatives, should be assisted by a co-operative cell with a Deputy Registrar and one or two Assistant Registrars.

For co-operation the recommendations of the Team were the following:

(1) Amalgamation of the cane societies with the village agricultural credit societies should be expedited so that there is a single financing agency at the village level. This will facilitate flow of funds from the Reserve Bank.
(2) The central co-operative banks should be enabled to attract deposits from the local bodies and trusts, etc.
(3) The programme of revitalisation and reorganisation of the village societies on the lines of Hyderabad Conference should be completed early.
(4) Crop loan system should be introduced early in the districts selected for this purpose.
(5) Arrangements should be made for providing long-term loans for development through the land mortgage banks in areas like Santhal Parganas and Chotanagpur where land is inalienable.
(6) The scheme of "decentralisation" for distribution of fertilizers through co-operatives under which more margin will be available to the primary units should be implemented early.
(7) The primary marketing societies should enrol more agriculturist members. The societies should be appointed as agents for foodgrains procurement.
(8) The policy of deofficialisation has not been fully implemented. This may be done early and the Government officers need not be *ex-officio* directors on the management of the co-operative institutions.

For the Fourth Plan the recommendations were:

(1) The setting up of an agriculture planning cell at Patna to help in formulating agricultural production plans should be expedited.
(2) The formulation of district and block plans for agriculture and allied programmes should also be expedited.

Shifting Cultivation

I
SHIFTING CULTIVATION AMONG THE ABORS

B.C. GOHAIN*

. Investigations into the economic conditions were carried out as a part of research programme of the Department of Anthropology, Government of India among certain groups of Abor, a primitive hill tribe on the north-east corner of Assam.

As the main economic basis of the Abors is the shifting cultivation, the purpose of this paper is to describe in short the methods by which various crops are raised by these people as a means of their subsistence.

The Assamese terms Abor which originally meant wild and unfriendly met, has applied to a group of Tibeto-Burman speaking hill-men inhabiting the hills between the Galongs on the west and the Mishmis on the east, on the north-east Frontiers of Assam. The Abors comprising several endogamous groups like the Padams, the Simongs, the Pangis, the Minyongs, the Pasis, the Milangs, the

*Department of Anthropology, Government of India, Calcutta.

Boris and others live in separate territorial zones and their whole territory extends roughly from the Syom, a tributory of the Dehang and the Chedo on the west to the Sesseri and the Dehang on the east, these last two being the tributories of the Brahmaputra. Their northern boundary extends as far as the Indo-Tibetan borders and on the south it encroaches the northern shore of the Brahmaputra.

For the British rulers in India during a period of over half a century, the relations with the Abors were not a happy one. Between 1848 as many as six expeditions were launched against the Abors by the British, but without any result. The crisis came in 1911 when the Political Officer of Sadiya, Leon Williamson and one Dr. Gregorson were murdered, that a military expedition was sent against the Abors and it was after that successful campaign that the Abor territory has been brought under the political control established over the hills.

According to their tradition, all the Abors have sprung from a common ancestor somewhere in the north and the cultural and linguistic similarity seem to support this theory of a common origin. Racially also they appear to be more or less homogenous.

The Abors whose approximate number is about 2,00,000 live in large communities and some of their permanent villages like Damroh, Karko, Riga, and Simong contain more than 350 houses in each. They are a democratic people and their socio-political unit is the village rather than the tribe or tribal groups. Each Abor village is run by a few elected 'Gams' or headmen assisted by the Kabang or the village council. The Kabangs are presided over by the Gams whose positions depend solely on their wealth, personality or force of character.

Almost all the Abors live in villages, the sites of which are always chosen on mountain sides or spurs with a view to satisfy the demands of water supply and defence.

They live in platform houses with low roofs, each family owning one for itself. The existence of dormitories for unmarried boys and girls called 'Moshups' and 'Rashengs' respectively are well-established institutions—and the latter particularly in the higher regions of the Abor Hills.

The main economic basis of the Abors is their shifting cultivation popularly known in Assam as Jhum and animal husbandry. Some of the Abors living on the foot hills are however taking to wet-cultivation and with good results. Of the live stock, the Abors keep methuns (bos Frontalis) and breed pigs, dogs and chickens and those living near the plains and have taken to wet-cultivation and have started keeping oxen for their plough cultivation.

Beset with the hilly nature of the country and handicapped as they are like so many primitive tribes by the absence of any suitable agricultural implement, the Abors who are essentially an agricultural people, have to depend for their livelihood on their ADI-ABIK or the JHUM Cultivation whereby forests are cleared and fired and cultivated for 2 or 3 successive years before it is allowed to lie fallow for a cycle of years which may vary from 10 to 20 years i.e., according to the amount of arable land available to each village as well as depending on the fertility of the soil.

The main staple food cereals of the Abors consist of rice and ANYAT (Coix Lachryma). But their cultivation varies in different regions according to the altitute and temperature. In the lower regions where the land is more or less flat and the climate warm, rice forms the staple food of the people. In the higher regions on the other hand the staple food consists of both rice and Anyat, the former crop being used more or less as a salable or exchangable commodity with the neighbouring groups of people for methuns, pigs, beads (Taddaks) and Dankis* which are regarded as property.

The staple drink of the Abors is the 'Apong' which is mostly brewed from 'MIRUNG' (Eleusine Coracana) millets and to a small quantity from a red variety of rice called 'AMKEL' and also from Ayak (Setaria Italica), ANYAT (Coix Lachryma) and SAPA (Zea Mays). The use of home-distilled liquor 'Fatik APONG' which is in vogue among the Padams of the higher regions are distilled in their homes.

Besides the main food and drink cereals, subsidiary crops like cotton (Sipyak), ginger, colocasia (Colocasia antiquorum), pumpkins, gourds, sweet potatoes, chillies, tobacco and other leafy vegetables though mostly grown inside the main rice fields are also grown in specially prepared plots called 'PAGLEK-ARIK'. Of these crops, ginger and the cotton rugs made from their home grown cotton are the main commercial commodity of the Abors which they bring to Pasighat market for sale.

*Dankis—Bronze bowls of Tibetan origin used as exchange for money.

Of the seasonal fruit gardens a large quantity of oranges are grown in the lower regions, but this crop is mainly raised as a salable commodity at Pasighat where it finds an easy market among the plains people. Jack-fruits are also grown throughout the region.

The Abor rugs called 'Gadu' made from the home-grown cotton are also brought by the Abors down to Pasighat market where it is sold through the Political Office at a price varying from Rs. 10 to Rs. 25 each according to size and quality.

The only narcotic ordinarily taken by the Abors is the tobacco-leaf which they either chew with lime and 'LIRANG' (bark of a tree) or smoke as tobacco.

The use of opium as narcotic is restricted to a few Abors of the lower regions where its cultivation is now prohibited by the Government. The cultivation of opium plants is mostly done in the higher regions, and especially at Adipasi and Damroh, on the narrow valley of the Yemne river. But the opium extracted from the fruits are used by the people for medicinal purpose only such as healing wounds and as an antidote for diarrhoea and dysentry.

Among the Abors the village forms the largest agricultural unit, each having its own 'jhuming' fields within its territorial boundaries, marked by such natural features as hills or streams. Generally, the 'Jhum' fields lie around the village and may not be at a great distance from it as cultivation of such land is carried out from the village.

Within the territorial division of the village, all arable lands are divided into two categories: The first which is called 'PATAT' or field is to make regional rotation of jhuming possible and the second which is called 'ARIK' is to facilitate allotment of a suitable area of 'PATAT' to each household in the village; and each village possesses a member of 'PATATS' which are brought under cultivation every year. The size and number of 'PATATS' cultivated each year depends on the arable land available for the village concerned and the period for which a 'PATAT' is opened up for 'ARIK' depends on fertility of the soil—which is generally cultivated for two to three successive years before allowing it to lie fallow, and also on the number of 'PATATS' available.

The small divisions into 'ARIK' to which a 'PATAT' is subjected may be called field plots. Originally one 'ARIK' is sufficient for one household to cultivate—which in average should give per adult an annual yield of one 'BARI*' of rice and one 'RERI' or 'ANYAT'—their main staple cereals besides 'MIRUNG' and other subsidiary food cereals.

The equitable division of land in most cases represent areas first cleared of virgin jungles by the household of the original squatters; and cultivation titles are passed over to the male descendants. The boundaries of these plots are always marked with heaps of stones placed at regular intervals to make the right of a permanent nature. But in case where the sub-division has occurred due to the partition or to the increased number of the family members of the original squatters and the original land is insufficient to meet the present needs of the family the 'GAMS' of the village summon the village to a council called 'ARIK-KEBANG' and there portion out some of the excess land from some of the clan or village members which have been lying fallow. This arrangement is however on a temporary basis depending on the number of years (two years in most cases) for which a field is cultivated. In such cases no compensation is paid to the owner of the land; and though temporary boundaries are laid across with felled trees, the hereditary right remains with the original owner and a newcomer enjoys only the usufactory rights.

But some villages possess certain common lands called 'MOLI-PATAT'. Here the ownership rests with the whole village; and in times when there is shortage of arable land, cultivation is carried on this land by the needy people of the village with the consent of the village council. No compensation or price is claimed by the council from the user and after the cultivation is over land reverts to the village. Besides the territorial rotation of fields the Abors also practise annual rotation of their crops both in the higher and lower regions. In the higher regions, where cultivation is carried on in high steep hills, the main cereal crop 'ANYAT' is sown together with maize and 'AYAK' millets in their new 'PATAT' which is opened after their regional rotational period. This is followed in the second year by sowing of rice and 'MIRUNG' before it is left as fallow.

At the foot hills the lands are more or less situated on gentle slopes or sometimes on flat lands. Here, rice which forms the main

*Bati—Large bamboo basket with capacity of about 20 maunds used for storing grains in the Granary.

staple cereal is grown by the people for two successive years intermixed with maize, 'MIRUNG' and 'AVAK' millets. The cultivation of 'ANYAT' also, is carried on to some extent and in such cases a field is generally used for three consecutive years, the first year being devoted to the raising of 'ANYAT' crop to be followed by rice and Mirung for the successive years.

The agricultural year begins sometime about January-February. Due to the rotational system of both land and crops the Abors have to prepare both the new and the old 'PATATS' simultaneously; and as the nature of work varies in both the fields there is a rough division of labour between the sexes. In the old field as the clearing entails little more than weeding the grass and uprooting the stems of the previous years' crops, before it is burnt for the sowing of seeds, the work is done mostly by women. But the opening of a new 'PATAT' requires lot of hard work in clearing undergrowth and felling trees both large and small and this strenuous work is carried out by men. In clearing a new forest for cultivation the men cut down all the trees at the root and put the felled trees in a line to mark the boundary line between different plots of land. It also gives them a good supply of firewood. The clearing of a new jhum-site generally takes about a month and when the clearing is done the jungles are left to dry for about a month before it is set to fire. The only implements used for clearing the new fields are the ABOR-DAOS and the heavy axes, both of them being purchased now-a-days from the Pasighat market.

When the clearing of the jungles is over the whole village join together and erect high fences round their common 'PATAT' where they intend to carry on their cultivation to prevent the 'MITHUNS' from getting inside the field.

The time for firing the new field varies in the higher and lower regions. In the higher regions where 'ANYAT' cereals are sown first the firing is done in April-May and 'ANYAT' seeds are sown one or two days afterwards together with maize and 'AYAK' millets. In the lower regions the sowing starts from the month of February, and the first cereals to be sown are maize and 'AYAK'. After a month when these plants grow to a height of about one foot, rice, the main cereal and 'MIRUNG' seeds are sown in their midst.

The ABOR-RICE is of two seasonal varieties. The summer variety called Amo is sown in April, and is harvested in August.

The winter variety of rice AMNE which is also sown in April-May is harvested from November onwards.

While sowing the party lines up at the bottom of the field, each person carrying his or her supply of seeds in small bamboo-baskets which is slung on the body and with a pointed 'DAO' or digging stick on the right hand; the party in bending position proceed forward thrusting the point of their implements at an angle towards the body thereby making small holes in which about 6/7 seeds of paddy are put from the bamboo-basket. The seeds are put in holes of about one foot apart. When the whole party reaches the top they come down to the bottom and repeat the process again till they finish the field. While this process is going on, one of the operations scatter the seed of MIRUNG millets between the paddy seeds and when this is over both paddy and 'MIRUNG' seeds are covered with soil with the help of a broom. In the lower regions, however, as rice and 'MIRUNG' seeds are sown in between the maize and 'AYAK' plants the use of broom, is not possible, and therefore, the paddy seeds are always covered with soil with the point of the DAC after sprinkling the seeds into the little holes made with the implement. The sowing of 'ANYAT' is done with a long pointed wooden pole by which holes are dung in which the seeds are sprinkled and covered with soil again from the point of a pole. Maize is also sown in between the 'ANYAT' crop with the wooden pole but the 'AYAK' millets are sown broadcast in between the above mentioned crops.

Vegetables like colocasia, sweet potatoes, ginger, chillies, beans, pumpkins, gourds etc., are planted along the field-paths. In the lower regions cotton seeds (SIPVAK) are sown with the summer variety of rice. But in the higher regions this crop is raised in a specially selected plot called 'PAGLEK-ARIK'. Another important leafy vegetable plant PATTU-OYING' (Lai-sak in Assamese) is grown almost throughout the year either in the main fields or inside the 'PAGLAKARIK'.

The weeding of rice and 'ANYAT' fields is done in the months of June and July. The operation is done with the help of a horseshoe-shaped bamboo scraper which is held tight at the joint and is moved forward and backward and also sideways to scrap the soil of the weeds.

The method of harvesting cereals and millets in most cases is primitive. The use of sickles is unknown except in the lower regions where a few Abors have now started using them in reaping paddy from their wet-cultivation fields. Generally, paddy and 'ANYAT' grains are stripped from the stock by hand straight into a large conical-basket. The 'MIRUNGS' ears are cut by a small knife called 'YOKSIK' and the 'AYAK' ears are plucked with hand. In the lower regions it has been seen that some people use their 'DAO' in harvesting the 'ANYAT' cereals. After gathering the crop they are thrashed, winnowed and cleaned in the fields before bringing the harvest to the village, to be stored in the granaries (KUMSUNG) which are built like miniature platform houses in groups usually built far enough from the dwelling houses as a protection against fire.

In families of average means most of the work in the field is done by the husband and the wife and their children as well as any relative or slave who may be a member of the household. But there are occasions when a family may require help from other members of the community and this kind of help is generally called RIGLAP. The usual practice is that if a person wants somebody to work in his field he usually approaches one of the Rashengs, i.e., a group of girls belonging to one of the village girls' dormitories or village Panus, i.e., a group of village girls and on the appointed day all of them work in the field of the plot-holder, who however as custom demands feed these workers with cooked rice and APONG, in the field. When the work is over the hirer usually given to this group of girls about 20 seers of paddy in return for their services, which the latter collectively use in SOLUNG festival, one of the main festivals of the Abors.

Then there is the EMGUL system by which a person may request his close friends or relations to help him for a day or two in his fields. No payment is made for such assistance except that the workers are fed with rice and Apong by the owner in his field.

Another method of using labour is by the exchange of service called ENPE-ENLE, where both the hirer and the hired have the right and obligations to work in each other's field.

But in the lower regions and especially in the Balek group of villages near Pasighat where wet-cultivation has been introduced, well-to-do persons with large holdings hire the services of Abors who come down to Pasighat during the winter from the upper regions to earn cash money by which they buy salt, tobacco, tea and other necessities.

In short, the main economic basis of the Abor life is agriculture which they raise by Jhumming and the implements used are only a dao and a digging stick, and the method of sowing and harvesting is done by hand. Of the other simple productive activities, the weaving of cotton blankets from their home grown cotton plays a large part and together with subsidiary crops like oranges, ginger and vegetables and sometimes in small quantities of rice, some of the Abors carry on trade with the plains of Assam; and from the cash which they get from these sellings they buy such articles as salt, dyed yarn, tobacco, aluminium and brass ports, iron and certain other luxuries for their daily use.

But the question is, can this system of shifting cultivation which is the main stay of not only the Abors but to many of the so-called aboriginals of India can be improved or replaced by such as terrace cultivation or permanent wet-cultivation in order to give them a better economic footing as well as to raise their standard of living? Criticisms have been levelled against this type of shifting cultivation from different quarters. Thus Mr. Nicholson, the Conservator of Forests, giving evidence before the Partially Excluded Areas Enquiry Committee of Orissa maintained that "the damage done to the forests by shifting cultivation was serious and that only under certain conditions where the area of land available is large and population small, such cultivation does little harm." Dr. N.L. Bor, Forest Botanist in the Forest Research Institute at Dehradun in his presidential address to the Section of Botany of the Indian Science Congress in 1942 observed that, "Of all practices initiated by man, the most anxious is that of Shifting Cultivation." He attributes the cause of soil erosion in the Assam Hills to the practice of Shifting Cultivation. Another writer in reviewing the 'Report of Forest Administration' in Assam for 1940-41, in Nature 1942 calls Shifting Cultivation "that most wasteful of agricultural methods." He attributes the backward condition of Assam tribes to the British policy of non-interference with tribal customs and observes that the consequence is that inspite of the lapse of well over half a century since forest conservation began to be introduced into parts of Assam, forest reservation has made little progress in the hill districts. He further says that the hill districts of Assam possess an adequate proportion of Reserved or Protected forests which provide one reason for erosion and flood damage.

Dr. Hutton also points out that the practice of bewar (shifting cultivation) is uneconomic and detrimental to the interests of the Indian Community as a whole, except perhaps in certain limited areas and under conditions of strict control. Dr. Elwin also thinks that the variety of shifting cultivation as practised by the Bhuiyas and Juangs do more permanent injury to the forests than the one favoured by the Baigas. Such are the criticisms that are levelled against the method of shifting cultivation of the Abor Hills. But considering the geographical surroundings in which the hardy Abor tribes live. Shifting Cultivation is the only method possible. To practise terrace or wet-cultivation, permanent water supply and necessary agricultural tools are of first consideration, and when all these conditions are wanting it is no use having only academic discussions on the evil effects of shifting cultivation; for the Abors must grow rice and other cereals to eat, he has no time to ponder over the merits or demerits of their methods of tillage when their stomachs starve.

But Sir S.H. Howard, the Inspector General of Forests while dealing with the question of 'Shifting Cultivation' holds different views. He suggests that instead of preventing this method of cultivation a tribal should be given by regulating it which means that if a longer period of rest is given between the fellings, there is little danger of soil erosion.

Mr. J.P. Mills with his lone experience in the Tribal areas of Assam is also of opinion that in the areas of that province where Jhum Cultivation has been carried out for hundreds of years there is no sign of the fields losing any of their fertility. He believes that wisely regulated, this Jhumming method can probably be carried on indefinitely without causing deterioration.

It has been seen that the Abors are by nature settled agriculturists. They have been living in their permanent villages varying from 50 to 400 houses for more than 100 years and have been carrying on their age-old shifting cultivation within their village boundaries without any detriment to their tribal economy. Their method of tillage on rotational basis which varies from 9 to 15 years or more, allows time for the regeneration of forest growth in the fallow lands and when their turn comes up again for re-cultivation, they are suitable enough for raising crops by burning the felled trees which serve as an important manure.

Another point which must be considered of this method of shifting cultivation, is that to the Abor, Rice Anyat (Jobs tears, coix lachryma) and Mirung (Ragi, Eleusine coracana) and cotton plays important part in their village economy. Subsidiary crops like leafy vegetables, ginger and taro are grown along with the above mentioned cereals. Milet-beer among the Abors, apart from its nutritive food value is the main-spring of their agricultural efforts. It is being used in all their social and religious functions. It is unthinkable to see the Abors without this all very important item of their diet.

The fact that the Abor spend most of his energies on his Jhum fields for his rice and millet crops which he uses in all phases of his life, is one of the reasons why new methods of their tillage or new crops suggested by officials do not always catch up with the speed that we would like. Such crops are of secondary interest to the Abor, as he cannot utilise them for his socio-religious activities so he does not give the willing attention necessary for their successful cultivation.

In short, if we are to see the agricultural development of the Abor tribe we must first have a thorough knowledge of the aspects of their culture far removed from the sphere of pure agriculture. New methods of their tillage and new crops can be introduced successfully only when physical conditions of land and local use of new crops have been found for them.

As regards the cause of soil erosion due to shifting cultivations—it is really doubtful how far this is true in the Abor Hills. During the survey in the Abor we visited quite a large number of Abor Villages and their Jhum fields and no where could we find any trace of soil erosion and the villagers also could not tell of any erosion effecting their fields within their living memories. Villages like Damroh, Karko, Riga, Simong, Adipasi and so many other villages have been established as long as 100 years or more, and the people of those villages have been carrying on their shifting cultivation from times immemorial without any detrimental effects of erosion on their fields. Even if we take it for granted that this system of cultivation does harm, it is in the fitness of things that the Agricultural Department should take active part in exploring new possibilities in improving their methods of existing system of cultivation. It is only then that they should guide them with proper tools to adapt to the new methods.

Last but not least it may be pointed out that a commission set-up by the Government to study the effects of soil erosion due to Jhum Cultivation in Assam has commented that the Shifting Cultivation as practised in Assam has no effects on soil erosion.

Another point that has to be considered while dealing in the productive field of the Abors is that though it is true that terrace or wet-rice cultivation ensures more produce than that of the Shifting Cultivation, it has been seen that most of the Abors though hardworking and devote almost all their time in their fields cannot get sufficient crops from their fields. Though this small yield is due partly to their existing system of tillage, it cannot be denied that sickness like malaria, dysentry, small-pox, etc. are rampant throughout the region, and it is not uncommon to find that sometimes half the population of a village is down with either of the above diseases. Being confined to bed without any medical treatment, it is no wonder that their activities in the field are restricted and that they cannot sometimes get even half the year's produce from the field. Abors are a verile race, and if free from any disease, most of the Abor families are quite capable of raising crops from their Jhum fields.

So considering all these above problems which are so mixed up not only with their physical environment but also closely intermixed with their social and religious structure, our aim in modernising them should not be at changing their old existing social and economic order but to improve upon it. With new scientific methods of Jhum cultivation, introduction of fertilizers, and with better varieties of cereals, the present existing yield of crops may be doubled and by introducing new and more numerous varieties of fruit trees and vegetables properly acclimatised to the locality a great difference could be made in the local diet. By improving the cotton crop and by using improved type of looms benefits could be achieved in the field of clothing also. There are a hundred and one ways by which the economic improvement of the Abors may be achieved but before doing that our duty is first to have a detailed knowledge of their spheres of life without which whatever good intentions we may have in introducing certain good things among them our efforts will not find any response from these people.

II
SHIFTING CULTIVATION OF THE BAIGA

PROF. D.S. NAG*

Meaning of Shifting Cultivation

The variety of soils, of climate and of vegetation is responsible for many types of agriculture existing in the world. The patch agriculture of the tropic forest without draught, animals and hoe cultivation prevailing in many parts of the globe are characteristically the most primitive among all the types. In the tropical regions the tribesman cuts the under-growth in order to make a small clearing in the forest. Either he leaves out the bigger trees or fells them or burns them. At the end of the dry season or just before the beginning of the rains he fires the cuttings and with the aid of hoe, digging stick or dibbler, he plants shoots tubers and roots or broadcasts seeds of cereals and millets. After raising two or three crops the village is shifting to another site where the fertility of the soil has not been exhausted. This type of cultivation is found extensively in the tropical forests of Africa, Southern Asia and in some Islands of the Pacific Ocean. The agricultural implements employed by the primitive cultivator are extremely simple and are made mostly out of locally available material. There are no more elaborate than a digging stick, hoe and axe- just to dig holes for seeds and cuttings or to cut the undergrowth and trees.

Sociological Implications

The foremost aim of primitive cultivation is a more reliable food policy. In the tropical forests apart from newly introduced crops, the cultivation of roots and the tending of fruit trees is dominant. In tropical regions their cultivation does not require any special period for they can be planted practically all over the year. The storage of agricultural produce for long periods is, therefore, unnecessary, save where large accumulations are required for social purposes, while the grain-cultivators have to store up stock in large quantities for their cultivation is of seasonal character. The primitive cultivators are universally found to supplement their

*Vice-Principal, College of Commerce and Economics, Jabalpur.

stock of cereals and fruits with hunting and fishing. Where agriculture is mainly carried on by women, men are free from these pursuits. Where however the intensity of agriculture is high and absorbs greater proportion of the community the importance of hunting and fishing declines.

On the one hand spread of agriculture reduces game, on the other it leaves very little time and energy in the male for hunting. Nevertheless, hunting and fishing are the usual source of supplementary food in the primitive communities. Where this instinct is suppressed, it finds expression in the shape of domestic animals for food supply or tending of pets just to satisfy the urge. The sociological implications of primitive agriculture are equally significant. Among root and fruit cultivators we do not find a fairly uniform level of civilisation distinct from grain growing people. There is less permanence and security in the life of the former and therefore less chances of steady social progress. Climate, topography and vagaries of nature introduce heterogeneity in their culture. Their technique of production is crude. They live a hand to mouth economy. The different operations in primitive agriculture are usually not initiated by the individual. In selecting seed, choosing of the time of sowing and harvesting, not the individual but the decision of the community as a whole directs the operations. The leader or priest of the village organises planting and harvesting ceremonies and propitiates Gods for the protection of crops and prosperity of the village. 'Primitive agriculture is a co-operative effort in which the community as a whole participates'. It has promoted culture not merely by providing food to the primitive, but is also responsible for closely knitting and disciplining humanity itself by bringing individuals together for observing rituals and ceremonies connected with agricultural operations.

Shifting Cultivation in Madhya Pradesh

India's tribal tracts are a part of the shifting cultivation belt which girdles tropical or sub-tropical countries. There is enough evidence which proves that patch agriculture was practised over wide areas by the tribals of Assam, Bengal, Bihar, Orissa, Central Provinces, Hyderabad and Madras till 30 to 40 years back. It has survived still in Assam, Orissa, Madhya Pradesh and Hyderabad in relic form.

Shifting cultivation was carried on over wide areas in the Central Provinces until it was stopped by a Government order in 1867. Among the important tribes associated with this system of cultivation were: Korkus in Betul, Melghat and Jagirs of Chhindwara and Hoshangabad, Baigas in Mandla, Balaghat, Northern Drug and Bilaspur; Kamars in Southern Raipur, Korwas in Bilaspur and the Marias in the Chanda and Drug Zamindaris. Among the merged States Kawardha and Bastar also permitted Bewar to the Baiga and Maria Gonds respectively in their jurisdiction. The bordering State of Rewa also allowed its Baigas to clear forest patches without any restriction as long as they paid the prescribed taxes to the State. The system of shifting cultivation was practically the same in all these areas of Central Provinces, with certain variations in accordance with the kind of local soil or forest growth. Bewar, of the Baiga, represented the main characteristics of shifting cultivation in this State.

Mythological Background of Bewar

A widely believed legend has given tremendous force to the Baiga cult of Bewar. To a Baiga shifting cultivation is not merely a means of livelihood but a tribal duty and responsibility with which he has been charged by the Supreme Power. For him it is an article of faith providing energy to his whole existence 'the symbol of their tribe, differentiating them from all others'. "All the kingdoms of the world," so said Bhagavan, "may fall to pieces, but he who is made of earth and is Bhumiaraja, lord of the earth, small never forsake it. You will make your living from the earth. You will cut wood and carry it on your shoulders. You will dig roots and eat them. You must not tear the breast of your Mother earth with the plough like the Gond and Hindus—you are to cut down trees and burn them and sow your seed in the ashes." However, opinion is divided on the extent of the hold which the legend has now over the tribe. Personal tour of the Baiga land and friendly discussions both with the older and newer generation of the Baiga revealed that the Baigas are fast forgetting the myth of the Bewar. The wiser among them explain 'without Bewar we are starving. It was the only means of livelihood for us for the soil below in the valley is barra. It does not give us good yield. Poor as we are, we have neither good plough or cattle to improve its fertility nor enough seeds to sow.' The urge for Bewar is not dead altogether among the traditional bewar-cutters. They yearn for it even now but a feeling of helplessness and indifference has overcome them; most probably due to repeated unsuccessful attempts to regain their 'freedom of the Forests'. Slowly he is shifting his emphasis from theological sanction to economic necessity.

Controversy Regarding Bewar

Shifting cultivation—known as bewar or dhya—was prohibited by law in this State as back as 1867. Since then official efforts and public opinion have tried to wean the aborigine from axe. Officially the issue has been settled, but as the facts will show this is an exparte settlement of the issue. The aboriginals have certainly yielded to the latter; but all through they have been demanding their right of freedom of the forest, even now the urge for bewar is there. The most common argument advanced against Bewar is that the system is responsible for the destruction of forest wealth of the country on very wide scale. Others apprehend that uncontrolled felling of trees will not only exhaust the forest wealth of the region, but also produce adverse effects on rainfall, flow of rivers and fertility of the soil. The system has been criticised even from the point of view of the axe-cultivator. It is often pointed out that with such crude methods the yield is low and precarious. Shifting cultivation, it is alleged, makes man lazy, nomadic and adverse to cultural progress.

The vehement criticism of bewar has not remained unanswered. Administrators, forest and agriculture experts and anthropologists have offered stubborn defence of the system. 'Shifting cultivation, was the only system under which races backward by modern standards could safely cultivate the tropical forest, and nomadism was the only system under which the grassland could be safely pasture.' The real question is; what type of forest trees have been too remote and inaccessible ever to be exploited and that, even though some fine timber has been sacrificed, much that has gone was hopelessly mature. In the absence of means of communication and general development of the tracts, much of the vegetation goes waste or there is any nearby market for minor products of the forests. The Baigas do not range through forests' clearing patches for cultivation at random; given adequate freedom to choose their plots they have more or less definite programme of rotations, and the clearings after two or three years' cultivation may get ten to twelve years' rest, at the end of which they have a dense forest growth. The population has been so sparse that natural generation has kept pace with the aboriginals' periodical feelings and little harm has resulted to either forest or soil. Messrs. Jacks and Whyte who completed a world survey of soil erosion analyse the problem in relation to population. It must be admitted that no agriculture system except shifting cultivation has yet been devised that will ensure lasting stability and fertility to tropical forest soils under human management." The yield on bewar patches is definitely lower than on ploughed and manured fields. But it may be remembered that crop production is not an absolute factor. It depends upon the fertility of the soil, investment of number of units of different factors of production, the traditional technique of cultivation and climatic factors. Baigas asserted that these grains sprout better on ash covered slopes and hill tops than in the level fields. Shifting cultivation is not so easy or lethargic as is presumed by certain persons. The aborigines has to walk on an average 7 to 8 miles per day to work on his bewar plot. He has to climb hillocks, pass through valleys and at times wade through the streams. It is most arduous task to clear a forest patch covered with heavy timber and impenetrable undergrowth. The firing of heavy trunks is not an easy job particularly under the scortching heat of the sun. He must fence his plot with logs, split bamboos and shrubs. Is Shifting cultivation an obstacle to the social progress of the Tribesmen?, 'we must remember', "that shifting cultivation is regarded in other parts of the world as the mark of a comparatively advanced stage of civilisation." The Bewar system is peculiarly suited to the aspirations of Baigas. If enough forest land is permitted to be cut, the Baigas say that they can manage for their food quite well and supplement it with fruits and roots from the forest.

Baiga's Viewpoint

Being illiterate and ignorant a Baiga cannot explain his attitude towards bewar in a cogent and scientific manner. Traditionally he is not in the habit of arguing or protesting against the law of the land. It is, therefore, no surprise that Baigas never gave an organised expression to their opposition to Government's anti-bewar laws. However personal tour of the Baiga land spread over a year and intimate talks with them revealed that the Baigas claim certain definite advantages of bewar cutting. 'We are forest-dwellers, for us bewar is what plough cultivation is for the kisan.' The system fits in their forest life remarkably. Since times immemorial he has been a food gatherer and partly a shifting cultivator. He had so harmonised his cultivation with forest activities that each supplements the other. Without bewar plots he cannot raise his staple food crop Kutki and without hunting, food gathering and fishing he cannot make his diet wholesome. The arrangement has one more significant implication. Through it the Baigas secure diversification of his employment, 'We Baigas do not sit idle, we work throughout the year either on the bewar or in the forest'. Thus the simple Baiga has solved one of the most complex problems of rural India namely underemployment. Thus bewar and forest work are the two sections of the Baiga economy securing diversification and the conditions of full employment. Plough cultivation is not within the means of an average Baiga. It requires investment of more units of factors of production which the poor Baiga at present do not possess. Unless their resources are augmented, the Baigas argue, profitable plough cultivation will remain a distant dream; while bewar cultivation, they suggest, is in full consonance with their economic capacity. Moreover, bewar is in tune with the technological condition of the Baiga tribe. Agriculture technique without mechanical aid is more of a traditional skill than the result of scientific training. It can be gained very slowly particularly when the heritage is in divergence with the plough cultivation. This is why the Baigas find themselves at a loss when they raise crops with plough. Soil conditions are another reason for this preference. The Baigas pointed out in many villages that the Barra lands were the poorest in their tract. In these circumstances, Baigas point out, Bewar and Kanda Koosa are the only means of livelihood in their country. Many Baigas, particularly the older ones strongly asserted it was wrong to presume that they are the worst enemy of forest. Given enough forestland, the Baigas argued, they would not use a plot for more than two years and would return to it not before 10 to 12 years when these plots have regained their vegetation. Some of them went to the extent that the regrowth is thicker and faster on the ash covered lands. Baigas tell they can raise crops for their requirements. If the patch is virgin the production is definitely more than sufficient for the average Baiga family. Baigani Kutki can be best grown on bewar plots and gives very good yield.

CONCLUSIONS

We are now in a position to draw certain conclusions and make some basic proposals to bring about an increase in the agricultural production of the Baiga land to general.

(i) There are certain forest areas in the Baiga land for example Northern parts of the Munngeli and Kawardha tehsils and pandaria Zamindaries, and upper region of the Baihar tehsils and joining with southern upland of Mandla—where poorest Barra soil predominates in valley lands. Besides, these forests are of not much commercial value due to inaccessibility of these areas and the high transport charges. In such areas bewar cutting or dhya cultivation and collection of forest produce can alone support the hill tribesmen like the Baigas. A bewar belt may, therefore, be demarcated here in which the Baigas may have the freedom to cut bewar on certain conditions discussed hereinafter.

(ii) The belt should cover sufficient area so as to permit necessary cycle of rotation of bewars. A restricted area like the Baiga Chak has proved that under such an arrangement there is little opportunity for leaving the bewar plot fallow for long. The real danger from shifting cultivation, as experience of other countries shows, arises when the scortched plots are used for more than two years and plots are not left fallow for recuperation. A sufficient area for bewar cultivation should be allotted to each village which may permit the customary cycle of rotation, i.e., 10 to 12 years between each period of cultivation.

(iii) As stated above, prolonged shifting cultivation on the same plot exhausts its fertility and breaks the soil structure. On no account should Baiga be required to use the same bewar either more or less than two years at a time. This will enable the forests to recuperate much quickly and also give good yield in the first two years.

(iv) The Baigas have developed an attitude of wrecklessness in felling trees for their bewars, probably due to their resentment against Government's anti-bewar policy. Efforts should be made by persuasion and propaganda, to remove this 'attitude of wrecklessness'. As far as possible bewar cutting should not be permitted in predominantly Sal patches. Mixed or bamboo forests should only be cut for bewar. They should not be cut on ridges enclosing the head waters of important streams. The Baigas should be encouraged to leave out the stamp unburnt so that off-shots may come out at the end of second year.

(v) Baigas, must also be made to realise their duties in regard to forest protection and development. It should be incumbent upon the Baigas to maintain fire lines between their bewars and forest zones. The protection of forests against fire in the bewar belt should be the responsibility of the Baigas residing in that particular area. Being the more important work, it should be made obligatory upon the Baigas. The experiment has been quite successful in Nigeria, in the Gold Coast and Sierra Leone. The axe-cultivator should be asked to definitely indicate the areas to be farmed during the next ten years, with the order in which they would be farmed. That on each plot so indicated a number of young forest trees of rapid growing indigenous or other species should be supplied by the Forests Department, and be planted by the owner of the plot after the manner prescribed by the Department. The cultivator should look after these plants during the period he occupied the area. When the latter moved on, the new young trees thus brought in would have definitely increased the density of the forest patch by the time it was again cut for bewar. In this fashion a regrowth of bewar patches could be brought about, at small cost, by the shifting cultivator himself with the help of the Forest Department, and with increasing success and resulting crop values, once the simple method is made popular among the Baigas. It would be necessary to establish forest nurseries in different parts of the bewar belt and more forest staff will have to be employed to supervise and guide the Baigas.

(vi) In view of the expanding population of the State, it is neither practicable nor desirable to isolate the Baiga or make him subsist on shifting cultivation for all times to come. It is, there, necessary to rehabilitate the plough-cultivator Baiga so that he may come up to the average standard of living prevailing in the State. This will involve a complete reorganisation of agricultural economy of the tribal areas. At present majority of the Baigas live in areas of barra soils which are awefully poor. The field areas in the forest villages are not large enough to allow of resting fallows. Therefore, larger areas for regular field cultivation should be allotted to enable the Baigas to give their barra lands adequate time for resting fallows. Simultaneously either through the co-operative societies or the Forest Department they should be advanced money (Preferably seeds and ploughs) for purchasing plough, bullock and seeds. A small council of village elders may be constituted to help in the distribution of this help and see that the money or the commodity advanced are put to their proper use.

III
SHIFTING CULTIVATION

DR. B.K. CHATTERJEE*

Serious attention should be given to the various problems arising out of the widely applied legislative measures regarding the shifting cultivation. The British Government in India applied the principle of preservation of the forest by introducing legislative measures most probably without giving serious considerations to different problems involved in such measure, particularly how it would affect the forest dwellers. Their primary consideration was the preservation of the flora and the fauna of the country and the

*M.Sc. (Cal.), D.Sc. (Paris), Department of Anthropology, Government of India.

revenue derived from the forest products. But another important aspect of the measure arising out of the adoption of such act—viz. the proper rehabilitation of the forest people involved in shifting cultivation was entirely left out of any serious consideration.

As a result of this people involved in it suffered in physical and cultural aspect of their lives. To a primitive group of people the method of procuring food is as important as his life. Every aspect of his culture, social and material is virtually connected with such method. Their religion, folk lore, customs, habits, and social organization are all based on the procurement of food. Therefore, a tribe which has been practising shifting cultivation from time immemorial in the forest cannot change its habit over night without detriment to its vital force. A certain area was declared as reserve by the Special power, and then people dwelling there was ordered to quit the land immediately, as a result of which the poor people were compelled to shift to some other forest either owned by the Government or by a private body. They faced new difficulties as certain new restrictions where imposed upon them by the new land lords, which had affected their customs and habits. Gradually we find degradation, and disintegration come in, due to extreme hardship caused by non-pursuing the shifting cultivation. Their misfortune came to a climax, when such forests also declared to be treated as "Khas Mahal" forest, and they were compelled to take shelter on the plains. The agricultural lands on the plains were already occupied by other people, who had been living there for generations and there was no suitable land for the refugees. So the refugees had to settle on lands rejected and unsuitable for agricultural purpose. They were deprived of their primitive methods of agriculture, and having no means for the new equipment, they were ultimately thrown into extreme miserable state of life, full of struggle for the bare necessities of life. Certain people were compelled to adopt plough cultivation to which they were not all accustomed, nor was the land suitable for the purpose, so they could not profit thereby and at last they were compelled to leave the new adventure. For the shifting cultivation, generally they utilised pointed sticks but when they were compelled to leave forest they were not provided with the ploughs, bulls, harrows or other material essential for such cultivation. Due to the failure in the struggle for existence sooner or later, an inferiority complex developed among the members of these uprooted tribes and their degradation commenced in rapid strides. Most of them had fallen an easy prey to the recruits of Tea Garden labours and they were scattered throughout tea grown area from where they were not allowed to return to their original places of birth. Some practical methods have to be found out in order to give relief to those people who had long left shifting cultivation, but failed to settle in other modes of life inspite of their best efforts. They could have been rehabilitated without detriment to their culture, habits and mode of living. Certain forest lands may be distributed to these landless tillers of the soil for the amelioration of their distress.

IV
SHIFTING CULTIVATION IN ORISSA

SHRI L.K. MAHAPATRA*

Definition and Differentiation

That shifting cultivation causes a very serious problem in the geo-economic life of India has been recognised for more than a century. But as late as in 1947 at the Fifth British Empire Forestry Conference there have been some misconceptions about definition.

Shifting cultivation may be defined as impermanent cultivation on hill slopes, often steep, after cutting and burning the vegetation for cropping for two or at best three years; then the people move somewhere else to begin the cycle.

It is called 'Jhum' in Assam, 'Bewar' in Madhya Pradesh, 'Podu' in the Deccan, 'Rama' by the Kondh and 'Dahi', 'Koraan', or 'Bringa' by the Bhuiyan of North Orissa, 'Gudia' or 'Podu' or 'Dongar chas' in South Orissa and 'Penda' in Bastar by the Hill Maria, and probably 'Dahi' of the Kharia in Mayurbhanj.

Taila Chas

In Central and Eastern Orissa it is similar to shifting cultivation but practised on usually level or slightly sloping ground.

*Joint Secretary-Cum-Research Scholar, Tribal Research Institute, Orissa.

Dahi

In West of Sambalpur it is a less pernicious practice of cutting branches from forest trees and spreading them on a level land for reducing them to ash-manure. This is practised also on 'Bewar' fields in the second or third year and is called 'Dahia' in Madhya Pradesh. The Hill Bhuiya also practise such manuring in his low land fields.

Gora

It is upland cultivation widely employed in Chotanagpur and Mayurbhanj, Keonjhar, Gangpur and Bonai. In the already impoverished soil only some miserable corp like highland rice or gundli or gulji is raised once on the ash of grass and shrubs allowed to grow for 3 to 4 years. This ends in what Dr. H.F. Mooney aptly discribes as 'soil mining'.

Taungya

Literally hill cultivation in Burma, it now applies to an admirable scientific method of raising tree plantation with field crops under skilled control and generally on level or moderately sloping grounds.

Shifting cultivation should also be distinguished from the burning of the trees and cultivation thereafter as a phase of reclamation of land before preparing it for cultivation. This method is a cheap way to reclamation and is indulged in by all classes of people in Orissa.

Extent of Shifting Cultivation

This type of cultivation is practised also in Assam, Madhya Pradesh, Madhya Bharat, Vindhya Pradesh, Madras, Hyderabad, Travancore and Nonkan.

Though it is perhaps most extensive in Assam, it may safely be called most intensive in Orissa, judging the pressure of population and lack of availability of cultivable land. Assam is lucky in having the Garo hills with density of population of six (6) per sq. mile or having its maximum density of 66 in the Khasi and Jaintia hills. But even in North Orissa (North of the Mahanadi) areas of shifting cultivation the density of population comes rarely below SO, unlike in the Naga hills (density 49). South Orissa with its greater density of population (Koraput district having 129 per sq. mile or Ganjam Agencies 113 or Khondmals Sub-division 107) has only though infinitely tiny patches of areas with 47 (Malkangiri Taluk and Ambadola P.S.), 52 (Nalaghat P.S.), 29 (Bamanigam P.S.) or 66 (Balliguda Taluk and Lanjigada P.S.) Drs. Verrier Elwin and H.F. Mooney have noted that it has gone to the extreme in most parts of Koraput especially on the 3000′ plateau and Puttasinghi Hills, and in Balliguda Agencies and South Kalahandi. Bare rock is visible where often little shrub fights out its existence in the crevices.

To magnitude of the problem will be apparent from the chart of shifting cultivation appended herewith, where the areas shown are directly affected when not exclusively devoted to shifting cultivation.

Altogether therefore about 1 million people depend on shifting cultivation in about $3^{1}/_{4}$ million hectares or 13,000 sq. miles of territory. Some neighbouring castes have been known to practise this method as a supplement to their wet cultivation.

Nature of Shifting Cultivation

A patch of forest is selected on a hill slope, often with divination and religious sanction. In February or thereabouts, trees are felled and left to dry. It is done either collectively by the men of the village or by each family on distribution of family patches. Towards the end of April or in May the wood is burnt after being helped in one place and then the ashes are spread out. In Bonai 'Koman fields' some trees are spread to act as supports for a climbing bean called 'Dhonk' (Mucuna sp.). But these trees are often girdled, that is, so severely burnt at the base that they stand like ghost trees beckoning desolution to a distance. These trees are generally cut down in the second year and burnt for ashes. Where people possess cattle as in South Orissa, the land is ploughed, provided the slope is not too steep or rocky. Saora of Ganjam uses a pick with an iron blade and others use hoes for cultivating the soul. Women also take part in this operation and sometimes exclusively. Immediately after the initial breaking of the monsoons seeds of mixed crops are sown broadcast, or like the Juang of Keonjhar Pal-lahara or the Kondh of Phulbani in former days seeds are inserted into the holes made with a dibble. In some places weeding is done in the first year. The crops begin to ripe one after another from August-September till January-February or even March-April as in Ganjam Agencies. The field is guarded against birds, wild animals and thieves right from August-September.

In the second year, grass, stray plants, stalks or stumps are again burnt and the ash spread out. Again the cycle goes on. But the crop yield diminishes.

Only where pressure of population is very high and restrictions, natural and administrative, are severe, the field is cultivated in the third year. But this has come to be more frequent now-a-days in Koraput, though in the last quarter of the 19th century Col. Beddome has noted that land was being cultivated generally for two years in the 3000′ plateau. In Malkagiri they have four croppings.

Then the patch of exhausted land is abandoned to recuperate in the natural process. The period of inactivity is 15 years to 20 years in parts of Bastar while in Koraput it has come to be 4 to 6 years. Col. Beddome had noted that in his days fields were abandoned for 8, 10 or at best 15 years.

Among crops there is a wild variety of them in South Orissa. In Malkangiri and 3000′ plateau and some other places in Ganjam and Koraput hill rice is grown but sparingly. In North Orissa, however, the Bhuiyan raise dry rice in their Koman and Delhi fields, more in the latter.

The most important crops are varieties of millet like Marua or Mandia, Gandli and gulji (Panicum miltare), Jahna or Johar (Sorghum Vulgare), Kangu (Pennisetum italicum) and also Suan (Echinochloa-crusgalli) and maize and another millet called Ghantia or Kosra (Pannicum Miliaceum). In August or early Sepember, when the first violence of the monsoon is spent, oilseeds like Jatingi, Olsi (orniger Guzotia abyssinica), and castor are sown. Rasi or Til (sesamum indicum) is generally grown on lower slopes. Various pulses like 'Kandul' (Cajanus indicus) and 'Kolthi' are cash-crops. In North Orissa maize, Kangu Marua and 'Dhonk' beans are grown. Besides these some vegetables like gourds, Janhi, redpepper, Jhata and Bailo beans, cucumber, etc., are mostly grown on the platform on which a watch-hut stands as in Ganjam Agencies. The Kondf manages to raise turmeric in two years on a sandy soil in the hill slopes of Phulbani.

Whatever may have been the conditions in the days of unlimited forests, the tribals have been known to practise shifting cultivation on a rotation basis so that the villagers returned to the same patch after an interval of about 8 to 10 years in North Orissa but after 4 to 5 years in the 3000′ plateau in Koraput.

The Causes of Shifting Cultivation

The following are widely given as the causes:

(1) Ignorance and reluctance to learn better methods;
(2) Indolence;
(3) Lack of suitable lands for settled cultivation;
(4) Alienation of better lands and thus being driven especially in South Orissa to the more remote hills and inhospitable regions by powerful foreigner, by opening of out posts (police) etc., or communications, or through a subtle process of money-lending, rack-renting, and subsequent alienation of land with the help of an alien 'rule of law', land tenure system or inheritance rules—as in Keonjhar, South Kalahandi and the Saora country and in many other areas;
(5) Unsuitability of the terrain as in East Bonai for alternative uses; (the pity is that in areas where Agency Tracts Interests and Land Transfer Act of Madras has been effective since 1917, land has been extensively transferred in clandestine processes to non-Saora money lending class, leading to the recent Gunupur rising of the Saoras);
(6) Lack of capital (cattle, plough, implements, manure and reclamation expenses for settled cultivation down the slopes. The Kondh of Ganjara had asked in 1908 for cattle so that they might be able to reclaim permanent fields);
(7) Lack of alternative employment; and
(8) Socio-Religious and cultural ties with the land, e.g. ideas about hurting the breasts of Mother Earth among the 'Baiga'. There is often mythological sanction of the custom as among the Gond, the Bhuiyan (who are mostly now plains cultivators) and the Lanjia Saora and Juang.

In the beginning there must have been plenty of forest land

on level ground, but curiously enough, the tribals have the tradition of taking to impermanent cultivation even in these primordial days. The Kondh learnt ploughing in their present habitat from the Kurmu. The Gond has learnt ploughing from a Dhoba Raja, according to their tradition. Therefore, shifting cultivation should be viewed as a very ancient and rather efficient cultural adaptation to food production in rocky slopes, often in inhospitable country, with little capital, little technological knowledge or knowledge of nature.

But to dismiss this cultural deficiency as mere ignorance is to make the matter look simple. Let me cite an interesting case. A hill Maria of Bastar practises shifting cultivation and Dahi (Dippa) cultivation on flat land and may have even permanent rice fields. While he hoes up or ploughs the 'dippa' land and permanent rice fields he never uses even a stick for sacrifying the soil after spreading the ash unevenly—not to speak of turning up the soil. He sows seeds broadcast. Only when seeds do not germinate (probably being washed down by rains) he roughly sacrifies the field and resows. His neighbour living lower down the valley—the Bison-Horn Maria—'practises Penda' cultivation with hoe and where workable with plough. The Bison-Horn Maria have taken to ways of the plains for few decades past. Similarly, the Saora are famous for their ingenious terrace cultivation with high revetments—of which practice points to a later but more efficient cultural heritage. But their wilder sections or the Kutia Kondh have little traditions in this regard. Practising this shifting cultivation for thousands of years they have developed a particular attitude towards life so that the tribals are reluctant to pickup the new thing which may be very obvious to others in the thick of the process. Wherever there has been any serious urge in a large scale to change and pickup the new way there has been a change over. Most of the Gond, the Bhuiyan, the Munda and all the Sental and the Bathudi have taken up settled cultivation in course of generations.

Indolence as a factor has been highly exaggerated. The arduousness of the process is convincingly shown by W.V. Grigson and Dr. Haimendrof. The rocky nature of the soil, the inefficient implements, the labour of cutting and firing in rather steep slopes, not to speak of travelling miles for preparing and attending to a new block every three years are rather heavy work in comparison with ploughing in the oft-cultivating lands of the plains. In weeding (but rarely) and broadcasting seeds only hill cultivators steal some advantage over the plains cultivators.

If the shifting cultivation is to be taken as a cultural phase and the fact of tribals sticking to it or even reverting to it as a case of denial of opportunities and not of in-capacities, then it should be made clear that this method of cultivation was the only efficient means of subsistence in their self-sufficient economy. We should not therefore wonder if this mode of existence has received all the stamp of religion, tradition and has been almost inseparable from life itself. If the Juang and the Baiga were debarred from shifting cultivation there was not only economic degradation —as also in the case of the Korku in Madhya Pradesh—but also lack of zest in life and a corrosive dependency and distrust. Personally I think the tribals are perhaps as much scared away by the thought of change to a new economy as by the peculiar associations of such change-over in the historic past—the new diseases, the exploitation by money-lenders and officials and middle men, the high rental and taxes, the disruption of social relations and recreation-ceremonial life, the cessation of forest freedoms though much shrunk now, and the lack of capital and may be the profanation of the sacred Grove in the forest and displeasure of the Godlings or the Manes. All these together present prospects too bleak to be mitigated by the uncertain though rosy one of affluence, security and luxuries of the plains.

It appears, not only lack of cattle and plough, but also the longer time that one will be required to wait before the crops are ready in the first year, the time and energy for reclamation of low lands and the need for manure and also the time and opportunity to learn the necessary skill in ploughing, weeding or transplanting, are very serious deterrent factors.

There is also another negative factor in such addiction to shifting cultivation. There is a lack of alternative employment in the hills except as an occasional day-labourer. That is mostly because each family or at least the village was a self-sufficient unit. Only in relatively recent times some Kondh have taken to pottery-making, some Saora to weaving or some Koya to basket and mat-making. There has been a recent illustration of reversion to shifting cultivation when some Gad aba could not keep their own against local competition in weaving. But there may be reasonable doubt if all these cases are mere specialists entirely depending on their craft for subsistence.

Thus we may sum up that cultural factors were probably responsible for tribals sticking to shifting cultivation for thousands of years. But the process of change has been effectively arrested by exploitation, alienation of land, lack of capital, lack of opportunities (like suitable land), lack of knowledge of improved methods and implements and not the least, lack of alternative employment and possibly also fears of socio-religious disruption in case of change to settled economy.

That a large number of non-tribals also practise some 'Podu' in South Orissa and Taila Chas in Central and Eastern Orissa is a question of smaller importance. Many 'Dom', 'Pan', 'Raut', 'Paik' or other castes in the agency get their patches cultivated by the tribals generally.

Effects

The evil effects of shifting cultivation have been admirably summed up by Mr. Harries, Agency Commissioner of Madras in 1918.

1. it causes the springs below the hills to dry up;
2. causes the soil on the 'podu' land to be washed away;
3. ruins valuable timber for the sake of much less valuable crops of grain;
4. causes very heavy floods in the rivers and then endangers life and property;
5. causes the hot weather supply in these rivers to diminish and this reduces the water available for second crop cultivation;
6. it brings down heavy silt into tanks and makes them useless on to fields and destroys crops;
   It has sometimes also been added that probably;
7. the consequent deforestation causes rainfall to diminish;
8. it also makes the climate a little more extreme; and
9. it deprives the people of benefits of the forest.

So mainly there are 4 kinds of evil effects, deforestation and soil erosion which in turn affect the supply of rivers and rainfall and the climate of the region. The feeders and the catchment basin of the Mahanadi, the Baitarani, the Brahman, the Nagabali, the

Vamsdhara, the Sileru, the Indrabati and the Jonk are affected by shifting cultivation.

But it will be fair to point out that shifting cultivation has kept together the body and soul of about one million tribals when they were driven to the hills at the end of a tragic tale and such cultivation had reconciled them to their luck without giving rise to inflagrations even greater than the recent Gunupur rising of the Saora. And when land was plenty, population sparse, the abandonment of fields for 20 or more years, as in the past it must have been, deforestation and erosion must have been negligible. Indeed in sparser parts of Assam shifting cultivation has changed the landscape but little, and "in the Garo hills, riddled with agelong 'jhum' cultivation one still sees streams carrying clear water after heavy showers" (vide Shifting Cultivation in Assam).

Now, let us examine the effects in some details. Soil erosion is governed by the factors of the nature of soil, the rainfall and its distribution, the physiography of land, the lack of green cover of forest or crop, and mechanical operations like grazing and cultivation. The Inspector General of Forests and the Commissioner of Agriculture in the Government of India have noted in the above mentioned report on Assam that it is the nature of the soils which is primarily determines the rate of erosion. Now the rock of Orissa is of the same category—as in Deccan the Central Massif of Assam (Garo, Khasi, Jaintia and Kachar Hills). This rock being by nature very hard yields to erosion relatively much less than the newer Himalayan upheavals like the Naga hills and Lusai hills, whose rock is liable to slips and slides. But, the nature of the ancient Deccan rock varies in Orissa. In South Orissa the Khondalite, the oldest and highly metamorphised sediment, yields a friable sand while the youngest of the series, prophyritic granite-gniess is extremely amenable to denudation. The latter covers most of the 3000′ plateau of the Koraput, South Kalahandi, while the former covers the upper slopes in South Kalahandi, Balliguda and Koraput. And in these upper slopes the cultivation and the devastation are most wide-spread. In Khariar—the Sonabeda plateau has a mostly thin and infertile soil covering, utterly devoid of vegetation due to shifting cultivation.

The only relieving features from geological stand point is that charnokite and born-blende schist appear as intrusive into the Khondalite and they are resistent to erosion yielding good crops.

In Keonjhar Bonai-Pallahara the Iron-ore series of the Dharwars, and in Bamra-Rairakhole tract epidiorite or fine-grained granetiferous gneiss of South Indian rocks stand up against erosion. The lateritized hill tops in North Orissa have been natural check; to shifting cultivation. Similar seems to be the position in Mayurbhanj hills.

But the picture appears not to be so black as it can be painted. The Koraput District Gazetteer (1945) while refuting Mr. Turner's exaggerations notes, "Though podu cultivation is by no means extinct the 3000 foot plateau is still well watered and Summer crops of rice are grown in nearly every village. Nor, it seems, has the appearance of the plateau greatly changed within the last 60 or 70 years."

Now, a word about the reactions of the politically conscious tribals to deforestation. It is reported, when requested to stop podu, an old Kondh asked, "Why not increase the jungle area in the plains? Why should we be starved to spare land for the jungle?" If he had read, 'The Rape of the Earth' by G.V. Jack and R.D. Whyte he could have also pointed out, "Continuous cultivation meant continuous depletion of the soil and always more deforestation to secure new land for the rapidly growing community and to replace worn-out soils."

None-the-less many tribals are now realising to their helplessness that forests meant a lot to them in food, fuel, raw materials for the market or the home and also medicinal herbs.

In the end we may be warned, though, with much exaggeration that the most flourishing civilisations of the world in Egypt, Persia and Mesopotamia and perhaps also in the Indus Valley as in the modern prairies of America had or have to succumb to the fate of desolation and decay due partly to an unwise depletion of forests.

The Cultural Background of Shifting Cultivators

As some habitual practices or characteristics of the tribals of different cultures and areas are great determining factors in their life and incidentally in shifting cultivation we should try to organise our knowledge of these factors or detect the lack of it before we suggest remedies.

The Kutia Kandh of Balliguda, North-East Kalahandi and Bissamkatak, the Savara of Koraput have their villages on hilltops, originally perhaps for purposes of defence; at any rate this partly saves them from rampant malaria, mostly of blackwater variety of the low valleys. Therefore, it is easy for them to practise shifting cultivation on the upper slopes and tops. Others like the Bhuiyan live in the valleys or down the slopes.

The Savara do not only know the better type of cultivation, i.e., settled cultivation by ingenious terracing and revetments, often 15′ high, but also they are more industrious than the Kandh. Therefore the hills in Puttasinghi area are more barren. The Savara are also known to be more obstinate and intractable than the simple and communicative Kandh.

On the 3000′ plateau the aggressive, greatly individualistic and a most homicidal tribe—the Bonda Poraja or naked Poraja live. Their area is known to be one of the worst-affected with podu. But even then their communal sense is reinforced in rituals, and village "sindibor" or Darbar, etc. Some of them make baskets and mats like the Gadaba, who are again obstinate.

The Bhuiyan and the Kandh of Phulbani were known to have their inter-village socio-juridical organisations called 'Bar' and communes respectively and almost all tribes have their village Panchayats.

Malkangiri with rather infertile, swampy and flooded lands and a malarious climate can hardly allow the Koya reap 4-year crops. Many Kandh have fled there in search of unrestricted 'podu' lands. Here the wild animals run amuck among cattle and crops and have driven away two or more villages. The Koya have herds of cattle and they plough their fields. They have functional sub-divisions like basket-makers, blacksmith or carpenter and brass worker or even beggar. The Koya like honey as also the sweet juice of Palmyra Palm which evidently does them good.

All of the tribes do not depend exclusively on shifting cultivation as the Kutiya and Dongriya Kandh, or Bhuiyan of East Bonai or the Juang does. The Desia Kandh of Rayaghada have taken to settled cultivation completely while their co-brethren in Narayanpatnam are in the intermediate stage. The Kandh in many cases in Kalahandi, Ganjam and Koraput as also many Saora in Ganjam cultivate, tearaced rice fields and upland or 'Padar' land. But a large number of them practise shifting cultivation along with the settled. The Saora, however, are more addicted to podu than the Kandh especially in North-western Ganjam Agencies. There are also functional groups among the Saora who weave, or make baskets and mats and among the Kandh who make pots or iron smithy. And the Kandh of Phulbani is reported to be more migratory than in Koraput. In the South-West of Koraput tribals have been known to be either very reluctant or ignorant in taking to terracing.

The tribes depend for food on the forest for fruits, like mahwa, mango, kend, etc. which sustain them in the Summer scarcity. Carytoa Palm not only yields a drink but also its pith is eaten. There is at least one ceremonial hunt in a year before sowing crops and success in hunting is in many cases an 'index' to successful harvest.

Facts like those described above are extremely valuable in planning rehabilitation of the people—for, rehabilitation of forests and improved land-use are only means to that end.

We are apt to forget the human factor in our eagerness to stop podu. Therefore, let us try to know, appreciate, integrate and enrich their vigorous life, communal sense, free enjoyment of life, women's economic roles and a much higher status than among us, or youth organisations, among with our attempts to satisfy their need of cattle and seeds or wells and kitchen gardens.

Remedies and Rehabilitation

To suggest a remedy in this case is to call for a change over to new life. Hence, it is as much economic as a human problem, involving all psycho-cultural stresses and strains inherent in the situation of change. Hence, there should be an integrated approach.

There is also a strong plea to change our attitude by the Inspector General of Forests and Commissioner of Agriculture to the Government of India, who have remarked, "The correct approach to the problem of shifting cultivation lies in accepting it not as a necessary evil, but recognising it as a way of life; not condemning it as an evil practice, but regarding it as an agricultural practice evolved as a reflex to the physiographical character of the land. Far too long, jhuming has been condemned out of hand as a curse to be ashmed of, a vandalism to be decried. This attitude engenders an inferiority complex, and an unhealthy atmosphere for the launching of any development scheme seeking to improve the current practices."

But on the other hand the problem cannot await generations to proceed on a process of gradual awareness, appreciation and change. The Partially Excluded Areas Enquiry Committee of Orissa under Chairmanship of late Thakkar Bapa had prescribed in 1940 for complete stopping of podu cultivation within 10 years. But practically nothing serious has been done except settling few thousands of families in colonies, with not always satisfactory success.

In the 5 Year Plan for Madhya Pradesh the late Thakkar Bapa had wisely remarked, ". . . this process of denudation of the hills should be prevented and stopped as early as possible without causing much disturbance to the old traditions of the Hill tribes. . ." But he also thoughtfully added, ". . . there is no reason why this tradition should not be disturbed, of course, taking the precaution of not doing it suddenly." Evidently, what he pleads for is to respect traditions in the beginning till the harmful or inefficient ones are weeded out through intelligent and patient approach.

There are two broad solutions. Either to give all of them land for settled cultivation which is obviously impossible except perhaps in some part of Assam and North Orissa, or, give land for settled cultivation to those who are willing to come down and to give others opportunities of alternative employment in fruit gardening (after controlled podu) and other arts, crafts and occupations on their habitations on the hill slopes or in the valley below. The latter method seems to be the only workable plan. But lands have to be found out especially in South Orissa which is rather thickly populated. The forest department has of course tried to find out a few thousands of acres in the Ganjam, Phulbani, and Koraput agencies. Specific areas will need specific planning and treatment. But on the whole to solve the land problem, not only improved production but also social justice should be secured without delay as Shri R.R. Diwakar, the Governor of Bihar, has pointed out.

We may reasonably hope to stop shifting cultivation and rehabilitate its tribal dependents, if we sincerely set out to work out the following suggestions of a 10 Year Plan with imagination, fact, and seriousness.

In the next ten years there may be controlled shifting cultivation and this may be secured by the following methods or measures.

A. Legislative Measures

1. To restore lands to tribals which were unjustly alienated since the famine of 1919.
2. To acquire surplus load from holdings in which each family member has more than two acres, in taluk or thana adopting a zone of shifting cultivation, subject to a minimum holding of acres.
3. To take advantage of Shri Vinoba Bhave's land gift plan.
4. To guarantee the shifting cultivators their right to forest produce for domestic use, or sale through forest labourers' co-operative and also the right to hunt on ceremonial occasions in forests nearby.
5. To cancel all debts above the initial capital of Rs. 10.
6. To grant exemption from rent and taxes for five years in case of all shifting cultivators.
7. To adopt strong measures against land alienation.
8. To reserve all hill tops and steep slopes of more than 45 degree in gradient for 'taungya' plantation; only where hill tops are used for cultivation, law will be effective after 15 years or less.
9. To stop shifting cultivation in other areas within 10 years.

B. Scientific Surveys

1. Soil and Land-use survey of the hills and nearby valleys.
2. Socio-economic survey to show what are the possible socio-economic-religious sources of resistance to change and methods of overcoming them, study of family requirements and earnings, co-operative institutions and the natural leadership as also the factors of spontaneous change to settled cultivation where it has been, and lastly, the possible alternative occupations and crafts to be taken up.
3. Survey of the colonisation schemes already in operation, 69 in number, in Orissa.

C. Rehabilitation Measures

1. Zoning of the areas according to factors of easy demonstration, economic returns, receptivity, available leadership and land and alternative employment.

2. Physical measures—Terracing, contour-bunding, minor irrigation projects and reclamation of nearby valleys.
3. Crop planning—for the middle slopes in the hills. The policy should be adopted in the T.V.A. to secure a protective soil cover "through thick-growing farm vegetation of soil improving and soil protecting crops in proper rotations or combinations, and by decreasing the proportion of tilled crops and bare lands." Cash crops should be encouraged, like pulses, citrus fruits, cashew-nuts, jackfruit (from 2000′ to 4000′), pine apples, oil-seeds, lac and tassar supporting trees. Potato should be introduced only after proper consideration of the grim fate of the denuded areas of the Khasi hills.
4. Sylvicultural practices—Inter-cropping with raising of a kind of wattle trees (Accacia Mollissima) on the hill tops and steep slopesor even in the middle slopes where those who live on the hill tops inveterately opposed taking to either colonisation schemes, crop planning and fruit orchardry or alternative occupations. This wattle has restorative qualities and its bark yields a very valuable tannin, imported from South Africa. It grows well in 8 to 10 years and its wood is not of much value. This has been found to be the ideal suggestion for areas of shifting cultivation in Assam.
5. Otherwise there will be 'taungya' plantations in the reserved hill tops and steep slopes of 45 degree gradient or more.
6. Land redistribution and colonisation schemes:
   (a) the policy should be to subsidise spontaneous colonisation as in many Bhuiyan areas;
   (b) to plan colonies on basis of receptivity local initiative and leadership, and available culturable land. Malaria control and land reclamation on the valleys and lower hill slopes should proceed before colonisation itself; and
   (c) to give terraced land to those who do not come down, if there be surplus.

In all these cases all capital and subsistence doles before the first harvest should be initially advanced by the

Government. The colonies should be provided with all necessary opportunities and facilities available in their home site. It is a very cogent suggestion to invite enterprising Munda, Santal or successful terrace-cultivators belonging to the same community as the colonists and permanently settle them in the localities. Thereby there will be ample opportunities of observation, example and imitation in a very comprehensible manner.

7. Providing alternate or subsidiary occupation:

   (a) Foremost place should be given to immediate formation of *Forest labourers' cooperatives* on the lines of those in Bombay State. This will give them almost all the essential things in organisational training as also material comforts.

   (b) Other suitable arts and crafts, e.g. carpentry for the Kandh, or weaving for the Gadaba or the Saora. Bee-keeping for the Juang or the Koya or Bhuiyan, dairying, piggery, or poultry, tailoring, making toys and fancy objects, lac and cocoon raising, spinning and weaving, sawing, oil pressing, bidi-making, etc. and employment as forest guards, or labourer in fire-line making road-building, house-building, etc. should be taught or provided.

   (c) Preferably under non-official missionary-spirited worker's co-operative undertakings in terraced and low land cultivation, fruit orchards, or organisation of crafts and communal reserves like grain-gola or aid-fund, etc. should be actively encouraged. In Girischandrapur colony in Rairakhol sugar-cane was cultivated by a co-operative organisation.

D. Other Measures

1. Propaganda by official and non-official workers.
2. Excursion by shifting cultivators to nearby colonies.
3. Social education should be vigorously pursued and should be oriented towards stopping of shifting cultivation.
4. Education of children in Ashram and Sevashram schools

where text books should incorporate shifting cultivation and its rehabilitation as a subject matter.

5. Demonstration farms serving the specific demands of the area and actively participating in the agricultural undertakings of the people, preferably in their own patches.
6. Sacred Groves or other haunted places in the slopes or hill tops and old fruit trees, etc. thereon should be protected and free access be given to the tribals.
7. Multipurpose co-operatives for giving marketing and' easy credit facilities should also immediately be started.
8. Transport system should also be improved.
9. Social customs or items of food and drink should not be banned indiscriminately, for, this may unnecessarily hamper proper understanding of our motives.

Mr. Mooney's Chart of Shifting Cultivation in Orissa

District and Sub-division	*Area affected by axe-cultivation*		*Name of tribe*	*Population*
1	2		3	4
North Orissa				
	Sq. miles	Hectares		
Keonjhar	460	117760	Bhuinyas	20000
			Juangs	8000
Sundergarh				
*Bonai	300	76800	Bhuinyas	10000
			Erenga Kols	1000
Dhenkanal				
*Pal-lahara	100	25600	Bhuinyas	2600
Sambalpur	60	15360	Bhuinyas	7000
*Bamra	300	76800	Kondhs	6600
*Redhakhol	50	12800	Kondhs	2200
Total North Orissa	1270	324120		57400
South Orissa				
Kalahandi	1800	460800	Kondhs	111000
			Kutiya	1300
			Kondhs	
Khariar	200	51200	Kamars	1600
			Bunjas	5400
Ganjam Agency:				
(Kondhmals, Balliguda and Parlakimedi)	4500	1152000	Kondhs	206100
			Saoras	95600
			Jatapas	600
Koraput			Kondhs	176500
			Saoras	52500
			Jatapas	15200
			Parjas	145700
Jeypore Estate	5000	1280000	Godabas	34300
			Koyas	28000
			Others	3800
Total South Orissa	11500	2944000		878300
Grand Total	12770	3268120		935700

*Axe-cultivation virtually stopped. Axe-cultivation well on the way to being stopped; it will probably be eradicated by 1953 or 1954.

Problem of Shifting Cultivators

It has been estimated by the Task Force on Shifting Cultivation set-up by the Ministry of Agriculture that approximately 9.95 million hectares in the tribal and hilly areas of the country are under shifting cultivation. About 223 development blocks in 62 districts in 16 States are affected by this practice. Shifting cultivation is a dominant production activity for approximately 12 per cent of the tribal population in the country. The shifting cultivators live a life of less than subsistence level. The period of rotation has dangerously come down from around 7 years a few decades back to about 3-4 years in several forest and hilly areas in the country. Though considered a wasteful activity from the environment and forest wealth point of view, the problem cannot be lightly brushed aside as over 6 lakh tribal families depend on this source for their living.

The problem of the shifting cultivators is enormous. We would recommend: (a) settlement, and (b) resettlement of the shifting cultivators during the Seventh Plan on the following lines:

(1) The States have generally not evinced enough interest in the programmes of settlement or resettlement of shifting cultivators. One of the reasons could be heavy cost of such schemes. We recommend that a Centrally

Sponsored Scheme with at least 60 per cent participation by Centre and the balance 40 per cent by State be instituted for the purpose during the Seventh Five Year Plan.

(2) Where the existing land under shifting cultivation is agriculturally productive and has already been well developed, *in situ* settlement of the tribal cultivators should be taken up. Such areas have not yet been identified and should be identified by the Forest Department of the State Governments by drawing up a cash programme. The Tribal Development Department of the State Government should monitor the progress of such identification. The identified tribal habitations and areas should be declared as revenue villages or part of revenue villages and brought within the fold of Block and Revenue administration. Possibility of providing irrigation facility to these areas should be explored. The attempt should be to convert shifting cultivation into settled cultivation. Special programmes of comprehensive development of the area and the tribal population involved should be drawn up.

(3) *Ex situ* resettlement of the shifting cultivators should be attempted in cases not falling under sub-para 2 above. The areas and the tribal population falling under this category should be first identified by a crash survey undertaken by Forest Department in consultation with the Revenue Development of the State Government as indicated above. Suitable land for such resettlement schemes will have to be found out—

(a) within forest areas in denuded patches, whether adjoining revenue villages or elsewhere; and
(b) within revenue villages.

Identification of this land will have to simultaneously done by Forest and Revenue Department of the State Government with the Tribal Development Department closely monitoring progress. Except where a tribal family is willing to move to an isolated village, resettlement should be by groups/community in the new site earmarked for such settlement.

(4) The programmes of comprehensive development to be undertaken for settlement/resettlement of the shifting cultivators should include agriculture, forestry, animal husbandry and village and small industries including arts and crafts suiting the tribal population and the environment, besides providing the much needed community and social services. Making the tribal families economically viable should be the main theme of the programme. Specific project reports for a group of villages or gram-panchayats should be drawn up with this end in view.

(5) In the Fifth and Sixth Plans, suggestions had been made for constitution of committees with representatives of forest, agriculture, soil conservation, revenue, planning and tribal development department to enable to prepare integrated plans for rehabilitation of shifting cultivators and for implementation in the field. As per the feed-back, hardly any State has constituted such committees. There should be a high level committee under the Championship of the Development Commissioner/ Chief Secretary of the State Government with Secretaries of Forest, Agriculture, Soil Conservation, Community Development, Rural Development, Revenue, Planning and Tribal Development Departments to review the progress of identification of shifting cultivators' families/area, formulation projects of settlement/ resettlement, earmarking of adequate funds from the State Plan towards the State's share of the Centrally Sponsored Schemes and to monitor and evaluate the schemes under implementation. Similar committees should be formed at the Head of the Department level with CCF of the States as the Chairman and at the district level with the District Collector as the Chairman. These committees at the respective levels could be same as for the programmes of rehabilitation of the forest villagers suggested elsewhere.

(6) In case of resettlement at a different location, no shifting of families should take place until the programme of resettlement has progressed sufficiently so as to provide reasonable living facilities in the new location.

(7) A programme of educating the shifting cultivators on the advantage of settled cultivation should be taken up alongwith implementation if the settlement/resettlement schemes for which provision of adequate material, financial and training input should be made.

We would suggest that a target of atleast 3 lakhs, i.e., 50 per cent of the total number of families be kept for the Seventh Plan and at an approximate cost of settlement of Rs. 30,000 per family (it is difficult to make any exact estimate), an amount of Rs. 55 crores be kept towards 60 per cent share of the Central Government under the proposed Centrally Sponsored Scheme. While approving the State Plans, provision of adequate funds for the purpose should also receive priority attention of the Planning Commission.

Agriculture and Animal Husbandry

SHIFTING CULTIVATION

Prior to the present settled agriculture that is found in the tribes today, the most popular method of growing crops in the tribal areas used to be shifting cultivation or axe cultivation. This is quite natural as shifting cultivation marks a stage of transition from hunting and food gathering to settled agriculture.

Shifting cultivation was practised by the Bhil in the south as well as the Saharia in the north. It must have continued since times immemorial, particularly among the Saharias. B.C. Mazumdar tells us, "It appears that the Savara-kol people in the highlands of Central India used sticks for a long time for digging the soil and only at a comparatively later date introduced the plough for agricultural purposes." Shifting cultivation continued to be practised on small-scale in the southern part of the State till about the mid-forties, though not openly. As late as 1943 shifting cultivation was detected in Alirajpur (Jhabua district) in small patches. Shifting cultivation was also widely practised in Kathiwada (Jhabua district) till about 1930, when it was stopped by the Ruler. But surreptitiously the practice continues even today and it is still a serious menace to proper forest management. But from the broad economic point of view the practice is a very minor one and does not constitute any topic of serious study.

Conditions among the Saharias are very different. They live mostly in the reserve forests or villages very close to them. In the absence of suitable land for cultivation due to competition from caste Hindus, and lack of other gainful sources of employment, they fall an easy prey to the temptation of shifting cultivation or *suradahiya,* as they call it. Among the Saharias shifting cultivation was very common until 1908 and "good forest crop was cut down and burnt to raise a crop or two of *tilli* (sesamum indicum) and *jowar* (sorghum vulgare)." With the tightening of the forest administration the *dahya* cultivation has diminished very considerably. It still occurs here and there but when detected by forest authorities it is severely punished. The process of cultivation is briefly as follows:

A suitable sloping land is selected on the hill side. The forest trees are cut down with an axe and burnt. The ashes are spread all over the field. After allowing the land to cool down, holes are dug at soft points in the soil with the help of a steel-pointed stick known as *khoria.* Then seeds, chiefly of jowar, are placed in these holes and covered with soil. *Ramasa, rotka* and other small millets are also grown this way. The land yields 4 to 5 maunds of jowar per acre.

This practice is being severely discouraged, and tribals all over the State are being settled on land. This has largely been achieved in the south, and Bhils and Bhilalas can now be termed as settled agriculturists. Gonds and Korkus are now largely employed as labourers on lands and forests, and whatever agriculture persists in them is mainly settled. The Saharia has little land and great love for shifting cultivation. Efforts are being made to give him the first preference in the allotment of new land. By far and large there is no shifting cultivation economy in the primitive tribes of the State. The dependence is always on the settled agriculture. Thus it can be said that in the course of last half a century or so, the tribal people in the State have made a transition from shifting cultivation to settled agriculture. For all practical purposes shifting cultivation is a thing of the past and whatever interest persists in the subject now is largely historical.

SETTLED AGRICULTURE IN THE TRIBAL BELTS

In the following pages it is proposed to discuss the various aspects of settled agriculture as it is found in the tribal areas of the State. For the sake of convenience the discussion shall be confined to the conditions in the areas where the tribals live and these areas may be designated as the tribal belts to distinguish them from the broad natural divisions. The Bhil-Bhilala belt would be the same as the Scheduled Areas of the State confined to the Hills division. The Gond-Korku belt would refer to the Kannod, Khategaon and Bagli tehsils of the district Dewas on the hilly section of Plateau division. The Saharia belt would refer to the tehsil Morena of the Lowland division and the tehsils of Shivpuri, Guna and Bhilsa on the north and north-east of the plateau division.

THB LAND

Soil Zones

Broadly speaking there are five main soil zones in Madhya Bharat. The first is the Alluvial zone comprising of the districts of Gwalior, Bhind and Morena. The soil is alluvial or sandy loam, very similar to the Agra, Etawah and Jhansi districts of the Uttar Pradesh. This zone is devoted mostly to wheat and rice, and where irrigation is plenty, to cash crops like potatoes and sugar-cane. The second is the Light Black Soil zone comprising the districts of Shivpuri, Guna and Bhilsa. This zone forms a sort of bridge between tne alluvial zone of the north and heavy black cotton soil of the Malwa Plateau, and has characteristics marking it out from both of them. This is a rich wheat area. The third is the Heavy Black Cotton zone comprising of the most of Plateau division growing cash crops like cotton and groundnuts and important grain crops like wheat and jowar. The fourth zone may be termed as the Nimar zone consisting of shallow black soil. This zone extends over a thin strip of land between the Vindhya and the Satpura ranges, running along the Narmada river. It is an alluvial of very high fertility and highly suited to the cultivation of cotton and groundnut. And finally we have the Hilly zone covering most of the districts of Nimar and Jhabua and parts of the district Dhar.

Tribal Area Soils

It has been discussed earlier that the tribal population is heavily concentrated in the hilly areas of the various natural divisions and the three tribal belts are spread over the Vindhyas and Satpuras and their numerous offshoots. Therefore, despite the soil zone they may be broadly classed in, they have for their sustenance the hilly soils. The Saharias, for instance, though living in the alluvial and light black soil zones, have mostly stony and hilly soils as their holdings. The Gonds and Korkus, similarly, inhabit the most infertile parts of Dewas district. So far as the Bhil belt is concerned it is over-whelmingly dependent on the hilly soils. Therefore, it is the last zone that is practically omnipresent in the three tribal belts of the State.

These hilly soils are laterites and laterities. These soils are deficient in potash, phosphoric acid and lime. On higher levels these soils are exceedingly thin and gravelly, but on lower levels and in the valleys they consist of heavy loams and clays. On the whole, these soils are very poor. These soils are equally poor in nitrogen and humus. Their capacity to retain moisture and nutrients is also severely limited. These soils occur on the summit of the Vindhyan and Satpura hills throughout the State. Thus, whatever be the distances separating one tribal belt from another the tribal areas have the same type of soil throughout.

Bhil Belt

But within these belts also there is a wide variety of soils—from most fertile to the most rocky ones. *Bhuri*, *Halki* and *Khardi* are the more common ones with occasionally the *Kali* thrown in between. This variety is due to the hilly terrain of the country. The rocky substratum plays a very important part in creating this variety. Hills, stony ridges, streams and nalas leave their own mark on the soil types. In these hilly areas the value of a soil depends largely on its depth, while in the plains the intrinsic quality of the soil is the prime determining factor. Where the rocky substratum is thickly over-laid with soil the soil is deeper and has greater power of retaining moisture. Due to the undulating nature of the terrain, the surface run-off during the rains is very large, resulting in excessive soil erosion. The fields on top of the hills and on the slope of the hills get denuded of rich silt. Near the nalas and rivers a good part of this silt gets deposited creating fertile valleys and banks rich in alluvium.

The *Khardi* is a red soil with little depth and poor retention. The *Halki* is relatively a poorer soil having rocks very close to the surface. And finally there is the *Bardi*, the poorest of the poor soils. It is shallow and stony.

These soils can retain moisture for very short periods. This shallowness has been brought out very picturesquely in a tribal phrase. Said a Bhilala cultivator to the author, "My soils, Sir, are thin, and even moonlight is sufficient to parch them up." They are suitable for shallow rooted kharif crops only which do not require much moisture for their growth and whose life span is shorter. We have therefore the risky spectacle of the Bhil and Bhilala cultivator of the hills sowing his maize soon after the first break of the monsoon as early as the last week of May. He does this to secure two rain fed crops counting on the average rain during the monsoons and liberal dose during the winter. *Khardi* can grow *jowar, bajra* and *makka*. *Bardi* is suitable for small millets like *kondon, savan, kulthi*, etc.—the typical dry crops of the draught areas. These crops yield food for the human being as well as the cattle.

Saharia Belt

The soils in the Saharia belt are subject to the same variability as in the Southern Hills. The main types in these areas are *Padua, Bhura, Dumat, Rankar* and occasionally the *Mar*. *Padua* is a greyish sandy soil. The *Bhura* is a yellow coloured soil suitable for small millets and other small grains. The *Rankar* is the stony soil found in most of the areas known as *Tarathi Dung* situated on the foot of the Vindhyan Hills. This soil like its counter-part the *Bardi* of the Bhil areas is very shallow and subject to quick exhaustion. It can be cultivated only once in three years. The sowing on *Rankar* is very early in order to make the best use of the moisture. In the tribal economy of the belt it is the *Rankar* that plays the most important role.

Gond-Korku Belt

The tribal people occupy the north-west and south-west of the Nemawar part of the Dewas district comprising of the tehsils of Kannod, Khategaon and Bagli. These parts are hilly and of little fertility. The level and fertile plains of the centre and the east are comparatively more fertile. In the hilly tracts only kharif crops are raised. Small millets like *kondon* and *savan* are the staple crops on the hilly soils which have the same characteristics as those of the hills in the south.

Soil Erosion

The soils of these submontane tracts are subject to heavy erosion. The slope being very steep, the surface run-off of the rain water during the monsoons constitutes the greatest eroding factor. Due to excessive run-off surface soil disappears and the soluble chemicals are bleached out. The rich humus bearing top soil gets washed-off, and rocky and raw sub-soil is continually exposed. This raw sub-soil gets little time to mature and become efficient in cropping capacity. Dr. Higginbottom had estimated a loss of twenty to fifty tons per acre of the top soil of the fields in central India.

In terms of individual income and national wealth the loss would amount to crores of rupees annually. In the context of the tribal economy this excessive denudation poses a serious socio-economic problem. It results in lower soil fertility which means less yield per acre and less income per cultivator. Finally, it results in poverty for the majority of the tribal cultivators. Their economic position worsens and moneylender's grip becomes tighter. Evil social consequences follow this destitution.

To a certain extent soil erosion is a beneficial process. Our soils are a result of this process over a long period. According to Jacks and Whyte 'geological erosion' or 'denudation' is a process necessary for soil formation. History of civilization is largely a history of the foot or two of the top soil that gives the man and animal his sustenance. But when "the same process is accelerated by human mismanagement, it becomes one of the vicious and destructive forces that have ever been released by man." This destruction threatens not only the well-being but the very existence of the tribal people.

The question that arises is not one of putting a stop to soil erosion but of reducing it. What is actually required is "an equilibrium between soil denudation and soil formation." If that is achieved the problem of soil fertility and soil stability would become easy to solve.

Contributory Causes

Besides the topographical and climatic factors causing erosion there are other important factors that have helped in the acceleration of this destructive process.

In the Bhil belt in the Hills division the large number of cattle results in serious grazing of the land. Particularly the goats prove most destructive. They eat every bit of greenery that they sight. Even the young sprouts are eaten, and new vegetation hardly gets a chance of survival. This excessive grazing deprives the soil of invaluable binding material that may hold the soil together and check the surface run-off.

The tribal cultivator loves to run his plough up and down the slopes of his field. This he would do, even at the cost of the life of his bullocks. This method of ploughing against the contour and along the slope, provides easy channel for rain water to run-off at great speed. This further increases the rate of denudation.

And finally, there is the factor of increasing pressure of population on land. Decrease in the size of holdings due to sub-division and fragmentation in successive generations now does not allow much land to lie fallow. Every tenant tries to use every bit of land in his tiny holding. In the past, fallow and uncultivated land used to be quite considerable and such covered land always protected the soil against excessive erosion. The reduction in fallows and uncultivated patches has further hastened the process of erosion. The smaller gets the average size of holding the greater the soil erosion.

Erosion and Agronomic Improvements

It is generally not fully realized that in the face of excessive soil erosion agronomic improvements by surface treatment would either fail altogether or succeed only very partially. No addition of manures would be of any avail because frequently its effect would be "negatived in the same season or another" depending on its topography. The maintenance of equilibrium in the soil erosion, thus, becomes the pre-condition of improvements in the quality of crops and yields per acre.

The soil erosion can be checked by following measures: Contour bunding, contour ploughing, provision of storm-water channels, regulation of grazing and better crop rotation.

These measures of preventing soil erosion would require for

their success some sort of joint land management. Small and scattered holdings do not lend themselves to proper contour bunding and scientific crop rotation.

Rainfall

The rainfall, together with soil and temperature, determines the nature of the agricultural industry. Rain water dissolves the salts and other nutrients present in the soil, and the plant utilizes these nutrients in solution form. The region being hilly, climate dry and hot, and the facilities of irrigation almost non-existent, the only source of water to the plant is through the rains. This importance of the rains to the agriculture is realized by the tribal cultivator. He wisely says, "*jaeso, bursego, waiso pakego* (if it rains well, it will grow well)."

The tribal folk, ignorant of the meteorological science, have, through observation and tradition, built up a vast store of sayings bearing on the forecast of the rains. The Jhabua fihil has a saying that if a particular type of cloud known as *Garab* is seen overhead in Bhadawa (August-September) then it must rain in *jeth* (May-June), believing that the cloud would require nine months to mature into a water bearing cloud. If the *Titahri* lays its eggs on the river bank, the rain is likely to be deficient; if it lays eggs on some high place the rains would be plentiful. If a peacock cries before dawn on the third *Vaisahh,* it is considered to be a sign promising as many months of rains as there are cries. The bathing of sparrows in the dust is taken as an indication of the stoppage of rains. These sayings have secured a deep nitch in the thinking of the tribal cultivator and he plans his operations very much on the predictions obtained from such signs and omnes. The science of weather forecast has yet to reach the tribal people.

From the point of view of rainfall the census of India has divided the country into five belts:

	Rainfall belt	*Annual Rainfall*
1.	Blue belt	Exceeding 75 inches
2.	Dark-green belt	Between 50 and 75 inches
3.	Light-green belt	Between 30 and 50 inches
4.	Brown belt	Between 15 and 30 inches
5.	Yellow belt	Below 15 inches

All the three tribal belts of Madhya Bharat fall in the Brown belt, generally averaging less than 30 inches of rains annually. The special feature of the Brown belt is frequent seasonal fluctuations at a more or less regular break. And when "they do occur, they cause a great deal of hardship to the people and expense to Government." This belt is exposed to special hazards which is a constant source of trouble. The table below gives the rainfall for the tehsil towns in the interior of the three tribal belts. For the Bhil belt two tehsil towns have been selected which represent the two areas of Nimar and Rath comprising the belt.

TABLE 6.1

Rainfall in Tribal Areas

Year	*Bhil belt*		*Saharia belt Pohri*	*Gond-Korku belt Khategaon*
	Jhabua	*Barwani*		
1948	29.6	31.16	35.87	N.A.
1949	28.0	24.8	42.67	N.A.
1950	41.0	21.10	27.60	45.85
1951	19.51	16.95	23.43	22.00
1952	32.96	11.89	16.60	23.66
1953	19.21	21.44	36.1	51.68
1954	30.98	28.56	33.74	37.09
Average	28.76	22.99	30.7	36.05

N.A.=Not Available.

The table indicates the uncertain nature of rainfall in the last seven years for which statistics are available.

The rainfall has gone as low as 11 inches and as high as 51.68 inches. Jhabua in the Bhil belt shows an average 28.76 and Barwani 22.99. Both these averages are within the range of the brown-belt. Pohri in the Saharia belt shows an average of 30.7, which is slightly higher than the maximum of the brown-belt. Khategaon in the Gond-Korku belt shows an average of 36.05. This is again higher than the brown-belt maximum. But a smaller sample appears to be the cause of this high average. The year 1953 had an unusually high precipitation which has raised the general average.

Distribution of Rainfall

From the point of view of agriculture the total rain is not the only determinant of the moisture supply of the plants. Equally important is the distribution of the rains. In Nimar the average rain of 25" is considered sufficient for a good crop of cotton, provided it is well distributed. Some rain in August-September is essential for a good crop. The failure of rain at this time of the year has led to widespread scarcities in many a season. Particular mention might be made of the crop-year 1952-53 when the letting up of the rains in the months of August-September caused a widespread failure of crops and resulted in acute distress in the tribal areas.

The *mavtha* (winter rain) is a godsent to the rabi crop. If the rain is average the cultivator expects to get a fairly good rabi crop without irrigation only if the *mavtha* is timely and liberal.

Temperature

Temperature plays an important part in the determination of the agricultural life of the people. The crop seasons are largely a result of the temperature and rainfall. Besides its influence on crops, it plays a not insignificant role in the determination of the character ot the people. High temperature retards physical activity and induces lethargy and indolence.

From the climatic point of view the State can be divided into three well defined zones; the North with extremes of heat and cold; the Plateau which is more or less temperate; and lastly the Hills which are extremely hot and dry.

The Saharia belt falls more or less in two climatic zones. Parts of the district Morena and Shivpuri lie in the Northern zone of the extremes. Hot winds start blowing from the month of April and continue till the middle of September. The temperature throughout the long summer is high at all times of the day. The winter commences from October and the mercury from now on starts contracting, often falling below freezing point. The extreme cold causes heavy frosting during the months of December and January resulting in immense harm to the Rabi crops. The mountainous sections inhabited by the Saharias are subject to even greater extremes. Part of the Saharia belt lies in the temperate Plateau. But here too, the hills are hotter than the plains. Saharia life is, thus, set in the hotter parts of the zones.

The Gond-Korku belt, falling as it does, in the temperate zone, should normally be expected to enjoy respite from the rigours of the climate. But that unfortunately, is not the case. Situated on the right side of the Narmada this belt is also confined to the Vindhyan offshoots. Thus, it is hotter than the rest of the Plateau.

The Bhil belt is almost entirely situated in the Hot zone. Here the climate is excessively hot during the summer. The summers set in the beginning of April, and last till the end of October.

Agricultural Year

The agricultural year is divided into two seasons. The *Sialu* or *Kharif* and the *Unhalu* or *Rabi:*

Sialu or *Kharif* extends from *Baisakh* (April-May) to *Kunwar* (September-October). The *Unhalu* or *Rabi* extends from *Kunwar* to *Chaitra* (March-April).

Sialu: The kharif season begins by the end of May when summer ploughing commences and lasts till October when the crops are harvested. The kharif crops require a higher temperature and plentiful supply of water. Cereals such as jowar, bajra, makka, kodon, etc. which are hardly and quick growing are the main crops of the season.

In the billy soils it is not possible to begin tillage until there has been a shower to moisten the land. As soon as the first monsoon breaks the ploughs are put into fields. Because of the hard nature of the soils, the general practice is to give a thorough ploughing to the field after the previous crop. As generally only kharif crops are grown, this ploughing is done somewhere in October or November. In case rabi is grown, the ploughing is done sometime in March. After this the fields are left as they are. In the month of May the field is dry-manured with cowdung-cake and other refuse. The manure is distributed over the whole field. No ploughing or *bakhering* is done after manuring. It is *bakhered* just after the first shower by the end of May or the beginning of June. Immediately after the second shower the sowing is done. In the areas where the soils are extremely shallow the sowing commences as soon as the first rain is received. The idea is to take advantage of the early rain so that there may be sufficient time to take a rabi crop.

In the alluvial tracts generally a *bakhering* is done in the fields before the commencement of the rains. This uproots the weeds and shrubs, etc. and the soil is in a better state to absorb rain. After the first shower, one good ploughing is done, and soon after the second shower the sowing is started.

The kharif crop is brought to maturity by the autumn rains received in the months of September and October. Failures of autumn rain results in fatal injury to the standing kharif crop and leads to short sowing of crops.

Sowing: The sowing is done with *tiphan* in Nimar and *nai* in Jhabua. For smaller grains and millets the sowing is done with *phadak* which sows two rows at a time. Cotton is sown in *phadak* as well as *nai.* Sometimes the seeds are simply broadcast and later covered with a light ploughing or *bakhering.*

Weeding: As soon as the seeds start germinating *nindai* (weeding) becomes necessary. Nindai is done either by hand or with *khurpis* or with a *dora* (harrow). Two weeks later, another weeding is done. When the plants are a month old the *qalni* or *iltani* (thinning) is done. This is done by hand leaving a distance of 4" to 6" between the plants. Sometimes a *Kolpa* (small plough) is also used for interculture.

Reaping: Generally the crops are harvested with a *karati* (sickle) or pulled out by the roots (as in the case of gram). They are then bound into sheaves and carried to the *khala* (threshing floor) and then stored till dry. In case of *makki* the cobs are allowed to be dried in the fields. When the cobs are matured and dry the whole plant is cut together with the cobs, tied into sheaves and heaped in the *khala.* The cobs are removed at leizure and the seeds separated. For other grains the separated heads are placed on the ground of the *khala* and either beaten with mallets or trodden by the muzzled bullocks. This process is known as *datvan pherna.*

The next process is *khalna* (winnowing). The trodden grains are separated from the chaff. This process requires three persons. One person stands on a stool and empties his basket of grains at a slow speed. Second person fans the falling grain which results in separating the chaff. The third person simply collects the grains below. If a good wind is prevailing at the time, fanning is not required. Sometimes the residue is re-trodden and rewinnowed.

The chaff is carefully collected and preserved as a cattle feed. The stalks of the dried plants are also stored as valuable roughages for the cattle.

The tribal agriculture is solely dependent on rains. In the Nimar district in the Bhil belt 91 per cent of the area is under kharif crops while only 9 per cent is under rabi crops. Nimar includes quite a sizable irrigated area. The rest of the belt has much less of irrigation. The dependence of the tribal belt on the kharif for us human needs as well as those of its large cattle population is a characteristic feature of tribal economy. In other belts also the tribal lands are suited for kharif only. Rabi in tribal cropping-scheme is a rarity. Even in the most interior tribal areas most of the rabi land is with non-tribals.

Unhalu: The preparation of the rabi starts soon after the kharif harvest. The field is ploughed or *bakhered* once to clear the stubble. Then it is given a planking with a plank 5 feet long and 9 to 12 inches wide and 3 to 4 inches thick, drawn by a pair of bullocks. Rabi crops, as a general rule, require comparatively less moisture and heat. The moisture is supplied by heavy winter dews and the *mavtha* (winter shower) which falls between December and February. But these sources of water can be depended upon only when the soil is sufficiently retentive and there happens to be a shower in November to suffice for the germination and growth of the plants, otherwise the rabi is coexistent with irrigation. The main crops of the season are wheat, gram, barley, etc. The Rabi crops do not require much of weeding and inter-culture. They are harvested from March to April. The harvest is earlier in the Bhil belt as compared to the Saharia belt.

CULTIVATED LAND

Of the total available land-area in Madhya Bharat roughly 38 per cent is under the plough. The rest of the 62 per cent is accounted for by fallows, culturable waste and uncultivable waste. Lack of irrigation, rocky nature of a large part of the terrain and primitive methods of cultivation are responsible for such a large wastage of land.

The present state of land utilization in the State is shown in the Table 6.2. In order to focus the attention on the tribal regions, the table deals with the natural divisions and the relevant districts in the three tribal belts only.

The table shows that in 1951 the total land per capita in the State amounted to 374 cents. The cultivated and cultivable land area per capita amounted to 233 cents. And in terms of cultivated area per capita it came to 123.9 cents only. This means that 150.1 cents of land area per capita lies uncultivated for one reason or the other.

TABLE 6.2

Land Area Per Capita and Trend of Cultivation in the Madhya Bharat (1951)

(Area in cents)

State, Divisions and Districts	*Land area per capita*		*Area of cultivation per capita*
	Total land area per capita	*Area cultivated and cultivable per capita*	
Madhya Bharat	374	233	123.9
Lowland	309	160	104.2
Morena	450	196	119.6
Plateau	381	259	123.7
Shivpuri	543	334	112.7
Guna	570	355	137.3
Dewas	512	296	161.4
Hills	422	233	145.0
Jhabua	424	228	129.1
Dhar	403	265	183.1
Nimar	433	215	159.3

Being the region of highest density the Lowland has only 309 cents of land per capita, out of which the cultivated area is only 104.2 cents per capita. Plateau, coming second in the scale of density, has 381 cents of land area per capita, out of which 123.7 cents per capita is cultivated. The Hills, which are least densely populated, have 422 cents of total land per capita, out of which the cultivated area amounts to 145 cents per capita. On the average 277 cents of land per capita goes waste here as compared to 150.1 cents per capita in the whole State. The corresponding uncultivated land per capita in lowland is 204.8 cents and in the Plateau 257.3 cents. *Thus, the Hills show the highest total land area per capita and the highest cultivated land per capita. The Hills, incidentally, also show the highest uncultivated land per capita.*

The same characteristics mark the per capita land position

in the relevant districts of the three tribal belts. Morena, Shivpuri and Guna in the Saharia belt show 450, 543 and 570 cents of land area per capita respectively. The Gond-Korku belt in Dewas shows 512 cents of land per capita, out of which only 161.4 cents per capita is cultivated. This belt also shows that a good deal of total land is not used for cultivation. In the Bhil-Bhilala belt covering the Hills, Jhabua shows the lowest area of cultivation with only 129.1 cents per capita. Dhar shows the highest cultivated land per capita with a figure of 183.1 cents. The poor quality of soils in the tribal areas in general and the Bhil-Bhilala belt in particular offsets the advantage of larger cultivated land per capita in these areas.

IRRIGATION

Madhya Bharat as a whole is hilly deficient in the sources of irrigation, despite the presence of numerous streams, including such mighty rivers as the *Narmada* and the *Chambal*. In 1953-54 the total area sown in Madhya Bharat was 12,390,931 acres. Of this only 1,74,241 acres or roughly 2.15 per cent was irrigated. The percentage of irrigated area to the total area sown presents a very dismal picture. The table below gives a belt-wise acreage under irrigation in 1953-54.

TABLE 6.3

Irrigated Area in the Tribal Belts in Madhya Bharat (in 1953-54)

	Total area sown (acres)	*Total area irrigated (acres)*	*Percentage of the irrigated area*
Bhil Belt			
Dhar	1027432	26401	2.56
Jhabua	512956	4441	0.86
Nimar	1362992	32836	2.40
Saharia Belt			
Morena	855643	86794	1.01
Shivpuri	653602	63267	9.67
Guna	811686	16567	2.04
Gond-Korku Belt			
Dewas	653042	9039	1.38

The Table 6.3 gives a good idea of the position of irrigation in the tribal belts. Jhabua district which is overwhelmingly populated by Bhils and Bhilalas has merely a percentage of 0.86. We do not have any data as to what percentage of this irrigated area is part of the holdings of the tribal people. But looking to the fact that most of the better quality of land is with the castes considered high in the social hierarchy, it would not be wrong to presume that major part of the irrigated area must be in the non-tribal holdings. That would leave almost unirrigated land in the hands of the tribal farmer. Thus, there is almost no protection against the drought, and irregular rain can result in nothing but utter scarcity and untold misery to the teeming tribals. Dhar and Nimar figures are comparatively higher, having a percentage of 2.6 and 2.4 respectively. These figures do not give the exact idea of the irrigability of land so far as the tribal is concerned. District Dhar includes parts of Malwa Plateau which grew opium at one time. Fertile and riverine parts of Nimar were also famed for its poppy cultivation. These poppy lands were and are in the hands of the non-tribals even today when poppy cultivation is highly restricted. Thus, even in these districts the irrigation does not play any role worth the name in the tribal economy.

Shivpuri in the Saharia belt has the highest percentage of irrigated area and Guna and Morena much lower. But the same tale is repeated here. Either the Saharia lives in the highlands where the sources of irrigation are extremely scanty, or if he happens to live in close proximity and in the midst of the sources of irrigation, he finds that the best of the land which could get the benefits of irrigation is in the hands of higher castes.

Sources of Irrigation

The chief sources of irrigation in the State are canals, tanks, wells and others.

Of the sources of irrigation wells are the most important. In 1952-53 wells accounted for 61.34 per cent of the total irrigated area of the State. Canals irrigated 32.41 per cent of the irrigated area, tanks 4.82 per cent and other sources 1.62 per cent.

The Table 6.4 gives the irrigated area in tribal belts in 1952-53.

The table shows that in the Bhil belt wells are the chief sources of irrigation. In Jhabua wells irrigate 4,069 acres of the

TABLE 6.4

Irrigated Area in the Tribal Belts of Madhya Bharat (1952-53)

(in acres)

	Canals	*Tanks*	*Wells*	*Other sources*	*Total*
Dhar	21	459	24555	471	25506
Jhabua	nil	nil	4069	317	4386
Nimar	nil	1903	28833	1951	32687
Morena	10557	2573	21410	549	35080
Shivpuri	4134	5830	52056	745	62765
Guna	4514	273	11277	543	16567
Dewas	50	733	8025	70	8878

Department of Land Records and Settlement, Madhya Bharat.

total 4386 acres of irrigated land in the district. Only 317 acres is irrigated by other sources. Thus, more than 90 per cent of the land is irrigated through wells. In Dhar and parts of Nimar also wells are the chief sources of irrigation. But in these two districts tanks are plentiful and they supplement the wells. Jhabua has a terrain very well suited to the construction of tanks, but this possibility has not been exploited by the former rulers of the areas. Strangely enough, Nimar does not show any irrigation by canals despite the presence of Narmada in a large part of the district. This is, as we have seen earlier, due to the high banks of the river. In the jungle areas of the Bhil-belt the number of wells is much smaller than in the open areas. Wells, generally, go with villages. The Bhils and the Bhilalas (mainly the Bhils) do not live in compact villages. As such there is little possibility of poor individuals digging their own wells. This socio-economic factor happens to coincide with the peculiar geology of the tribal habitat. In the archean terrain of the Bhil belt the wells are not likely to yield sufficient water for irrigation in future as well. The hope here lies in the construction of small bunds and tanks.

In the Saharia belt, particularly in Morena, canals irrigate nearly 10,557 acres of land coming next to wells which irrigate 21,410 acres. Shivpuri and Guna also show a relatively greater development of irrigation through canals and tanks, but wells continue to be the chief source here as well.

In the hilly tracts of the belt, where the tribals live, there is a dearth of wells, and canals are few. Rarely do we come across a Saharia with an irrigated piece of land, Kirars, Gujars, Kachhis and Ahirs—the four main cultivating castes of the area have the best of land divided between them.

The Gond-Korku belt is also predominantly dependent on the wells for irrigation. In the rocky areas the wells are very few. The tribals generally live in these rocky areas subject to acute water scarcity for drinking as well as irrigational purposes.

LAND TENURES

Of the covenating States of Madhya Bharat, Gwalior State had most of the area under Zamindari system. The rest of the States had Ryotwari system. Most of the States had a number of small Jagirdars who followed either the Zamindari or the Ryotwari system.

Historical

The land revenue system in the Madhya Bharat is a very complicated one as a result of the peculiar history of the region. Originally, the Central India had the Ryotwari or the peasant proprietorship system in common with the rest of the country. All land belonged to the Ruler or the State, and the man who cleared and tilled the land had the right of use as a tenant. This right of cultivating the holding was hereditary. The revenue was collected by the village headmen known as *Patels, Choudhries* or *Mandlois* in Central India.

The incursions and invasions from other parts of India have been a peculiar feature of the history of Central India. Mohammedans, and later the Marathas conquerred this area. These influences largely destroyed the existing ryotwari system. During these unsettled years the inalienable rights of the *ryot* were violated and rights of alienation were transferred or assigned to others. These assignees generally were:

(a) outsiders who came with the conqueror, and now required appeasement,
(b) old village headman who had obliged the Ruler in some way and had come to exercise great influence over him,

(c) fareign contractors who replaced hereditary village headman who had disappeared from their posts owing to war and other pauses.

These factors gave rise to Zamindari system in the Saharia belt. In the Bhil and Gond-Korku belt, the middlemen came to be known as *Ijardars, Malguzars* and *Lambardars.* These middlemen had no respect for the rights of the cultivators and were only interested in keeping them attached to land and paying land revenue. By usage, sufferance, administrative indifference and other causes, these men gradually acquired rights and powers in the land they occupied, and over the heads of the people who cultivated them.

On the return of peace and tranquility in the region the Ijardars and other middlemen except the Zamindars in the northern parts of the State, were gradually liquidated and hardly held any rights in the land. The ryotwari system was reinstituted.

While land was being assigned to middlemen the conquerring chieftains created *jagirs* in favour of their relatives and powerful leaders. The cultivator was worst-off in these jagirs where he was subjected to various levies and exactions unfair in the extreme. In these semi-independent and alienated areas the number of middlemen was even greater. These jagirs were sub-divided again and again to provide for junior members of the ruling families.

Recent Legislation

This state of chaos was brought to an end by the various ordinances issued by the State and several Acts passed by the legislature. With a view to bring uniformity in the Ryotwari area, the *Land Revenue and Tenancy Ordinance* was issued in 1948. Later in 1950 the *Land Revenne and Tenancy Act* (Act No. 66 of 1950) was enforced. This was followed by *Zamindari Abolition Act* and the *Abolition of Jagirs Act* in 1951. These Acts created uniformity in the tenancy and revenue administration throughout State.

Types of Tenures

At present the tenancies in the State are as follows:

(i) *Pakka* tenant,
(ii) Ordinary tenant,

(iii) Sub-tenant,
(iv) Concessional holder, and
(v) Special tenures.

(i) *Pakka tenant:* It is a tenant who holds land for agricultural purposes and enjoys hereditary rights over his holding. He can sublet or sell the whole or a part of his holding if he so desires on certain conditions. But he cannot hold more than 50 acres of land and is not permitted to have a holding with less than 5 acres of irrigated land and 15 acres of non-irrigated land. He is also termed as *Pukhta Mauroosi.*

(ii) *Ordinary tenant:* It means a tenant other than a *Pakka* tenant, but does not include the sub-tenant. This includes all types of temporary tenures.

(iii) *Sub-tenant:* It means a person who holds land from a *Pakka* or an ordinary tenant or from a holder of service-holding or from a concessional holder.

(iv) *Concessional holder:* It means a person who holds land on a revenue less than the revenue, which, but for a special tenure he would have been assessed.

(v) *Special tenures'.* This class includes Jagirdars, Inamdars, Istamurardars and Muafidars who enjoy certain proprietary rights in land free of revenue or on favoured assessment. Besides the above it also includes special leases granted by the Government for the development of land.

Tenancy in Tribal Economy

The tenancies relevant to the tribal economy belong to the first three categories.

The proportion of the *Pakka* tenants is relatively the largest in the Bhil belt as this tract has been under ryotwari since long. The proportion of this type of tenure is very small in the Saharias and the Gonds and the Korkus.

Ordinary tenure, (including all types of temporary terms but not including sub-tenancy) is not very common in the Bhil belt. It is most common in the Saharia belt, where Saharia is a relatively new convert to settled agriculture. The most typical form of ordinary tenure is that which is known locally as *Arazi Ahatmal.* Generally, holdings of *ḍanda* and *rankad* soil are not held in *pakka* tenure as these poor soils can be cultivated for not more than two years in succession. Next five years they are left uncultivated to allow them to recoupe their fertility. The landless Saharia is interested in cultivating this type of land to supplement his meagre incomes, The State allows this land to be leased for short leases of one year under ordinary tenancy. But the process of securing such a tenancy is so long and cumbersome that instead of going through the regular procedure the Saharia cultivates it without a tenure. Since it is now a well established irregularity the Revenue Department takes a lenient view of the practice, although technically it amounts to trespass, punishable by the dispossession of the trespasser or an imposition of fine upto Rs. 50. He is given the lightest penalty under the Act, and is charged only twice the normal annual rent of the land. This, the Saharia has no hesitation in paying promptly.

Sub-tenancy is common in all the tribal areas. This goes by the name of *sajhedari* (partnership) or *bati* (crop sharing) with minor differences. The *sajhedari* is offered when the number of male members in the owning family is very small, so far as the regular *pakka* tenant is concerned. On the other hand, it is accepted by the *sajhedari* only when the number of the members in his family is large. It is profitable only when domestic labour is sufficient to meet the demand and no outside labour is employed. The land generally let out on *sajhedari* is of a poorer quality and rarely manured. The terms of contract are generally these: The *patta* continues to be on the name of the *pakka* tenant but the land revenue is paid on the fifty-fifty basis. The plough-cattle and the implements belong to the incoming partners. The pattedar himself does not share in the cultivation of this land but supplies half the seed required for sowing. If labour is employed on the land the expenses are borne equally by the two partners. But this is rarely permitted by the pattedar. The gross produce is divided equally between the *pattedar* and the *sajhedar*. In case the pattedar supplies the plough cattle he gets 2/3 of the produce and the *sajhedar* gets only 1/3. The contract is generally oral and is renewable after every agricultural year. There are instances where *sajhedari* has been continuing for more than 10 years.

The *batai* differs from the *sajhedari* chiefly in that the *pattedar* in *batai* bears no share of the expenses of production except paying half the land rent. All the expenses are borne by the *bataidar.* The gross produce is shared equally by the two.

CROP PRODUCTION

The conditions of topography, soil, climate and rainfall, that we find in the three tribal belts of the State, fashion the pattern of crop production to a great extent. Lack of irrigation facilities under such conditions makes the dependence on rains even more pronounced. In these areas of inadequate and uncertain rains, both with regard to the amount and its distribution, crop failures, scarcities and famines are common phenomena. The stage in the tribal areas is thus set for an acute struggle between the mean and the miserly nature on one hand and the adaptable and adamant tribal on the other. In his struggle for existence the tribal has adopted the only form of agriculture possible in the land inhabited by him. From the point of view of the source of water supply it may be termed as 'Rainfed Farming', from the consideration of lack of artificial sources of water, it may be termed as Dry Farming, and from the point of view of the crops grown it may termed as Millet Farming. As generally such mode of farming goes by the name of Dry Farming in our country we shall stick to the use of this term in our deliberations.

Dry Farming

Dry Farming has been going on in the tribal areas of the State since times immemorial. The agricultural techniques in vogue in the areas are a result of the long process of adaptation spread over scores of centuries. But the rapid growth of population in the recent decades has exerted a very heavy pressure on the tribal land. Per capita land has diminished and the holdings have gone down. The pressure of population and the regulation of forest management has led to the use of marginal and sub-marginal lands for agricultural purposes. "Now many crops of exhaustive nature have been introduced and the cultivation of the whole land has continued year after year without any rest or without any effort to recuperate or maintain the fertility of land." At the same time, acute soil erosion has been going on reducing the fertility of land.

Under such conditions of low and precarious rainfall, lack of irrigation and low fertility on the land, draught resistant and shallow rooted crops mainly the millets, are grown in these areas They form the staple food for both the man and the cattle. The

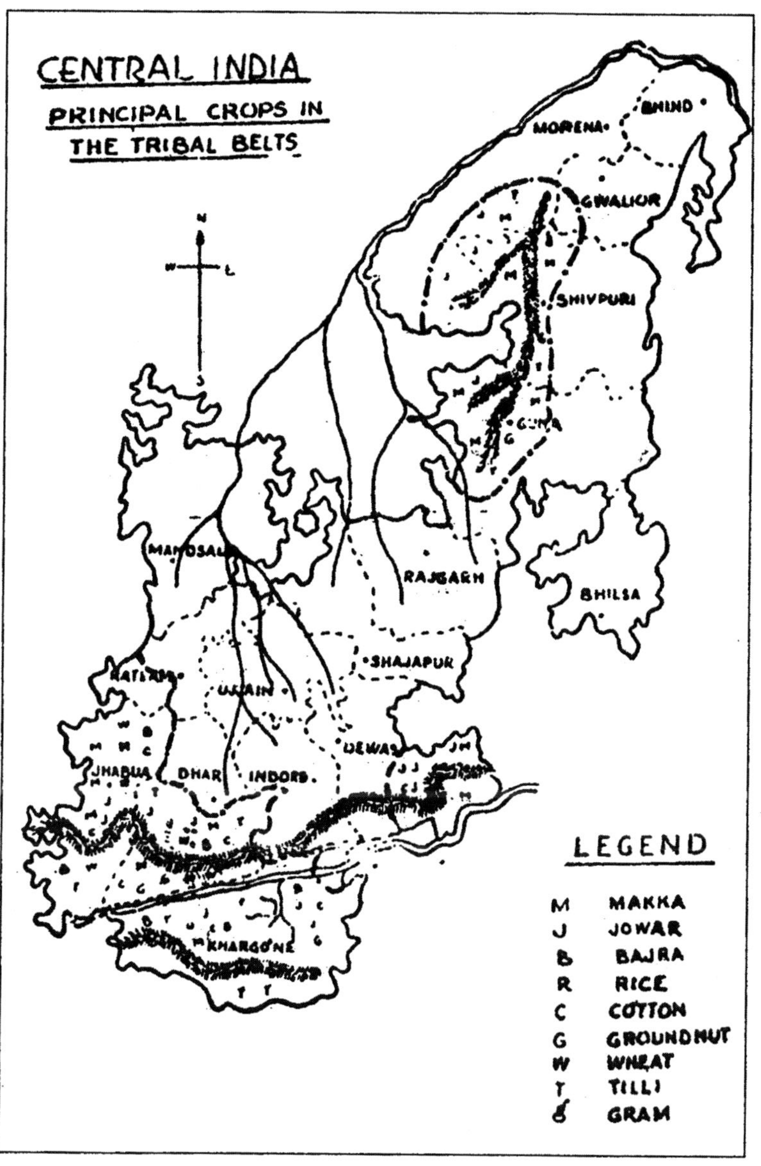
CENTRAL INDIA
PRINCIPAL CROPS IN THE TRIBAL BELTS
BHIND
MORENA
GWALIOR
SHIVPURI
GUNA
RAJGARH
BHILSA
SHAJAPUR
UJJAIN
DEWAS
DHAR
INDORE
JHABUA
KHARGONE
LEGEND
M MAKKA
J JOWAR
B BAJRA
R RICE
C COTTON
G GROUNDNUT
W WHEAT
T TILLI
G GRAM

most important crops grown are *Jowar* (Andropogon sorghum) *Bajra* (Pennisitum typhoideum), *Maize* (Zea mays), *Sevan* (Panicum milihare), *Kulthi* (Dolichos biflorus), *Tilli* (Sesamum indicum) and other small millets like panicum frumentaceum, paspalum scrobiculaturo, etc.

Besides these, where conditions are suitable, the following crops are also grown on a minor scale: *Dhan* (Oryza sativa), Tuar (Cajanus indicus), Groundnuts (Arachis hypogea), *Cotton* (Gossypium indicum), *Chilies* (Capsicum annuam) and *Urd* (Phaseolus mungo).

Bhil Belt

The table below gives the total area under the main crops in this belt in 1953-54:

TABLE 6.5

Total Area Under Various Crops in the Bhil Belt: 1953-54

	Jhabua	*Dhar*	*Nimar*
Cereals	334282	526250	660197
Pulses	69814	176883	199049
Oilseeds	54797	92860	132916
Fibres	49487	125212	357566
Fodder crops	1	2283	1905
Total area sown	508381	923488	1351633

The largest proportion in this belt is under cereals, accounting for more than half the total sown area. The predominantly tribal district of Jhabua gives a better idea of the typical picture of tribal crops. Of the 5,08,381 acres of total sown area 3,34,282 is under cereals, pulses coming next, followed by oilseeds and fibres. It is notable that area under fodder crop in the year under consideration was only 1 acre.

Table 6.6 gives the acreage under various cereals in the belt in 1954-54.

Table 6.6 shows that of the total acreage of 3,34,882 under cereals in Jhabua 1,43,136 acres is under makka. In Dhar and Nimar also it accounts for a considerable area. Makka is the most favourite cereal of the Bhils and the Bhilalas. It is grown on the

TABLE 6.6

Area Under Various Cereals in the Bhil Belt: 1953-54

(In acres)

Cereals	*Jhabua*	*Dhar*	*Nimar*
Makka	143136	96506	52549
Jowar	41251	228512	412500
Bajra	24810	45815	108894
Rice	32322	21595	21505
Wheat	4018	109365	50256
Barley	439	279	14
Other cereals	88306	24178	14479
Total	334282	526250	660197

gorma or manured land. Generally the land around the Bhil hamlet is used for this crop. This land gets the manure from the cattle kept by the cultivator. The reason for the importance attached to makka in tribal agriculture is probably due to the fact that makka takes much shorter time to ripen requiring nearly 100 days for the cobs to be ready. After Makka is harvested there is ample chance of taking a wheat crop in the field, provided the winter rain is timely. But if jowar is grown the field is occupied 4 to 5 months and there is hardly time for the rabi crop.

The other crop next in the scheme of tribal agriculture is jowar, which these people reverently call as *jowar mata* or 'Mother Jowar'. The jowar has magico-religious significance in tribal life. Small millets also occupy an important place in the tribal agriculture. Dhan is grown near streams or low places where rain water can be stored.

Commercial crops like cotton and groundnut are grown in the black soils occurring in the area. In ordinary laterites these heavy crops are not grown.

Wheat, likewise, is grown in the heavier soils with or without irrigation. Possibility of growing wheat on retentive soils without irrigation depends on the good rains preceding the rabi and liberal winter rains afterwards. These two conditions sometimes enable the Bhil cultivator to take an additional crop of wheat or gram after makka. The income so had is in the nature of a windfall and is very rare—once in many years.

The average seed rate and yield per acre in the belt are shown the following.

Crop	*Average seed rate per acre*	*Average yield per acre (unirrigated)*
Makka	8 to 10 seers	3 to 4 mds.
Jowar	6 to 7 seers	3 mds.
Bajra	3 to 4 seers	3 rods.
Barley	8 to 12 seers	4 mds.
Tilli	2 to 3 seers	3 mds.
Tuar	6 to 8 seers	3 mds.
Wheat	10 seers to 1 md.	4 mds.
Gram	32 seers to 1 md.	3 mds.

The seed rates are rather high and yields very low. The proportion of seed weight to total yield in kharif varies from 1:10 to 1:20. In rabi crops the average seed rate is higher. This is due to poor rate of germination of rabi seeds in the low-fertility and low-moisture content of the tribal soils. Due to unsuitability of the soil for rabi crops the proportion between seed weight and yield drops down considerably.

Saharia Belt

In the Saharia belt cereals occupy the largest portion of cultivated land with pulses coming next and oilseeds after that. Fibres occupy a minor place in this belt, with fodder coming last. In the Saharia agriculture *jowar, makka, bajra, dhan, tilli* and *kutki* and other millets are the staple crops. Tilli is generally grown as a commercial crops which the Saharia sells in the market either to get his other requirements or to get some cash to pay the land revenue, etc.

Jowar is grown where the *mar* land is available. Sometimes it is grown on *danda* as well. Makka is generally grown on *kitat kheda* or land near village sites which are manured in the normal course by the village cattle. Millets like *fikar* and *rameli* are generally grown on the *danda* and *rankad* land. Tilli and Bajra are also grown on this type of soil.

The average seed rate and yield per acre in the Saharia belt are shown on next page.

Seed rates on the whole are higher in this belt also. The yields are proportionately lower. As we go from kharif to rabi crop the seed rate increases without a corresponding increase in the yield.

	Average seed rate per acre	*Average yield per acre (unirrigated)*
Makka	10 seers	3 mds.
Jowar	3 seers	4 mds.
Bajra	4 seers	3 mds.
Tilli	3 seers	3 mds.
Alsi	8 seers	4 mds.
Wheat	1 md.	4 mds.
Rice	1 md.	5 mds.

This pattern again underlines the unsuitability of the average tribal holding for rabi crops.

Gond-Korku Belt

In this belt more or less the same crops are grown as in the Bhil belt. Cereals occupy the first place in this belt with fibres coming second. Pulses come third and the oilseeds last. This pattern is due to the fact that next to cereals cotton is grown extensively. Groundnut and *tilli* are not major crops in this area. Of the cereals jowar is the most important, occupying about 2/3 of the land under cereals. Jowar is the staple crop in this belt which supplies grains to men and fodder to the cattle. In the Gond-Korku economy, next to jowar comes makka and then bajra. The *khardi* soil of the region is suited to these drought resistant crops only. The God and the Korku cultivators are very indifferent to their crops. They are always running to forest either for employment as labourers or for illegal felling. Consequently, the crops are neglected and the yields are extremely poor.

Seeds: The quality of seeds plays a very important role in agriculture. Improved seeds, suitable to the soil and climate of the tract concerned, ensure good germination, better plant growth and higher and better quality of yield. In the rural economy of the tribal countryside this aspect of agronomy is very sadly neglected. There has not been sufficient research to evolve suitable strains for the hilly and the hot areas of the State. The Institute of Plant Industry at Indore has been doing excellent work in this field, but its activities are mainly confined to wheat, cotton and groundnut. For dry crops like *jowar, makka, bajra* and *millets,* etc. it has not done much work. After the formation of the Madhya Bharat the State Agriculture Department paid some attention to this problem. But as the Department was not equipped with a competent plant-breeding section, its work has largely been confined to acclimatisation and selection of more suitable strains from the existing ones.

Secondly, the seed-types found suitable by experimentation could not be popularised on a large scale. The tribal cultivator generally gets his seeds from the village *mahajan* on credit basis. After harvest the seed is returned to the *mahajan,* one and a half times or twice the weight of the seed borrowed. Seed is rarely purchased in cash from open market. Therefore, the seed type depends on the village *mahajan* who has no scruples in supplying the worst quality of grain for this purpose. Unless this source is regulated, the seed quality has no early chance of improving.

And thirdly, the tribal cultivator has become so fatalistic and so pessimistic about possibilities of improvement in his hereditary lot that even when he can afford to buy seed on cash he does not bother about any particular variety. He takes what he can get from the nearest *hat* or the village *bania.* The correlation between seed type and crop yield is not understood by him.

Manures: Manuring does not find important place in tribal agriculture, though it cannot be denied that the tribal cultivator is quite aware of its usefulness. The most familiar manure in the tribal countryside is the common farm yard or cattle manure. Green manuring is generally unknown. Even if it is made known it would have no chance in the tribal agriculture where only kharif crop is taken. It would be a suicidal luxury for the tribal cultivator to devote any part of his small holding for the entire season for green manure. The crop rotation practised in these areas does not generally include fallows that might be used for the purposes of green manuring. Chemical fertilizers are also unknown. In the absence of irrigational facilities there does not appear to be much scope for them as chemical fertilizers, particularly ammonium sulphate, are considered to be injurious to crops with sufficient irrigation.

Farm yard manure is the only manure that is generally used. But composting is not done. Sometimes plants and shrubs are burnt *in situ* to provide ash manure to the soil. The Bhils and the Bhilalas keep a large number of cattle and goats for the purposes of manure. Among them cattle folding is also practised. But the manurial attention is generally confined to fields round the hamlets. Among the Bhils the manuring is mostly confined to Makka. Among the Saharias, Gonds and Korkus where agriculture is minor and tenures are temporary, generally few cattle are owned. This source of valuable organic manures is, thus, denied to them. Poverty prohibits purchasing manure from market. And the lands continue to poorer and poorer every year.

Besides poverty the biggest factor discouraging use of manures is the form of tenure. The nature of tenure determines the duration of the interest of the cultivator in a particular holding. Manures have a residual effect, that is, there is a time lag between the application and the total utilization of manure. If the cultivator has a temporary tenure of a holding, he is not likely to invest in it by manuring it. In the *arazi ahatmal* land in the Saharia-belt, manuring is not done. Likewise, no manuring is done in the holdings cultivated on *batai* or crop sharing basis. Thus, all such land which is sublet, generally goes without manures. The proportion of temporary tenure (sub-let or held for a short stipulated period only) is quite considerable in the tribal areas. High prevalance of this form of land-rights leads to pauperisation of land.

Crop rotation: Crop rotation *(panwa)* is practised by the tribal people in all the belts. The scope of the rotation is, however, very restricted due to one-crop economy and dry farming. Wherever land is very poor and suited to only one crop, the question of crop rotation does not arise. Crop rotation is not done on the *gorma* or *kitat kheda* which gets manure. The common crop rotation when practised, is as follows:

Bhil belt: 1. Jowar, cotton, tilli, jowar, 2. Jowar gram, cotton, 3. Jowar, tilli and rameli, 4. Jowar, bajra, cotton, 5. Cotton, wheat, jowar, groundnuts.

Saharia belt: 1. Tilli, jowar, chana, 2. Dhan, jowar, matar, masur, 3. Makka, jau, wheat, 4. Jowar, wheat.

The crop rotation in the Gond-Korku belt is the same as in the Bhil belt.

Mixed cropping: Mixed cropping is resorted to guard against the total failure of crops. Generally, crops maturing at different periods are mixed together. The most common mixtures are jowar and tuar, cotton and tilli, tilli and jowar, jowar and cotton, wheat and gram, unseed and wheat.

AGRICULTURAL HOLDINGS

Before proceeding to discuss the size and nature of holding in the tribal areas, we can profitably spend some time in discussing the size and nature of holdings in the State on the whole.

The table below gives the percentage of holdings and total area under various grades of holdings:

TABIE 6.7

Grades of holdings (in acres)	*Percentage of Area under personal cultivation*			
	Percentage of holdings		*Percentage of area*	
Less than 5	46.4	81.1	10.3	42.1
5-10	22.7		16.7	
11-15	12.2		15.1	
16-30	13.2		28.0	
31-45	3.3		12.3	
46-60	1.2		6.1	
Above 60	1.2		11.5	

Source: Second Five Year Plan, p. 216.

The table shows that holdings with less than 5 acres from 46.4 per cent of the total holdings in the State. Holdings between 5-10 acres account for another 22.7 per cent and holdings in the grade 11 to 15 acres amount to 12.0 per cent. These three grades account for 81.1 percent of the total holdings. But they cover only 42.1 per cent of the total land. Holdings in the grade 16-30 acres account for 13.2 per cent of the total holding covering 28.0 per cent of total cultivated land. Holding in the grade 31 to 60 acres account for 5.7 per cent of the holdings only but covering 29.9 per cent of land.

The sample survey conducted by the author among the various tribes reveals the real position of land holdings in the tribal areas. Table 6.8 gives the results of this survey.

TABLE 6.8

Percentage of Land Holdings in Various Grades Among the Various Tribes

Sr. No.	*Tribe*	*Percentage of holdings in various grades*				
		Less than 5 acres	*5-10 acres*	*11-15 acres*	*16-20 acres*	*21 acres and above*
1.	Bhil	22.8	26.1	32.6	13.5	5
2.	Bhilala	24.6	25.5	28.0	14.7	7.2
3.	Saharia	57.4	28.6	14.0	—	—
4.	Korku	20.0	20.0	60.0	—	—
5.	Gonds	20.0	40.0	20	—	20

Source: Sample Survey.

Despite the very small size of the sample taken, the table does indicate the broad pattern of the distribution of land among the tribes. In the Bhils 22.8 per cent of holdings are below 5 acres. And in the Bhilalas 24.6 per cent of holdings are in this grade. The Korkus and Gonds show that 20.0 per cent of their holdings are in this grade. As compared to the general picture of the State we find that whereas the State percentage in this grade is 46.4 the tribes mentioned above have a much lower percentage in this grade. Only Saharias show a percentage of 57.4 in this grade which is higher than the State average. In the grade 5-10 acres the State average is 22.7 per cent. All the tribes excluding Gonds show a much higher percentage in this grade. Among the tribes next to Gonds come the Saharias with a percentage of 28.6. Bhils with 26.1 come next and Bhilalas with 25.5 come last. In the grade 11-15 acres the State average is 12 per cent. All the tribes show higher percentage in this grade. The highest average is among the Korkus, 60 per cent of whose holdings are in this grade. Bhils have 32.6 per cent, Bhilalas 28.0, Gonds 20 and Saharias 14 per cent. Despite difference in frequencies in the various grades there is broad similarity in the pattern. In the State as a whole land holdings of 15 acres and less account for 81.1 per cent of the total holdings. Comparing this pattern with that of Bhils we find that 81.5 per cent of holdings are of 15 acres and less. In Bhilalas 78.4 per cent of holdings are of 15 acres and less. Thus, in both these main tribes nearly 80 per cent of the holdings are 15 acres and less. Only 20 per cent of the holdings are above 15 acres.

The lower frequency of smaller holdings, particularly in the grades below 10 acres, and higher frequency in the grade 11-15 acres in the tribals need an explanation. Going by absolute size tribal holdings appear to be larger. But when we consider the actual cultivated and uncultivated land in the tribal holdings in general, this notion is dispelled. Most of the tribal holdings, particularly in the Bhils and Bhilalas, have quite a high percentage of *banjar* (waste) land, generally consisting of bare rocks. We had occasion to refer to this characteristic of land-use earlier in our discussion on land *per capita* in various divisions and tribal districs. We had seen the great wastage of land in the tribal areas due to its rocky nature. Secondly, these holdings contain quite a good proportion of thin land of such poor fertility that after every two crops or so it has to be rested. This every holding contains a lot of land that is not put under the plough every year. Consideration of this aspect of actually cultivable and cultivated land tends to make holdings larger—so that each holding may have some fertile land included into it. Another contributory cause is that subdivision of holdings is much less in tribal areas. Larger families being a rule and splitting up of families after the father's death being rare, the brothers stick together and add new lands to their holdings and cultivate them jointly. The State regulation subdivision of holdings into units smaller than 15 acres again acts in favour of the maintenance of bigger holdings.

Saharias, on the other hand, show the typical State pattern as they are new in the field of settled agriculture. Due to the appropriation of the most of the cultivable land by old cultivating castes, they are content to have smaller holdings. Korku and Gond pattern, as shown in the Table 6.8, is to be considered with the pre-condition that the size of sample in this case was small. They, therefore, show very broad patterns only. Gonds having 20 per cent of holdings above 21 acres, show very high proportion of big holdings. To some extent it is explained by the small size of sample and to some extent by the fact that some Gonds in this area are descendants of rich Gonds of the former ruling caste of Gondwana in Madhya Pradesh. Raj Gonds, as these castes are called, have large estates in land even now.

The general conclusion would be that of the various tribes

Saharias are the worst placed in the matter of land size. Relatively, Bhils and Bhilalas are better-off. Between the Bhils and Bhilalas the latter have generally higher percentage of bigger holdings. Generally they have better land as they are an old agricultural class, whereas the Bhil is relatively a newcomer to the field,

ECONOMIC HOLDING

Keating had defined economic holding on the basis of the net income that would accrue to a man to support him and bis family on a reasonable standard of comfort. Dr. Baljit Singh on the other hand thought that "the conception of an economic holding with reference to the standard of living of the worker is not capable of any definiteness or precision." He accordingly, suggested, "A better way of approach would be to define an economic holding for a family as one which provides remunerative employment to the members." But he warns that the economic family holding would be a moving point and would in practise be indeterminable. He then goes on to consider the size of holding from the operational point of view. This he terms as optimum cultivation unit and defines it as "of a size at which the relationship between costs and yields gives the maximum of profits per acre to the worker." The Planning Commission of India seems to have synthesized these two view points to give a new definition of family holding.

The Commission considers it from two view points;

(i) as an operational unit, and
(ii) as an area of land, which can yield a certain average income. Proceeding on this concept the Commission defines family holding as "an area equivalent, according to local conditions and under existing conditions of technique, either to a plough unit for a family of average size working with such assistance as is customary in agricultural occupations."

However extensive and well worded, the definition does not succeed in getting out of a series of abstractions. In practise, as Dr. Singh had stated earlier, the concept remain 'indeterminable.'

In the absence of detailed information regarding the

productivity of soil, value of crops raised and expenses incurred, it is not possible to suggest any exact size of economic family holdings in the various tribes of the State. The tribal people are not given to keeping quantitative estimates of the various expenses they incur and the produce they collect. Therefore, it becomes all the more difficult to arrive at an exact quantitative answer to this problem.

The Madhya Bharat Revenue and Tenancy Act laid down that no holding could be reduced to a size smaller than 15 acres of dry land and 5 acres of wet land. This probably, indicates that for the State as a whole 15 acres of dry land or 5 acres of wet land was considered to be some sort of a minimum holding. In the tribal areas irrigation is almost absent, therefore the 15 acres limit would be the only relevant prohibition. Now, the soil in the tribal areas is so poor, and a good part of the holding so rocky, steep and eroded that 15 acres here would not compare in yield with 15 acres, say, on the Plateau or the Lowland. Considering the fertility of the soil, usable proportion of the holding, and the uncertain nature of rains, the economic family holding in the tribal areas would in no case be less than 20-25 acres of dry land. Larger size of average family among the tribals and deplorable standards of capital investment would also support this contention. This finds support it the researches made in similar tracts elsewhere. For instance, in the jowar-cotton tracts of Gujarat where dry farming is practised, Desai considered a holding of 15-20 acres as economic. In case of the aboriginal tribes he considered up to 25 acres as uneconomic. Not allowing extremely bad areas to get an undue weightage we can safely take the lower limit of the range and regard holdings below 20 as uneconomic. Taking roughly 21 acres and more as the size of economic family holding in the tribal areas, the picture we get is a very dismal one. More than 74.2 per cent of the Bhils have uneconomic holdings, 73.2 per cent of Bhilala holdings are uneconomic. Among the Saharias, Korkus and even Gonds more than 90 per cent holdings are uneconomic. In these last three tribes a very small fraction of cultivation is found in the group having economic holdings. Relatively speaking, the Bhils and the Bhilalas are better placed in this matter than the Saharias, the Korkus and the Gonds.

LAND REVENUE

Land revenue is the most important State tax. Land revenue is the oldest of all taxes known to us from the early Vedic period. It was charged as the king's share in the agricultural produce of the cultivator. Manu had fixed this share between 1/6 to 1/12 of the gross produce depending on the quality of soil. Kautilya had fixed the Royal share as 1/6 of the produce. This share was termed as *ball* or *bhaga.*

In Madhya Bharat, the different regions had different systems of land administration. The former Gwalior State had large areas under the zamindari system and the rest of the States, including Holkat State (Indore State), had ryotwari systems and were duly surveyed and settled. Areas like Alirajpur and Jobat (district Jhabua) were largely non-surveyed and non-settled. According to the system of land administration the methods of land rent assessment were also different in different areas. The settled areas had adopted more or less empirical methods of assessing the land revenue. The areas that were not settled had either summary settlements or *ad hoc* settlements.

In the southern part of Madhya Bharat, which covers the Bhil and the Gond-Korku belts, the most advanced State in this respect was the Holkar State. It had carried out elaborate and painstaking settlements periodically and its land administration was emulated by other States like Dhar and Dewas.

Settlement reports of the Holkar State provide us with a good source of the study of the various aspects of land revenue. It is relevant from the point of view of tribal economy also, as the Holkar State included large Bhil-Bhilala areas in Khargone (now District Nimar) and Petlawad (now district Jhabua), and the Gond-Korku areas of Nemawar (now district Dewas).

The land revenue in the Holkar State was assessed on the following consideration:

(i) character and capacity of soils,
(ii) the caste, character and economic condition of the tenantry,
(iii) the character of the crops produced,
(iv) the distance from the market,
(v) the means of communications, and

(vi) the paying capacity of the cultivators.

Assessment done on this basis yielded very divergent incidences of land revenue. In Khargone, for instance, the assessment per acre was as high as Rs. 3 and as low as Annas 5. The fertile Indore district had an all round incidence of Rs. 3-12-0 per acre. In Nemawar it was Rs. 1-12-4 and in Nemar only Rs. 1-6-3. The wet incidence was about $4^1/_2$ times as much as the dry one. For the State as a whole the all round incidence was Rs. 2-1-0 per acre. Considering that 30 per cent of the occupied area was uncultivated, the incidence was in effect much higher. The share of the State amounted to not more than 1/11 of the gross produce from agriculture.

This was in 1929. Coming to the more recent past we have no settlement data to go by for the discussion of the incidence of land revenue in Madhya Bharat. We can, however, get some idea of the incidence of land revenue per acre by the size of the agricultural population, acreage under cultivation and the total land revenue assessed. The table below gives these figures with relation to the Madhya Bharat in general and the tribal district of Jhabua in particular.

TABLE 6.9

Land Revenue Per Capita and Per Acre

	Madhya Bharat	*Jhabua Dist.*
1. Agricultural Population	4896788	330934
2. Land Under cultivation (acres)	10916951	467103
3. Land revenue (Rs.)	30997676	603009
4. Per capita cultivated land (acres)	2.23	1.41
5. Per capita land revenue (Rs.)	6.33	1.80
6. Per acre land revenue	1.80	1.28

Above table shows that per capita cultivated land in Madhya Bharat 1971-72 was 2.23 acres, but in Jhabua per capita cultivated land was only 1.41 acres. On the basis of this land distribution the per capita land revenue in the whole state worked out to Rs. 6.33 whereas in the tribal Jhabua it was only Rs. 1.80. Taking the incidence of land revenue per acre of land we find that in the state as a whole this insidence was Rs. 1.80 and in Jhabua it was Rs. 1.28. As compared to the state as a whole Jhabua has a lower per capita land revenue and per acre land revenue. This is explained by the fact that the cultivated land as related to total cultivating population is lower in Jhabua. Lower quality of land means lower assessment of land revenue per acrce. The state as a whole shows a high per capita land revenue as it includes land of better grades with higher quality of soil and more proportion of irrigation. Various cash crops like cotton, wheat and groundnut are grown in these areas. Communications are better and the markets are nearer. The general level of economic activity is at a higher pitch and the economic condition of the cultivators in general is much better than in Jhabua.

The tribal setting throughout the state presents the same characteristics so far as the various factors affecting land revenue are concerned. Therefore, with very slight variations the per capita incidence of land revenue would be about the same in the Saharia and the Gond-Korku belts as in the Jhabua.

New Technology and Agricultural Development in Tribal Areas

L.N. BHAGAT*

INTRODUCTION

The increasing role of new technology for agricultural development has been well established by the results of agricultural research stations. They claim that an optimum package of new technology consisting of High Yielding Variety (HYV) seeds, chemical fertilisers, insecticides, etc. leads to substantial increases in the yields, especially of paddy and wheat. A fast-growing population and frequent drought and floods have made it absolutely essential to raise the level of agricultural output and maintain it so. In fact, "the man who is bounded by traditional agriculture cannot produce much food, no matter how rich the land. Thrift and work are not enough to overcome the niggardliness of this type of agriculture. To produce an abundance of farm products requires that the farmer has access to and has

*The author is indebted to Dr. (Mrs.) V. Mukerji, Professor of Economics, Calcutta University, for her guidance.

the skill and knowledge to use what science knows about soils, plants, animals, and machines," (Schultz, 1964). Therefore, the study of the problems of transforming traditional agriculture in tribal areas, particularly where the farmers are generally accused of practising the traditional method of agriculture owing to their rigid socio-economic attitudes, deserves special attention.

The present paper attempts to examine the problems and prospects of agricultural development in the tribal-concentrated Chota Nagpur region through the use of New Agricultural Practices (NAPs). The Chota Nagpur Plateau is one of the three natural divisions of Bihar with characteristics distinguishing it from the rest of Bihar. It also facilitates the identification of some regional characteristics responsible for the differences in the adoption behaviour and the pace of agricultural development. Besides this, some *ad hoc* studies conducted[1] at village level, related to the Chota Nagpur region, have been used with a view to collecting some information about the motivation, awareness and adoption of NAPs and specific problems faced by them with tribal and non-tribal disinctions.

The tribal concentration in the Chota Nagpur region is borne out by the fact that about 92.3 per cent of all the tribals of Bihar reside in this region, as per the 1971 census. This is why the region is also called "Tribal Bihar." The concentration is the highest in the Ranchi district where 58.1 per cent of the total district population is tribal, followed by Singhbhum, Santhal Pargana, Palamau, Giridih, Dhanbad and Hazaribagh districts with 46.1 per cent, 36.2 per cent, 19.1 per cent, 13.7 per cent, 10.6 per cent and 8.7 per cent of tribals respectively. Oraons, Kharias and Mundas are the major tribals settled in the Ranchi district, Santals in the Santhal Pargana and the Ho tribe is to be found in the Singbhum district. These five major tribes together cover about 83 per cent of the total tribal population in Bihar as per the 1961 census.

It may be noted, at the very outset, that the tribals of Chota Nagpur significantly differ from other Indian tribals in many respects: (a) Most of the tribals of Chota Nagpur are settled agriculturists and possess land. There is evidence that many of them (32.5 per cent as per 1971 census) possess more than 5 acres of cultivable land (Draft Sub-Plan for Tribal Region of Bihar, 1974-79). (b) The tribal farming system is almost the same as that of non-tribals in the region. Though living amid hills and forests

(41.6 per cent of the total area is covered with hills and forests), the tribals of Chota Nagpur prefer to live in villages and do not practise shifting cultivation, except for a few minor tribal communities like the Hill Kharia of Singhbhum and the Souria Paharia of Santhal Pargana (Vidyarthi, 1964). As per the information available for the year 1960-61, we find that only 5.9 per cent of the total tribal population engaged in cultivation used shifting cultivation as against 73.5 per cent, 66.6 per cent, 59.7 per cent, 51.1 per cent and 47.7 per cent in Manipur, Orissa, Tripura, Andhra Pradesh and Assam (Report of the Scheduled Areas and Scheduled Tribe Commission, 1961). (c) The system of communal ownership of land among the tribals, except among the Ho tribals[2] is also not found in Chota Nagpur but observed by others in other Indian states in their respective studies. (Goswami and Saikia, 1970 and Roy Burman and Sharma, 1970).

Sachidananda (1964) has observed that "the social background of the Chota Nagpur tribes is very much different from that of African, Melanesian or even NEFA and Assam tribes. In the latter areas in tribal regions we have only tribals and no one else, at least till recently. In Chota Nagpur in most areas, we have numerous Hindu communities living in the tribal village for many centuries." Prasad (1961) has also noted that "with improved communication and technical developments and through significant changes in the attitudes and beliefs the tribal people of Chota Nagpur came more and more in touch with the forces of contemporary society elsewhere." In fact, all these special characteristics of the Chota Nagpur tribals distinguishing them from other Indian tribals are mainly attributable to the rapid social changes observed in Chota Nagpur over the last few decades or so.[3]

NEW TECHNOLOGY AND AGRICULTURAL DEVELOPMENT IN CHOTA NAGPUR

In this section we examine the extent of adoption of NAPs and agricultural performance as measured in respect of agricultural productivity per unit of area in the Chota Nagpur region as compared to that of other regions of Bihar during 1976-77. A brief sketch of the recent village survey conducted by the author is also presented. This gives some idea of the extent of adoption of NAPs by the tribal and the non-tribal farmers of Chota Nagpur.

Table 7.1 showing the regional disparities in the level of adoption of NAPs reveals that the adoption index (see Appendix A for methods of preparing the adoption index) for Chota Nagpur is remarkably lower than that of other regions of Bihar even though the average size of operational holdings is higher for this region. This may be so because the farmers though having sufficient land lack capital which is essential for purchasing new seeds, fertilisers and machines. The level of agricultural productivity is closely associated with the level of adoption[4] which emphasises the role of NAPs in agricultural development in Bihar. The lower level of adoption of NAPs in Chota Nagpur has resulted in lower agricultural productivity, leading to stagnation and backwardness of the region (Chota Nagpur). It should be noted, however, that the average agricultural productivity per unit of area in the Chota Nagpur plateau region as compared to that of the plain regions of Bihar is not so low as observed in the case of the average adoption index. This indicates that the Chota Nagpur farmers, who mostly grow traditional varieties of seeds using organic manures and traditional agricultural implements, are quite efficient in their own traditional method of cultivation.

Table 7.2 showing the adoption behaviour of 41 wheat-growing farmers in a tribal village indicates that both tribal and non-tribal farmers are using NAPs. The use of chemical fertiliser and HYV seeds is much more widespread than that of insecticides and machines in both the communities as shown by the total adoption index of the individual practices. The table also reveals that the tribal farmers hold landed property but other concomitants are lacking, resulting in a lower average adoption index (2.79) as compared to that of the non-tribal farmers (4.08).[5] It should be noted, however, that even though the average adoption indices of tribal and non-tribal farmers differ significantly (though marginally at 10 per cent level of significance), it has not resulted in so much difference in the average yield-rate observed by the farmers in the village. This might be attributed to the fact that the tribal farmers who mostly grow traditional varieties of wheat are quite efficient in this respect of farming wheat, using their own traditional methods of cultivation supplemented by the nominal use of chemical

TABLE 7.1

Adoption of NAPs and Agricultural Productivity in Bihar During 1976-77

Region	*Adoption of NAPs (individual items)*			*Adoption index (Regional average)*	*Agricultural productivity** (in Rs./ha.)*	*Index of agricultural productivity (Regional averages)*	*Average size of operational holdings (in ha.)*
	Per cent of area under HYV seeds of paddy and wheat	*Total consumption of fertiliser (nutrient) per ha. of gross sown area (in kg.)*	*Total value of machines* used for agricultural purposes per ha. of net sown area (in Rs.)*				
North Bihar							
Plain Region	33.64	18.74	169.36	110.43	387.11	104.22	0.84
South Bihar							
Plain Region	38.03	31.99	186.66	130.02	577.91	112.99	1.01
Chota Nagpur							
Plateau Region	11.02	4.27	30.93	36.20	321.89	73.00	1.91
Bihar State	25.82	18.65	134.58	100.00	435.52	100.00	1.11

Notes: The figures are computed from the original values collected from various sources: (1) *Bihar Statistical Hand Book, 1978,* (2) Office of the Directorate of Statistics and Evaluation, Government of Bihar, Patna, (3) Office of the Directorate of Agriculture, Government of Bihar, Patna, (4) Agricultural Census (1976-77), Revenue (Agricultural Census) Department, Government of Bihar, (mimeo), (5) *Fertiliser Statistics, 1977-78.*

* Machines used for agricultural purposes, included in this study are tractors, power tillers, pumping sets, (diesel and electric), sprayers and dusters, and the value of machines is evaluated as per average market price.

** Gross value of agricultural output (the value of 10 major crops grown in Bihar, covering about 85 per cent of the gross sown area) at constant (1961) prices per unit of area is taken to indicate roughly the level of agricultural productivity.

TABLE 7.2

Adoption Index of 41 Wheat Growing Farmers in a Tribal Village (Kutua in Ranchi District) During 1979-80

Farming Community	*Number of wheat growing farmers*	*Total adoption index of individual practices*				*Total adoption index (all practices)*	*Average adoption index*	*Average yield rate (in quintal per acre)*	*Average from size (in acre)*
		Fertiliser	*HYV seeds*	*Insecti-cides*	*Machines (diesel pumps)*				
Tribal Farmer	28	54	22	2	—	78	2.79	4.70	10.86
Non-Tribal Farmers	13	23	14	8	8	53	4.08	5.22	8.46
All Farmers	41	77	36	10	8	131	3.20	4.91	10.10

Note: The adoption index of a farmer for a specific agricultural practice is taken as the number of years he has been using that practice. Thus, if a farmer uses fertiliser for 3 years, HYV seeds for 2 years and insecticides for 1 year, his overall adoption index is 6.

Source: Bhagat (1981a).

fertilisers. The tribal farmer, as the interview reveals, also uses organic manures, besides using chemical fertilisers in growing wheat. It was noticed that the average yield-rate of the traditional variety of wheat was considerably higher for the tribal farmers (3.53 quintal per acre) than that for non-tribal farmers (2.36 quintal per acre) in the village. It was also noticed that the average yield-rate of HYV wheat was almost the same for both the communities, which might be because the problems faced by the farmers with regard to the use of NAPs are almost the same for both the communities (for details see Bhagat, 1981a).

PROBLEMS OF AGRICULTURAL DEVELOPMENT

In fact, the proper use of new technology requires motivation towards the innovation, awareness and intensity of adoption, investment capacity, infrastructural facilities for using the practices managerial capacity and, of course, the appropriateness of the new technology for the users. Therefore, in an attempt to identify the real cause of the low level of adoption in the Chota Nagpur region (as noted earlier) we have examined the problem in the light of the following tentative hypotheses: (i) Chota Nagpur farmers are sufficiently motivated to use NAPs, (ii) adequate infrastructural facilities necessary for using the new practices are not available, and (iii) the package of new technology is not appropriate in the sense that it does not suit the pockets of the poor farmers, specially tribals.

Motivation of Chota Nagpur Farmers Towards the Innovation

Though the level of adoption of the NAPs in the Chota Nagpur region is very low as compared to those of other regions of Bihar, there is sufficient evidence at the village level that the farmers are gradually adopting the practices and sharing the benefits of the Green Revolution. Our village survey (Bhagat, 1981a) indicates the late adoption of NAPs in the Chota Nagpur region. It was also observed that one non-tribal farmer had adopted the practice in 1975-76 and then other non-tribal and tribal farmers used the practice in producing wheat. It is interesting to note that in the village under survey, about 57.7 per cent of the total farmers (50 per cent of the tribal farmers and 61.5

per cent of the non-tribal farmers) introduced wheat in their crop-portfolio for the first time in 1979-80, motivated, as the interview revealed, mainly by the failure of kharif cereals caused by the monsoon failure. The study indicates that all the 41 farmers used the chemical fertiliser but none of them followed the prescribed dose. From the interview with the farmers it was clear that they had used the chemical fertiliser without knowing its specific role and nutrient value. Thus, the late adoption of NAPs in the tribal village might indicate the fact that the diffusion of innovation takes time to reach the poor farmers in rural areas owing to various social, financial and informational constraints.[6]

The use of chemical fertiliser by the farmers, without being informed of its use, was also established by the findings of an earlier study relating to this region made by the Xavier Institute of Social Service (1978), Ranchi during 1977-78.[7] In an another survey (Xavier Institute of Social Service, 1979) they observed that none had adopted the practice but 15.5 percent of respondents expressed their willingness to learn the NAPs. Lavania and Srivastava (1978) have noted that "the farm people particularly the tribal farmers are now responsive to new innovations in farm technology and are introducing new strains of high-yielding seeds on their farms." A van Exem (1973) has also indicated that in some parts of Chota Nagpur the farmers have taken to the use of fertilisers on a fairly large scale.

Availability of Infrastructural Facilities in Chota Nagpur

Infrastructure in its broad sense, used in this study, covers the items which are needed for the successful use of NAPs and provide external economies to the farmers as a whole. The existing infrastructural facilities (main items) in Bihar during 1976-77 are presented in Table 7.3.

Table 7.3 indicates that the infrastructural facilities are relatively more abundant in the South Bihar Plain region (which may be due to the vicinity areas of State capital) followed by the North Bihar Plain and the Chota Nagpur region in that order. The basic facilities like irrigation and credit are absymally lower in Chota Nagpur as compared those of the other regions. The Chota Nagpur farmers, because of their socio-economic backwardness, deserve special attention as regards the provision of extension services but they have been unfortunate in this respect. In fact,

TABLE 7.3

Infrastructural Facilities in Bihar During 1976-77

Region	*Some Selected Items of Infrastructure*			*Composite index of infrastructure (regional averages)*
	Percentage of total irrigated area to gross area sown	*Availability of Agricultural credit through various agencies (viz. government co-operatives and commercial banks) per rural family (in Rs.)*	*Number of Composit demonstrations for paddy and wheat per block*	
North Bihar				
Plain Region	25.4	45.2	19.40	92.54
South Bihar				
Plain Region	57.5	65.8	18.55	143.88
Chota Nagpur				
Plateau Region	9.2	23.4	11.46	50.51
Bihar State	31.8	46.3	16.54	100.00

*Composite index of infrastructure includes seven items. Other items, besides those presented in the table, are: (i) the rural literacy rate in percentage, (ii) percentage of villages electrified, (iii) road length per thousand square kilometers, and (v) the number of regulated markets per block.

Note: The presented figures are computed from original values collected from various sources such as: (i) Office of the Directorate of Agriculture, Government of Bihar, Patna, (ii) *Bihar Statistical Hand Book, 1978, and Bihar Through Figures, 1977,* both published by the Directorate of Statistics and Evaluation, Government of Bihar, Patna.

the human capital of Chota Nagpur has been neglected by the Government through its discriminating policies. Singh (1979) has already noted that "imbalances in investment patterns since the beginning of the First Five Year Plan have led to the neglect of the human capital in tribal Bihar."

In our study (Bhagat, 1981b) it has been observed that irrigation and credit facilities in the district during 1976-77 significantly explain the inter-district variations in the level of adoption in Bihar (the coefficients of irrigation and credit variables in the multiple regression equation came out significant at 0.1 per cent level of significance). But unfortunately, these facilities are greatly lacking in the Chota Nagpur region, resulting in a lower level of adoption of NAPs. The empirical evidence presented above sufficiently indicates that the Chota Nagpur farmers are not irresponsive to NAPs but that they do not get an opportunity to respond in the sense that a viable minimum of infrastructural facilities does not exist. Adoption of NAPs might be forthcoming if adequate infrastructure was made available.

It may also be noted that special assistance in the form of removing the acidity characteristics of the soil is needed as a prerequisite for adoption of NAPs for the farmers of Chota Nagpur because "the acidic soils of Bihar[8] not only give low yields of crops without manuring but also show a poor response to fertilisers" (Mathur and Srivastava, 1980). Schultz (1978) in his editorial remark has noted that wihout optimum incentives it is not possible for farmers in many low income countries to produce the potential supply of food.

Appropriateness of New Technology for the Chota Nagpur Farmers (Specially Tribals)

The crux of the problem of modern technology is the cost involved in using it. We shall examine the appropriateness of the new technology, keeping in view the amount that the Chota Nagpur farmers are ready to invest.

From the discussion the author had with the relevant officials it appears that the scientists of the experimental station blame the extension officers for not extending the technology to the farmer's plot. On the contrary, the extention officers allege that the package of modern technology is not acceptable to the poor farmers. Recent findings of the Operation Research Unit of the Birsa Agricultural University,[9] Ranchi, provide a partial solution to this prolonged dispute. The chief scientific officer at the Operational Research Unit claims through various experiments on farmer's plots using four-plot techniques, that the available technology is beyond the reach of the pockets of the poor farmers. Though some farmers used the HYV technology by diluting the recommended package according to their need and ability, they could not succeed in getting a good yield owing to their poor management and perhaps the inappropriateness of the package finally used in the place of the recommended package (experimental results are given in Appendix B).

Moshin (1978) has rightly argued in favour of intermediate technology for tribal farmers and emphasised the need for developing different levels of technology even for a particular crop, to suit the investment capacity of the farmer. We find in village survey (Bhagat, 1981a) that the farmers invest on an average Rs. 400 per acre in growing wheat whereas the op.timum package of modern technology consisting of HYV seeds, fertilisers, insecticides and machines, etc. developed at the Ranchi Experimental Research Station requires an investment of at least Rs. 1000 per acre at the 1979-80 prices. It is recommended, therefore that a package of technology costing only Rs. 400 (approximately) with emphasis on simple cultural practices be offered to begin with. Once the farmers observe a viable increase in yield, they will automatically select a better technology costing Rs. 500 and upwards according to their choice. Their choice among the options available to them, will reveal the appropriateness of the technology for them. Thus the level of technology will increase with the socio-economic growth of the farmers.

Prospects of Agricultural Development

The prospects of agricultural development through the use of new technology, specially dry land farming technology developed at the Dry-Land Agricultural Research Unit of the Birsa Agricultural University at Ranchi, is examined in terms of the latent yield potential of the crops grown in the region and the possibility of introducing new crops suitable for the soils of Chota Nagpur.

Table 7.4 showing the average (actual) yield-rate and potential yield-rate of selected crops, sufficiently indicates that the technology developed by the scientists at Ranchi can sufficiently be transferred to other areas of the Chota Nagpur region as indicated by the yield performance at the pilot project area situated at Chandwa in the Palamau district. As much as 100 per cent transfer is observed in the case of upland rice (Bala), sorghum, groundnut and maize. But if we compare these results with what the Chota Nagpur farmers are actually getting, the results are very disappointing. Utilisation of yield potential in the case of major cereals grown in the region like upland rice, brown gora, ragi and maize is only 38.9 per cent, 32.0 per cent, 45.0 per cent, and 36.7 per cent respectively of their potential values. Groundnut, soyabean, sorghum and safflower are promising new introductions but the cultivation of these crops seems to be very difficult without special assistance and care because the risk-averter farmers first want to secure the minimum for their subsistence rather than introduce new crops on experiment. Adequate marketing facilities are, however, essential for crops like soyabean and safflower.

TABLE 7.4

Crop Yield at the State (Regional) Level, Plot Project Level and at the Research Station

Sl. No.	*Crop*	*Average yield in quintal per hectare*		
		State (Regional)	*Plot project area (Chandwa)*	*Research station (Ranchi)*
1.	Uplad rice (Bala)	7	18	18
2.	Brown gora	8	20	25
3.	Ragi	9	15	20
4.	Sorghum	*	25	35
5.	Groundnut	*	15	15
6.	Soyabean	*	10	15
7.	Maize	11	30	30
8.	Linseed	2	4	6
9.	Safflower	*	6	8
10.	Gram	7	12**	10
11.	Barley	8	10	15

Note: *New crops.
**On heavier soils.

Source: Mohsin and Sinha (1979), Table 2.

It should be noted that in some special varieties of crops the use of the recommended dose of fertiliser alone (Linseed T-39 and safflower A-300 are responsive to nitrogen only) raises the yield considerably and earns good profit. As per the estimate available[10] we find that upland rice (Bala), maize (GS-2), ragi (A-400), groundnut (AK-12-24), soyabean (Punjab-1), linseed (T-39) and safflower (A-300) earn as profit per rupee spent on fertiliser 2.80, Rs. 2.00, Rs. 3.00, Rs. 2.60, Rs. 2.40, Rs. 1.50 and Rs. 1.50 respectively. It may also be noted that the land productivity in the Chota Nagpur region can be increased manifold simply by removing the acidity characteristics of the soil through the appropriate liming procedure. At Kanke, a series of studies was made with a large number of crops and the results clearly indicate that liming increased the yields of crops like cereals, pulses, cotton, groundnut, fodder crops and vegetables 5 to 16 times. Response to fertilisers also increased considerably in the presence of lime (Mathur and Srivastava, 1980).

CONCLUSION

We find that the level of adoption is associated with the level of agricultural productivity in Bihar and a very low level of adoption had led to the low level of agricultural productivity in the Chota Nagpur region as compared to that of other regions of Bihar. The low level of adoption in the Chota Nagpur region does not, however, mean that the farmers are irresponsive to the NAPs but that they do not get an adequate opportunity to respond in the sense that the viable minimum of infrastructure needed for the successful use of the NAPs does not exist. There is sufficient evidence to show that the farmers of Chota Nagpur, including tribals, have made an initial attempt to change over from traditional to modern agricultural practices. In most cases they have used the practice after diluting the recommended package as per their choice and ability, resulting in a lower yield than what would have been possible with the same amount of money and effort spend under proper guidance. Therefore, one would expect that the adoption of NAPs that promote agricultural productivity might be forthcoming when adequate infrastructure is made available. The study indicates that only a small percentage of the latent yield-potential has been utilised by the farmers owing to various social, financial, institutional and informational constraints. Until these constraints are removed by the Government through heavy investment and special care, Chota Nagpur farmers can not be blamed for being unresponsive to NAPs and ultimately for their backwardness and poverty.

The study emphasises the need for providing necessary

infrastructural facilities to the farmers on a large scale not only in the form of increased irrigation and credit facilities but also in the form of crop-management instructions and soil-management facilities. What type of irrigational system and what institution for credit distribution would suit the requirement of the region and farmers of the region respectively is again a matter for social science research to determine through intensive field studies. In his recent model of agricultural development Ruttan (1977) has emphasised the need for institutional innovations and noted that "unless social science research can generate new knowledge, leading to viable institutional innovations and more effective institutional performance, the potential productivity growth made available by scientific and technical innovation will be underutilised." The study also emphasises the need for a simultaneous attempt at transforming the traditional agriculture in the Chota Nagpur region by removing social, economic, institutional, technical and managerial constraints.

NOTES AND REFERENCES

1. By the author and some others relating to the village of Ranchi and Singhbhum districts of the Chota Nagapur region.
2. It should be noted, however, that even among the Ho tribals this attitude has undergone change in the process of transition. "Today the family has become the dominant element in their social organisation, that is, the interests of the family are regarded as of greater importance than that of the Hatu (village) or even a Killi clan," (Prasad, 1961, p. 108).
3. Studies indicating social change among the tribals of Chota Nagpur are Bougaert (1975), Ivern (1969), Lall (1963), Prasad (1961), Sachidananda (1964), Sen (1968) and Vidyarthi (1971).
4. A log-linear regression of agricultural productivity (Y) on adoption index (X) estimated from the data of 31 districts during 1976-77 is given below: Log Y = 2.94+0.3651 Log X: $R^2 = 0.753$

   (t = 9.4098)

   The coefficient of log X is significant at 0.1 per cent level of significance.
5. Though the total adoption index of 28 tribal farmers is higher than the total adoption index of 13 non-tribal farmers, the average adoption index is lower for tribal farmers (2.79) than non-tribal farmers (4.08), which has been used for measuring the relative level of adoption of NAPs (i.e., adoption rate) of the two farming communities in the village.
6. For a detailed analysis of the lag in "acceptance" of innovation, see Griliches (1957).

7. They have interpreted the estimated correlation coefficient between aware, ness and adoption (r = 0.35) by saying that only 12 per cent of adoption of modern practices can be explained though their adequate knowledge of modern agricultural practices.
8. The problem of acidity is particularly severe in the Chota Nagpur Plateau region where the uplands and to a great extent medium lands are acidic.
9. It refers to the old Ranchi Agricultural College, Kanke Campus, a unit of the Rajendra Agricultural University, Bihar. Recently, it has been converted into a university and named Birsa Agricultural University, Ranchi.
10. Through personal communication from Dr. R.K. Sinha, Senior Scientist-Cum-Associate Professor and Head, Department of Agronomy, Birsa Agricultural University, Ranchi.

REFERENCES

A. Van Exem, S.J. (1973), *Basic Socio-Economic Attitudes of Chota Nagpur Tribals,* The Catholic Co-operative Society, Ranchi.

Bhagat, L.N. (1981a), "Adoption of New Agricultural Practices in TRIBAL BIHAR—The View from a Village," *The Economic Studies,* Vol. 22, No. 2, August 1981, pp. 147-56.

———, (1981b), "Adoption of New Agricultural Practices in Bihar—A Study of Socio-economic Implications" (mimeo).

Bougaert, V.D. Michael, (1975), "Training Tribal Entrepreneurs: An Experience in Social Change," *Social Change,* March-June.

Draft Sub-Plan for Tribal Region of Bihar, 1974-79, Chota Nagpur-Santhal Pargana Autonomous Development Authority, Ranchi, March 1974, p. 46. (mimeo).

Geogaonkar, S.G. (ed) (1979), *Problems of Development of Tribal Areas,* Leela Devi Publication, Delhi.

Goswami, P.C. and Saikia, P.D. (1970), "Problems of Agricultural Development in Tribal Areas," *Indian Journal of Agricultural Economics,* Vol. 25, No. 3, pp. 140-48.

Griliches, Z. (1957), "Hybrid Corn: An Exploration in the Economics of Technological Change," *Econometrica,* Vol. 25, No. 4, pp. 501-22.

Iven, F. (1969), *Chotanagpur Survey,* Indian Social Institute, New Delhi.

Lal, R.B. (1963), "Social Change among Urban Oraon," *Bulletin of the Bihar Tribal Research Institute,* Vol. 5, No. 1, pp. 24-37.

Lavania, G.S., and Srivastava, G.G. (1978), "Production and Resource Use Pattern on Tribal and Non-tribal Farms in Hill Area of Chota Nagpur (Bihar)," abstracted in *Indian Journal of Agricultural Economics,* Vol. 33, No. 4, pp. 53-54.

Mathur, B.S. and Srivastava, L.L. (1980), "Increasing Productivity of Acid Soils in the Eastern Region—Bihar," in Symposium on Increasing Productivity of Acid Soils in the Eastern Region, The Fertiliser

Association of India, Eastern Region, pp. 89-100.

Mohsin, M.A. (1978), "Choice of Technology for Tribal Farmers," *Journal of Social and Economic Studies,* Vol. 6, No. 1, pp. 111-14.

———, and Sinha, N.P. (1979), "Rainfed Agricultural Technology for Bihar," paper presented at the Kharif Workshop of the Department of Agriculture, Government of Bihar held at Patna on April 27-29 (mimeo).

Operation Research Project Experiments, 1978-79, Operation Research Unit, Birsa Agricultural University, Ranchi (unpublished).

Patel, M L. (ed.) 1972), *Agro-Economic Problems of Tribal India,* Progressive Publishers, Bhopal.

Prasad, N. (1961), *Land and People of Tribal Bihar,* The Bihar Tribal Research Institute, Government of Bihar, Ranchi.

Report of the Scheduled Area and Scheduled Tribes Commission, Government of India, New Delhi, 1961.

Roy Burman, B.K. and Sharma, P.S. (1970), "Tribal Agriculture in India," *Indian Journal of Agricultural Economics,* Vol. 25, No. 3, pp. 149-60.

Ruttan, V.W. (1977), "Induced Innovation and Agricultural Development," *Agricultural Development Council Staff Paper,* 77-1, reprinted from Food Policy, Vol. 2, No. 3, pp. 196-216.

Sachidananda (1964), "Social Change in Chota Nagpur," *Bulletin of the Bihar Tribal Research Institute,* Vol. 6, No. 2, pp. 220-39.

Schultz, T.W. (1964), *Transforming Traditional Agriculture,* Yale University Press, New Haven, Indian Edition (1970) by Lyall Book Depot, Ludhiana.

——, (ed.), (1978), *Distortions of Agricultural Incentives,* Indian University Press.

Sen, J. (1968), *Community Development in Chotanagpur,* The Asiatic Society, Calcutta.

Singh, B. and Bhandari, J.S. (ed.), (1979), *The Tribal World and it's Transformation,* Concept Publishing Company, New Delhi.

Singh, G. (1979), Economics of Human Capital of Tribal Bihar," Abstracted in the Conference Issue of the *Indian Economic Journal,* Vol. 1, No. 2, p. 106.

Vidyarthi, L.P. (1964), *Cultural Contours of Tribal Bihar,* Punthi Pustak, Calcutta.

——, (1971), *Socio-Cultural Implications of Industrialisation in India,* Ranchi University.

Xavier Institute of Social Service (1978), "Report of the Bench Mark Survey of Eleven Villages in Kanke and Ormanjhi Blocks of Ranchi District in Bihar, 1977-78," Ranchi (mimeo).

——, (1979), "Action Proposal for Rural Reconstruction Based on Potential Recource of Five Villages in Chandil Block (Singhbhum District), March 1979," Ranchi (mimeo).

APPENDIX

ADOPTION INDEX

Adoption indices for each district are simple indices of weighted standard scores of different items of NAPs, the weights being the simple correlation coefficients between agricultural productivity (roughly measured by the gross value of agricultural output per unit of area) and different individual items of NAPs. The formula used for computing weighted standard scores of the ith district using the jth item is given below:

$$Z_{wi} = \frac{\sum_{i=1}^{m} r_{oj} z_{ij}}{\sum_{i=1}^{m} r_{oj}} \qquad \begin{array}{l} i = 1, 2, \ldots n \\ j = 1, 2, \ldots m \end{array}$$

where,

Z_{wl} = weighted standard scores of the ith district,

z_{ij} = $(x_{ij} - x_{iz})/Sx_{ij}$ = standard scores of the jth items in the ith district,

x_{ij} and S_{lxij} are mean and standard deviation of the jth item (of the ith district) of NAPs respectively,

r_{oj} = correlation coefficient between the agricultural productivity in the ith district (central value) and jth items of NAPs. An index was then prepared, adding two to it to avoid the minus sign and multiplying by fifty (the same method was employed for computing a composite index of infrastructure).

APPENDIX B

EXPERIMENTAL RESULTS

The following table shows some of the results of experiments under dry-seeding during the kharif season of 1978-79, conducted by the Operation Research Unit of the Birsa Agricultural University at Ranchi:

Experiment number	*Village (district)*	*Crop (variety)*	*Area (in acre)*	*Yield-rate (q/ha under) different treatment*			
				IVIM	*IVFM*	*FVIM*	*FVFM*
1	Barhu (Ranchi)	Paddy (Bala and Local)	0.48	17.6	6.9	15.7	5.1
6	Bara Semar-toli (Ranchi)	Ragi (A-404 and Local)	0.40	14.4	1.8	12.6	1.5

Notes: IVIM = Improved Variety and Improved Management.
IVFM = Improved Variety and Farmer's Management.
FVIM = Farmer's Variety and Improved Management.
FVFM = Farmer's Variety and Farmer's Management.

Source: Operational Research Project Experiments, 1978-79, Operation Research Unit, Birsa Agricultural University, Ranchi (unpublished).

Problems in Agricultural Development in Tribal Areas

SUBODH HANSDA

The tribal people popularly known as adivasis are scattered all over the world except the European continent. The largest concentration can be found in the African continent and the second largest concentration is in India. The total population of tribals in India is more than 45 million which is nearly 6.5 per cent of the total population of India. There are another 15 million tribal people who are unfortunately not recognised as scheduled tribes for no fault of their own. These tribes are mainly found in the states of Assam, Andhra Pradesh, Bihar, Gujarat, Maharashtra, Madhya Pradesh, Orissa and Rajasthan. This is mainly due to the defect in the Scheduled Tribes Modification Order of 1956 and 1976. In this order a tribe is recognised as a scheduled Tribe only on an area-wise or state-wise basis and not on all-India basis. Thus a particular scheduled tribe of an area or a state may not be recognised as a Tribe in another area or a state. This is entirely against the fundamental principles of Article 15(1) and (2) and Article 19(d) and (e) of the Constitution of India.

This discrimination has deliberately been made to meet the

vested interests of the so-called politically and socially advanced sections of the society to deprive them of political and socio-economic benefits guaranteed under Articles 330, 332 and 335 of the Constitution.

There is another doubt about the genuineness of the Census figures. In all the past Censuses tribe-wise enumeration was not done due to which the real or actual tribal population is not known. However, whatever figures are obtained on the basis of the present Census document have been considered.

There are hundreds of tribal communities scattered all over the country. The largest group come from the Gonds, Santals, Bhills, Oroans, Khonds, Hols, Mundas, Boro-Kacharis, and the Nagas concentrated in the states of Assam, Andhra Pradesh, Bihar, Gujarat, Madhya Pradesh, Orissa, Rajasthan, Tripura, Manipur, Nagaland and West Bengal.

There have been several theories about the original home of the tribal people, but none seem to have established why they migrated from the hills to the plains and from the plains to the hills. Normally they are all peace-loving people not accustomed to any kind of outside interference in their socio-economic life. The political and administrative changes in the recent past have had a certain impact on their way of life resulting also in loss of landed property and frequent change of their habital place. The growth or increase of their population and the pressure on land is also responsible for their movement from place to place or area to area. Thus with the passage of time they divided themselves into three main groups:

(a) Those scattered over the South-West in the hill slopes and plateaus of the Western Ghats.
(b) Those occupying the Central belt of the hills and plateaus of Central India, south of the Indo-Gengetic plains.
(c) Those living in the mountain valleys of North-East India and the Eastern frontier of India.

Originally except for a certain percentage, all the tribal people were good agriculturists and practised shifting cultivation. It is possible that the tribals were the first to introduce plough cultivation. They are not only good agriculturists but good artisans as well. Nearly two-third of the tribal people live in the Central zone of India. This zone (Bihar, Orissa, Madhya Pradesh, Maharashtra, Gujarat, and Rajasthan) is full of natural resources. It is rich with forest and mineral wealth. The annual earnings from the forest wealth are more than Rs. 150 crores but the tribal people enjoy a very small percentage of this income. The income from mineral wealth is also not less than Rs. 10,000 crores mainly from coal and iron ore.

Various mineral wealth development projects have been located in tribal areas by which thousands of tribal families have been displaced from these areas. Neither have been displaced families been properly rehabilitated nor provided with any kind of jobs. Although no definite figure of displacement is available, it is presumed that more than 50,000 families have been displaced from various project areas to date resulting in a loss of approximately 250,000 acres of cultivable lands.

The following projects give an idea of tribal displacement.

Sl. No.	*Name of Project*	*Number of ST families displaced*	*Areas from which displaced*	*No. of ST families settled*	*Areas on which ST families settled*
1.	Maithondam (W.B.+Bihar)	3296	13138	464	2286
2.	Mayurkashkhi (Bihar)	2910	7215	—	2082
3.	Panchayat (Bihar & West Bengal)	1916	1951	—	—
4.	Hirakud (Orissa & M.P.)	1636	1116	300	—
5.	Machkund Power Project (Orissa)	1500	13705	450	2250
6.	Rourkela Steel Plant (Orissa)	1231	8158	1696	—
7.	Manindradam (Orissa)	817	4225	447	1696
8.	Sindhri Fertiliser	597	1228	973	—
9.	H.E.C., Ranchi (Bihar)	210	1502	—	—
		14113	62238	3477	8314

Source: ST Commission's Report.

The figures show that approximately 25 per cent of the displaced families have been rehabilitated on 13 per cent of their total displaced land. Thus it is presumed that nearly 40,000 families are yet to be provided with any kind of rehabilitation from among those who have been dispossessed of more than two lakh acres of cultivable land. These people have been reduced to almost homeless and landless beggars. At many places they were at the mercy of unscrupulous money lenders whose only interest was to exploit the social as well as economic condition of these people. How much land has been alienated by this process of money lending is difficult to assess for want of an extensive survey, but there is no doubt that this kind of alienation has been substantial.

Various land reform acts have been passed by all the state Governments to protect tribals from such land alienation, but these acts have not been very helpful to them. Many tribals have had to hypothicate their land against various debts contracted by them or have had their land transferred and become tenants or mortgagees on their own land.

The per capita land holding varies from state to state and from 0.5 acres in Bihar, Nagaland, Mizoram, Arunachal and Manipur to 2.5 acres in Madhya Pradesh and Maharashtra. In the absence of details of the economic survey reports of the whole country, it is difficult to give area-wise estimates of tribal land holdings. In any case they need to supplement their income either from the sale of forest products or from daily labour wage earnings.

Of the 45 million tribal people in India 90 per cent, i.e., approximately 40 million are agriculturists and 10 per cent, i.e., five million are landless agricultural labourers who depend on the sale of forest products for their living. Though there are no definite statistics, their land holdings are small and fragmented having mostly poor soil and poor irrigation facilities. During the pre-independence days their method of cultivation was elementary. This has gradually changed and in many places they are now using modern technology and science for better cultivation of their land. But this percentage is very small in comparison with other advanced sections of society in spite of the execution of the four Five Year Plans at the national level.

Nearly four million people practice shifting cultivation in the States of Assam, NEFA, Bihar, Orissa, Madhya Pradesh and Andhra Pradesh. This cultivation is popularly known as "Jhum" or "Podu." This is normally practised in the hilly forest slopes. In this system the hilly forest slopes are cleared of all existing trees or bushes. The felled trees and bushes are burned to ashes and the desired seeds are broadcast in the ash covered areas before the onset of the rainy season. After the rainy season when the crops are ripe, they are gathered and stored in houses for their consumption. This method of cultivation is very simple as no plough is used for lifting the soil, thus retaining the fertility of the soil. This cultivation is continued for two to three years or as long as the fertility of the soil remains. Then this area is abandoned for another new area. Even after 33 years of Independence this process of cultivation still continues in a number of areas.

This system may help four million people survive, but is causing serious damage to the forests. How far this problem has been solved by the Government can be well judged by the performance to settle these families permanently through Five Year Plans. In the last few years there has been little impact on the life and living of these normatic type of tribes.

On the hill slopes the agricultural land has a steep gradient and the rain water drains out instantaneously to lower regions. Therefore, it is very difficult to cultivate such lands in the normal way. Previously this was done by Terracing. Terracing is done to protect the land from soil erosion and also facilities irrigation.

The hill tribes draw water from the upper ridges through small canals to their paddy fields. Normally only paddy and wheat are grown in these areas but this was not found sufficient to sustain a family. After Independence the Government has come forward to provide more irrigation facilities to the hill people. This has on the one hand, improved their paddy fields and on the other, increased the yield due to modern methods of cultivation and irrigation. But as already pointed out the land area is so small in comparison to the tribal population, that it is difficult for a family to depend entirely on land. That is why the younger people from the hills, come down so the plains for alternate occupation. The Kumayun hills in Uttar Pradesh are a glaring example, where one sees only the women or the old people working in the paddy and wheat fields whereas the young go out of their village to the plains for alternate occupation.

Moreover, due to their difficult economic conditions, it is impossible for the tribals to go in for costly and better methods of cultivation by using improved seeds, chemical fertilisers, insecticides and better tools. This fact is borne out in that less than even 10 per cent of the total tribal population has not adopted the modern techniques of cultivation. Only the big rayots among the tribes whose percentage is very small go in for better or improved methods of cultivation but this too, in a very limited way. The reasons are obvious.

Firstly, they are mostly illiterate, the literacy rate being less than 10 per cent of their total population. Therefore, they are ignorant of the present scientific development in agriculture. Whatever they see or learn from others they try to adopt. But the most important factor of their non-adoption is their lack of faith in the advanced sections of the society who have exploited them for generations. This was proved further when the special multipurpose tribal blocks were introduced in different states during the Second Five Year Plan for the overall benefit of the tribal people. The entire benefit was enjoyed, however, by the advanced sections of the society as pointed out by the Dr. Varier Elwin Survey Committee Report of 1960.

Secondly, one of the greatest bottlenecks in switching over to modern methods of agriculture is the cost factor. The economic condition of tribals does not permit them to purchase the costly fertiliser, insecticides and agricultural implements.

Thirdly, the Government has constructed a number of irrigation schemes. But the tribal lands being small and fragmented and of poor quality, get little advantage of the irrigation schemes. Most of the Tribal lands are situated at such high places that irrigated water can rarely reach them. The water tax is also very high. The above reasons are mainly responsible for low adoptibility of modern methods of cultivation. This is also the reason why tribals still live below the poverty line.

The co-operative movement has also not made much headway among the tribal community. It is also difficult for them to take advantage of agricultural finance due to legal difficulties. The Land Alienation Act stands in their way for freely mortgaging their land to the financing institutions. In every case they need to take written permission from the Government, if they are to mortgage their land against a financial institution. This being a lengthy and time-consuming process, they are always reluctant to take advantage of such loans. All this makes very clear the fact that tribals have not been able to benefit much from the Government schemes during the Five Year Plans.

Issues in Agricultural Development in a Tribal Area—A Study of Panchmahals District

SUDARSHAN IYENGAR*

I

Every fifth tribal in Gujarat State has a home in Panchmahals and four persons out of ten in the district are tribals. For quite sometime now, the tribals have taken to agriculture as their main occupation. Almost every tribal owns a piece of land. The district as a whole has only 7 to 8 per cent agricultural labourers of the total working population. The Panchmahals tribals have been attended to by voluntary agencies since 1925 and by the government since Independence. Legislations have been passed to ensure the ownership of land to tribals and to stop illegal transfers. Soil treatment has been given to as many tribal holders as possible, irrigation potentials have been created (both big and small works), co-operatives for credit have been formed, demonstration in crops have been held, and input subsidies have

*The author wishes to thank Dr. Ravindra H. Dholakia for useful discussion on the subject.

been granted in lakhs of rupees. In spite of all these efforts, the response of tribals to modernise agriculture and improve productivity has been rather sluggish. The variation in agricultural output continues with the vagaries of monsoon. Poverty and unemployment are rampant. The seasonal migration has continued, grown and is reaching alarming magnitude. Every year representations (Political) about the drought situation in one or the other area are incessantly made at the state level.

The officialdom functions with a resigned attitude; planners are perplexed since, none of the formulae yield results when tested on the field. The political stalwarts limit the topic of tribals to speeches. The future of tribal areas thus seems quite bleak.

Is it true that tribals do not want to develop? Is it true that they do not respond to technological change in agriculture because they do not want? Is it true that tribals are not interested in increasing the productivity of land? These questions will be better answered if a tribal population is studied within a definite geo-physical context. Most of the studies so far have attempted to analyse the problems keeping in view the tribal population only. What has been overlooked is the area which tribals inhabit and the available degree of freedom to take decisions for agricultural activity. It is also worthwhile exploring whether tribal areas and tribal population have some comparative advantage in certain areas of agricultural production and other activities.

The paper attempts to examine:

1. Geo-physical features of the area under study.
2. Status of agriculture in tribal areas *vis-a-vis* the district and state.
3. Attempts made by government for agricultural development.
4. Response of tribal farmers.
5. Factors responsible for slow response.

II

Panchmahals is the eastern most district of Gujarat State. It is a border district of the state surrounded by the Banswara district of Rajasthan in the north-east and the Jhabua District of Madhya Pradesh in the south-east. The district has an area of 8866 km^2 and a population of 18.48 lakhs according to 1971 Census Reports. The district has 11 talukas of which five are tribal and are located towards the border. The distribution of tribal area and population is as under:

	Tribal talukas	*Non-tribal talukas*	*Total (district)*
Area (Per cent)	59.12	40.88	100
Tribal population to total population (Per cent)	64.90	11.68	38.55

The tribal population of the district is spread over a larger area relative to the non-tribal population. The tribal population inhabiting these areas are Bhils (73 per cent), Rathwas (6 per cent), Patelias (7 per cent), Naikdas (12 per cent) and other clans (2 per cent). The adjoining districts of Rajasthan and Madhya Pradesh are also inhabited by tribals.

The Geography

The tribal talukas of Panchmahals (Santrampur, Jhalod, Dohad, Limkhada and Devgadh Baria) form part of the Aravali range of hills. The entire district is at some height. The tribal area is a part of an undulating landscape with a height range of 150 to 300 metres. At some places the land elevates to more than 300 metres. This topography explains the spread of tribal population in a relatively larger area.

The weather conditions in the tribal area are extreme. The maximum temperature ranges between 38°C and 45°C during April, May and June and the minimum reaches 5°C in December and January. The wind velocity (annual) recorded in 1970 was 16.3 km/hour. In June it was maximum (29.6 km/hour). The district has an average annual rainfall of about 920 mm. The South-West monsoon brings the rains. The average rainfall of the tribal talukas is 875 mm. The average annual rainfal of the non-tribal talukas is 950 mm. Most of the areas in Gujarat receive rainfall from the South-West monsoon with a different variation. The coefficient of variation of rainfall is 30 to 40 per cent for the district. This variation is related to the total precipitation. About 95 per cent of the annual rainfall in the district is received during the monsoon months from June to September. July has the highest rainfall. On an average, there are 43 rainy days in a year. The statistical probability of insufficient rains is nearly 35 per cent. Every third year in the last three decades has seen drought conditions.[1] Good and even rainfall is experienced once in three to four years.[2]

Apparently, 920 mm. of rainfall seems to be sufficient for normal crop growth. What needs to be examined is whether enough water is available in the root zone of the crops after the losses run-off and deep percolation. One such rough estimate tends to conclude that the water available to the root zone of the Maize crop is not sufficient.[3] With 30 to 40 per cent variation in the total precipitation, it is thus obvious that there will be drought in certain years.

The textural status of the soil in the district is almost uniform. Barring Santrampur, which is a tribal taluka, 40 to 50 per cent of soil is of medium texture. In Santrampur taluka 60 to 80 per cent of soil is of high or light texture. The status of tribal talukas is slightly affected since Santrampur is in the class of high or light texture, the other tribal talukas have undulating topography and medium texture.

The fertility status (NPK) of soils in the district is as under:[4]

Tribal talukas	*NPK*	*Grade*	*Non-tribal talukas*	*NPK*	*Grade*
Santrampur	LLH	E	Godhra	MMH	B
Dahod	MMH	B	Shehera	LMM	D
Jhalod	MMH	B	Lunawada	LMM	D
Limkheda	LMH	D	Kalol	HMH.LMH	AD
Devgadh Baria	LMM	D	Halol	LMH	D
Jambughoda	LHM	D			

L = Light M = Medium H = High

The overall fertility status of the district is not very rosy. The majority of the area has 'D' class status which adds negatively to the overall land productivity. Santrampur taluka is again the worst with 'E' class fertility status. The tribal talukas of the district other than Santrampur seem to have an edge over the non-tribal talukas as far as fertility status is concerned.

The land productivity for the whole district which is calculated after taking into account the climate, topography, fertility, texture, etc. is as under:[5]

Tribal taluk as Talukas	*Class*	*Non-tribal*	*Class*
Santrampur	V	Godhra	III
Dahod	IV	Shehera	IV
Jhalod	IV	Kalol	III
Limkheda	IV	Halol	III
Devgadh Baria	IV	Lunawada	V
		Jambughoda	III

The productivity status of tribal talukas than the non-tribal talukas.

III

The major occupation of the workers in the district is agriculture. According to the 1971 Census, 86 per cent of the working population were engaged in agriculture, and 8 per cent were engaged as agricultural labourers. The tribal workers have still greater concentration in these two activities. Of the total tribal working population in 1971, 89 per cent were cultivators and 9 per cent were engaged as agricultural labourers. One of the features that did not get reported in the general Census was the seasonal migration of tribals to other rural and urban areas of the district as well as the state. Separate studies from time to time have been carried out to examine the migration aspect. This will be dealt with in detail later in this paper.

In the Light of the geo-physical and agro-climatic features, and the occupational structure of the population, it will be appropriate to examine the land use, cropping pattern, productivity and other related aspects of agriculture.

An end of the nineteenth century, the district area was covered with thick forests. In 1980-81, of the total cultivated and uncultivated area, 27 per cent was cropped area, 36 per cent was forest and rest was either fallow or culturable waste. By the beginning of the century, the forests area started declining. In 1900-01, the area under forest was reduced to 21 per cent of the cultivated and uncultivated area; the cropped area also came down to 20 per cent. However, by 1947 the trend became clearer and steadier. In 1947-48, the area under crops amounted to 55 per cent and under forests to 20 per cent. Within a decade (1960-61) the total cropped area to the total reporting area went upto 62 per cent and forest area came down to 12 per cent. The extensive use of land for agriculture had caught up. The *Gazetteer* (1970) states that the trend towards better utilisation of land was set in the 1960s.

The current status of land utilisation is available only upto 1974-75. It is possible to review the status of tribal and non-tribal areas separately for these years. In 1960-61 the area under forests accounted for 18 per cent of the total reported area and net area sown accounted for 54 per cent. In 1967-68 these figures were 26 per cent and 53 per cent respectively. In 1970-71, the area under forests accounted for 14 per cent in tribal talukas and 16 per cent in non-tribal talukas. The net area sown accounted for 52 per cent and 60 per cent respectively for tribal and non-tribal talukas. The area sown more than once in 1970-71 for tribal talukas accounted for 20 per cent of the net area sown and for non-tribal talukas it accounted for 13 per cent. In 1974-75, the area under forests accounted for 10 per cent and 19 per cent respectively for tribal and non-tribal talukas and net area sown accounted for 51 per cent and 59 per cent respectively. The area sown more than once to net area sown were 8 per cent and 2.4 per cent for tribal and non-tribal talukas.

It is worth noting that forests are depleting fast in the tribal areas without any substantial increase in the area under cultivation. If the culturable waste is brought under the plough in the tribal areas, the maximum area that can be sown will reach 60 per cent of the total reporting area.

The percentage of net area that is sown in Panchmahals since 1960-61 onwards is on an average higher than the percentage of net area sown in the state as a whole. In 1961-62, the net area sown in the state constituted 52 per cent of the total reporting area. The situation was identical in 1970-71.[6] The average share of net area sown in the state and the tribal areas of Panchmahals is almost the same. It seems that there is hardly any scope for extensive use of land for cultivation unless, of course, a big technological breakthrough is achieved.

Current statistics of *Land Holdings and Operations* are not available. Since the ownership pattern does not change very fast one can still continue to draw relevant meanings from the available data. The distribution of holders, area cultivated and the tenancy data for 1971 are presented in Tables 9.1 to 9.4.

TABLE 9.1

Percentage Distribution of Land Holders by Size of Operational Holdings in 1970-71 in Tribal-Non-Tribal Panchmahals and Gujarat State

Size of holding (Hectares)	*Tribal*	*Non-tribal*	*State*
0 to 4.99	74.58	72.03	—
5 to 9.99	19.79	19.14	80.82
10 and above	5.63	8.83	19.18
	100.00	100.00	100.00

Sources: 1. DPAP 1974-75 to 1978-79, Panchmahas.
2. Report of the Gujarat Land Commission.

TABLE 9.2

Percentage Distribution of Cultivated Area by Size of Holding (1971)

Size of holding	*Tribal*	*Non-tribal*
Upto 4 Hectares	81.47	75.27
4 to 12 Hectares	15.71	22.03
12 Hectares and above	2.82	2.70
	100.06	100.00

Source: DPAP 1974-75 to 1978-79, Panchmahals.

TABLE 9.3

Percentage Distribution of Owners, Farmers and Tenants in Panchmahals (1971)

Category	*Tribal*	*Non-tribal*
Owner farmers	90.10	68.90
Protected tenants	1.18	20.15
Unprotected tenants	8.72	10.95
Total farmers	100.00	100.00

Source: DPAP 1974-75 to 1978-79, Panchmahals.

TABLE 9.4

Average Size of Holding in Panchmahals and Gujarat (1971)

Area	*Size of holding (hectares)*
Tribal Panchmahals	2.81
Non-Tribal Panchmahals	2.42
Gujarat State	3/77

Sources: 1. DPAP 1974-75 to 1978-79, Panchmahals.
2. Report of the Gujarat Land Commission.

Almost 75 per cent of the total land holders in tribal Panchmahals hold land somewhere between 0 to 5 hectares. Considering the topography of the area this is not a large holding. The statistics regarding the percentage area held by them is not available. Twenty per cent of the holders hold land between 5 to 10 hectares. Big farmers in the tribal area constitute 5 to 6 per cent of the total holders. The pattern is not significantly different in the non-tribal area. However, at the state level, there is relatively a bigger class which holds more than 10 hectares of land. Since data about area held are not available at disaggregated level, one cannot comment on the skewness in the distribution of land.

Table 9.2 shows that of the total cultivated area in tribal Panchmahals 81 per cent is held by size class of 0 to 4 hectares. In non-tribal talukas, the middle size class farmers cultivate more area (to total cultivated area) than their counterparts in the tribal areas. The percentage area cultivated by the big farmers is almost the same in both tribal and non-tribal areas.

Table 9.3 reveals one more peculiar feature of the tribal Panchmahals. On record, there are more owner farmers in tribal areas relative to the non-tribal areas. Tenancy practice is relatively less in tribal areas.

Table 9.4 suggests that an average holding of the tribal area farmer is slightly higher than that of his counterpart in non-tribal areas but is considerably less than that of his counterpart in the state.

The land is cultivated with the help of a pair of bullocks. The draught animal is the bullock. In tribal areas the Malvi variety which is short and lean is extensively seen. In the non-tribal areas the Kankrej variety is seen. The Malvi variety has a special formation of heels that helps it to traverse undulating rough land strata.

The tribal area seems to be rich as far as the number of drought animals is concerned. The total number of draught animals has grown from 20 per cent in the past to 25 per cent (1951-77). Of the total draught animals in the district in 1972 and 1977, 64 per cent were enumerated in tribal areas. The area that is tilled with a pair of bullocks has registered a downward trend. This implies that bullocks have been growing faster than the net area sown in the district.

TABLE 9.5

Average Area to be Covered by a Pair of Bullocks

(Average area in hectares)

Year	*Tribal*	*Non-tribal*	*District*	*Gujarat state*
1951	NA	NA	2.64	NA
1956	NA	NA	2.40	NA
1961	NA	NA	2.40	6.30
1966	NA	NA	2.20	6.33
1972	1.74	2.8	2.20	6.30
1977	1.88	2.72	2.20	NA

NA = Not available.

The distribution of draught animals among tribal and non-tribal areas is not available for earlier years. If we assume the same proportions as 1972 and 1977 the change in number of animals is peculiar in tribal areas. For two quinquennial censuses from 1951 onwards, the population of the animal has remained less than the 1951 population. In between years it has grown over the previous census. To make it more explicit, assuming 64 per cent of animals in tribal areas in 1956, the total animals were less than the 1961 figures by 2.5 per cent.

In 1961 it grew by 12 per cent, 1966 and 1972 again register positive growth. In 1977 the animals in the entire district declined in number.

Table 9.5 shows that tribal bullocks are slightly better off as they have to till a relatively lesser area than their counterparts. This is as far as the quantum goes. The quality and draught capacity of the animal in these areas are not known. It is therefore, difficult to comment on the performance of a pair of bullocks on the field and thus the relative position of tribal farmers in this regard. The physical numbers suggest that the district in general and tribal area in particular is relatively better-off than the State, since, a pair of bullocks in the state has to cover 6.33 hectares of land (1972).

Agricultural Implements

The implements in use are generally traditional. They are light, portable, locally manufactured and mended and relatively inexpensive. Mechanised farms are yet not very often seen on the district canvas. The number of implements will not be of much help in understanding the availability and status of agriculture. The area under each implement may be of some relevance when reviewing the implements in use.

TABLE 9.6

Average Area (Of the Net Area Sown) Under Each Implement

(Area in hectares)

Implement Code		*1951*	*1961*	*1972*	*1977*
1		*2*	*3*	*4*	*5*
1.	T	2.64	2.3	1.69	1,70
	NT			2.74	2.45
	S	NA	6.10	5.64	NA
2.	T	15.00	16.00	18.00	21.00
	NT			13.00	13.00
	S	NA	13.50	11.70	NA
3.	T	NA	466	272	353
	NT			276	438
	S	NA	NA	NA	NA
4.	T	NA	NA	7.8	7.44
	NT			3.7	3.50
	S	NA	NA	NA	
5.	T	NA	NA	61	70
	NT			10	9
	S	NA	NA	NA	NA

(Contd.)

TABLE 9.6 (*Contd.*)

1		2	3	4	5
6.	T	—	—	28	24
	NT			9	7
	S	NA	NA	NA	NA
7.	T	—	—	65	12
	NT			10	10
	S	NA	NA	NA	NA
8.	T	1610	654	383	136
	NT			82	35
	S	NA	213	26	NA
9.	T	7446	2794	2223	1116
	NT			696	233
	S	NA	1535	198	NA
10.	T	—	—	785	778
	NT			510	135
	S	NA	NA	NA	NA
11.	T			1797	2133
	NT			486	186
	S	NA	NA	NA	NA
12.	T	264777	26555	23039	11504
	NT			6722	2596
	S	NA	4770	1007	NA
13.	T	—	—	—	4485
	NT				987
	S	NA	NA	NA	NA

NA = Not Available, T = Tribal, NT = Non-Tribal, S = State.

Note: (1) Plough (Iron and Wooden), (2) Carts, (3) Rahats or Persian wheels. (4) Improved Harrow, (5) Improved seed drill, (6) Wet land pudlers, (7) Earth levellers, (8) Oil engines, (9) Electric pumps, (10) Maize shellers, (11) Sprayers and Dusters, (12) Tractors, (13) Other modern implements such as Disc Harrows, Cultivators, Scrappers, Trailers, Threshers, etc.

Source: 1. Gazetteer Panchmahals, 1970.
2. District Statistical Abstract relevant years.
3. Report of Gujarat Land Commission.

The average area that a plough either wooden or iron has to tackle has remained the same since 1951. The change is very marginal. It seems that the ploughs have grown more in non-tribal areas. The usage of iron plough is also more in non-tribal areas.

On an average 4 to 5 per cent of total ploughs in non-tribal areas are cast from iron, whereas in tribal areas the percentage is only 0.3. It is to be noted that the state is poorer with regard to the number of ploughs. The state plough had to tackle around 6 hectares of land in 1961. This figure has declined in 1972 to 5.6 but is still high compared to Panchmahals.

The District is poorer in carts. Tribal areas are more so. In the tribal area each cart had to cover 18 hectares of land in 1972, and 21 hectares of land in 1977 as against 13 hectares in non-tribal areas. Carts in the state are growing faster and cover less area than the district. Nothing can be definitely commented on the trend of marketable surplus and interaction with market. It is likely that other modes of transport are developing faster in Panchmahals.[7]

The Persian wheels or Rahats have been in operation in the district for some time. They had become popular in 1961. By 1972 the number increased, but towards 1977, the numbers declined. The oil engines and pump sets seem to have taken their place. In the case of other implements the tribal area has registered relatively slower improvement than the non-tribal area. The only exception seems to be earth levellers. Since, this is a wooden device, tribals may have a relatively easy hold over wood in its manufacture. The pace of modernisation is higher in the non-tribal area at least as far as farm implements ownership is concerned. The state, of course, is showing trends of modernisation with increased use of tractors. The increased use of tractors implies that other related implements must also be growing in number and use.

Irrigation

The district is prone to drought. Rainfed cropping is the practice of the day. Wells are shallow and the yield is poor. No study has been undertaken to work out the potentials of surface water and ground water. Since Independence some investment has been made to develop irrigation facilities.

As in the state so in the district, wells dominate whatever irrigation is provided to the crops. The dominance of area covered by wells is more pronounced in non-tribal areas. In spite of the fact that the number of wells is more in the tribal area, their performance is relatively poor. The ground water availability and the soil strata with given undulating topography in the tribal area

TABLE 9.7

Source of Water Supply

(In number)

Year	*Implement Code*	*Canals*	*Wells*	*Tanks*
1967-68	T	28	16158	446*
	NT	3	14422	500*
1971	T	28	14576	455*
	NT	3	14266	507*
1971-72	T	30	24817	79
	NT	6	13010	48
1972-73	T	30	25361	79
	NT	6	14900	48
1973-74	T	30	25613	79
	NT	6	15411	48
1974-75	T	30	25690	79
	NT	6	15662	48
1979-80	T	30	23346	NA
	NTT	6	18804	NA

*Include tanks, ponds not used for irrigation purposes. Their number in 1974-75 was 827.

Sources: 1. Gazetteer Panchmahals, 1970.
2. DPAP 1974-75 to 1978-79, Panchmahals.
3. District Statistical Abstract (available years).

TABLE 9.8

Area Irrigated by Source as Percentage to Gross Cropped Area

Year		*Canals*	*Wells*	*Tanks*	*Others*	*Total*
1950-51		0.16	0.69	0.43	—	0.98
1960-61		0.30	1.05	0.23	—	1.59
1967-68	T	0.81	1.16	0.77	—	2.74
	NT	0.65	2.66	0.18	0.02	3.51
1971-72	T	0.97	2.43	0.71	0.16	4.27
	NT	1.70	4.47	0.86	0.14	7.17
1974-75	T	0.66	1.62	0.70	0.09	3.07
	NT	0.71	5.60	0.57	0.21	7.09

Sources: 1. Panchmahals Gazetteer, 1970.
2. District Statistical Abstracts.

may be leading to poor yield of water from wells in the tribal area. However, the overall coverage of cultivated land by irrigation is poor. The district in general and tribal belt in particular, grows mostly rainfed crops.

The Agricultural Credit Scene

The old *Gazetteer of Kaira and Panchmahals* prepared in 1879 and 1980 narrates the institutional structure for credit. The local money lenders were Vanias, Brahmans and Bohras. Rich Kanbis also advanced cash loans and grains. Kanbis were considered to be more liberal lenders than the Vanias. Of the total local money lenders, 10 per cent dealt with towns people, only 60 per cent with Kolis, Bhils and the poorer classes; and 30 per cent dealt with both. The repayment of loans by the tribals and poorer communities was by crops. This means that tribals and poorer communities were totally dependent on money lenders and the transaction cycle continued *ad infinitum*.

The co-operative movement was started by Shri Thakkar Bapa (one of Gandhiji's associates) in the 1920s. In 1921, there were 33 agricultural credit societies. The number increased to 52 in 1922. In 1947, there were 221 agricultural credit societies in the district. Since the area of operation of Shri Thakkar Bapa was tribal, we can say that the movement started in tribal areas first. In 1960-61, there were 800 societies with a paid-up capital of Rs. 16.99 lakhs and working capital of Rs. 58.87 lakhs. Total advances were worth Rs. 40.66 lakhs. By 1972 the number of societies went upto 885 but the advances came down to Rs. 21 lakhs. By this time the Co-operative Bank had gained an important position. The advances by the Co-operative Bank in 1972, amounted to Rs. 11,740 lakhs. Though, the figures for tribal and non-tribal areas are not available separately the business was brisk in non-tribal areas.[8]

Commercial banking started only in the 1960s. There were three to four branches of the State Bank (then the Imperial Bank) and Dena Bank in the earlier decades. The advance for agriculture started only in 1968-69. The spread of commercial bank branches still have a relative bias towards the non-tribal areas. In June 1979, the tribal areas had 23 commercial bank branches and non-tribal had 35 branches.

The primary agriculture credit societies also deal to some extent in handling fertilizers and storing grains.

Cropping Pattern, Production and Yield

In the context of the land utilisation pattern, land holding and operation, draught animal availability, implements ownership, available irrigation facility and agricultural credit, let us turn our attention to what the population of Panchmahals grew and grows, in what quantity and at what rate.

Maize was the staple food in the district. It still continues to be so in the tribal areas. Maize, paddy, wheat, jowar, bazra and kodra are the main cereal crops. Tur and gram are the pulse crops, groundnut and sesamum are the oilseed crops and cotton and tobacco the main cash crops.

TABLE 9.9

Cropping Pattern of the District and State Percentage to Total Gross Cropped Area

Year		*Total Cereals*	*Total Pulses*	*Total Oilseeds*	*Total other cash crops*
1980-81	D	70	20	8	2
1900-01	D	77	14	7	2
1930-31	D	72	12	13	3
1950-51	D	69	14	14	3
1962-63	T	64	18	13	5
	NT	62	7	20	11
	S	48	6	23	23
1971-72	T	70	15	8	7
	NT	65	5	12	18
	S	50	5	22	23
1974-75	T	73	13	'5	9
	NT	65	4	10	21
	S	48	4	23	25
1978-79	D	70	13	8	9
	S	45	6	26	23

D = District, T = Tribal, NT = Non-Tribal, S = State.

Sources: 1. Panchmahals Gazetteer, 1970.
2. Directorate of Agriculture, Gujarat State.

Compared with the state the district is still a foodgrain producing area with 80 to 90 per cent of the total cropped area being under foodgrains. The distinguishing features of the district in generel and tribal area in particular, is the growing of pulses. The area under pulses has been around 12 to 15 per cent for most years. The state on the other hand, has 4 to 6 per cent area under pulses. The tribal area continues to have a relatively higher area under pulses. The non-tribal area seems to be following the state pattern by growing more of oil-seeds and other cash crops. In the case of oilseeds, the area was significant in early years and has come down in recent years. This may be because castor, which must have been popular because of the forests, is losing the ground continuously in the tribal areas. Cotton, Tabacco and other cash crops are more popular in non-tribal areas of the district.

TABLE 9.10

Yield of Crops

(Yield/hectare in kg.)

Year		*Total Cereals*	*Total Pulses*	*Total Oilseeds*	*Cotton*	*Tabacco*
1950-51	D	430	386	560	124	769
	S	NA	NA	NA	NA	NA
1960-61	D	742	425	599	121	917
	S	417	331	613	139	700
1971-72	D	1216	584	723	329	990
	S	901	375	828	222	1359
1972-73	D	693	600	365	233	685
	S	532	295	218	139	1262
1973-74	D	857	743	914	156	649
	S	816	393	757	156	1446
1974-75	D	442	365	544	117	1560
	S	583	327	324	155	1440
1975-76	D	1293	657	914	137	996
	S	939	401	1153	160	1483
1976-77	D	941	633	687	161	1196
	S	902	417	953	161	1659
1977-78	D	724	577	655	148	1127
	S	925	330	846	180	1538
1978-79	D	852	771	546	213	2021
	S	1055	423	860	203	2060

NA = Not Available, D = District, S = State.

Sources: 1. Panchmahals Gazetteer, 1970.

2. Directorate of Agriculture, Gujarat State.

The characteristic feature of the yield both in the district as well as the state is that the variation in the yield is high. Neither the state nor the district can claim a definite trend in productivity, What is worthnoting, however, is the superiority of the district over the state in cereals, pulses and cotton. During the 1970s, the state yield average bettered over district in the case of oilseeds and other cash crops. The yield of pulses without exception has been high in the district right from 1951. The productivity of the district should not be rated low considering the physical productivity standard discussed earlier.

Within the district, the tribal areas show a slightly higher variation in yield. The yield differentials are there, for the majority of crops and most of the years the non-tribal talukas' yields are better than the tribal talukas. In case of maize, in average rainfall years the tribal areas, yield is either the same as or higher than the non-tribal areas. In bad years the tribal areas' yield becomes very low.

The greater concern thus, is the variation in the yield, which has a definite impact on the total production. The drought years in the district in general and tribal area in particular affect the yield and out-turn most severely. The impact of the drought gets carried over to the next years thus affecting the resources management of the farmer permanently. The effect of drought must have been much more damaging in the years before Independence, when no systematic attention was paid to the semi-arid tracts. The efforts of the Government began with the First Five Year Plan.

IV

The government efforts at development started from the scarcity relief works. During the drought years, the construction department of the PWD was assigned the task by the Goverement of undertaking road laying, tank digging and deepening works to provide employment to the affected masses. The scarcity works continue to date. It is just an impression that today the scarcity hit people seeking employment are greater in number than they were in the 1950s and 60s. This can easily be taken as the sum and substance of the government efforts in the district in general and tribal area in particular. However, one must account for the crores of rupees that have been spent on the development of district. This will be discussed by way of narrating the different programmes under which the areas of the district were covered and then the available financial figures will be furnished.

What happened during the First Five Year Plan in the district is not known. In the Second and Third Plans the district and the state plans were prepared keeping in view the objectives of the national plan which in tern was based on the welfare state. For each scheme of development a target was fixed and the estimates of expenditure were worked out. Till 1970 this kind of efforts continued. The areas that were covered were agricultural production, land development, minor irrigation, warehousing and marketing, animal husbandry, forest soil conservation, fisheries, community development, co-operation, irrigation and power, industry and mining, transport and communication, education, health, housing, other social services and scientific and industrial research.

In the early 1950s one major event occurred—the launching of the much spoken of and Celebrated Community Development Blocks Programme (CD). The community development programme in India was a measure to rectify structural deficits in the rural economic and civics system with a view to build a modern infrastructure of productives and institutions, and to integrate the same with an expanding urban-industrial economy and society.

The concept was to direct and strengthen the planned programme for rural upliftment. The areas covered by the programme were agriculture, animal husbandry, minor irrigation, health and rural sanitation, social education, womens' programme, communications, village and small industries, co-operation and other general activities.

The CD blocks covered in detail, distribution of improved seeds, fertilizers, implements and agriculture demonstrations under agricultural production programme. Under animal husbandry, new breeds of animals and birds were distributed and animals were castrated and artificially inseminated. Under minor irrigation, Kutcha, Pucca wells were constructed, repaired and renovated and tanks, tubewells were dug. Under other categories, health centres were built, roads were laid, co-operatives were formed and other services were established.

How Much was Done?

The physical targets for planned expenditure are not available. *The Panchmahals Gazetteer* gives an account of physical achievement in CD blocks. Since inauguration in 1952, the achievements till 31st March, 1970 were as follow (this again is not available for tribal and non-tribal areas separately):

	Unit	*Achievements*
I. *Agriculture*		
(a) Distribution of improved seeds	Qutl.	325006
(b) Distribution of fertilizers	"	215924
(c) Distribution of improved implements	No.	14148
(d) Agriculture demonstrations	"	29243
II. *Animal Husbandry*		
(a) Improved bread of animals supplied	"	1036
(b) Improved bread of birds supplied	"	111897
(c) Animals castrated	"	81653
(d) Animals artificially inseminated	"	6393
III. *Minor Irrigation*		
(a) Kutcha wells constructed and repaired	"	9174
(b) Pucca wells constructed and repaired	"	8519
(c) Tanks constructed and repaired	"	43
(d) Tubewells and pumps installed	"	2790
(e) Area to be irrigated (estimated)	ha.	14321
IV. *Health and Rural Sanitation*		
(a) Primary health centres	No.	23
(b) Rural latrines built	"	1789
(c) Drinking water wells	"	1235
(d) Drinking water wells disinfected	"	3235
(e) Hand pumps installed	99	435
V. The Kutcha Roads constructed and renovated covered 882 km. Over and above this about 2575 literacy centres were started, adults were educated, reading room, library, Mahila mandals, youth clubs, etc. were taken up.		

From How Much Financial Resources?

The expenditure by sector is available for the plan periods. For CD Blocks the expenditure is available by stage and not by the sectors or area covered. The plan expenditure and the CD

Blocks expenditure till March 1970 are given in Tables 9.11 and 9.12.

The plan money went mainly for construction, irrigation, power, communication and health and education. This implies that structures were created in these sectors. The post-third plan expenditure trend registered a change. Health and soil conservation were concentrated upon in a bigger way.

TABLE 9.11

Expenditure Pattern During the Second and Third Five Year Plans and from 1-4-1966 to 31-3-1970

Sl. No.	*Name of head*	*Percentage to total expenditure Second and Third Plans*	*Percentage to total expenditure 1966 to 1970*
1.	Agricultural development	1.91	0.63
2.	Land development	0.02	—
3.	Minor irrigation	5.66	17.38
4.	Warehousing and marketing	0.69	—
5.	Animal husbandry	0.17	0.45
6.	Forest	5.05	—
7.	Soil conservation	7.63	27.08
8.	Fisheries	0.01	—
9.	Community development	14.52	7.96
10.	Co-operatives	2.31	0.17
11.	Irrigation and power	21.34	—
12.	Industry and mining	0.65	1.38
13.	Transport and communication	15.20	5.03
14.	Education	11.32	1.31
15.	Health	4.50	32.66
16.	Housing	1.10	0.50
17.	Other social services	7.89	0.36
18.	Scientific and industrial research	0.03	5.12
	Total per cent	100.00	100.00
		Rs. 78266700	67088600

Source: Panchmahals Gazetteer, 1970.

TABLE 9.12

Expenditure in CD Blocks upto 1970

(Rs. in lakhs)

Type	*Block No.*	*Expenditure incurred*	*Contribution by people*
Non-Tribal Area	9	145.60 (55%)	28.60 (85%)
Tribal Area	13	120.04 (45%)	4.71 (15%)
Total	22	265.64 (100%)	33.34 (100%)

Source: Panchmahals Gazetteer, 1970.

In the CD Blocks relatively less was spent in tribal areas. This may be because of lack of popular contribution to the desired extent. The non-tribal blocks have contributed almost 17 per cent towards the total efforts. While the tribal blocks could muster only 4 per cent of the total finance deployed. It seems that in the tribal blocks more programmes were taken up that did not require popular contribution because the difference in total finance deployed by the government in tribal areas and in non-tribal areas is not in the same proportion as the popular contribution in both the areas.[9]

The Seventies

The Seventies witnessed a whirlwind in the realm of rural upliftment programmes. It started with the Drought Prone Area Programmes (DPAP). It also brought the Integrated Rural Development Programme, Small Farmers' Development Agency, Marginal Farmers' and Agricultural Labourers and other centrally sponsored schemes. The tribal area received much attention with the introduction of The Tribal Sub-Plan. Since, all these programmes are centrally sponsored, there is uniformity in pattern all over the country and a detailed discussion on each of the programmes is not essential.

The financial implications of two of the above mentioned programmes were significant. The DPAP had an annual budget of about Rs. 1.25 crores from 1974-75 to 1978-79 and has Rs. 1.05 crores from 1979-80 to 1983-84. The tribal Sub-Plan had an annual budget of about Rs. 5.70 crores in the 1973-78 plan and has about

Rs. 12.76 crores for the 1978-83 plan period. The other programmes have annual budgets of a few lakhs since their inception,

A glimpse of what actually has been attempted in the DPAP and Tribal Sub-Plan in the period 1973-79 is necessary. This is concisely reported in the 1978-83 Draft Project Report of the Tribal Sub-Plan, a portion of which is reproduced here.[10]

"Soil conservation which provides for the sheet anchor of the programme for rejuvenating the predominant sector of the tribal economy was reoriented on the watershed basis. Under this new approach 2145 hectares were covered by 1978. 5981 farmers were trained in 200 one day camps and 520 farmers were trained in 16 five day camps. The two soil testing laboratories in the tribal area tested 10,606 samples and advised farmers on crop selection. 16,582 kits containing improved seeds, fertilizers, and pesticides for 0.2 hectare area were distributed. Chemical fertilizers purchase was subsidised by worth Rs. 11.04 lakhs and insecticides subsidy of Rs. 0.11 lakhs was granted worth. Implement purchase subsidy was of Rs. 0.05 lakhs, and oil engine and pumpset subsidies were of 9.25 lakhs.

The spillover of irrigation works of the Fourth Plan was completed with an expenditure of Rs. 51.05 lakhs creating 61 tanks and 13 check dams. The potential added was 1631 hectares.

3395 hectares were planted and advance action for 1697 hectares was undertaken. 58 km. roadside plantations were done and 180 hectares in 45 villages were covered under village forests. 9 poultry farming societies were registered enabling 250 tribals to have production units. The reorganization of primary co-operatives into 7 FSS, 8 LAMPS and 76 villages primaries has been done. Development of roads during the Fifth Plan period has added 106 km. to the all whether road length.

Two primary health sub-centres were upgraded and medical officers were placed regularly. Five Ayurvedic dispensaries have been opened, the medicine quota has been raised, a 30-bed hospital in a village has been built and 12 PHCs have been provided with a motorcycle. 330 new school teachers have been appointed, 152 additional school rooms have been provided and 34 teacher's quarters have been built. Assistance was provided to voluntary agencies running high schools in construction of building, etc. ITI has opened new courses providing 76 seats per annum. A multipurpose workshop in trades such as welding gas, soldering, boring, etc. has been opened with an annual capacity of 107 trainees.

Four of the five talukas of the project area (tribal project) are covered under the Drought Prone Areas Programme. Under this the main thrust of activities has been minor irrigation (Rs. 73.23 lakhs), afforestation (Rs. 79.80 lakhs), soil conservation (Rs. 7.07 lakhs), co-operatives (Rs. 6.68 lakhs) and water supply schemes (Rs. 3.38 lakhs).

Over and above these major programmes the area has been covered by various other programmes aiding the tribals with individual beneficiary schemes.[11] From the point of view of financial expenditure, the efforts are highly significant. How the tribal population has responded to all these efforts is the next most relevant question.

V

A direct answer to check the impact of the efforts is to evaluate the programme with a socio-economic survey. This is yet to be done. However, there are certain indicators which speak of the agricultural development that has or has not taken place in the area in question.

The Cropping Pattern

With the development of agriculture which means land improvement, augmented irrigation facility, input supply and credit supply, it is generally observed that the cropping pattern in the area changes in favour of cash crops, both edible and non-edible. More grain or same quantum of grain is grown with relatively less area. That is to say the intensive agriculture has replaced the traditional extensive cultivation. The area that gets released in the process is brought under cash crops that would augment the income of the farm family. The marginal and average productivity per unit of land and labour thus register a positive change.

Assuming that the 1950s and 1960s were the periods when the government spread its extension network and built the necessary infrastructure (dams, roads, tanks, wells, co-operatives), the 1970s should have registered a change in cropping pattern. If we go back to Table 9.9 which displays the cropping pattern of the district as well as tribal and non-tribal areas of the district, it can be observed that the cropping pattern has failed to register a change. The area under cereals in the district has not undergone a change over a century. In 1880-81 the area under cereals was 70 per cent and it is the same in 1978-79. In 1962-63 the area under cereals in the tribal belt was 64 per cent of the total area under cultivation and it was 62 per cent in the non-tribal area. In 1974-75, these areas respectively covered 73 per cent and 65 per cent of total area cultivated in both the groups of talukas. The area under pulses has however come down both in tribal and non-tribal talukas. The fall in non-tribal talukas is sharper than the tribal talukas. For the district as a whole the area under pulses which was 15 per cent in 1962-63 had come down to 9 per cent in 1974-75. Now it is somewhere between 10 to 11 per cent. The area under oilseeds also has registered a decline after 1962-63. However, the non-tribal talukas have been able to keep up with the past to some extent. The area under cash crops has gone up by a small margin in the tribal belt but it is not very significant. The non-tribal talukas have responded significantly in this regard. Thus, in spite of the concentrated efforts in the 1950s the 1960s the cropping pattern has not changed significantly in the tribal areas.

The Myth of the Cropping Intensity

Cropping intensity is used generally as an indicator for agricultural development. Conceptually, the indicator has a very limited use and must be used discretely. This is so because the ratio of gross cropped area to net area sown has relevance only when the cropping pattern is known. The high cropping intensity may not necessarily reflect better agriculture. To illustrate this point, the cropping intensity figures for tribal and non-tribal areas are given below:

TABLB 9.13

Cropping Intensity in Panchmahals

Year	*Tribal Talukas*	*Non-Tribal Talukas*
1962-63	1.30	1.09
1963-64	1.33	1.10
1971-72	1.21	1.11
1974-75	1.10	1.09

The land utilisation statistics beyond 1974-75 are not available at the desired disaggregated levels. The tribal talukas show that cropping intensity came down to 1.1 in 1974-75 from 1.33 in 1963-64. In non-tribal areas it was in the range of 1.09 to 1.11. The tribal area has remained above its counterpart in this regard. This is not because agriculture has developed but because traditionally, tribals grow a local variety of maize (Dudh Mogra or so) that matures in under three months and then sow gram that grows with the moisture retained by the soil through late monsoon rainfall. The year 1974-75 was the worst drought year and hence gram may not have been grown. The cropping intensity may be working out low for non-tribal areas because long duration kharif crops (cotton, etc.) may have been taken. Since the coverage of irrigation is not very high, the cropping intensities will not serve as an indication of agricultural development in this specific context.

Irrigation Intensity

This concept, too, has relevance only when a significant area of the total cultivated area is covered under irrigation throughout the agricultural seasons. Since, the percentage area irrigated has gone up since 1950-51 both in tribal as well as non-tribal talukas, one may have a look at the irrigation intensities. Once again the data constraint is to be mentioned. The data are available only upto 1974-75.

TABLE 9.14

Irrigation Intensities in Panchmahals

Year	*Tribal Talukas*	*Non-Tribal Talukas*
1962-63	1.000	1.000
1963-64	1.000	1.000
1970-71	1.005	1.054
1971-72	1.012	1.095
1972-73	1.005	1.050
1973-74	1.009	1.150
1974-75	1.010	1.100

The relative position of non-tribal talukas is slightly better since with better augmented irrigation, hot weather crops are becoming popular in non-tribal talukas.

Area Under HYV and Use of Other Inputs

Another indication of agricultural development in an area is given by the adoption of high yielding varieties replacing the local varieties and the use of chemical fertilizers, pesticides and other inputs. The popularisation of improved seeds, fertilizers and pesticides was attempted since the CD Block days. This statistics relating to this should throw some light on the adoption of newer varieties in the tribal area.

TABLE 9.15

Area Under HYV in Tribal and Non-Tribal Panchmahals

Year	*Tribal*		*Non-Tribal*		*Total*	
	A	*P*	*A*	*P*	*A*	*P*
1966-67	NA	NA	NA	NA	3092	NA
1971-72	NA	NA	NA	NA	79703	NA
1974-75	12311	5.1	47607	15	59918	13
1980-81*	33974	10.0	42527	18	82501	15

A = Area, P = Percentage to Gross Cropped Area.

*For 1980-81 gross cropped area is taken as that of 1974-75.

Sources: 1. DPAP, Panchmahals, 1974-75 to 1978-79.
2. District Agriculture Office.

The area under high yielding varieties has significantly and dramatically gone up. In the last 15 years the area under HYV has registered an impressive increase. In tribal areas improved varieties for wheat have been accepted and hence, the area under HYV in rabi shows an increase. In non-tribal areas HYV in kharif and hot weather crops have picked up. However, there has not been an overall complete replacement.

TABLE 9.16

Use of Chemical Fertilizers (1978-79)

Fertilizer Type	*Tribal Talukas*		*Non-Tribal Talukas*	
	Total in tonnes	*Kg. per hectare of gross cropped area*	*Total in tonnes*	*Kg. per hectare of gross cropped area*
Chemical Fertilizer	483.7 (22)	1.42	1710.5 (78)	7.07

Figures in brackets indicate percentages.
Source: District Agriculture Office.

The district farmers do not generally use chemical fertilizers and tribal farmers seem much more reluctant. In the case of insecticides and pesticides, both talukas have shown a tendency to go in for liquid replacing the usage of powder. This may be due to availability. Though the use has gone up in tribal as well as non-tribal areas it seems that tribals are again not prone to use this practice much.

TABLE 9.17

Use of Insecticides and Pesticides

Year	*Tribal Liquid Litres*	*Taluka Powder Kg.*	*Non-Tribal Liquid Litres*	*Talukas Powder Kg.*
1974-75	1158	11186	5821	53301
1978-79	60699	1041	106574	7912

Source: District Agriculture Office.

The Agronomic Practices and their Adoption

The new varieties and inputs yield results only when a set of agronomic practices are strictly followed. For dry farming as well as irrigated farming considerable recommendations have been made by the department to the farmers. The extension worker at the village is supposed to instruct the farmers about the practices.

The tribals have not responded to this very significantly. This was revealed when a sample village was studied for the purpose.

The adoption of the recommended practices for maize and paddy was studied. The study reveals that neither the general agronomic practices nor the crop specific practices were followed. The improved seeds were used and fertilizer (chemical) was also sparsely used. But none of the respondents showed any systematic adoption of practices.[12]

The Productivity

The signals of agricultural development are received when the productivity per unit of land displays an upward trend or stability at a higher level. This is one of the soundest indicators of agricultural development. Referring to Table 9.10 one can say that the average productivity in the last decade has increased to some extent in the district compared to the trend of earlier decades. A similar trend is true for pulses, oilseeds and other cash crops too. However, the averages may be elusive and one will have to look into the variations in the productivity trends for the past years.

The government which has made efforts in introducing high yielding varieties and distributing and supplying other inputs should have aided the reduction of variation in productivity.

Due to augmentation in irrigation and use of improved seeds and fertilizers and other inputs, the average yield in the 1970s has gone up most of the crops in the district. The tribal area also seems to have experienced an increase in average yield over the 1950s. However, these improved averages do not score over the previous bests and hence, whether the credit of improving averages should be given to inputs or rainfall still remains a question. This is more so because the fluctuation in output has shown no visible change. Tables 9.18 to 9.20 make it clear that the co-efficient of variation for the major crops in the district is higher than the state and continues to be so even in the seventies. The uncertainty of yield still continues. Maize and paddy which are two major kharif crops in tribal areas continue to have a high co-efficient of variation (50 per cent and more).

This implies that agricultural development in the tribal areas of Panchmahals has not taken place with the pace at which it was assumed. The huge amount of investments in building irrigation structures, laying out roads, constructing hospitals, school buildings and wells have yet to pay dividends to society. As stated

TABLE 9.18

Variation in Productivity of Some of the Major Crops in Panchmahals (1961-62 to 1978-79)

Name of crop	*Mean yield Kg./Ha.*	*Standard deviation*	*C.V. per cent*
Maize	824	459	56
Paddy	622	358	57
Wheat	1202	423	35
Gram	640	228	36
Groundnut	665	230	34

C.V. = Co-efficient of Variation.

TABLE 9.19

Variation in Productivity of Some of the Major Crops in Tribal and Non-Tribal Areas (1965-66 to 1970-71)

Name of crop	*Mean yield Kg./Ha.*		*Standard Deviation*		*C.V. per cent*	
	T	*NT*	*T*	*NT*	*T*	*NT*
Maize	898	928	457	450	51	58
Paddy	427	470	325	359	76	76
Wheat	1109	1201	248	220	22	18
Gram	518	503	139	127	27	25
Groundnut	600	614	282	294	47	48
Cotton	776	823	266	258	34	31

T = Tribal, NT = Non-Tribal.

earlier droughts still occur, unemployment is still prevalent and tribal migration that has drawn statewise attention still continues. Once again the need for intervention calls for re-examination.

VI

It is thus apparent that the interventions by the government in tribal areas has not been able to bring about a significant change in the socio-economic conditions of the tribals. No recent study is available that gives the figures, estimates or guesstimates about the extent of poverty and unemployment in the area in question. Some symptoms nevertheless, direct one's attention and acceptance of the existing problems. The cropping pattern, productivity and adoption of practices have been briefly discussed. There is one more major symptom that draws our attention and that is the seasonal migration of the tribal farmers to other parts of the state in search of employment either on-field or off the field.

TABLE 9.20

Variation in Productivity of Some of the Major Crops at District and State (1971-72 to 1978-79)

Name of crop	*Mean yield Kg./Ha.*		*Standard Deviation*		*C.V. per cent*	
	D	*S*	*D*	*S*	*D*	*S*
Maize	951	995	459	438	48	44
Paddy	746	1000	403	346	54	35
Wheat	1467	2006	403	269	27	13
Gram	811	705	218	158	27	22
Groundnut	695	772	214	325	31	42
Cotton	187	172	64	26	34	15

D = District, S = State (Gujarat).

The Extent of Migration

The magnitude of migration gives some idea about the problems of un/underemployment in tribal areas. Many studies have been conducted to assess the extent of migration. One such survey was conducted in 1971 by the Bureau of Economics and Statistics of the state government. Three sample villages were selected from one of the five tribal talukas in Panchmahals. The results state that 86 per cent of the sample households were migratory at one time or another during the reference period.[13] It was observed that at least one person from each household was migrating. If we assume an average family size of five members and two workers, the persons migrating in the reference period (1971-72) will amount to nearly 40 per cent of the total working population.

One more study was conducted by the Tribal Administrator's Office in 1974. Ten sample villages from two talukas of the tribal area were selected for the purpose. Of the sample working population, 36 per cent migrated seasonally.[14] In yet another study[15] the estimate for five sample villages of Dahod taluka showed that 40 per cent of the working population of the sample seasonally migrated.

A much more systematic study was conducted in 1977-78 by the Gujarat Institute of Area Planning. According to the reports[16] of this study, the estimates show that of the 10 sample villages of Dahod, Devgadh Baria, Jhalod, Santrampur, and Limkheda (two villages from each of the tribal talukas) about 27 per cent of the sample population migrated. This study may be considered nearer the reality since entire tribal belt was covered.

Who Migrate?

Generally, the rationale behind the migration or mobility of labour is a search for better alternative employment opportunities in order to strengthen, support or fully substitute the opportunities and earnings at the place of origin. Hence, one may infer that the migrating members of the households may not be in a position to meet the household requirements by working at the place of origin or migrating members may not be having any productive employment at the place of origin.

The average holding of the migrating households in the villages studied by the Bureau was 0.70 hectares. The Institute for Area Planning study suggests that the lower the land holding, the higher were the households and members from each household who migrated. The percentage households migrating, who owned less than 2.5 hectares of land, was above 60. The persons migrating from the migrating households formed 35 to 40 per cent of their total population. Among the households who owned 2.5 to 4 hectares and 4 hectares and above, 42 per cent migrated and the migrating members of these households formed 15 to 20 per cent of their total population. Details about the ownership for the other two studies mentioned above are not available. One more study speaks for this.[17] The study examined the variables that affect the extent of migration. Of the 100 sample households studied, 86 per cent of the households owned less than 3 hectares of land. The migrating households that were owning one or less than one hectare of land were 43 in a sample of 100 households. In short, one can conclusively say that the small and marginal farmers have a higher tendency to migrate.

The Interventions Helped Whom?

Since seasonal migration of tribals is a common and a regular phenomena today, it should be asked, "who were the beneficiaries of government programmes"? It now seems obvious that the big farmers owning 5 hectares and above benefited most from the government programmes. In most of the government programmes, the target beneficiary is a tribal without any prescribed limit of land holding. This is so because even some of the relatively big holders are not in a position to better their agricultural prospects, since most of the land owned is undulating and not very good for cultivation purposes. In any case, generally, a bigger farmer has better accessibility to resources than small and marginal farmers.

Why Small and Marginal Farmers did not Reap the Benefits?

Looking at the investment pattern of the past 30 years one can least say that the tribal area has been provided with sufficient infrastructure. As a matter of fact a watershed study done by the Cell[18] suggests that the infrastructural status of watersheds in tribal areas is relatively better than that of their counterparts in non-tribal areas. The minor sources of irrigation, the roads, the other services (health and education, soil conservation, etc.) have been well taken care of in the tribal areas. The magnitude of capital investment in infrastructure development of the tribal area has been significant against the total allocation for the district as a whole. Why then has agricultural development not picked up and small and marginal farmers not responded?

The Interventionist's Strategy has Failed

The administrator-*cum*-planner-*cum*-implementor at the district and departmental level is given the allocation and objectives. He is free to opt for strategy. If one goes through the implementation of the majority of the programmes in the district in general and tribal area in particular one realises that the strategy has been almost non-existent. *Ad-hoc* decisions suiting the working convenience of the district officials have prevailed. Irrigation facilities have been created without consulting the agricultural department. Inputs have been distributed without looking into other necessary conditions and infrastructure. Soil has been treated in the areas where agricultural department scarcely tried to reach. The distribution of schemes over a space is based on administrative units such as talukas rather than watershed basis which provides a better homogeneity of the spatial unit. The efforts have been, thus, so scattered that whatever potential they originally had by design have been lost. The benefits, therefore, have been reaped by big and resourceful farmers who could salvage something of the efforts made by the government departments.

There were and are a couple of programmes which aim at benefiting only small and marginal farmers in a given administrative spatial unit. They also seem to have proved ineffective because of two major reasons. One reason is that these programmes have not been dovetailed with the other major programmes which were designed and implemented to create broad infrastructures. The logical combination and sequencing of the programmes and schemes have not been attempted at all in any meaningful way. To quote B. Sivaraman, "The mere fact that the various amelioration programmes have only been prepared in part and there is so far no sign of the integrated area approach to support the families in the programme, shows either unwillingness or an inability of the system to tackle the problem."[19] Hence, the entire expenditure has tickled down without creating any desired multiplier effect in the given spatial unit.

Mere delegation of power to plan and implement at lower levels does not mean decentralization of planning. Each district and/or the tribal area cannot have an omniscient planner, who can turn entire effort into mathematics and print out a readymade formula for success. However, unless and until the planner exercises his freedom to design and consider alternative strategies, no programme can become a successful one in achieving the objectives. If the district administration cannot spare time for planning activity (the implementation is time consuming and planners with vision are not often available at lower levels) the strategies should be designed, tested and then passed on to the implementing authorities by way of clear-cut well-defined guidelines.

The second reason, which is much more fundamental in nature and has far reaching repurcussions, is the design of the programmes/schemes themselves. As far as the infrastructure creating programmes are concerned, one may get away by saving that whether planned or unplanned the structure has been built. The social assets have been created. But here too, the programme design can easily be questioned. One should not forget that the objective was not to create assets but to see that they are optimally utilized so that the desired agricultural development takes place. When it comes to utilisation, the basic designs have no answer. For instance, the DPAP all the while maintained that they were there to build assets and not manage the assets and help utilisation. The planning for management and utilisation of the assets such as irrigation structures, dairies, farm ponds, cattle units is entirely absent in the grand schemes of the DPAP. Similar is the case of the Tribal-Sub-Plan. The result is that the utilisation of water from minor irrigation tanks in the district is 30 per cent of the potential created.[20] If command area development is not necessary for huge projects to ensure success, it is all the more so for the smaller projects. Thus, the incomplete designs have led the programme to failure *vis-a-vis* the objectives.

In case of the designs of individual beneficiary projects/schemes, the issues are much more fundamental. The potential target beneficiary in most of such programmes is a small farmer, marginal farmer or an agricultural labourer. The upper limit for land holding is determined but nothing is stated about the lower limit. However, these individual beneficiary schemes have overlooked certain basic constraints within which the small farmers, marginal farmers and especially tribal farmers base their decisions. It has now been well recognised that unless there is a minimum holding of land, the farmer family cannot become a viable one even if it is fully subsidised in the initial stages. Even the technology will have some limitations. To quote Dr. V.K.R.V. Rao, "The marginal and sub-marginal farmers' viability cannot be secured even by the new technology unless they go in for some kind of co-operative or community operation of their uneconomic holdings."[21] Overlooking this constraint the implementing agencies have tried to pass on some subsidy schemes to these marginal and sub-marginal farmers.

The content of these programmes is of much further interest. The individual beneficiary programmes such as the Integrated Rural Development Programme contained mainly subsidy schemes for milch animals, agricultural inputs, crop demonstrations, crop protection demonstrations, bullocks, implements, carts and storage bins. As far as milch animals and poultry schemes go, it is argued that they provide a subsidiary occupation and an additional income to a marginal farmer's or an agricultural labourer's family. The argument needs a little examination. The animal husbandrying and poultry activities in rural areas have not been taken up in the past as independent activities, especially, animal husbandry. Cows or buffalloes are maintained not because agriculture is bad but because agriculture is good. In the past and even today farmer's prosperity is judged by how many cattle are tied in his yard. The necessary inputs for animal husbandry are supplied by the farm. The feed for chicks comes from corn that is grown in the fields. The marginal and small farmers who do not have good agriculture will also not be in a position to maintain cattle. How is an agriculture labourer who as such, has a meagre earning that is not sufficient to survive, expected to enter into cash transaction for feeding the chicks or the cattle? A dairy is a possible answer to this. But in tribal areas like Panchmahals where fodder is generally a scarce commodity even for relatively well-to-do farmers, a dairy would remain a far cry for the small and marginal farmers. To supply milch cattle and poultry birds without providing for the feed and fodder, may unnecessarily burden the farmer with the institutional credit which he has to seek to obtain subsidy. The guarantee for feed and fodder cannot be given in a scarcity area like Panchmahals. If such a guarantee is provided somehow, it will only give rise to problems in planning at the macro-level.

The second set of schemes is based on the agricultural inputs. As stated earlier, improved seeds, chemical fertilizer, pesticides, etc. have been subsidised. Crop demonstrations and crop protection demonstrations have been held. The subsidising of seeds, fertilizers and pesticides would imply working capital subsidy. The farmer may like to deploy these inputs till they are subsidised, since he does not have to bear the cost directly. The tribal farmers especially small and marginal farmers have been reluctant to invest in this working capital because they are not sure of the success in output. Their economy may undergo a change and will put them in a negative quadrant of earnings if the rains fail. It is not the irrationality of the tribal farmer that prevents him from using HYV and fertilizers but experience which makes him decide against the risk of new experiment.

One may argue at this juncture that the tribal farmer does not take risks because he is not aware of the new technology and crop care. This argument loses ground once we accept that tribal farmers have been migrating to neighbouring districts for quite sometime, especially to rural areas. The studies that have been mentioned earlier confirm to one more important aspect, that majority of migration that is taking place is rural to rural. The majority of the migrants are hired on a season basis by the well-to-do farmers of Kaira and Vadodara district who practice modern agriculture. The employers mainly oversee the activities carried on by the hired labour. Thus, the tribals of Panchmahals, who form the majority of the hired labour are exposed to modern cultivation techniques. The same set of labourers when they return to their own land with the first monsoon rains do not adopt the practices. They consider the new varieties to be more risky with regard to output. There is also an additional factor which requires to be studied in detail. Some general remarks, however, can be made for this factor.

The migrating population is younger as compared to the non-migrating population. Each migrating household sends out a young couple to labour in other fields. The old people, parents or relatives stay back to look after cattle, kids and small pieces of holding. The young couple returns with the first monsoon, sows the local variety that matures soon, and goes back to their employers. They come again within three months to harvest and take grain with them. They also sow grams that grow with the available moisture. It seems most likely that the value of output differential between the high yielding variety and the local variety is not greater than or equal to the value that is added by labouring outside. This may be mainly true for the arid tracts where irrigation facility is not available. In arid tracts, without irrigation a farmer also has to bear a greater risk in cultivating HYV than the local variety. One thing is confirmed that in the case of crucial shortfall in rains, the HYV yields nothing whereas the local variety yields are very low.[22] Also, the local variety provides for fodder, which the farmers value equally. The HYV plants, the farmers say, are not suitable as fodder. If the rains fail then the farmer has to lose not only the HYV crop, but also the next crop of grams due to late maturing of the kharif HYV. In case of the local variety, the farmer can resort to the gram crop. This is his rationality and should not be mistaken for the traditional value system and lack of extension and knowledge on his part.

Coming back to our issue on scheme/project designs, is its enough to ensure the farmer with working capital to be used as inputs? The productivity of land, the texture, the soil strata, the topography also play a significant role in agricultural development. No specific dry farming agronomic practices have been developed by researchers for tribal areas that have special topographical features. The tribal farmers contend that even the iron plough bends when taken deep below the crest soil. When a farmer is not equipped with a good pair of bullocks with sufficient draught and suitable implements why is he subsidised for other inputs like seeds and fertilizers?

There are also a bunch of small and marginal farmers who are pitted against potentially low productivity soil. If the arguments in the light of real situation are accepted thus far, then, the more relevant issue crops up. Is agriculture viable in the stated area with the given geophysical characteristics of soil and the given distribution of land holding? Will it be possible to support the existing population with agricultural development alone?

It can now be well understood why the cropping pattern has remained unchanged and productivity variation continues at a significant rate in tribal Panchmahals. The decision of tribals to migrate is thus, highly rational in the context of the situation. However, if the pressure on land is released somehow (either by migration or by alternative non-agricultural employment opportunities) the area has some potential even in agriculture. For instance, the yield variations in pulses has been less compared to the state and tribal areas of Panchmahals grow most of the pulse in the district. The Panchmahals contributes of an average about 25 per cent of the total state's pulse output by covering only 12 per cent of the state's land that is under pulses. The Panchmahals definitely have a comparative advantage in pulse production over the state. Surprisingly, this factor has not been noted by any of the agricultural experts in the state. A pulse processing factory could provide employment to un/under-employed persons in the area. Similar possibilities need to be explored.

Unless a thorough re-examination of the geophysical characteristics of tribal unit is carried out and a study of tribal population and their capacities and abilities in agriculture is attempted, the ongoing efforts by the government will only widen the gap between (i) the non-tribals and the tribals, and (ii) the elite and resourceful tribals and the resourceless tribals. Only a scientific and systematic well-organised planned programme based on some concrete physical aspects (such as watersheds or water or land) will bring overall socio-economic health to the tribal area and population.

Notes and References

1. *Panchmahals Gazetteer*, 1970.
2. Drought Prone Area Programme, 1974-75 to 1978-79.
3. Girija Sharan, *Some Physical Characteristics of Drought in Panchmahals*, (mimeo,) People's Centre of Education and Development, February 1980.
4. *Report of the Gujarat Land Commission*, Government of Gujarat, May 1979, Appendix II.
5. *Ibid.*, Appendix II describes the way in which the productivity status is determined and how different weights are attached to different characteristics.
6. *Statistical Abstract of Gujarat*, 1977, Director, Information, Government of Gujarat, p. 60.
7. Panchmahal's progress in road construction is enviable. It has achieved 96 per cent of the targets set in the 1961-81 Master Plan by the Indian Road Congress as against the 75 per cent achievement of the state. Bus connections are also relatively better in the district in general and tribal areas in particular. See for details ; Sudarshan Iyengar and Ravindra H. Dholakia, 'Planning for Special Programmes—An Exercise in DPAP Planning in Panchmahals,' (mimeo) DPP Cell, October 1979.
8. Private Communication, Manager, District Central Co-operative Bank, Panchmahals, Godhra.
9. KC. Panchnadikar, and J. Panchnadikar, *Rural Modernisation in India*, Popular Prakashan, Bombay, 1978.
10. For details kindly refer; *Tribal Area Sub-Plan*, Integrated Tribal Development Project, Dahod, Distt. Panchmahals—*Draft Project Report, 1978-83* (mimeo.), Project Administrator's Office.

11. The voluntary agencies are not discussed since most of them are there for social and educational purposes. Recently, Sadguru Seva Sangh Trust has made a significant dent in the area with lift irrigation schemes. This will require attention at a future date.
12. For details refer, Sudarshan Iyengar and others in *Dry Land Agriculture —Diagnosis and Prescription,* (Mimeo.) DPP Cell, Godhra, Presented at the 12th Annual Conference, The Gujarat Economic Association.
13. "Final Report on Survey of Seasonal Migration of Labour in Panchmahals District, 1971-72," *The Bulletin of Economic and Statistics,* April-June 1973, Vol. XIV, No. 2, Bureau of Economics and Statistics, Government of Gujarat.
14. Private Communication, Tribal Administrator's Orifice, TSP, Dahod.
15. Anil D. Bhamania, *A Study of Migrating Rural Adivasi Bhil Labourers of Dahod Taluka,* MSW Unpublished thesis, Gujarat Vidyapith, Ahmedabad, 1976.
16. R.D. Gandhi, *Rural Seasonal Migration,* Gujarat Institute of Area Planning, Ahmedabad, March, 1979.
17. T.K. Jayaraman, "Seasonal Irrigation of Tribal Labour—Irrigation Project in Gujarat," *Economic and Political Weekly,* October 13, 1979.
18. Sudarshan Iyengar and Ravindra H. Dholakia, *op. cit.*
19. B. Sivaraman, The Alternative? *Kurukshetra,* Oct. 1, 1984.
20. The DPP Cell has arrived at this figure, Class I tanks having more than 100 hectares of potential command have been studied.
21. V.K.R.V. Rao, Growth with Social Justice, *Kurukshetra,* May 16 1978.
22. Private Communication Agriculture Officer, District Agriculture Office, Panchmahals, Godhra.

Tribal Economic Formations Based upon Settled Agriculture and their Modes of Dissolution

S.N. MISHRA

SETTLED AGRICULTURE

The tribal economy based upon settled agriculture as it emerges from shifting agriculture usually comes to have two forms: one in which cultivated land continues to be under communal appropriation and the other in which it has passed under private appropriation. In due course, the former form itself passes into the latter. Such a change occurred in past as in the case of the N.W. Frontier tribes and it is occurring today in the case of the N.E. Frontier tribes and the Eastern Central Belt of India. The more delayed the change, the more is the impact of external factors upon it. Of the two forms, the former is more primitive and therefore less dynamic than the latter. The mechanism of its transformation into the latter it taken up subsequently. Here our attention is focused on the dynamics of the second form. This needs to be prefaced, however, by an outline of the patterns of settlement and associated divisions of the community territory.

Irrespective of the form of the economy, the village emerges as a key economic unit concomitant with the emergence and development of settled agriculture. The village emerges on the one hand as the "being together" of the producing families, on the other the clan, and in the absence of the clan the community begins to appear as the "coming together" of the villages. The village which gets formed as spatial cluster of producing family units itself becomes the basic unit of the primitive state organisation, having its own territorial jurisdiction with judicial and penal powers exercised by a chief or village council. The village territory which is fluid at the outset takes definite shape, however, as the density of the village increases. Further, being a part of the wider division of the community's territory, it exists alongside the clan or the community land. Wherever due, perhaps, to the large size of the community, clans have come to acquire territorial dimension, clan territories together replace the community territory and the village territory appears as a sub-space of the clan territory. The clan territory not covered by village territories obviously exists as *common clan land* open for common use of the villages and for the formation of new villages. As the families setting in these villages belong to the same clan, the villages take the mono-clan form. In the absence of territorial dimensions of clans, village territory appears as a sub-space of the community territory and in the like manner uncovered portions of it exists as *common community land*, open again for common use and for the formation of new villages. The village in this case is more likely to take a multi rather than mono-clan form.

The territorial division patterns just outlined emerge only in those natural environments in which the introduction of settled agriculture leads to the formation of cluster villages of mono or multi-clan composition. Natural conditions which make individual families settle in a dispersed manner but nonetheless at an approachable distance to each other, eliminate from the outset the village as an economic or social unit. The lands of the families appear as sub-spaces of the community territory or of the clan territories. And the uncovered territory appears as *common community or clan land* available for common use of the families and settlement of new families. Though uncommon, a scattered family pattern of settlement is attested to by the Nayars of the

Malabar Coast and by the Germanic tribes before these invaded Rome, Gaul and Spain, etc.[1]

PRIVATE APPROPRIATION AND ITS DISSOLUTION

The primitive economy based upon settled agriculture with cultivated land under private appropriation can be briefly described now. It emerges after overcoming all the limitations arising out of communal mediation, on the one hand between the producer and his land and on the other between him and the product of his labour. This economy, thus, can be assumed to consist of independent family producers who face the material conditions of their living—means and material of labour including land—as their own. The aim of production, as in all hitherto primitive economies, is reproduction of the family alongwith the material conditions of its reproduction. Each family is self-sufficient; so is the village and still above it the clan and the community consisting of such clan. Each family engages itself not only in securing the food it needs but all other goods—cloth, house, cooking utensils, storage bins, articles of personal use, implements, tools and weapons of war, etc. required for living directly or indirectly. Cultivated land is inherited within the family through successive generations. When the family size outgrows its inherited land that is when the inherited land fails to meet the food needs of the family, daughter families and so also daughter villages spring up on the common community lands, in the territory of the original village or of the clan. This way of expansion of the economy reaches, however, a dead end as soon as the cultivable portion of the common community land has been brought under cultivation. Thereafter any change in the economy must occur through a change in its basis; *the basis being the self-sufficient family producers who labour on the land they own without any division of labour among them.* The manner in which the basis is changed we shall return to discuss soon. Meanwhile, in order to round-off the picture a few observations on its primitivity are in order.

The primitivity of this economy lies in the fact that *common land* irrespective of whether it is in the village or clan jurisdiction continues to be under *communal appropriation*. Not only is it used as common means of production—as hunting and food gathering grounds, grazing land, collection of wood for odd types of needs, etc. but it is also commonly defended from other communities.[2] The other evidence of primitivity is that alienation of land under private appropriation is contingent upon *common blood* ties. The blood ties may be very direct as within the family, further removed as within the village or still farther removed as within the clan. The legitimacy of alienation is directly proportional to the nearness of the two individuals between whom the land passes. Indeed often it is restricted to direct blood relations. And in case of alienation where this condition is not met, *land passes from private to communal appropriation.* It becomes common village or clan land. From the viewpoint of fully developed private property such as in the capitalist economy where a private owner has an unfettered right of alienation, the unredeemed, primitive character of private appropriation in this economy is only too clear. The restricted nature of private property in land here is nevertheless quite consistent with the absence of any division of labour and exchange. Land like everything else is not a *commodity* in this system.

The foregoing is still an abstract and general reconstruction. The real economies are its modifications, essentially brought about by a certain degree of division of labour usually at the village or clan level and some amount of intercommunity trade. A village or clan may be better placed in respect of availability of a particular material or may have acquired better skill in a particular craft such as in pottery, weaving, tool-making, etc. and thereby is able to meet not only its own needs but also those of other villages or clans in varying degrees. But there is no village or clan which could be said to be composed full-time specialists engaged in any one of such crafts. In fact, crafts are only supplementary to the main activity—agriculture. In any case, there is a certain amount of exchange, therefore, of craft goods for craft goods and for food, modifying in the process the self-sufficiency of the family, the village and the clan. It is also modified by the exchange relations of the community with other communities which may be more or less primitive than itself. It obtains from games of hunt, gathered food and non-food items, wood, stone tools and other crafts goods from the hunting and food gathering neighbours and also from the community of shifting cultivators in exchange for produced food. From the advanced class-community, again in exchange for produced food, the community obtains items like suit, metal and metal tools, kerosene oil, electric-torches, mill-made cloth and other manufactured goods. It is evident from the nature of these exchange relations that the economy produces a certain amount of surplus food.

Simple exchange relations of this kind, while modifying in varying degrees the self-sufficiency of the primitive economy based upon settled agriculture, do not, however, contradict its original basis wherein family producers stand as owner-workers in relation to the means of production including land. The real threat to the original basis arises when the economy reaches the limit of its cultivable land and there remains no scope for further appropriation of land through labour. *From here on any change in the private appropriation of land at the family level can come only through attention of land among the families.* The precondition for such alienation—that there exist families which come to own more or less land than they can and need to cultivate with their own labour—is also created from here on, in course of the reproduction of the community. Since the total food production of the community reaches its upper limit along with the cultivable land, its population too may stabilise at its upper limit; but this does not prevent the population of the families and villages to vary among themselves. This fact, couple with the inheritance of cultivated land within families sooner or later creates the precondition just mentioned. And no sooner than this precondition is created, alienation of land between the families becomes a social necessity. It is effected through the traditional medium of exchange, on payment of a lumpsum tribute or gift in the form of a cow, mithan, goat, pigs, garment, grain, etc. For the first time land in this way acquires a certain, though token, nominal *exchange value.* So long as, and to the extent that, private land under the vestige of the blood ties, is transferred in this manner, the tendency is towards a pattern of land redistribution that reasserts the economy's original basis in which families *own the land they cultivate by their own labour.* The prospect of exchanging the food surplus specially with the class community, (which, as if, lies in waiting at the door with its armoury of merchandise, money and credit), however, *favours alienation of surplus food rather than land* between the families. The land, in view of this prospect, is transferred without the ownership right and on payment of a part of the produce for the right to cultivate. The producer faces the land transferred in this way *not as his own*. Instead, his relation to this land is mediated by the owner who, as owner, appropriates a part of the produce which is the product of the producer's labour. Here for the first time, crystalise a new set of production relations which contradict the original basis of the economy, and in which are laid the foundation of a class society. The development of the primitive economy based upon settled agriculture to this class-form is one among several ways in which its dissolution occurs. Its distinguishing characteristic is that the dissolution in this case results solely from the internal logic of production and reproduction of the primitive economy. The other forms of dissolution that are attested to by history and produced by the external relations—violent or peaceful—of the community can be briefly described as follows:

(1) When the primitive agricultural community conquers the territory of the other neighbouring community, it expropriates the conquered population from the ownership of land, and if the population is not expelled, it either becomes the slave of the conquers as during ancient Roman or Greek times, or it is allowed to cultivate its land on payment of tribute or regular rent to the suzrain community as among the NEFA villages.[3] In either case, the original basis of the community gives way to an inferior, exploited population which becomes the basis of the primitive class community.

(2) When the primitive community is conquerred by an alien Raja or a prince belonging to a class community, the tribal chief's lands become Raja's demesne land, the subjugated population is reduced to the status of serfs in part and in part of tenants. It may also be required to give *corvee* either for military service or public works. As the Raja's own people usually of alien origin, family members, administrators, revenue collectors, etc. increase, a class of landlords, at first through assignment of rent, labour service and finally of demesne lands and common lands of the community, develops, breaking the old basis of the community.[4]

(3) When the chief of the primitive community, wherever there is a chief, accepts the Brahmanic system and,

through an initiation ceremony, is admitted to the Kshatriya caste and consecrated to the status of a king, the community gradually gets differentiated into a class-community. The chief usually introduces the administration pattern of the caste society with the help of aliens who are allowed to own land in the territory of the community besides grant of shares in the traditional tribute which becomes land rent in due course.[5]

(4) When the community admits members of other primitive communities and allows them to cultivate land in its territory on payment of rent to the clan or village chief or to the private owners of land it contradicts its original basis and lays thus the foundations of class society.[6]

(5) When the community allows its members or is forced to allow by the State power of the surrounding, suzrain class-community, the right to alienate its lands to outsiders, especially to the members of the latter community, its original basis gives way to a class-community. The outsiders, who initially come to own land usually against cumulating balance of payments liability which results from adverse terms and unfair manipulations on account of trade, in the process of appropriation convert the expropriated into a class of bonded labourers who provide the necessary labour power for the cultivation of the appropriated land. A prior phase may be to allow the original community members to cultivate the appropriated land on rent. Besides the resulting formation of classes, the alien appropriators stand out as a class by itself, for they pay no allegiance to the primitive community while they own land in the territory of the community. The presence of their culture in the primitive community subverts the culture of the community. This process of dissolution of the primitive community has been quite extensive and occurring steadily, specially since the inception of the British rule in India. It received a new fillip when, following freedom from the British rule, the primitive communities became subjects of planned development.

The modes of dissolution just described occur over long periods of time before the primitive community of settled agriculturists based upon private appropriation of cultivated land forever passes into a class-community. Until the primitive community has thus vanished it may continue to give the appearance of a primitive form more so because the exploited carry the burden of their memorable past in the stray primitive traits and practices of their dying culture.

COMMUNAL APPROPRIATION AND ITS DISSOLUTION

The second form of primitive economy based upon settled agriculture is the one in which cultivated lands remain under communal appropriation. The reader may be remained that survival of communal property relations in the production conditions of settled agriculture is basically due to the community's inability to discard the principle of equality of all its members. The cause of this inability may be the small size of the community wherein producers are usually cognate kins. Occasionally the equality principle may be retained after the size has surpassed the limits of cognate kins in order to keep alive the consciousness of blood ties, and the resultant unity, as among the Pathan communities of the N.W. Frontier. This way a community is able to mobilise greater collective force—a larger unity free from contradictions—against external attacks, dismemberment and threats of expulsion.

The survival of the communal property relations may indeed be reinforced further by specific preconditions of settled agriculture arising out of specific geoclimatic conditions of a community's territory. These preconditions—such as construction and maintenance of irrigation channels in the precarious arid soil of Beluchistan and southern portions of the N.W. Frontier region: quick, effective utilisation of short-lived inundations by embankments of fields in the trans-Indus regions; controlling of hill torrents for seepage of water over the successive terraces as in the Dera-Ismail-Khan district; renewal of old and adding of new terraces in the Kangra district of Himachal Pradesh[7]—call for co-operative labour of the producers. At some places some of the preconditions can be so severe as to force the producers even to cultivate the land in common and share the produce according to family contributions of labour and ploughs.[8]

In the more prevalent form for which evidence is readily available from Pathan and Baluch communities in N.W. Frontier, Nayars[9] in the south and Kangra villages in the north, while grazing grounds, forest and waste lands, are left as common means of production, cultivated land is divided among the producing families on an equal share basis: per capita or per working male basis as the case may be. This principle of division works under the given territorial divisions and sub-divisions of the community. The smaller the population size of the community, the smaller are the number (levels) of its territorial divisions. The primary division is among clans and secondary among sub-clans and further among villages. The respective divisions are known as *llaqua, Tappa* and *Khel* in the Pathan communities. At the base level, i.e., *Khel,* the cultivated land is partitioned off into compact blocks of good, medium and bad quality lands. These blocks are called *Wand(s).* The divisions of the community territory and of its arable lands into *Wands* are permanent.

At the time of any redistribution called *Vesh* (Wesh), two types of changes, in general, occur: (a) clans, sub-clans or villages interchange their territories leaving behind their immovable property; and (b) cultivated lands (Wands) are shared on equal per capita basis among the families or groups of families of close kindreds (Kandi) belonging to a clan, sub-clan or the village. A family or group of families may receive its share of land in one or more Wand(s), with land area duly adjusted for quality differences among the *Wands.* Both changes aim at community members sharing equally the advantages and disadvantages of territorial divisions and land quality differences.

Since differences arising out of natural causes cannot be eliminated under the prevailing methods of production no one redistribution is final. And as the differences can be shared equally among members only by rotating, periodic, redistributions are a logical necessity. Also as in course of time family holdings become unequal either due to changes in family size resulting from population change,[10] admission of new families through initiation (as among Baluch and Oraon), or change in the total cultivated area, redistribution is required to re-establish equality. There are thus constant opposite movements of the forces of equality and inequality. At regular intervals of 5, 10, 15 or 20 years, a community replaces a situation of inequality by that of equality through redistribution but only to face the problem again. The length of the interval depends upon the communal forces seeking equality, its urgency, etc. on the one hand and undisturbed objective conditions of production and reproduction on the other. At the time of redistribution (Vesh) the community reappropriates, in the general case, all lands under family possessions, territories of the villages, sub-clans and clans, makes a fresh allotment in such a manner that clans exchange their territories and *ipso facto* therefore the sub-clans and villages. Within the territory of a village, then, the cultivated land is divided among the families that come to occupy it, on an equal share basis. The allotments of territories and division of the cultivated lands remain valid until the next redistribution.

The communal authority is exercised by the village, clan and the community chief at the respective levels. The chief's authority is based upon popular consent; in fact, the chief in discharging his functions is assisted by a council of members at his level. The chief and his family's own share of land is governed by the same general rule of distribution that applies to the rest of the community. In communities where the institution of a chief does not exist, the exercise of communal authority rests with a council of elders at different levels or with the popular assemblies of all adult male members (*Jirga* of the Balooch and Pathans).

The contradictory basis of the above economy lies in the antithetical nature of communal appropriation (manifest in periodic redistribution) of its land and private mode of agricultural production. This antithesis develops, with the development of the community, into a conflict which is eventually resolved through the dissolution of communal appropriation. A new unitary basis with private appropriation alongside private production replaces the old basis of the economy. The conflict comes to surface when development on the old basis begins to face its limits. The population approaches a size at which blood bonds, apart from those of close kindreds, become very weak and there remains little scope for increasing the cultivated land of a family, a village, sub-clan and a clan, except at the expense of another family, another village, another sub-clan and another clan. Private producers see no reason to develop the land, houses and other immovable assets under their possession when they realise more and more that the fruits of such development may, at the time of the next redistribution, accrue to those with whom they have no or very distant affinity of blood. All such conditions crystalise into opposition to communal appropriation and redistribution of land. As a result, redistribution gets confined at first to the clan and sub-clan, then to the village and finally to a family group and is eventually abandoned. In this way, the dissolution of the old and the formation of the new basis of the economy is completed.

This general description is attested to by specific steps that were taken among the N.W. Frontier communities in order to counter the force of communal appropriation and redistribution of land. Among the Marwats of Bannu[11] every man attempted to increase his family size by taking in as many wives as he could for claiming a larger share in land. In the Swat valley[12] where redistribution of land and exchange of territory covered almost the whole valley, villagers far from refurbishing their houses would not even plant a tree whose fruits they knew they would not reap. In fact, wherever improvements in land, houses, etc. were undertaken, redistribution was at first sought to be deferred and the period of redistribution enlarged. Lands specially so improved came to be recognised as *quabza* land and were made exempt from communal appropriation and redistribution.[13] In the beginning such exemption may have looked like a harmless concession to the special expenditure of private labour. But this could easily open the gate for private efforts to increase the share of *quabza* lands and inevitably to progressive reduction of land area still subjects to communal appropriation and redistribution. This dissolution process of communal property in land is endogenous to the economy. External forces may sometimes reinforce it or set aside the old basis of the economy altogether such as when the community becomes a subject community. An example of the first sort of impact comes from the Pathan villages of Dera-Ismail-Khan which let out the common lands to alien tenants and divided the produce rent among the families according to their shares in the cultivated lands at the time of the last redistribution (Vesb). The village community *vis-a-vis* alien tenants becomes a collective landlord contradicting thus the original basis of the economy in which all working individuals were independent producers. Periodic redistribution remains restricted to lands under the possession of community members.[14] When, due to the causes described above, it is finally given up, the basis of a feudal economy emerges directly from the communal system.

Conquest of the community, when its members are not expelled from the conquered territory, lays the basis for an intermediary class between the conquerers and the community members. As it happened with the Sikh conquest of some trans-Indus communities, this class is usually formed of the chiefs and leading families who are entrusted with the task of collecting state-taxes and in lieu are given a share in it. Their power being now less based on common consent and more derived from the state above, this class attempts to appropriate the common lands for itself. Even if communal redistribution of lands under the possession of community members continues, appropriation of common lands in this way changes the original basis of the economy and marks another step in the direction of the feudal system. Communal authority having been undermined, opposition to communal redistribution fails to be countered, leading to its defferment and eventual abandonment. Wherever expropriation of common lands has been successfully resisted, abandonment of communal redistribution leads to the emergence of independent peasant proprietors. Finally, as with the British, when the conquerers force upon a system of law and administration resting on private property conceptions, they sound the death-knell of communal appropriation and redistribution. The settlement reports of the N.W. Frontier districts annexed to the British territories of India speak volumes on the subject. D.G. Barkley, in the *Administration Report, 1872-73* wrote, "Since the country (N.W. Frontier district) came under British rule, every opportunity has been taken to get rid of these periodical exchanges on a large scale (i.e., inter-village and inter-clan exchanges), by substituting final positions or adjusting the revenue demands according to the value of the lands actually held by each village but the custom is in few cases still acted upon among the proprietors (in fact holders holding on behalf of the village community) of the same village, though probably no cases remain in which it would be enforced between the proprietors of the distinct villages."[15] The next step the conquerers took was to prepare and give legal status to a record of private rights for the lands under family possessions within the village. Besides granting proprietary rights and putting an end thus to communal appropriation and redistribution at the village levels, tenants, where these had been taken in on common lands, were given occupancy rights. Further where revenue assessments were settled with chiefs and village heads, a supervisor landlord right with power to dispose of former common waste land was recognised. In other cases village forests and wastes were appropriated as state property, with provision, for limited common use of the community members. All these measures finally put an end to the primitive communal system and cleared the way for agriculture based upon private property in land.

NOTES AND REFERENCES

1. Karl Marx, *Grundrisse*, Penguin Books, 1973, pp. 483-84. Marx says this form was not original but a product of historical evolution since back in Julius Caesar's lime in the Germanic community, "there was already annual re-division of the cultivable field among the groups—the gentes (clans) and tribes—but not yet among the individual families of a community; probably cultivation was also in groups, communal. See his letter (Third Draft) to Veza Zasulich in Eric Habsbaum (Ed.) Karl Marx *Precapitalist Economic Formations*, p. 144. Lawrence and Wishart, London, 1964. Marx may well be right in his guess but the fact of scattered family settlement and cultivation is not inconsistent with periodic exchange or redistribution of clan territories. Moreover, a historical case of this nature is provided by the N.W. Frontier tribes.
2. From the vantage point of the class community such defence appears to be an act of rebellion and is accordingly suppressed.
3. B.K. Roy Burman, "Dimensions of Land Problem" (mimeo.), Registrar of Census Office, New Delhi.
4. B.H. Baden Powell, *Indian Village Community, op. cit.* See the land tenures of Kulu Valley, Oraon under the Dalbhum Kingdom and Ahom in Assam. In ancient India, the kingdom of Magadh arose out of a similar process. Kosambi, *Introduction, op. cit.*
5. S.C. Roy, *The Mundas and Their Country*, Calcutta, 1912. See also J.H. Hutton in O'Malley, (Ed.) *Modern India and the West*, and also the discussions of Ahom and Kooch in B.H. Baden Powell, *Indian Village Community, op. cit.*
6. Besides many cases such as Oraon, Pathan, Naga, etc. the case of Maler and Mala-Paharia is pertinent. It is described in Saileshwar Prasad, *Where the Three-Tribes Meet*, Indian International Publications, Allahabad, 1974.
7. B.H. Baden Powell in the *Indian Village Community*, quoting P. Lyall's *Kangra R.S.*, also his *Land Systems of British India*, Vol. 2, Part IV, Chapter II.

8. The 'Halara' system of cultivation among the Pathan tribes of the northern part of Dera-Ismail-Khan District; See B.H. Baden Powells, *Land Systems, ibid.*, p. 653.
9. B.H. Baden Powell, *Indian Village Community, op. cit.*, p. 17.5.
10. The total population of the community need not change for changes to occur in the size of the families.
11. L.S.S. O'Malley, *India's Social Heritage*, Chapter III, first published 1934; Reprint, Vikas Publishing House, Delhi, 1976.
12. *Imperial Gazetteer of India*, Vol. XIX, North-West Frontier Province, Clarendon Press, 1908, p. 138-220.
13. B.H. Baden Powell, *Land Systems, op. cit.*
14. It should be interesting to compare it with the opposite case of Oraon in which redistribution was restricted to the lands given to non-community members, cf. Baden Powell, *Indian Village Community, op. cit.*
15. Quoted in B.H. Baden Powell, *Land Systems of British India*, Vol. II, Clarendon Press, Oxford, 1982, pp. 628-29.

Cattle and Livestock

The role of livestock in general and the cattle in particular in the tribal economy is directly connected with agriculture and tenures. In the tribes where settled agriculture is practised and the proportion of land owning tillers is large, the cattle population is also large. But in tribes where shifting cultivation was practised until recently and where the tribals have not been able to make the transition to settled agriculture, either because of long traditions of axe cultivation or because of the paucity of cultivable land the livestock population is very small. Wherever the cultivator has land of his own, even it be very small, he acquires livestock. In the tribal economy the cattle find the greatest use. They supply the draught necessary for various tillage operations and for transport. Another important use of cattle relates to manure. In the peculiar soil conditions of the tribal areas manuring becomes a necessity. Their staple crop, the makka, and the various cash crops like cotton and groundnut require good doses of manure. The tribal cultivator is so poor that he can rarely afford to purchase manure. The easiest way out for him is to rear his own cattle. Since he does not feed his cattle on costly concentrates, the rearing of cattle does not involve any extra expenditure. Even roughages he gets as a by-product of the makka and jowar that he grows. Rest of the roughages the cattle get from grazing on the *charnoi* (pasture) land. Manure is the primary consideration for rearing large number of cattle, goats and buffaloes. The second consideration relates to draught power and the third to milk and milk products.

BREEDS OF CATTLE IN THE TRIBAL AREAS

In the Bhil belt of State the main breeds of the cattle are *Malwi, Nimari* and *Khillari* with local breeds dominated by these strains. Malwi breed is found mainly on the Plateau and the adjoining areas. The Nimari breed is found in the district Nimar of the Hill division.

Malwi is chiefly a draught breed. Its dominating colour is pure white. The size is medium. The bullocks are strong but not fast.

The Nimar cattle are found all over the Nimar district of the State. Nimari breed is also prized for draught purposes. The milch capacity of Nimari cows is very limited. The cattle bred on the Satpuras are smaller and lighter as compared to those bred in the Narmada valley.

Satpuras in the Nimar have another breed of cattle for draught purposes known as the *khillari* breed. This is a hardy and rather wild breed used mainly for dragging carts.

In the hilly tracts of Nimar, Dhar and Jhabua many local breeds are found which are much smaller. These local breeds are dominated by several strains but mainly by the dominant breed of the region. In Sailana, for instance, the local breed is dominated by the *Dongri* breed of adjoining Rajasthan. In Alirajpur tehsil of Jhabua district Gir blood is visible in the local breed. In Jhabua most dominant strain is the Malwi, although the cattle are small and weak.

In the Gond-Korku belt the Gondi or the Gondwani is the chief breed. The Gondi cattle are very hardy, though smaller in stature as compared to Malwi and Nimari.

In the Saharia belt the main breed of cattle is the Malwi. In Morena and Shivpuri there are local breeds of cattle which are hardy. These local breeds are also mainly of draught type.

DENSITY OF LIVESTOCK

Each tribal belt has its own characteristics regarding the density of livestock. But all the tribal belts show a remarkable high density of cattle population.

The table below gives the density of livestock in the three tribal belts as the number of livestock per 100 acres of cultivated land.

TABLE 11.1

Density of Livestock in the Tribal Areas

Sl. No.	*District*	*Net cultivated area (in acres)*	*Total livestock (1951)*	*Density of livestock (per 100 acres of cultivated land)*	
1.	Jhabua	467103	552591	11	
2.	Dhar	923305	687092	73	84
3.	Nimar	227539	752009	61	
4.	Dewas	610305	417507	67	67
5.	Shivpuri	597408	919517	153	
6.	Guna	731501	801198	109	121
7.	Morena	795000	813935	102	

District Jhabua in the Bhil belt shows a density of 118, the highest in the belt. Dhar with 73 comes next and Nimar last with 61. Dewas, in which lies the Gond-Korku belt, shows a density of 67. The districts of Shivpuri, Guna and Morena show a density of 153, 109 and 102 respectively.

This indicates that in all the tribal belts density of livestock population is very large from the point of view of the carrying capacity of the land. The poor soils of these areas can hardly be expected to keep the livestock in good health and vigour. As a region the Saharia belt shows an average density of 121, which is the highest of all the belts. The Bhil belt has an average density of 84 and the Gond-Korku belt only 67. From this picture of density one would normally expect the largest number of livestock per household in the Saharia belt, with Bhil belt coming second and the Gond-Korku belt coming last. But sample survey shows that the pattern of livestock keeping in the three belts is altogether different. The Table 11.2 shows the average number of livestock (excluding poultry) per household among the various tribes.

Table 11.2 shows that Bhilalas have an average of 12.1 livestock per household. The Bhil comes close second with 10.2 livestock per household. The Saharia has an average of 1.87 only. The Korku has an average of 3.7 and the Gond 4.6.

TABLE 11.2

Average Number of Livestock in each Tribal Household

Sl. No.		*Average number of livestock per family*
1.	Bhil	10.2
2.	Bhilala	12.1
3.	Saharia	1.87
4.	Korku	3.7
5.	Gond	4.6

The Saharia, although inhabiting the region of highest livestock density has the least number of livestock per household. The reason is that in the Central India settled agriculture and cattle go together. The Saharia has been used to forestry and shifting cultivation till very recently. Neither of these occupations need very many cattle. Populations practising shifting cultivation have a certain amount of nomadism which not facilitate rearing of a large number of livestock. Now, when the Saharias have been deprived of shifting cultivation they do not have sufficient land to settle down to agriculture, cultivating their own land. In the absence of ownership of land and no possibilities of availability of enough cultivable land they cannot afford to keep many animals with them. It would be unnecessary and wasteful. The historical reasons and present pressure of population on land have made Saharias an anachronism—a tribe in the land of over-populated livestock having very little livestock of its own.

The Bhils and the Bhilalas on the other hand keep large number of animals. They live in compact groups in the south and outnumber the non-tribals. They hold most of the land in their region and even if the holdings are small, the hills and wastelands are plenty and the Bhil and the Bhilala can afford to keep many animals. They like to keep cattle, goats and sometimes buffaloes. These animals supply invaluable manure free of cost, provide cheap draught and even yield some milk for the household. At times their bullocks may be offered for rent. If the tribal gives a pair of bullocks on hire for the Rabi he can easily earn about thirty rupees for the season. In kharif he would get about twice the above amount. The young ones may be reared and sold on maturity, bringing additional income to the family coffers. The Bhil and the Bhilala is so conscious of the economy of the cattle that he rarely milks Ms cows. The heifer and the calf are allowed to suck all the milk they can so that they may grow strong and vigorous.

The Gond with 4.6 livestock per household and Korku with 3.7 shows that relatively they have more animals per household (as compared to Saharias). But as compared to Bhils and the Bhilalas they have fewer animals per household.

EVIL EFFECTS OF LARGE LIVESTOCK POPULATION

It is apparent that the large livestock population in the Bhil belt, under the present circumstances of land fertility and the plethora of uneconomic holdings, cannot but lead to a gradual deterioration in the breed of the livestock particularly the cattle which is most numerous. Although, the number of cattle in this belt is large, its performance as draught and milch cattle is deplorably poor. Neglected feeding and indiscriminate breeding are sure to make the breed poorer and poorer. Merely cheap supply of manures does not justify such a large livestock population, most of which is superfluous and redundant. The tribal cultivator here has been caught in a vicious circle where he can not replace the quantity with quality. Given an economic unit of cultivation he would not need so many useless cattle for dung alone. As Dr. Baljit Singh has remarked, "a petty holding and an inferior pair of bullocks go together. We cannot eliminate the one without doing away with the other."

APPENDIX

CATTLE STATISTICS

TABLE 1

Statement Showing the Number of Livestock in Bihar According to Last Four Livestock Censuses

Livestock	*1956*	*Percentage of increase (+) or decrease (–)*	*1961*	*Percentage of increase (+) or decrease (–)*	*1966*	*Percentage of increase (+) or decrease (–)*	*1972*
1. Cattle							
(a) Males over 3 years	6379154	(+11.27)	7098123	(–2.35)	6930719	(+5.26)	7295418
(b) Females over 3 years	4301393	(+ 1.26)	4351597	(–5.67)	4104770	(+ 1.97)	4185650
(c) Young stock	3717852	(+25.19)	4654366	(–11.46)	4120967	(–16.76)	3430035
2. Buffaloes							
(a) Males over 3 years	683402	(–0.22)	681866	(+7.36)	732018	(–1.93)	717867
(b) Females over 3 years	1618700	(+1.96)	1650458	(+0.74)	1662685	(+14.45)	1903079
(c) Young stock	1124848	(+21.48)	1365908	(+7.78)	1259661	(–16.03)	1157701

TABLE 2

Statement Showing the Bovine Population in the Selected Districts as per Livestock Census of 1972

Livestock	*Name of the districts covered under I.A.D.P.*				*Remarks*
	Patna	*Shahabad*	*Monghyr*	*State*	
1. Cattle					
(a) Males over 3 years	263420	462131	354554	7293428	
(b) Females over 3 years	105194	240750	265592	4185659	
(c) Young stock	103072	216009	239629	3430035	
2. Buffaloes					
(a) Males over 3 years	26295	1152	32131	717867	
(b) Females over 3 years	137803	214567	103130	1903079	
(c) Young stock	86563	128255	52045	1057701	
	723148	1262864	1057101	18589759	

TABLE 3

Statement Showing the Bovine Population Covered by the I.C.D.P. and R.C.D. Centres in the State

Name of the units	*Cattle*			*Buffalo*			*Total*
	Males over 3 years	*Females over 3 years*	*Young stock*	*Males over 3 years*	*Females over 3 years*	*Young stock*	
1. I.C.D.P. total	184204	146011	124680	623	95333	58250	609101
2. Barauni-Begusarai Project	74103	83861	75146	112	30854	20423	284499
3. Patna-Arrah Project	110101	62150	49534	511	64479	37827	324602
4. R.C.D. Centres							
4.1 Barauni	16593	26041	18055	7	8447	5079	74122
4.2 Begusarai	18493	20498	19500	24	7221	5133	70859
4.3 Manjhoul	15745	15502	16568	30	5136	3489	56471
4.4 Khagaria	23271	21820	21023	51	10150	6722	83037
4.5 Danapur	18729	16687	14389	160	14673	8259	72897
4.6 Bikram	33876	13292	11286	170	19517	10899	89740
4.7 Arrah	27727	16205	12170	131	13855	7753	77841
4.8 Sahar	29769	15266	11689	50	16434	10919	84124

TABLE 4

Statement Showing the Breedable Bovine Population of the Selected Stockman Centres

Sl. No.	Name of the I.C.D.P. Projects	Name of the R.C.D. Centres	No. of Reporting Stockman Centres	No. of breedable animals		Other bovine pouplation		
				Cows	Buffaloes	Bulls	Bullocks	Male Buffs
1.	Patna Arrah	1. Danapur	9	4701	4267	14	57/9	314
		2. Bikram	8	3666	5022	19	8092	21
		3. Arrah	10	8324	6568	56	10288	272
		4. Sabar	7	2155	4932	16	9081	14
	Total		34	19346	20789	105	33240	621
2.	Barauni Begusarai	1. Barauni	8	8528	1874	1	4039	353
		2. Begusarai	8	6661	2414	16	4128	4
		3. Khagaria	7	6254	2375	90	6781	421
		4. Manjhoul	5	3783	880	9	3991	nil
	Total		28	25226	7543	116	19939	778

TABLE 5

Statement Showing the Number of Cattle Inoculated and Vaccinated under the Projects

Name of the LCD.P./ Regional Centres	*No. of Stockman Centres*	*No. of Cattle inoculated and vaccinated against different deseases*			
		H.S.		*B.Q.*	
		1970-71	*1971-72*	*1970-71*	*1971-72*
1	*2*	*3*	*4*	*5*	*6*
Patna-Arrah					
1. Danapur	9	10040	7026	4023	3528
2. Bikram	10	23395	19530	9607	6697
3. Arrah	8	15743	32286	11071	20871
4. Sahar	7	8617	12381	4642	11579
Total	34	61795	71223	29243	42675
Barauni-Begusarai					
1. Barauni	9	N.A.	5575	N.A.	4586
2. Begusarai	8	52	28644	37	6104
3. Khagaria	7	N.A.	4190	N.A.	20
4. Manjhoul	5	1000	6131	N.A.	17285
Total	29	1052	44980	37	27994
Grand Total	63	68847	115755	23380	70669

(Contd.)

TABLE 5 (*Contd.*)

Name of the I.C.D.P./ Regional Centres	*No. of Cattle inoculated and vaccinated against different diseases*					
	Anthrax		*R.P.*		*Total*	
	1970-71	*1971-72*	*1970-71*	*1971-72*	*1970-71*	*1971-72*
1	*7*	*8*	*9*	*10*	*11*	*12*
Patna-Arrah						
1. Danapur	1699	1613	3049	5811	18811	17978
2. Bikram	7205	5121	30319	58821	74526	90169
3. Arrah	478	3807	27624	64331	54916	121295
4. Sahar	60	274	21336	26439	34655	50873
Total	9442	11015	82328	155402	182908	280315
Barauni-Begusarai						
1. Barauni	N.A.	4027	N.A.	4390	N.A.	18578
2. Begusarai	N.A.	857	N.A.	16929	89	52534
3. Khagaria	N.A.	N.A.	N.A.	11762	N.A.	13972
4. Manjhoul	N.A.	2143	N.A.	14840	1000	39888
Total		7027		47541	1089	126972
Grand Total	9442	18047	82828	202828	183997	405237

TABLE 6

Name of the Region	Total Bovine population	Inoculations and vaccinations done during 1970-71 and 1971-72 against contagious diseases in percentage			
		HS		B.Q.	
		1970-71	1971-72	1970-71	1971-72
1	2	3	4	5	6
1. Danapur	72897	13.77	9.64	5.52	4.84
2. Bikram	89740	30.53	21.76	10.70	7.46
3. Arrah	77841	20.22	41.47	10.42	26.81
4. Sahar	84124	10.24	14.71	5.52	13.76
5. Barauni	74122	N.A.	7.52	N.A.	6.18
6. Begusarai	70869	Nil	40.41	Nil	8.61
7. Khagaria	83037	N.A.	5.04	N.A.	0.02
8. Manjhoul	46471	NA	10.83	N.A.	30.60

(Contd.)

TABLE 6 (*Contd.*)

Name of the Region	*Inoculations and vaccinations done during 1970-71 and 1971-72 against contagious diseases in percentages*					
	Anthrax		*R.P.*		*Total*	
	1970-71	*1971-72*	*1970-71*	*1971-72*	*1970-71*	*1971-72*
1	*7*	*8*	*9*	*10*	*11*	*12*
1. Danapur	2.33	2.21	4.18	7.97	25.80	24.66
2. Bikram	8.03	5.70	33.78	65.54	83.04	100.46
3. Arrah	0.61	4.89	35.49	82.64	66.74	155.81
4. Sahar	Nil	0.56	25.36	31.42	41.12	60.45
5. Barauni	N.A.	5.43	N.A.	5.92	N.A.	25.05
6. Begusarai	N.A.	1.20	N.A.	23.88	Nil	74.10
6. Khagaria	N.A.	N.A.	N.A.	14.16	N.A.	19.22
8. Manjhoul	N.A.	3.79	N.A.	25.39	N.A.	70.61

TABLE 7

Statement Showing the Incidents of Epidemics Spread under the Jurisdiction and the Number of Victims under Different Diseases

Name of the I.C.D.P./Regional Centres	*No. of stockman centres*	*No. of hospitals and dis-pensaries*	*No. of stockman centres reporting spread of different type of epidemics since the inception*				
			B.Q.	*H.S.*	*Anthrax*	*R.P.*	*F.M.D.*
1	*2*	*3*	*4*	*5*	*6*	*7*	*8*
A. Patna-Arrah							
1. Danapur	9	4	9	9	5	—	—
2. Bikram	8	3	8	8	3	—	1
3. Arrah	10	4	10	10	8	9	—
4. Sahar	7	3	7	7	3	4	—
Total	34	14	34	34	19	13	
B. Barauni-Begusarai							
5. Barauni	9	4	9	9	—	—	9
6. Begusarai	8	3	8	8	—	—	8
7. Khagaria	7	3	7	7	—	—	7
8. Manjhoul	5	—	5	5	—	—	5
Total	29	13	29	29	—	—	
Grand Total	63	27	63	63	19	13	30

(Contd.)

TABLE 7 (*Contd.*)

Name of the I.C.D.P./ Regional Centres	*Death during 1970-71 and 1971-72*				
	B.Q.	*H.S.*	*Anthrax*	*R.P.*	*F.M.D.*
1	*9*	*10*	*11*	*12*	*13*
A. Patna-Arrah					
1. Danapur	N.A.	N.A.	N.A.	N.A.	N.A.
2. Bikram	7	29	—	—	9
3. Arrah	12	34	8	—	9
4. Sahar	4	11	—	—	—
Total	50	74	8	—	18
B. Barauni-Begusarai					
5. Barauni	N.A.	N.A.	N.A.	N.A.	N.A.
6. Begusarai	N.A.	N.A.	N.A.	N.A.	N.A.
7. Khagaria	N.A.	N.A.	N.A.	N.A.	N.A.
8. Manjhoul	N.A.	N.A.	N.A.	N.A.	N.A.
Total	—	—	—	—	—
Grand Total	23	74	8	—	18

TABLE 8

Statement Showing Total Milk Supply, No. of Societies and Amount of Loan and Subsidies Distributed Till 31-3-1972

Name of the Project	*Total milk supply per day (in litres)*	*No. of co-operative societies (Dairy) functioning*	*Amount of loan and subsidies distributed (in Rs.)*
1. Patna-Arrah Project	140200	96	52955
2. Barauni-Begusarai Project	202306	120	302600
Total	342506	216	355555

TABLE 9

Statement Showing the Percentage of Distribution of Milk by the Different Agencies and the Prevailing Prices

Name of the R.C.D. Centres	*Co-operative societies*			*Milk Supply scheme*		
	Per cent of milk sold	*Price*		*Per cent of milk sold*	*Price*	
		Highest	*Lowest*		*Higest*	*Lowest*
1	*2*	*3*	*4*	*5*	*6*	*7*
1. Danapur	Nil	Nil	Nil	100	1.10	1.00
2. Bikram	Nil	Nil	Nil	100	1.10	0.90
3. Arrah	25	1.25	0.90	Nil	Nil	Nil
4. Sahar	75	1.00	0.80	Nil	Nil	Nil
5. Barauni	N.A.	1.25	1.00	N.A.	N.A.	N.A.
6. Begusarai	N.A.	1.25	1.00	N.A.	N.A.	N.A.
7. Khagaria	N.A.	1.25	1.00	N.A.	N.A.	N.A.
8. Manjhaul	N.A.	1.50	1.25	N.A.	N.A.	N.A.

(*Contd.*)

TABLE 9 (*Contd.*)

Name of the R.C.D. Centres	*Private Contractor*			*Local Contractor*		
	Per cent of milk sold	*Price*		*Per cent of milk sold*	*Price*	
		Highest	*Lowest*		*Highest*	*Lowest*
1	*8*	*9*	*10*	*11*	*12*	*13*
1. Danapur	Nil	Nil	Nil	Nil	Nil	Nil
2. Bikram	Nil	Nil	Nil	Nil	Nil	Nil
3. Arrah	50	1.12	0.75	25	1.25	1.00
4. Sahar	12	1.00	0.75	13	1.25	1.00
5. Barauni	N.A.	N.A.	N.A.	N.A.	1.25	1.00
6. Begusarai	N.A.	N.A.	N.A.	N.A.	1.25	1.00
7. Khagaria	N.A.	N.A.	N.A.	N.A.	1.25	1.00
8. Manjhoul	N.A.	N.A.	N.A.	N.A.	1.50	1.25

TABLE 10

Statement Showing the Different Types of Fodder Demonstrations Under the R.C.D. Centre During 1970-71

Name of the R.C.D. Centre	*Gwar*		*Cowpea*		*Teosente*		*Barseem*	
	Kg.	*Acre*	*Kg.*	*Acre*	*Kg.*	*Acre*	*Kg.*	*Acre*
1. Dinapur	—	—	56	7.30	116	9.00	764	33.70
2. Bikram		—	110	20.00	60	26.00	509	45.65
3. Arrah	—	4.00	28	15.80	151	26.00	243	50.00
4. Sahar	5	2.00	68	47.55	273	25.00	356	74.80
5. Barauni	15	2.00	12	20.00	161	52.00	105	23.00
6. Begusarai	5	—	298	82.00	105	25.00	60	18.00
7. Khagaria	88	12.00	176	19.00	50	10.00	—	—
8. Manjhoul	50	19.00	30	40.00	2	2.00	30	5.00
Total	163	39.00	783	251.65	918	174.00	2067	247.15

(*Contd.*)

TABLE 10 (*Contd.*)

Name of the R.C.D.	*Dinanath*		*Hybrid Maize*		*Bhirni*		*Barghin*		*Total*	
	Kg.	*Acre*	*Kg.*	*Acre*	*Kg.*	*Acre*	*Kg.*	*Acre*	*Kg.*	*Acre*
1. Danapur	—	—	—	—	126	50.00	42	42.00	1104	142.80
2. Bikram	—	—	40	4.00	285	73.00	221	44.00	1225	212.65
3. Arrah	—	—	88	8.50	75	18.00	—	—	595	122.30
4. Sahar	—	—	210	28.50	25	3.50	—	—	937	180.35
5. Barauni	12	6.00	58	19.00	—	—	63	17.00	426	136.00
6. Khagaria	—	—	—	—	—	—	72	33.00	535	158.00
7. Begusarai	—	—	—	—	80	—	430	54.50	824	95.50
8. Manjhoul	—	—	—	—	—	—	128	29.00	240	95.00
Total	12	6.00	396	60.00	591	145.30	956	219.50	5886	1142.60

TABLE 11

Statement Showing the Different Types of Fodder Demonstrations Under the R.C.D. During 1971-72

Name of the R.C.D. Centres	*Gwar*		*Cowpea*		*Teosente*		*Barseem*	
	Kg.	*Acre*	*Kg.*	*Acre*	*Kg-*	*Acre*	*Kg.*	*Acre*
1. Danapur	—	—	132	9.50	133	9.50	—	2.00
2. Bikram	—	—	111	20.00	40	—	3.00	15.00
3. Arrah	—	—	91	38.50	132	45.50	—	1.00
4. Sahar	—	—	75	35.25	25	31.50	90	12.00
5. Barauni	171	9.00	20	3.00	127	81.00	259	61.00
6. Begusarai	554	123.00	392	77.00	159	49.00	—	—
7. Khagaria	444	93.75	87	19.00	56	20.00	—	—
8. Manjhoul	24	28.00	36	6.00	41	16.00	—	—
Total	1193	253.75	944	208.25	713	252.50	649	91.00

(Contd.)

TABLE 11 (*Contd.*)

Name of the R.C.D.	*Dinanath*		*Hybrid Maize*		*Bhimce*		*Barghin*		*Total*	
	Kg.	*Acre*	*Kg.*	*Acre*	*Kg.*	*Acre*	*Kg.*	*Acre*	*Kg.*	*Acre*
1. Danapur	—	—	—	—	20	5.00	9	4.00	294	30.00
2. Bikram	—	—	10	—	70	50.90	—	36.50	531	122.40
3. Arrah	—	—	—	—	—	—	—	—	223	85.00
4. Sahar	—	—	66	—	—	—	—	—	256	78.75
5. Barauni	6	7.00	71	20.00	—	—	37	8.00	691	189.00
6. Begusarai	—	—	—	—	—	—	64	14.00	1169	263.00
7. Khagaria	—	—	—	—	101	20.00	378	57.10	1065	209.85
8. Manjhoul	—	—	—	—	—	—	20	4.00	121	54.00
Total	6	7.00	147	20.00	191	75.90	508	123.60	4351	1082.00

TABLE 12

Statement Showing the Artificial Insemination Work done and the No. of Calves (Male and Female) Born from 1967-68 to 1971-72 as per Stockman Schedule

Name of the Regional Cattle Dev. Centre	*No. of Artificial insemination done and Calves born*					
	1967-68			*1968-69*		
	No. of A.I. done	*Calves Born*		*No. of A.I. done*	*Calves Born*	
		Male	*Female*		*Male*	*Female*
1. Dinapur	5296	599	612	5684	526	567
2. Bikram	2654	182	186	2971	368	407
3. Arrah	2572	514	456	3650	610	581
4. Sahar	391	81	32	364	42	46
5. Barauni	4206	88	985	4437	32	599
6. Begusarai	2825	796	667	4383	580	410
7. Khagaria	1878	249	288	2267	400	388
8. Manjhoul	1515	270	333	1820	197	264
	21337	2728	3559	25576	2755	3262

(*Contd.*)

TABLE 12 (*Contd.*)

Name of the Regional Cattle Dev. Centre	*No. of Artificial insemination done and Calves born*								
	1969-70			*1970-71*			*1971-72*		
	No. of A.I. done	*Calves Born*		*No. of A.I. done*	*Calves Born*		*No. of A.I. done*	*Calves Born*	
		Male	*Female*		*Male*	*Female*		*Male*	*Female*
1. Danapur	5548	621	659	5576	515	517	5140	533	508
2. Bikram	3518	451	383	3502	541	429	3187	526	447
3. Arrah	926	642	638	3967	741	869	3858	861	910
4. Sabar	498	71	64	802	175	136	584	134	81
5. Barauni	4644	42	1089	6369	42	866	1549	26	216
6. Begusarai	3506	403	396	5065	490	637	3357	450	337
7. Khagaria	2481	508	505	3148	506	486	2111	522	812
8. Manjhoul	1874	144	194	1823	95	88	1764	349	42
	25985	2882	3928	20252	3105	4028	21550	3421	3422

TABLB 13

Statement Showing the No. of Pedigree Bulls and Buff Bulls Available During 1971-72

Name of the Project	*No. of Bulls available under the Project*	*Required No. of Bulls to be maintained*	*No. of Buff. Bulls available under the project*	*Required No. of Buff. Bulls to be maintained*
1. Patna-Arrah	49	50	18	50
2. Barauni-Begusarai	23	46	14	22
Total	72	96	32	72

TABLE 14

Statement Showing the Natural Services done and the Calves Born from 1967-68 to 1971-72

Name of the R.C.D. Centre	*1967-68*		*1968-69*		*1969-70*		*1970-71*		*1971-72*	
	No. of N.S. done	*Calves born*	*No. of N.S. done*	*Calves born*	*No. of N.S. done*	*Calves born*	*No. of N.S. done*	*Calves born*	*No. of N.S. done*	*Calves born*
1. Danapur	401	78	742	36	373	53	449	95	32	12
2. Bikram	128	21	887	98	776	273	1362	222	854	241
3. Arrah	—	—	182	94	623	343	772	489	1084	1022
4. Sahar	339	58	1192	74	1201	203	1389	453	731	522
5. Barauni	393	74	75	20	146	44	107	66	—	—
6. Begusarai	106	59	118	63	93	53	100	61	36	22
7. Khagaria	340	110	275	63	467	257	874	233	528	130
8. Manjhoul	—	—	—	—	—	—	—	—	—	—
Total	1707	400	3471	448	3679	12-6	5033	1619	3265	1958

TABLE 15

Statement Showing the Number of Animals Castrated During the 1967-68 to 1971-72

	Name of the Regional Centre	*Animals Castrated*					
		1967-68	*1968-69*	*1969-70*	*1970-71*	*1971-72*	*Total*
1.	Danapur	711	1275	1371	2000	1947	7304
2.	Bikram	446	924	1197	1281	1369	5217
3.	Arrah	912	1844	1815	2202	2405	9178
4.	Sahar	811	750	823	936	827	4147
5.	Barauni	300	28	41	422	154	1035
6.	Begusarai	180	140	195	306	479	1300
7.	Khagaria	291	324	584	914	524	2637
8.	Manjhoul	87	64	148	209	388	896
	Total	3828	5349	6174	8270	8093	31714

TABLE 16

Statement Showing the Loans and Subsidies Distributed Under the Jurisdiction of the Regional Cattle Development Centres

	Name of the R.C.D.	*Loans and Subsidies distributed (in Rs.)*					
		1967-68	*1968-69*	*1969-70*	*1970-71*	*1971-72*	*Total*
1.	Danapur	5800	3000	600	—	—	9400
2.	Bikram	—	4000	—	5000	—	9000
3.	Arrah	—	14300	11600	—	15000	40900
4.	Sahar	—	—	—	—	—	—
5.	Barauni	13550	—	—	—	8000	21550
6.	Begusarai	—	—	—	—	—	—
7.	Khagaria	11800	—	5000	—	—	16800
8.	Majhoul	14200	—	—	—	—	14200
	Total	45350	21300	17200	5000	23000	111850

TABLE 17

Statement Showing the Percentage of Distribution of Milk by the Different Agencies and the Prevailing Prices

Name of the R.C.D. Centres	*Co-operative Societies*			*Milk Supply Scheme*		
	Per cent of milk sold	*Price*		*Per cent of milk sold*	*Price*	
		Highest	*Lowest*		*Highest*	*Lowest*
1. Danapur	Nil	Nil	Nil	100	1.10	1.00
2. Bikram	Nil	Nil	Nil	100	1.00	0.90
3. Arrah	25	1.25	0.90	Nil	Nil	Nil
4. Sahar	75	1.00	0.80	Nil	Nil	Nil
5. Barauni	50	1.25	1.00	Nil	Nil	Nil
6. Begusarai	50	1.25	1.00	Nil	Nil	Nil
7. Khagaria	50	1.25	1.00	Nil	Nil	Nil
8. Manjhoul	50	1.50	1.25	Nil	Nil	Nil

(*Contd.*)

TABLE 17 (*Contd.*)

Name of the R.C.D. Centres	*Private Contractor*			*Local Contractor*		
	Per cent of milk sold	*Price*		*Per cent of milk sold*	*Price*	
		Highest	*Lowest*		*Highest*	*Lowest*
1. Danapur	Nil	Nil	Nil	Nil	Nil	Nil
2. Bikram	Nil	Nil	Nil	Nil	Nil	Nil
3. Arrah	50	1.12	0.75	25	1.25	1.00
4. Sahar	12	1.00	0.75	13	1.25	1.00
5. Barauni	Nil	Nil	Nil	50	1.25	1.00
6. Begusarai	Nil	Nil	Nil	50	1.25	1.00
7. Khagaria	Nil	Nil	Nil	50	1.25	1.00
8. Manjhoul	Nil	Nil	Nil	50	1.25	1.25

TABLE 18

Statement Showing the Fodder Area and Fodder Seeds Distributed as per Project Schedule

Name of the Project	*Position at the time of inception of the project (According to preliminary survey)*			*Achievement till 31-3-1991*		
	Fodder area (in acres)	*Fodder seeds (in Kg.)*	*No. of chaff cutters*	*Fodder area (in acres)*	*Fodder seed (in Kg.)*	*No. of chaff cutters*
1. Patna-Arrah	3497.50	34639	N.A.	N.A.	170937	345
2. Barauni-Begusarai	8242.00	16595	N.A.	14701	178203	286

TABLB 19

Statement Showing the Area Under Fodder, Fodder Seed Supplied, etc. as per Regional Schedules

Name of the Regional Centres	*Area under Fodder (acres) from 1965-66 to 1971-72*	*No. of fodder demonstrations (1965-66 to 1971-72)*	*Fodder seed distributed (1965-66 to 1971-72) (Kg.)*	*Number of chaff cutters (1965-66 to 1966-67)*
1. Danapur	6069	15816	76403	146
2. Bikram	3845	64563	49200	60
3. Arrah	16033	39253	37975	107
4. Sahar	Nil	Nil	1649	76
5. Barauni	2327	N.A.	34994	Nil
6. Begusarai	5811	N.A.	83069	42
7. Khagaria	3049	N.A.	8263	103
8. Manjhoul	2715	N.A.	51873	141
Total	40649	119632	343425	675

TABLE 20

Statement Showing the Different Types of Fodder Demonstrations Held During 1971-72 as per the Stockman Centre Schedules

Name of the R.C.D. Centres	Gwar		Cowpee		Teosente		Barseem	
	Kg.	Acre	Kg.	Acre	Kg.	Acre	Kg.	Acre
1. Danapur	—	—	132	9.50	133	9.50	—	2.00
2. Bikram	—	—	111	20.00	40	—	300	15.00
3. Arrah	—	—	91	38.50	132	45.50	—	1.00
4. Sahar	—	—	75	35.25	25	31.50	90	12.00
5. Barauni	17	9.00	20	3.00	127	81.00	259	61.00
6. Begusarai	554	123.00	392	77.00	159	49.00	—	—
7. Khagaria	444	93.75	87	87.00	56	20.00	—	—
8. Manjhoul	24	28.00	36	6.00	41	16.00	—	—
Total	1193	253.75	944	208.25	713	252.50	649	91.00

(Contd.)

TABLE 20 (*Contd.*)

Name of the R.C.D. Centres	*Dinanath*		*Hybrid Maize*		*Bhirnee*		*Barghin*	
	Kg.	*Acre*	*Kg.*	*Acre*	*Kg.*	*Acre*	*Kg.*	*Acre*
1. Danapur	—	—	—	—	20	5.00	9	4.00
2. Bikram	—	—	10	—	70	50.90	—	36.50
3. Arrah	—	—	—	—	—	—	—	—
4. Sahar	—	—	66	—	—	—	—	—
5. Barauni	6	7.00	171	20.00	—	-	37	8.00
6. Begusarai	—	—	—	—	—	—	64	14.00
7. Khagaria	—	—	—	—	101	20.00	378	57.10
8. Munjhoul	—	—	—	—	—	—	20	4.00
Total	6	7.00	147	20.00	191	75.90	508	123.60

Total demonstrations—4351 Kg.
Average covered—1032.00 Acres.

TABLE 21

Statement Showing the Total Area Sown, Area Under Fodder and Area Irrigated of the Selected Cattle Owners

Name of the Project	*No. of cattle owners*	*Total area sown*	*Area sown with fodder*	*Per cent of area under fodder*
Patna-Arrah	380	4156.50	142.92	3.41
Barauni-Begusarai	339	4646.07	16.05	0.04
Total	719	8802.57	158.97	1.81

TABLE 22

Statement Showing the Improved Variety of Cattle Maintained, Breeding Practices Adopted, etc. of the Selected Participants

Name of the R.C.D. Centres	*No. of selected participants*	*No. of improved variety of cattle maintained*		*Breeding practices preferred*		*Amount of dry fodder purchased*	*Amount of concentrates purchased*
		Cow	*Buffalo*	*A.I.*	*N.S.*		
Dinapur	95	12	1	33	57	30%	25%
Bikram	84	3	3	45	39	5%	5%
Arrah	116	Nil	3	N.A.	N.A	25%	20%
Sahar	85	1	Nil	85	Nil	10%	Nil
Barauni	106	2	Nil	106	Nil	Nil	Nil
Begusarai	88	Nil	1	88	Nil	Nil	Nil
Khagaria	83	Nil	Nil	83	Nil	Nil	Nil
Manjhoul	62	Nil	Nil	62	Nil	Nil	Nil

TABLE 23

Statement Showing the Gross Area Under Cultivation, Area Under Fodder, etc. of the Selected Participants

	Name of the R.C.D. Centres	*No. of the selected participants*	*Gross area under cultivation (acres)*	*Area under fodder (acres)*	*Area irrigated (acres)*	*Fodder seed used (Kg.)*	*Source from where obtained*
I.	Dinapur	95	1146.70	51.70	337.25	267	Market
2.	Bikram	84	959.00	21.80	777.50	201	"
3.	Arrah	116	1142.35	51.65	614.40	229	"
4.	Sahar	85	907.85	30.75	778.35	237	"
5.	Barauni	106	1205.50	9.95	187.95	44	Vety. Officer
6.	Begusarai	88	1240.00	0.20	55.00	10	"
7.	Khagaria	83	1149.50	1.00	70.00	15	"
8.	Manjhoul	62	983.10	4.40	147.00	28	"

TABLE 24

Statement Showing the Feeding Practices of the Cattle Maintained by the Participants

	Name of the Regional Cattle Dev. Centre	*No. of the selected participants*	*No. of participants adopted recommended practices in feeding*	*Reason for not adoption*	*Time of feeding*		*Type of feeding*		*Remarks*
					Morning	*Evening*	*Stalled*	*Grazing*	
1.	Danapur	95	25	No means and knowledge	95	95	93	95	
2.	Bikram	84	22	"	84	84	84	84	
3.	Arrah	116	28	"	116	116	116	116	
4.	Sahar	85	10	"	85	85	85	85	
5.	Barauni	106	9	"	106	106	106	106	
6.	Begusarai	88	14	"	88	88	88	88	
7.	Khagaria	83	12	"	83	83	83	83	
8.	Manjhoul	62	8	"	62	62	62	62	
	Total	719	128 (17.6%)		719	719	719	719	

TABLE 25

Statement Showing the Source of Income of Selected Participants

	Name of the R.C.D. Centres	*No. of Selected participants*	*No. of participants derived their income from*				*No. of participants Consumed the Milk*
			Selling of calves	*Selling of Cow Dung*	*Selling of milk*	*Selling of Ghee etc.*	
1.	Danapur	95	—	32	55	3	40
2.	Bikram	84	3	39	51	2	33
3.	Arrah	116	4	45	67	3	49
4.	Sahar	85	3	33	41	4	44
5.	Barauni	106	2	59	61	5	45
6.	Begusarai	88	1	44	80	4	8
7.	Khagaria	83	3	46	67	8	16
8.	Manjhoul	62	5	22	41	9	21
	Total	719	21	320	463	38	256

TABLE 26

Statement Showing the Items on which Expenditure was Incurred

	Name of the R.C.D. Centres	*No. of selected participants*	*No. of participants purchased fodder*	*No. of participants paid grazing and service charge*	*No. of participants paid other charges*
1.	Danapur	95	89	25	3
2.	Bikram	34	75	20	2
3.	Arrah	116	101	29	3
4,	Sahar	85	61	10	Nil
5.	Barauni	106	97	17	2
6.	Begusarai	88	76	23	Nil
7.	Khagaria	83	58	21	Nil
8.	Manjhoul	62	52	10	Nil
	Total	719	609	155	10

Index